THE PACIFIC SERIES

TEACHERS NOTES for English

GRADE SIX

Tandi Bloxam

Melbourne
OXFORD UNIVERSITY PRESS

OXFORD UNIVERSITY PRESS AUSTRALIA

Oxford New York
Athens Auckland Bangkok Bogotá Buenos Aires
Cape Town Chennai Dar es Salaam Delhi Florence
Hong Kong Istanbul Karachi Kolkata Kuala Lumpur
Madrid Melbourne Mexico City Mumbai Nairobi
Paris Port Moresby São Paulo Shanghai Singapore
Taipei Tokyo Toronto Warsaw

and associated companies in
Berlin Ibadan

First published 1983
Reprinted 1984, 1987, 1991, 1998, 1999, 2001, 2015(D)

National Library of Australia
Cataloguing-in-Publication data:

Bloxam, Tandi.
Teachers; notes for English, grade six.
(Pacific series).
ISBN 0 19 550495 X
I. English language – Study and teaching (Elementary)
– Papua New Guinea. I. Title. (Series)
372.62' 21

Printed and bound in Australia by Ligare Pty Ltd.
Published by Oxford University Press, 253 Normanby Road, South Melbourne

Contents

Introduction

This book is designed to cover the skills outlined in the Papua New Guinea Department of Education's English Syllabus for Grade 6. It is a *guide* to help teachers use Grade 6 *Using English Pupil's Books One*, *Two* and *Three* of the Pacific Series, which follow on from Grade Five.

You do not have to follow the instructions in this book exactly, since they are only suggestions. You should vary the work to suit your pupils, because some children learn much quicker than others.

Remember that *not all pupils* will be able to do *all the work* set out in the *Using English* books. This does not matter. However, brighter pupils who work faster should be given extra exercises to do when they have finished set lessons. Exercises not used during school hours could be used for homework but *do not* allow children to take the *Using English* books home.

Each unit of work takes one week.

Method

There are Lesson Suggestions at the end of this book. They give general instructions for teaching each type of lesson. Each lesson in the units of work refers you to the relevant Lesson Suggestion, e.g: Unit 1, Lesson Five, see Lesson Suggestion 1C. The **Method** section of each individual lesson does not repeat the general instructions. It gives only the points which are important for that particular lesson.

Answers

All answers to lessons are set out in this book. Where only one answer is correct, answers are headed **Answers**. The answers do not always have to be *exactly* the same as the ones given in this book. The teacher must decide whether an answer given by the pupil is acceptable.

Where *several* answers are possible, answers are headed **Possible Answers**. You should use these as *examples* to help you mark the pupils' work.

Where a letter or written composition is required, a **Model Answer** is given as a guide to help you.

Where two (or more) words are correct for the same answer, the two words are written but divided by a line, e.g: they/them. Note the following abbreviations used in the lesson plans:

T = teacher
C = children
P = pupil
Q = question
A = answer
e.g. = for example
i.e. = that is
etc. = and so on

Programme of Work

The syllabus for Grade Six English is divided into seven different topics:

Listening	Oral Expression	Spelling	Handwriting
Talking	Written English	Reading	

You could divide up the time spent each week on each topic like this:

Subject	*Total Lesson Time* per week:	*Divide Total Time into Lessons* as follows:
Listening	20 minutes	2 lessons of 10 minutes each
Broadcasts	60 minutes	3 lessons of 20 minutes each
Talking	75 minutes	5 lessons of 15 minutes each
Oral Expression	60 minutes	3 lessons of 20 minutes each
Written Sentences	100 minutes	5 lessons of 20 minutes each
Written Composition	30 minutes	1 lesson of 30 minutes or 2 lessons of 15 minutes each
Spelling	30 minutes	2 lessons of 15 minutes each
Handwriting	15 minutes	1 lesson of 15 minutes
Reading	130 minutes	5 lessons of 20 minutes each and 1 lesson of 30 minutes

Note

These times are *suggestions* only. You should vary these times to suit the particular needs of your class.

You could make use of block time to complete any English work not finished. Timetable block time immediately after English lessons.

TERM ONE

WEEKLY UNITS OF WORK: LISTENING

Unit 1 1 Everyday sounds: game
2 Consonant sounds
Unit 2 1 Following directions
2 Identifying musical sounds
Unit 3 1 Understanding a story
2 Identifying known sounds
Unit 4 1 Following directions
2 Telling how someone *feel*s by the way he speaks
Unit 5 1 Remembering 'key' words
2 Classifying (odd word out – sound)
Unit 6 1 Listening to unseen speaker
2 Remembering names
Unit 7 1 Order of events
2 Identifying everyday sounds
Unit 8 1 Vowel sounds
2 Syllable stress in words
Unit 9 1 Rhyming words
2 Word stress in sentences (who, what happened, whose, what)
Unit 10 1 Word stress in sentences
2 Remembering messages

WEEKLY UNITS OF WORK: TALKING

Unit 1 Revision: What can I cut this paper with? You can use these scissors.
Revision: Can I borrow your pencil please? Yes, you can./No, you can't.
New sentence pattern: What can you see in the mirror? I can see myself in the mirror.

Unit 2 Revision of last week's work
Revision: Can you tell me the time? It's a quarter past eight.
New sentence pattern: Can you see yourself in the water? Yes, I can see myself.

Unit 3 Revision of last week's work
Revision: What are you doing tomorrow? I'm going to town tomorrow.
New sentence pattern: What's he doing? He's washing himself.

Unit 4 Revision of last week's work
Revision: When the bell rang what did they do? When the bell rang, the children went to assembly.
New sentence pattern: When Waru looked in the mirror, he saw himself.

Unit 5 Revision of last week's work
Revision: Who did you see when you went to the market? I saw Raka.
New sentence pattern: Who did they buy peanuts for? They bought them for themselves.

Unit 6 Revision of last week's work
Revision: What did he say? He said that . . .
What did he tell us? He told us that . . .
New sentence pattern: Did he build that house for himself? No, he built it for his brother.

Unit 7 Revision of last week's work
Revision: What will you do when/after/before the bell rings?
New sentence pattern: What did he do? He poured water on himself.

Unit 8 Revision of last week's work
Revision: What does he need? He needs a comb. What will he need? He'll need an axe.
New sentence pattern: What did he buy himself? He bought himself a shirt.

Unit 9 Revision of last week's work
Revision: Why does he need some wood? To make a fire.
He has a new shirt. He doesn't need another one.
New sentence pattern: Did anyone help Malu to carry the box? No, he carried it by himself.

Unit 10 Revision of last week's work
Revision: Can you go swimming now? Yes, I can. No, I can't because . . .
New sentence pattern: Can you make a kundu by yourself? Yes, I can.

WEEKLY UNITS OF WORK: ORAL EXPRESSION

Unit 1
1 Class discussion (holidays)
2 Class discussion (about things they hear outside)
3 Class discussion (on classroom improvements)

Unit 2
1 Describing how to get somewhere
2 Giving opinions
3 Thinking up imaginative stories

Unit 3
1 Describing objects
2 Giving oral directions
3 Giving accurate explanations

Unit 4
1 Telling a story about a picture
2 Asking questions to obtain information
3 Greetings/Farewells

Unit 5
1 Asking politely
2 Introductions
3 Apologizing

Unit 6
1 Telephone conversations
2 Answering the telephone
3 Telephone conversations

Unit 7
1 Oral descriptions
2 Describing contrasts
3 Describing contrasts

Unit 8
1 Giving opinions
2 Arguing effectively
3 Making logical connections

Unit 9
1 Telling the time
2 Sentence word game
3 Discussion (helping the local community)

Unit 10
1 Using imagination
2 Inventing an alibi
3 Giving instructions

WEEKLY UNITS OF WORK: WRITTEN SENTENCES

Unit 1
1 Completing sentences
2 Beginning sentences
3 Using 'many' or 'much'
4 Substituting one word for a group of words (optional)
5 Using known phrases in sentences
6 Sentences about a picture (revising grammar)

Unit 2
1 Completing sentences (adverbial clauses)
2 Choosing the correct word (optional)
3 Contractions
4 Opposites
5 Adjectives
6 Making sentences

Unit 3
1 Apostrophes (possession)
2 Changing from singular to plural
3 Matching sentence beginnings and endings
4 Questions and answers about pictures
5 Choosing the correct word (optional)
6 Using adjectives

Unit 4
1 Choosing the correct form of the verb
2 Similar sounding words
3 Writing questions and answers
4 Changing from past to present
5 Punctuation
6 Using nouns in sentences (optional)

Unit 5
1 Writing telegrams
2 Using known phrases
3 Completing sentences
4 Answering questions about pictures
5 Choosing the correct description
6 Adverbs (optional)

Unit 6
1 Choosing the right words
2 Quotation marks
3 Answers to questions (optional)
4 Choosing the correct word
5 Choosing the correct word
6 Choosing adverbs

Unit 7
1 Contractions
2 Adverbial phrases
3 Joining sentences
4 Descriptions about a picture
5 Using 'after' or 'before'

Unit 8
1 Reflexive pronouns
2 Jumbled sentences
3 Apostrophes (to show possession)
4 Answers to questions about pictures
5 Punctuation

Unit 9
1 Reflexive pronouns
2 Answers to questions (reflexive pronouns)
3 Using prepositions
4 Writing direct speech
5 Writing questions and answers (optional)
6 Choosing the correct pronoun

Unit 10 1 Choosing the correct form of a verb
2 Changing from singular to plural/plural to singular
3 Sentence pattern: How long have . . . been . . .
4 Sentence pattern: Are you sure they will . . .
5 Sentence pattern: Are you sure they won't . . .

WEEKLY UNITS OF WORK: WRITTEN COMPOSITION

Unit 1 1 Correct order of ideas
2 Choosing the correct sentence to match the picture
Unit 2 1 Imaginative writing
2 Understanding directions
Unit 3 1 Story writing from sentence beginnings
2 Writing directions
Unit 4 1 Observation — answering questions about a picture
2 Descriptive passage
Unit 5 1 Writing a personal letter
2 Perception — writing sentences about a picture
Unit 6 1 Writing a story to match sequence pictures
2 Looking at the main ideas in a paragraph
Unit 7 1 Writing a descriptive passage
2 Writing a business letter
Unit 8 1 Finishing a play
2 Filling in forms
Unit 9 1 Writing a business letter
2 Filling in forms
Unit 10 1 Writing a report
2 Writing a personal letter

WEEKLY UNITS OF WORK: SPELLING

Unit 1 harm harmful hard harbour ('har' group)
above abandon ability about ('ab' group)
Family Group: The Sea
Written Exercises
Unit 2 accident accept account accommodation ('acc' group)
decide deceive declare decorate ('dec' group)
Family Group: Fishing
Written Exercises
Unit 3 arrange arrest arrive arrow ('arr' group)
wrap writing wrong wreck ('wr' group)
Family Group: Space
Written Exercises
Unit 4 east beast least feast ('east' group)
example expect except expand ('ex' group)
Family Group: Post
Written Exercises
Unit 5 excellent explanation exercise explore ('ex' group)
brave cave save waved ('ave' group)
Family Group: Clothes
Written Exercises

Unit 6 instrument instructions instead injured ('in' group)
uncomfortable until untidy underneath ('un' group)
Family Group: Town
Written Exercises

Unit 7 consider constable condition contest ('con' group)
knife knock knot know ('kn' group)
Family Group: Sea Transport
Written Exercises

Unit 8 beak beard beach beat ('bea' group)
sound sour south soup ('sou' group)
Family Group: Airport
Written Exercises

Unit 9 employ employer employee employment ('employ' group)
plantation relation situation station ('ation' group)
Family Group: Tools
Written Exercises

Unit 10 deserve describe despair destroy ('des' group)
tough rough enough cough ('ough' group)
Family Group: Animals
Written Exercises

WEEKLY UNITS OF WORK: HANDWRITING

Unit 1 Practise letter combinations 'ff' and 'os'
Copy model passage about a Wild Boar

Unit 2 Practise numbers 1–10
Copy model letter

Unit 3 Practise letter combinations 'fl' and 'ie'
Copy model passage about Traffic

Unit 4 Practise letter combinations 'ion' and 'ld'
Copy model passage about the Highlands Drought

Unit 5 Practise letter combinations 'cks' and 'wi'
Copy model passage about Eskimos

Unit 6 Practise letter combinations 'eet' and 'and'
Copy model passage about the Kula Exchange

Unit 7 Practise letter combinations 'me' and 'woo'
Copy model passage about the Cyclone

Unit 8 Copy model passage — conversation

Unit 9 Copy model passage about Flying

Unit 10 Copy model passage about the Dog

WEEKLY UNITS OF WORK: READING

Unit 1
1 Reader: '*Grumble, Grumble, Grumble*'
2 Comprehension
3 Context clues
4 Learning the meanings of new vocabulary
5 Poetry
6 Reading for enjoyment

Unit 2
1 Reader: '*Deruma's Dream*'
2 Comprehension

	3	Comprehension
	4	Following written instructions
	5	Poetry
	6	Reading Games
Unit 3	1	Reader: '*The Carving*'
	2	Comprehension
	3	Reading exercise
	4	Arranging sentences in correct order
	5	Reading Games
	6	Poetry
Unit 4	1	Reader: '*The Letters*' Part 1
	2	Comprehension
	3	Understanding written directions
	4	Getting information from a notice
	5	Reading for enjoyment
	6	Poetry
Unit 5	1	Reader: '*The Letters*' Part 2
	2	Comprehension
	3	Arranging sentences in correct order
	4	Comprehension
	5	Reading exercise
	6	Reading for enjoyment
Unit 6	1	Reader: '*Machele and the Heron's Leg*'
	2	Comprehension
	3	Reading exercises
	4	Work on Telephone Directory
	5	Reading for enjoyment
	6	Reading Games or Poetry
Unit 7	1	Reader: '*The Mark of the Borowei*'
	2	Comprehension
	3	Fact and opinion
	4	Headlines
	5	Supplementary reader
	6	Reading Games or Poetry
Unit 8	1	Reader: '*Kemuse and the Strike*'
	2	Comprehension
	3	Comprehension exercise
	4	Reading exercise
	5	Context clues
	6	Reading for enjoyment or Poetry
Unit 9	1	Reader: '*The Hermit and the Rajah's Crown*'
	2	Comprehension
	3	Context clues
	4	Examining the Table of Contents
	5	Reading Games
	6	Reading for enjoyment or Poetry
Unit 10	1	Reader: '*Kamapua*'
	2	Comprehension
	3	Context clues
	4	Getting information from a notice
	5	Following directions
	6	Reading Games or Poetry

LISTENING 1

LESSON ONE

Objective
The children will listen carefully and name different sounds the teacher makes.

Preparation
Collect a number of things which will make different sounds. (There are some examples below.) Keep them hidden from the class.

Method
1 Tell the children to sit quietly with their eyes shut and their hands over their faces.
2 Make a sound a few times and ask the children: What makes this sound? What am I doing? Some sounds you can make:

sharpen a pencil
turn the pages of a book
shut a book
drop a pencil
knock on the desk
tear a strip of paper
tap sticks or stones together
strike a match
hit a tin can, cardboard box or glass jar
clap, whistle, hum
pour water into a cup
jingle coins

Note
This game is fun to play and it is a good way to start the term.
1 If the children find the game difficult, *show* them all the things you are going to use before you begin the game.
2 Choose individual children to make one of the sounds.

LESSON TWO

Objective
The children will be able to hear the difference between consonants which sound similar.

Preparation
Make a list of words or sounds which the children often get mixed up. (You can add to this list all through the year.) Write them on the blackboard, e.g:

Beginning sounds:

1 'b' and 'p' sounds:	bad	pad
	big	pig
	back	pack
	bill	pill
	buy	pie
2 'c' and 'd' sounds:	came	game
	cave	gave
	cane	gain
	could	good
3 'bl' and 'pl' sounds:	blank	plank
	blight	plight
4 'br' and 'pr' sounds:	brick	prick
	bride	pride

Ending sounds:

1 'ck' and 'g' sounds:	lock	log
	back	bag
	pick	pig
	peck	peg
2 'd' and 't' sounds:	thread	threat
	laid	late

Method

1 Read down the list; the children repeat after you.
2 Read across the list; the children repeat after you.
3 Read one word and ask the children to write it down or point to the word you have read.

Note

This exercise is good listening practice, but do not do it for too long, or the children will get bored.
You could also use these words in sentences and ask the children to pick out the word you have used from the list on the blackboard, e.g:

T: I wish I could be good
C: could and good

TALKING

LESSON ONE (Lesson Suggestion 1C)

Objective

The children will practise a sentence pattern they already know:
What can I cut this paper with? You can use these scissors.

Method

1 Show the children a piece of paper. Ask the question: What can I cut this paper with?
2 Encourage a child to answer: You can use these scissors. If a child does not give the correct answer, say: I can use these scissors. (Hold up a pair of scissors.)
3 Children repeat the question and answer.
4 Give other examples, e.g:
What can I comb my hair with?
What can I clean my teeth with?
What can I wash my face with?
What can I fix this chair with?
5 Ask individual children to ask another child a question.
6 Divide children into groups. Group leaders must make sure that each child in the group has a turn to ask a question and answer a question.
7 Walk round the room listening to the group work, giving help where needed.

LESSON TWO

Objective

The children will practise a sentence pattern they already know:
Can I borrow your pencil please? Yes, you can./No, you can't.

Method

1 Pick up a piece of paper and say to a child: Can I borrow your pencil please? The child answers: Yes, you can.
2 The class repeats the question and answer.
3 Give another example: Can I borrow your umbrella please? Child answers: No, you can't.
4 Class, or smaller groups, repeat the question and answer.
5 Give other examples:
Can I borrow your spear please?
Can I borrow your spade please?
Can I borrow your canoe please?
6 Ask individual children to ask another child a question.
7 Divide children into groups. Group leaders must make sure that each child in a group has a turn to talk.

LESSON THREE

Objective

The children will be able to use a new sentence pattern:
What can you see in the mirror? I can see myself in the mirror.

Preparation

Have a mirror ready for this lesson.

Method

1 Show the mirror to the class. Look into it and say: I can see myself in the mirror.
2 Give the mirror to a pupil and say:
Q: Karo, what can you see in the mirror?
A: I can see myself in the mirror.
T: Karo can see herself in the mirror.
Q: What can she see?
A: She can see herself in the mirror.
Q: What can Taku see in the mirror? (Holding the mirror in front of Taku.)
A: He can see himself in the mirror.
3 Continue with this pattern using yourself, itself, ourselves, themselves.
4 Work in groups using tin lids as mirrors.

Pronounciation Note

Normally there is no stress in words like *themselves*. Correct children who say herself or ourselves.

LESSON FOUR

Objective

The children will practise this sentence pattern:
What can they see in the glass window? They can see themselves in the glass window?

Method

1 Say the sentence pattern. The class repeat it.
2 Give other examples:
Q: What can they see in the water?
A: They can see themselves in the water.
Q: What can they see in the mirror?
A: They can see themselves in the mirror.

3 Substitute with other reflexive pronouns: she/herself, he/himself, we/ourselves, it/itself, we/ourselves.
4 Other examples could be:
Q: What can she see in the photograph?
A: She can see herself in the photograph.
Q: What can he see in the water?
A: He can see himself in the water.
Q: What can they see in the shiny window?
A: They can see themselves in the shiny window.

LESSON FIVE (Lesson Suggestion 1C)

Objective
The children will practise Lessons Three and Four using a substitution table.

Preparation
Write the following substitution table on the blackboard:

	SHE		WASH	SHE		HERSELF
	THEY		PICTURE	THEY		THEMSELVES
What can	HE	see in the	WATER	HE	can see	HIMSELF.
	IT		MIRROR	IT		ITSELF
	WE		PHOTOGRAPH	WE		OURSELVES
	YOU		GLASS	YOU		YOURSELF

Note
If possible, leave this substitution table on the blackboard until next week for revision in Lesson One.

ORAL EXPRESSION

LESSON ONE

Objective
The children will talk about what they did in the holidays.

Method
Ask each child to tell you something that he or she remembers from the holidays. Encourage them to use questions and complete sentences, e.g:
Q: Tam, what did you do in the holidays?
A: I went to visit my uncle in Lae.
If the children find this difficult, tell them what *you* did and then ask if they did similar or different things.

LESSON TWO

Objective
The children will talk about what they can see and hear outside the classroom.

Method
1 Discuss with the children what they can see and hear outside the classroom, e.g: children playing, boys shouting, people walking down the road, birds singing, teacher carrying books to class.

2 Encourage the children to make complete sentences, using interesting words, about what they can see and hear, e.g:
C: I can see three small boys playing football and shouting very loudly.
C: I can hear the beautiful birds.

Note
Encourage the children to use the words they have been learning this week: very, much, many, first, next, then.

LESSON THREE

Objective
The children will talk about the things they would like to do this term to improve their classroom.

Method
Ask each child to make a suggestion. They should use the words: I think we should . . . I think it would be a good idea to . . . Remind the children that you use the words I think when you express an *opinion*.

Note
Encourage the children to use the words *first, next, then*, to say in what order they want to do things.

WRITTEN SENTENCES

Note
Remember, you will teach only FIVE of the lessons. Choose one lesson for homework, or for fast workers to do.

LESSON ONE (Lesson Suggestion 6)

Objective
The children will write sentences beginning with phrases which tell you *when* something happened.

Preparation
Give out *Pupil's Book 1* to each child (page 3, Lesson 1).

Note
The children may find it easier if you tell them to make their sentences all about one topic, e.g: the sea.

Possible answers
1 After a long time the sea grew calm again.
2 The next day the waves were much bigger.
3 A few hours later the tide turned.
4 As the people arrived the boats became very crowded.
5 All of a sudden the child fell into deep water.
6 Many years later we found another old canoe on the beach.
7 Before we could move the boat crashed on the rocks.
8 When the time came for us to leave we felt very sad.
9 Before we left the village we had one more swim in the sea.
10 By the time we were ready to go the tide was in.

Note
This is a good chance to use the words in this week's Spelling Family Group.

LESSON TWO (Lesson Suggestion 6)

Objective
The children will write suitable phrases to begin sentences.

Preparation
Give out *Pupil's Book 1* to each child (page 3, Lesson 2).

Method
Suggest that they use some of the phrases from Lesson 1 in their answers.

Possible Answers
1 The next day ...
2 By the time we were ready to go ...
3 After capturing us ...
4 Before we left the village ...
5 Not long after ...
6 When they looked back ...
7 Over the years ...
8 When the funeral was over ...
9 All of a sudden ...
10 Before we could move ...

LESSON THREE

Objective
The children will know when to use *many* or *much* in a sentence.

Preparation
Give out *Pupil's Book 1* to each pupil (page 3, Lesson 3).

Method
1 Remind the children that for things we can count, we use *many*. For things we cannot count, we use *much*. Encourage pupils to give examples. Make a list on the blackboard, e.g:

[*Many*]			[*Much*]	
books	bilums	sand	sugar	flour
canoes	shells	water	tea	money

Answers
1 much
2 many
3 much
4 much
5 many
6 much
7 much
8 many
9 many
10 much

LESSON FOUR (optional)

Note
Use this lesson as an extra lesson for the children who work fast. Do Lessons Five and Six before you let the children do Lesson Four.

Method
1 Discuss the meanings of each word in the list. They are all words that the children have used in earlier Pacific Series work, except *peeled* and *poked*.
2 Read the instructions and explain the example.

LESSON FIVE (Lesson Suggestion 6)

Objective
The children will complete written sentences using phrases they have learned from the Pacific Series in Grades 4 and 5.

Preparation
Give out *Pupil's Book 1* to each pupil (pages 4–5, Lesson 5).

Method
Discuss each phrase with the class to make sure they understand the meaning.

Answers
1 try it out
2 wide open
3 flash of lightning
4 one by one
5 lost his way
6 just in time
7 as usual
8 by then
9 burst into tears
10 looking forward to

Note
In sentence 5, 'short cut back to the village' means 'a quicker way home'.

LESSON SIX (Lesson Suggestion 2)

Objective
The children will write sentences about a picture.

Preparation
Give out *Pupil's Book 1* to each child (page 5, Lesson 6).

Method
1 Remind the children that:
verbs are *doing* words, or words that tell you about actions, e.g: walking, jumping, looking.
nouns are *naming* words, for things, people and places, e.g: chair, woman, river.
adjectives are words which describe things, e.g: tall, short, round, silly, beautiful.
2 Ask the children to suggest some verbs, nouns and adjectives for the picture. Write lists of these words on the blackboard to help the children in their written work, e.g:
Verb: running, kicking, playing, cleaning, watching, collecting.
Nouns: boy, girl, broom, playground, football, hut, tree, dress.
Adjectives: young, tidy, dirty, lazy.
3 Ask the children to write six sentences about the picture. Explain the examples in the book. The children must underline the doing words, naming words and describing words in their sentences.

Possible Answers
1 A girl is *cleaning* the window.
A boy is *collecting* the rubbish.
The children are *playing* football.
2 One *girl* is cleaning the window.
The *children* are playing with the football.
The *children* are tidying the playground.
3 The *good* girl is sweeping the *untidy* playground.
The *helpful* boy is kicking up the *dirty* rubbish.
The *lazy* girl is watching the children play.

WRITTEN COMPOSITION

LESSON ONE (Lesson Suggestion 38)

Objective
The children will sort out sentences and put them in the correct order to make a sensible story.

Preparation
Give out *Pupil's Book 1* to each child (page 6, Lesson 1).

Method
1 Read through the introductions.
2 Let the children work in groups and discuss what order they think the sentences in each story should be written in.
3 Select one or two groups to tell you what order they have decided for one of the stories. Discuss with the class whether they are right or wrong.
4 Repeat 3 to discuss the next story, and so on.

Note
If your children do not know about how frogs grow, miss out story A and begin with story B.

Answers
A Tadpoles go through many stages before turning into frogs. First of all the two back legs appear. Next the front legs grow. The long tail begins to disappear after the legs have grown. Changes also take place inside the body.
B John woke up early and began to get ready for work. He washed and dressed. Then he ate some pawpaw for breakfast. After breakfast he walked to the bus stop.
C Kewon saw a wild pig in his garden and decided to kill it. He approached the gardens very quietly so as not to frighten the pig away. Aiming carefully, Kewon threw the spear at the pig's body. The pig sank to the ground, dead.
D Bop and Anis went fishing in their canoe. When they were a long way out from the beach, they threw their nets and lines into the water. Suddenly both boys felt a strong tug on their lines. They pulled in their lines excitedly. They found that instead of a big fish, they had caught each other's lines.

LESSON TWO (Lesson Suggestion 15)

Objective
The children will choose the best sentence to describe a picture.

Preparation
Give out *Pupil's Book 1* to each child (page 7, Lesson 2).

Answers
1 Why won't this stupid car start?
2 Hey, you've put mud all over my dress!
3 Are you all right old man?
4 That plane is on fire! It's going to crash!

Note
If there is time, pupils could write a paragraph about one of the pictures.

SPELLING

Note
Do not try to do all the exercises in each week's unit. Choose the ones which give your pupils the kind of practice they need most.

LESSON ONE (Lesson Suggestion 22)

Objective
The children will learn to spell this week's words.

Preparation
Give out *Pupil's Book 1* to each child (page 8, Spelling List).

LESSON TWO

Select from Exercises A–E.

Preparation
Give out *Pupil's Book 1* to each child (pages 8–9).

Exercise A (Lesson Suggestion 29)

Objective
The children will be able to spell the list of words correctly and know what they mean.

Answers

1 harmful
2 shallow
3 abandon
4 tide
5 ability

Exercise B (Lesson Suggestion 23)

Possible Answers

1 bar car far jar star bark dark market
2 bore sore tore fork more pork stork for morning
3 water daughter sister butter faster
4 burn turn fur hurt
5 fir stir skirt shirt dirt

Exercise C (Lesson Suggestion 27)

Answers

1 after have out park queen rain smell
2 coastal grass king storm village why
3 dance holiday market singsing yesterday

Exercise D (Lesson Suggestion 23)

Possible Answers

1 Information: form mat formation inform ration nation fort main in for
2 Altogether: to get the that got goal gale halt hog rag rot lot gate

3 Conversation: sat ration not tin cat on stir stove cast can cannot
4 Announcement: an noun ten men to announce cement ounce cent meant mount

Exercise E (Lesson Suggestion 33)

Answers

Clues Across	**Clues Down**
1 climate	1 coastal
3 palms	2 mission
5 sago	4 soil
6 nation	

HANDWRITING (Lesson Suggestion 33)

Preparation
Give out *Pupil's Book 1* to each child (page 10).

Note
Always encourage the pupils' best work by giving plenty of praise to those children who have really tried to produce neat work.

READING

INTRODUCTION (Lesson Suggestion 34)

Objective
The children will be able to understand the background to the story, and the meaning of new words. They will read the story silently.

Preparation
Give out *Reader 1* (pages 4–6), *'Grumble, Grumble, Grumble'*.

Method
1 Introduce the story. Discuss the word *grumble* (which means to complain a lot) and talk about some people who are never happy, whatever happens to them. Ask the children if they know people like that. Next, talk about *wishing*. Can wishes really come true? Ask the children what they think.
2 Follow Lesson Suggestion 34B.

LESSON ONE (Lesson Suggestion 34C)

Objective
The children will be able to answer questions to show that they understand the story.

Preparation
Give out *Reader 1* (pages 4–6) and *Pupil's Book 1* (page 11, Lesson 1) to each child.

Possible Answers

1 The wife wished for a large coconut.
2 The husband used the last wish to remove the coconut from his wife's head. (*Remove* means to get it off.)
3 The husband and wife began to laugh because they had been so silly.
4 No, the woman did not expect the first wish to come true. (*Expect* means to think something will happen.)
5 The husband was angry because his wife wasted the first wish.
6 The man wished that the coconut was stuck on top of his wife's head.
7 No, he didn't expect the wish to come true. He said it because he was angry with his stupid wife.
8 A married couple lived in a small village high in the mountains.
9 When they put the log on the fire, a little old man stepped out from the flames and gave them three wishes.
10 The husband wished that the coconut would stick on top of his wife's head.

LESSON TWO (Lesson Suggestion 35)

Exercise A

Objective

The children will be able to work out the meaning of a word from the context.

Preparation

Give out *Pupil's Book 1* to each child (page 11, Lesson 2, Exercise A).

Method

1 Read each sentence.
2 Read the sentence again, saying the word 'something' in place of the word in heavy print.
3 Ask the children questions about that word, to help them work out its meaning, e.g:
   1 Q: What is another word meaning to catch or seize a person?
     A: Capture, captured – meaning caught, taken prisoner
   2 Q: How would you move if you didn' want to wake someone?
     A: creep – walk quietly on tiptoe
   3 Q: If Sali was frightened he would not be happy about going with the sorceror. He would go . . .
     A: reluctantly – unwillingly, not wanting to do something.
   4 Q: If you were hungry, what would you look for?
     A: something edible – something that can be eaten
   5 Q: How do you feel when you have been walking and then sitting in the hot sun?
     A: drowsy – sleepy, tired
   6 Q: How do you put on something that is sticky?
     A: smear, smeared – wiped on
   7 Q: What do you call people who buy things in a store?
     A: customers – people who come to buy goods
   8 Q: What do you do when a singer has sung very well?
     A: applaud, applauded – clapped their hands
   9 Q: How would you feel if someone dropped your radio in the river?
     A: furious – very angry
   10 Q: What do you call people who live in a place?
     A: inhabitants – people living there

LESSON THREE

Objective
The children will learn the meanings of new words.

Preparation
Give out *Pupil's Book 1* to each child (page 12, Exercise B).

Method

1 Explain the meaning of each word in brackets, e.g:
Encyclopedia – a book of information on every subject
Dictionary – a book containing the words in a language and their meanings
Library – a place where you can borrow books to read
Museum – a building where interesting objects or artifacts are put on show
Basin – a bowl for holding water; a place to wash your hands
Cup – you drink out of this
Performance – a play acted in front of an audience
Audience – the people who watch a play (or other kind of performance)
Policeman – a man who belongs to the Police Force
Politican – a person interested in politics (government)
Scholarship – an award you can win which helps pay for further studies
Reward – if someone loses something precious, they may offer a reward (perhaps K10) to the person who finds it, and returns it to the owner

Answers

1 dictionary
2 museum
3 basin
4 performance
5 politican
6 scholarship

LESSON FOUR — Poetry (Lesson Suggestion 40)

Objective
The children will listen to a poem and think about what it means.

Preparation
Give out *Pupil's Book 1* to each child (page 13) *'Child's Moon'*.

Method

1 Read the poem out loud, slowly and clearly.
2 Read it again (or ask a child to read it).
3 Ask the children whether they like it and understand what it means.
Q: What is the poem about?
A: The moon.
4 Explain that poets often use words in unusual ways to try to make you understand their feelings about something, e.g: This winter calls the moon 'the eye of the night' because he feels as though the moon is watching him.
5 Discuss the questions and answers at the end of the poem.

Answers

1 sunny
2 The light from the moon would make the mountains pale.
3 a large golden ball or a spirit
4 calm, sweet

LESSON FIVE

Objective
The children will be able to play Reading Games.

Preparation
Give out *Reading Games for Grade 6* (pages 3–5, Unit 2).

Method
Choose games for the children to play.

LISTENING 2

LESSON ONE

Objective
The children will follow directions given by the teacher.

Method
T: Bring me a/the . . . or, Who can bring me a/the . . .? Ask a child to carry out the order, e.g:
Who can bring me a red book?
Bring me the longest stick.
Who can bring me a thick red book?
Bring me the third stone from the left.
Who can bring me the third book from the left on the second half?

LESSON TWO

Objective
The children will be able to identify musical instruments by their sound.

Preparation
Bring any instruments you can find to the class. These could include a guitar, ukeleli, Jew's harp, kundu, Tobo, garamut, etc. Keep them hidden from the children. You could also have a radio cassette on your desk.

Method
1 Ask all children to put their faces down on their desks while you play an instrument. They must not see you. Tell them to raise their hands when they think they can identify the sound.
2 Play a song from the radio cassette and ask children to identify the instruments used in the song, e.g: Elvis cassette –
Q: What instruments can you hear?
A: Guitar, piano, drums, etc.

TALKING

LESSON ONE (Lesson Suggestion 1C)

Objective
The children will practise last week's sentence pattern:
What can you see in the mirror? I can see myself in the mirror.

Method
1 Use the substitution table that is still written on the blackboard from last week and revise it thoroughly with the class.

LESSON TWO

Objective
The children will practise a sentence pattern they already know:
Can you tell me the time? It's a quarter past eight.

Preparation
Bring a demonstration clock to the class.

Method
1 Show the children the clock and ask: Can you tell me the time?
A child will answer: It's half past nine.
2 Make different times on the clock and each time ask: Can you tell me the time?
3 Divide class into groups. Each group will use a demonstration clock, or draw a clock on paper or blackboard. Children must ask the question and give the answer using this sentence pattern.

LESSON THREE

Objective
The children will be able to use a new sentence pattern:
Can you see yourself in the water? Yes, I can see myself. No, I can't.

Preparation
Have mirrors, lids of tins or coconut shells of water ready.

Method
1 T: Can you see yourselves in the water?
C: Yes, we can see ourselves in the water.
2 Point to one group and ask the rest of the class:
T: Can they see themselves in the water?
C: Yes, they can see themselves.
3 Organize children into groups to practise this pattern.

LESSON FOUR

Objective
The children will practise this sentence pattern:
Can you see yourself in the water? Yes, I can see myself. No, I can't see myself.

Method
1 Continue as for Lesson Three with further examples. This time, teach negative answers, i.e: No, I can't see myself in the water.
Q. Can you see yourself in the photograph?
A: No, I can't see myself in the photograph.
Q: Can she see herself in the picture?
A: No, she can't see herself in the picture.
Q: Can we see ourselves in the water?
A: No, we can't.

LESSON FIVE (Lesson Suggestion 1C)

Objective
The children will practise Lessons Three and Four using a substitution table.

Preparation
Write the following substitution table on the blackboard:

	SHE		HERSELF		PICTURE?		SHE		HERSELF
	THEY		THEMSELVES		WINDOW?		THEY		THEMSELVES
Can	YOU	see	YOURSELF	in the	WATER?	No,	I	can't see	MYSELF.
	WE		OURSELVES		MIRROR?		WE		OURSELVES
	HE		HIMSELF		PHOTOGRAPH?		HE		HIMSELF

Note
If possible, leave the table on the blackboard for next week's Talking Lesson One.

ORAL EXPRESSION

LESSON ONE

Objective
The children will be able to describe how to get somewhere.

Preparation
Give out *Pupil's Book 1* to each child (page 18, Lesson 2).

Method
1 Ask children to study the plan of Burimur Village.
2 Ask a child for directions, e.g: If I were at house number 6, how would I get to house number 3?
3 Ask a child to give directions to reach somewhere in your district, e.g: How would you get to the river from our school?

LESSON TWO

Objective
The children will discuss a given topic, expressing their own point of view.

Preparation
Write the following heading on the blackboard:
SCHOOL RULES AND WHY WE SHOULD HAVE THEM.

Method
1 Read out the heading and then ask the class if they think school rules are necessary.
2 Encourage children to give arguments for or against school rules.
3 What kind of rules should our school have? Ask children for suggestions.

Note
If the school has no formal rules, this may be the time to make a list. These could then be shown to the Headmaster and, with his approval, could be presented to the rest of the school. If school rules already exist, pupils may suggest changes to these.

LESSON THREE

Objective
The children will tell a story using their imagination.

Method

1 Introduce a story by saying something like: The other night I had a dream. I dreamed that I was digging in my garden when a huge worm twenty metres long slid up to me.
2 Then ask one child to continue the next part of the story.
3 Then ask someone else to carry on the story, and so on until the story is ended.

Note

If the children cannot think of ideas, ask questions which will help stimulate their imaginations, e.g: Where do you think the worm could have come from?

WRITTEN SENTENCES

Note

Teach only five of the lessons. Choose one for homework, or for fast workers to do.

LESSON ONE (Lesson Suggestion 6)

Objective

The children will be able to complete sentences.

Preparation

Give out *Pupil's Book 1* to each child (page 14, Lesson 1).

Method

1 Read through the sentence beginnings with the children, e.g:
T: They went home . . . *When* did they go home?
C: They went home after dark.
2 Ask children for suitable endings. When they have answered all the questions orally, instruct the children to write down the completed sentences in their exercise books.

Possible Answers

1 They went home after they shot two pigs.
2 They caught two fish with their spears.
3 Henao didn't go to school yesterday because he was sick.
4 I am going to build a new house next year.
5 I am going into town by truck.
6 I have to visit the dentist because I have a toothache.
7 I am going to see Uncle Ramu in Rabaul at Christmas.
8 We are going to Manus Island by boat.
9 Father has to go to hospital to have an operation.
10 We will have lunch at twelve o'clock.

Note

It is important to collect books at the end of this lesson for marking.

LESSON TWO (Lesson Suggestion 7)

Objective

The children will be able to choose the correct form of the verb.

Preparation

Give out *Pupil's Book 1* to each child (page 14, Lesson 2).

Method

1 Read out the example given and the answer.
2 Read out several more as examples and ask the children to choose the correct verb.
3 Ask the children to write the completed sentences in their exercise books.

Answers

1 flew	4 seen	7 owned	10 thinking
2 give	5 find	8 danced	
3 feeds	6 buy	9 sang	

LESSON THREE (Lesson Suggestion 10)

Objective

The children wil be able to shorten words by using apostrophes.

Preparation

Give out *Pupil's Book 1* to each child (page 15, Lesson 3).

Method

1 Explain that when we talk in English we often shorten words.
2 Read the example. Work out several other examples with the children before asking them to write down the answers.

Answers

1 wouldn't	4 can't	7 doesn't I'll	10 you'd wouldn't
2 didn't	5 they'll	8 doesn't	
3 won't	6 I'd	9 I'd	

LESSON FOUR

Objective

The children will be able to find words which have opposite meanings to words given.

Preparation

Give out *Pupil's Book 1* to each child (Page 15, Lesson 4).

Method

1 Read out the example to the class.
2 Discuss several other examples with the class orally before instructing them to write down their answers in their exercise books.

Answers

1 stupid	4 hot	7 broken	10 deep
2 sad	5 long	8 dirty	
3 wild	6 poor	9 dry	

Note

Make sure that the children fully understand what is meant by *opposite* before doing this work. Give simple examples, e.g: up – down, fast – slow.

LESSON FIVE

Objective

The children will be able to think up suitable words to describe things.

Preparation

Give out *Pupil's Book 1* to each child (page 16, Lesson 5).

Method
Read the example given and then ask children to complete other examples.

Possible Answers

1 tall/huge
2 sweet/fragrant/fresh
3 tired/exhausted
4 blue/white
5 exciting/interesting
6 long/black/shiny
7 lively/loud/gay
8 exhausting/tiring
9 exhausted/sweating/puffing
10 broken/untidy/messy

LESSON SIX

Objective
The children will be able to use nouns, verbs and adjectives in good sentences.

Preparation
Give out *Pupil's Book 1* to each child (page 16, Lesson 6).

Method
1 Revise Unit 1, Lesson 6 on page 5.
2 Read the example and explain how this sentence was made from the lists, e.g: Take the first words listed under nouns, verbs and adjectives. These are: boy ice-cream licked young cold.
3 Ask the children to arrange all these words and use them with other words to make a good sentence: The young boy licked the cold ice-cream.
4 Work out several more answers before children write in their books.

Answers
1 The cruel man kicked the black cat.
2 The clever thief stole the valuable book.
3 The excited children swam in the cool sea.
4 The old man chewed the bitter betel-nut.
5 The colourful birds flew in the air.
6 The hungry cow swallowed the prickly leaf.
7 The angry mother smacked the naughty baby.

WRITTEN COMPOSITION

LESSON ONE (Lesson Suggestion 16)

Objective
The children will be able to write a story about a day-dream.

Preparation
Give out *Pupil's Book 1* to each child (pages 16–17, Lesson 1).

Method
1 Read the story at the beginning of the lesson and refer to the illustration.
2 Ask children to tell about any strange dreams they have had.
3 Talk about day-dreaming.
4 Tell children to pretend that they are the girl or boy in the picture and write about the day-dream that they are having.
5 If they do not have enough time to finish their story, ask children to complete it for homework.

Note
Collect all books for marking.

LESSON TWO

Objective
The children will be able to understand written directions.

Preparation
Give out *Pupil's Book 1* to each child (page 18, Lesson 2).

Method
1 Study the plan of the village together. This should already have been discussed during Oral Expression Lesson 1.
2 Read out the first direction and ask who can find the house. Child gives the number of the house for his answer.

Answers

1 Bob	4 John	7 Tom	10 Kewa
2 Wamp	5 Pila	8 Anis	
3 Toa	6 Puk	9 Guan	

SPELLING

LESSON ONE (Lesson Suggestion 22)

Objective
The children will learn to spell this week's words.

Preparation
Give out *Pupil's Book 1* to each child (page 19, Spelling List).

LESSON TWO

Select work from Exercises A–E. Some of these exercises could be given as homework.

Preparation
Give out *Pupil's Book 1* to each child (pages 19–20).

Exercise A (Lesson Suggestion 29)

Answers

1 decide	3 account	5 decorate
2 trawler	4 bait	

Exercise B (Lesson Suggestion 23)

Possible Answers
1 what who which white what wheat whale where while whole
2 shout shake show shine sheep shed shell ship shelter
3 thing that thought think the throat three threw though
4 church cheese chin change chase chew chicken child chain

Note
There are many more possible answers to the above exercise.

Exercise C

Answers

1 tide
2 rough
3 current
4 waves
5 shallow

Exercise D

Possible Answers

1 His father was very cross when he heard the news.
Do you think we can cross the river?
2 We will wave goodbye from the verandah.
A huge wave overturned the boat.
3 I would like to lie in bed this morning.
He told the teacher a lie instead of telling the truth.
4 We saw a ship on the horizon.
They used a saw to cut up that tree.
5 This work is too hard for me.
That biscuit is too hard to bite.

Exercise E (Lesson Suggestion 23)

Possible Answers

top – pin – not – tan – nap – put – tip – pat – half – fork – kind – down – nest -thin – neck – keep – path

HANDWRITING (Lesson Suggestion 33)

Preparation
Give out *Pupil's Book 1* to each child (page 21).

READING

INTRODUCTION (Lesson Suggestion 34)

Objective
The children will be able to understand the background to the story, and the meaning of new words. They will read the story silently.

Preparation
Give out *Reader 1* to each child (pages 7–9), *'Deruma's Dream'*.

Method
1 Introduce the story. Talk about Cargo Cults. Explain that because some people didn't understand that modern-day things (cargo) were made in factories in other countries, they believed that the cargo came on boats or planes which were sent by spirits. This story is about a man who has a dream about some cargo coming in a ship.
2 Follow Lesson Suggestion 34B.

LESSON ONE (Lesson Suggestion 34C)

Objective
The children will be able to answer questions to show that they understand the story.

Preparation
Give out *Reader 1* (pages 7–9) and *Pupil's Book 1* (page 22, Lesson 1).

Answers
1 presents
2 wanted it to be true
3 wasn't coming
4 He dreamed that a ship was coming loaded with presents.
5 His wife heard him say, 'When the moon is brightest'.
6 They stopped working because they thought the ship would bring them gifts.
7 No, he just pretended he had the dream so that everyone would go back to work.
8 He felt very sorry that he had told them about it.
9 The old man told everyone about his dream so that they would go back to work and forget about Deruma's dream.
10 The old man was very wise.

LESSON TWO

Objective
The children will be able to choose the correct statement about a story they have read and understood.

Preparation
Give out *Pupil's Book 1* to each child (page 22, Lesson 2, Exercise A).

Method
1 Read the first short story and ask children to choose the correct statement. If they suggest the wrong one, read through the story again so that children can see why it is not correct.
2 Work out the second one with the children.
3 Ask them to write down the answers in their exercise books.

Answers
1 Kura wasn't sick.
2 I caught a cuscus.
3 Maria's voice is high.
4 Uncle Tau and Tom made the outrigger.

LESSON THREE (Lesson Suggestion 37)

Objective
The children will be able to understand written instructions.

Preparation
Give out *Pupil's Book 1* to each child (page 23, Exercise B).

Method
1 Read the directions and make sure the children understand them.
2 Explain the first two examples. Then ask a child to write the next answer on the blackboard. Discuss what he or she has done.
3 Children write down the answers in their exercise books.

Answers

hat cat catch hatch at atlas at last last lost lot plot

LESSON FOUR – Poetry (Lesson Suggestion 40)

Objective

The children will be able to listen to a poem and think about what it means.

Preparation

Give out *Pupil's Book 1* (page 24) *'Canoe Song'*.

Answers

1 The sea is rough.
2 The sea is calm.
3 There are no adults in the poem because the first line says 'paddle, paddle children, Oldio'.

LESSON FIVE

Objective

The children will be able to play Reading Games.

Preparation

Give out *Reading Games for Grade 6* to each child (pages 3–5, Unit 2).

Method

Choose games for the children to play.

LISTENING 3

LESSON ONE

Objective

The children will listen to a story and answer questions about it.

Method

1 Ask the children to listen carefully, then read or tell them a short story. Ask the children questions about the story.

Example

Of the nine children in Grade 5 at the Mambu Community School, two girls and one boy came from Selep. The Head Teacher of the school was Mr Pawea. The class teacher was Mrs Sewi. The Selep children liked English and scored good marks for English in their exam. Every day they brought fresh fruit to school for their lunch, except on Friday when they brought peanuts and kaukau.

Questions

1 How many children in Grade 5 came from Selep? (three)
2 Who was the Head Teacher of the Mambu school? (Mr Pawea)
3 What did the children eat for lunch on Wednesday? (fresh fruit)
4 Which school subject were the Selep children best at? (English)

LESSON TWO

Objective

Children will listen carefully to identify sounds.

Method

1 Tell the children to close their eyes and listen.
2 Make a sound, several times, loud enough for everyone to hear.
3 Tell the children to put their hands up if they know what the sound is.

Examples

knocking on the door, closing the door, sharpening a pencil, writing on the blackboard, clapping, whistling, running water, walking, running, dropping a pencil/ruler/book, lighting a match, heavy breathing, coughing.

TALKING

LESSON ONE (Lesson Suggestion 1C)

Objective

The children will practise last week's sentence pattern:
Can you see yourself in the water? Yes, I can see myself. No, I can't.

Method

Point to the substitution table that is still on the blackboard from last week and resire it thoroughly with the class.

LESSON TWO

Objective

The children will practise a sentence pattern they already know:
What are you doing tomorrow? I'm going to town tomorrow.

Method

1 Ask a child: What are you doing tomorrow?
The child answers: I'm going fishing.
The teacher answers: No, you're not. You're coming to school.
2 Ask other questions like:
What are you doing on Thursday after school?
What are you doing in the school holidays?
What are you doing this afternoon after school?
What are you doing in the week-end?
3 Divide the class into groups. Each pupil has a turn to ask a question and answer a question.

LESSON THREE

Objective

The children will be able to use a new sentence pattern:
What's he doing? He's washing himself.

Method

1 Ask a child to pretend to wash himself.
T: What's he doing?
C: He's washing himself.
T: What's she doing?
C: She's washing herself.
2 Tell the pupils in the front row to rub themselves to get warm. Ask the others: What are they doing?
C: They're warming themselves.

T: What are you doing?
C: I'm warming myself.
T: What is she doing?
C: She's warming herself.

3 In groups, pupils must mime something and the others must guess, e.g: What am I doing? You're drying yourself.

LESSON FOUR

Objective
The children will practise this sentence pattern:
What's he doing? He's washing himself.

Method
1 Tell children to think of something to do to themselves, e.g: scratch, tickle, smile, whistle, hum.
2 Now point to a child and ask: What are you doing? or What's she doing? Children must answer: I'm scratching myself, or She's smiling to herself.
3 In groups, children must ask each other: What are you doing? or point to another child and say: What's he doing?
Other examples could be: I'm tickling myself.
I'm whistling to myself.
I'm humming to myself.
I'm pinching myself.
I'm helping myself.
I'm admiring myself. (in a mirror)

LESSON FIVE (Lesson Suggestion 1C)

Objective
The children will practise the new sentence pattern, using a substitution table.

Preparation
Write the following substitution table on the blackboard and leave it on till next week:

What's	SHE	doing?	SHE'S	washing	HERSELF.	
	HE		HE'S	scratching	HIMSELF	
	IT		IT'S	licking	ITSELF	(dog)

What are	THEY	doing?	THEY'RE	admiring	THEMSELVES.
	YOU		I'M	pinching	MYSELF
	WE		WE'RE	enjoying	OURSELVES

ORAL EXPRESSION

LESSON ONE

Objective
The children will be able to describe objects.

Method
1 Choose a pupil to *describe* an object to the class (e.g. a canoe) without telling the class what it is.
2 The others must try to guess what that person is describing.
3 The child who guesses correctly has the next turn at describing something.

Note
If the pupil cannot think of anything to describe, give help by saying: describe something in the classroom, or something that can be found in the village.

LESSON TWO

Objective
The children will be able to give oral directions.

Preparation
Give out *Pupil's Book 1* to each child (page 30, Lesson 2).

Method
1 Choose two pupils, one to be a stranger to town and the other to be a local.
2 The stranger must ask the local how to get somewhere.
3 The local must give the stranger directions, e.g:
Stranger: Excuse me, I'm a stranger here. I'm at the Post Office now, could you tell me how to get to the Bank from here?
Local: Yes, of course, just continue down Rua Street . . . etc.

LESSON THREE

Objective
The children will be able to give accurate explanations.

Method
1 You are the 'Magician'. You have the power to grant wishes to children as long as they give you good reasons why their wish should be granted.
2 Choose a pupil for a wish to be granted, e.g:
P: I wish I could go to Port Moresby during the next holidays.
T: Why do you want this wish?
P: So that I can see what a big city is like. I would like to see big buildings and lots of traffic and I would like to visit my wantoks who live there. I would like to go to the drive-in movies and buy ice-creams when I'm hot.
T: Very well then, your wish will be granted.

WRITTEN SENTENCES

Note
You should teach only FIVE of the six lessons. Choose one lesson for homework, or for fast workers to do.

LESSON ONE (Lesson Suggestion 9)

Objective
The children will be able to use apostrophes to show possession.

Preparation
Give out *Pupil's Book 1* to each child (page 25, Lesson 1).

Method
1 Explain the examples to the children. (See step 1 of Lesson Suggestion 9)
2 Work out several more examples on the blackboard asking the children where to put the apostrophe.
3 Children write the answers in their exercise books.

Answers

1 Mele's	4 dogs', pigs'	7 pig's	10 hen's
2 boys'	5 truck's	8 sister's, mother's	
3 father's	6 John's	9 teacher's	

LESSON TWO (Lesson Suggestion 11)

Objective
The children will be able to change sentences from singular into plural.

Preparation
Give out *Pupil's Book 1* to each child (page 25, Lesson 2).

Method
1 Follow steps 1–4 of Lesson Suggestion 11.
2 Write the examples given at the beginning of the lesson, on the blackboard. Put a circle around each word that is changed in the answer, i.e: The *men* raised *their spears*, ready to throw them.
3 Work out the next two examples in the same way, on the blackboard. When you are sure that the pupils know how to do them, then they can write down their answers.

Answers
1 These loaves of bread are stale.
2 The women were sitting beside the fire/s.
3 The men's wives burned the food for the singsing/s.
4 The boys had to sharpen their knives before they could cut the grass.
5 The PMV trucks were waiting to take the children into town.
6 The babies were asleep in the baskets under the mango trees.
7 When it began to rain, the men cut down large leaves to use as umbrellas.
8 Gawi cut his feet on giant clam shells lying on the beach.
9 The girls' teeth were sore after they ate so many sweets.
10 The mice had eaten all the rice in the cupboards.

LESSON THREE (Lesson Suggestion 6)

Objective
The children will be able to match sentence beginnings with the most suitable endings, to make good sentences.

Preparation
Give out *Pupil's Book 1* to each child (page 26, Lesson 3).

Method
1 Read the instructions to the class. Do the example orally with the children. Explain why none of the other endings would make a sensible sentence.
2 Ask the class for the correct answers for the next three or four sentences. Make sure they think about the *meaning* of the sentences.
3 Children write their sentences in their exercise books.

Answers
2 The men were out hunting for wild pigs.
3 The baby cried when his mother went away.
4 The pupils read books in the school library.
5 Kipa cleaned the fish ready for dinner.
6 They paddled the canoe out to sea.
7 The boys dived into the water to look for crayfish.
8 The helicopter rescued the people from the wrecked plane.

9 They bought taro and kaukau at the market.
10 Tau opened a tradestore in his village.

LESSON FOUR (Lesson Suggestion 2)

Objective
The children will be able to write suitable questions and answers to match illustrations.

Preparation
Give out *Pupil's Book 1* to each child (page 26, Lesson 4).

Possible Answers
2 What are the children doing? They are choosing library books.
3 What is the nurse doing? She is washing the boy's foot.
4 What is the policeman doing? He is directing the traffic.
5 What is grandmother doing? She is sewing a dress.
6 What are the women doing? They are washing clothes in the river.

LESSON FIVE (Lesson Suggestion 8)

Objective
The children will be able to choose the correct word to fit in a sentence.

Preparation
Give out *Pupil's Book 1* to each child (page 27, Lesson 5).

Answers
1 allowed
2 break
3 threw, blew
4 peel
5 hole
6 seen
7 know
8 cheap
9 plane
10 tires

LESSON SIX

Objective
The children will be able to choose the most suitable adjectives to describe things.

Preparation
Give out *Pupil's Book 1* to each child (page 28, Lesson 6).

Method
1 Read all the words and make sure that the children understand what they mean.
2 Look at each picture and ask the pupils to tell you about each one.
3 Which of the words in the list describe the first picture?
4 Children write down their answers.

Answers
1 stormy thundery windy
2 large heavy wrinkly
3 broken-down deserted old
4 shy pretty young

WRITTEN COMPOSITION

LESSON ONE (Lesson Suggestion 16)

Objective
The children will be able to write an imaginative story.

Preparation
Give out *Pupil's Book 1* to each child (page 29, Lesson 1).

Method
1 Discuss the picture with the children, asking them the questions listed underneath.
2 Read the instructions given.
3 Tell children that they do not have to use the sentence beginnings given, but they can if they wish to.

Follow Up
Choose pupils to read their finished stories to the class.

LESSON TWO

Objective
The children will be able to follow written directions.

Preparation
Give out *Pupil's Book 1* to each child (page 30, Lesson 2).

Methoa
1 Ask the children to study the map carefully.
2 Read out the directions for getting to the market from the hotel. Ask the children to follow them, using their fingers on the map in their books.
3 Next ask the children to give directions for getting to the Bank from the Post Office.

Answer (*Should be something like this.*)
You are at the Post Office. Walk along Rua Street to Rowa Street. Now cross over Rowa Street on the pedestrian crossing. Turn left, then turn right into Dika Street by the hotel. Walk right down to the other end of Dika Street. Cross over the road into Rewa Street and turn right. You will find the Bank on your left, on the corner of Rewa Street and Muruk Street.

SPELLING

LESSON ONE (Lesson Suggestion 22)

Objective
The children will learn to spell this week's words.

Preparation
Give out *Pupil's Book 1* to each child (page 30, Spelling List).

LESSON TWO

Select from Exercises A–E. (Choose the ones which will give your pupils the practice they need.)

Preparation
Give out *Pupil's Book 1* to each child (pages 30–1).

Exercise A (Lesson Suggestion 29)

Answers

1 arrange
2 wrap
3 arrest
4 arrive
5 wrong

Exercise B

Testing in pairs.

Exercise C (Lesson Suggestion 27)

Answers

1 apple elephant parrot pen seventy underneath
2 bank change queen sand soft window
3 diamond fairy gather gentle gold wide

Exercise D

Answers

silent b: comb dumb lamb numb limb
silent w: wrestle wreck wrong wring writing
silent k: knee knock knob know knew

Exercise E

Answers

1 trawler
2 outrigger
3 bait
4 sinker
5 spear

HANDWRITING (Lesson Suggestion 33)

Preparation
Give out *Pupil's Book 1* to each child (page 32).

READING

INTRODUCTION (Lesson Suggestion 34)

Objective
The children understand the background to the story, and the meaning of the new words. They will read the story silently.

Preparation
Give out *Reader 1* to each child (pages 10–13), *'The Carving'*.

Method
1 Introduce the story. Ask the children to name some traditional artifacts, e.g: carvings, masks, drums, etc. Discuss why these things are valuable, not

only in terms of money but because they are a part of our culture and heritage. Explain that very old artifacts are more valuable than most modern artifacts, because they are rarer. Some pupils may know of old artifacts that are kept in their village. Discuss them.

2 Follow Lesson Suggestion 34B.

LESSON ONE (Lesson Suggestion 34C)

Objective

Children will be able to answer comprehension questions to show that they understand the story.

Preparation

Give out *Reader 1*, (pages 10–13) and *Pupil's Book 1* (page 33, Lesson 1) to each child.

Answers

1 For years the rain had wet the carving and the sun had dried it. These things had made the carving wear and begin to crack.
2 Toku bought baskets, paintings, wooden masks, carved crocodiles, birds and pigs from the villagers.
3 Matias did not want the carving sold because it belonged to his ancestors and he thought it should stay where it belonged, in his village.
4 Toku gave Matia K10 for the carving.
5 Matias chopped up some old wood and told Toku that it was the carving.
6 Toku was dishonest and greedy.
7 dishonest
8 wise, clever, proud
9 cracked, old, grey
10 The villagers became interested in the carving because Matias had shown them how important and valuable it was to them.

LESSON TWO

Exercise A

Objective

The children will be able to write a paragraph about what one of the story characters thought.

Preparation

Give out *Reader 1* (pages 10–13) and *Pupil's Book 1* (page 33, Lesson A).

Method

1 Read out what Toku thought.
2 Read the instructions and then ask the children for answers.
3 After they have given oral answers, they must write a paragraph in their exercise books.

Answer

Matias would have thought something like this: 'You are a very dishonest man Toku. You know very well that this is a very old and valuable carving. You don't really want it for firewood at all. You will take it and sell it for a lot of money and cheat us.'

LESSON THREE (Lesson Suggestion 38)

Exercise B

Objective
The children will be able to arrange the sentences in the correct order.

Preparation
Give out *Reader 1* (pages 10–13) and *Pupil's Book 1* (page 33, Exercises B & C) to each child.

Method
1 Read the instructions.
2 Read the sentences and ask the children to put them in the correct order orally.
3 They may have to look at the story in the reader to remind them.

Answers
1 Matias dug a hole around the carving and pushed it back and forth until it came loose.
2 He lowered the carving to the ground and dragged it off into the bush.
3 He covered it with leaves and branches.
4 Next he searched around amongst the trees until he found an old dead tree trunk.
5 He chopped up the old trunk into pieces of firewood.

Exercise C (optional)

Method
1 Read the instruction.
2 Discuss the meanings of these phrases. If necessary, find each one in the story to demonstrate its meanings.
3 Ask the children to suggest suitable sentences to use these phrases.

Possible Answers
1 I was beginning to fall asleep in my chair.
2 I wiggled my loose tooth back and forth.
3 He fell over on his way home from school.
4 We knew that the Head Teacher was coming to deal with us for breaking our chairs.
5 The teacher gave them time to talk amongst themselves.

LESSON FOUR — Poetry (Lesson Suggestion 40)

Objective
The children will listen to a poem and think about what it means.

Preparation
Give out *Pupil's Book 1* to each child (page 34), '*Flames*'.

Answers
1 The poet imagines the flames to be dancers.
2 The wind would make the flames dance wildly.
3 The wood had all been burned.

If there is more time left in this lesson, give out supplementary reading material for enjoyment.

LISTENING 4

LESSON ONE

Objective
The children will be able to listen carefully and follow the directions given them.

Preparation
Give each pupil a piece of paper and crayons or coloured pencils.

Method
1 Say: Listen carefully and do exactly as I say.
2 Then give directions for the children to follow, e.g:
Draw a red line near the top of your page. Draw a blue cat near the centre of the page. With your pencil, draw a square near the bottom of your page. Print the word FRIEND on your paper with a space between each letter. Draw a circle around the letter that comes after R. Draw a square around the last letter, etc.

LESSON TWO

Objective
The children will be able to tell what kind of mood the teacher is in by the way he or she talks.

Method
1 Explain to the children that you can tell a lot about someone's mood (how he feels) by the way he talks.
2 Say something to the class and they must guess how you feel, e.g:
T: (In a very tired voice) I don't think I'll be able to go to the party tonight, I'm sorry.
C: You are feeling tired.
T: (In a very happy voice) Good morning everyone. Isn't it a lovely sunny day today!
C: You are feeling happy.
T: (In an angry voice) Nobody is going to play with the sport's equipment today!
C: You are feeling angry.

Other emotions you could express are: fear, sadness, disappointment.
3 After several examples, choose pupils to say something while the rest of the class guess how they feel.

TALKING

LESSON ONE (Lesson Suggestion 1C)

Objective
The children will practise last week's sentence pattern:
What's he doing? He's washing himself.

Method
Point to the substitution table on the blackboard and revise it with the class.

LESSON TWO

Objective
The children will practise a sentence pattern they already know:
When the bell rang, what did they do? When the bell rang, the children went to assembly.

Method
1 Say this pattern. Ask children for different answers.
2 Ask similar questions, e.g:
When the fire started, what did they do?
When the storm broke, what did they do?
When the car broke down, what did they do?
When the rain started, what did they do?
Encourage children to give good answers.
3 Divide the class into groups. Each child must ask her own question and choose someone in the group to answer it.

LESSON THREE

Objective
The children will be able to use a new sentence pattern:
When Waru looked in the mirror, he saw himself.

Method
1 Ask a child to look in the mirror. Say to the class: When Tom looked in the mirror, what did he see?
Answer: When Tom looked in the mirror he saw himself.
2 Give other examples for the children to repeat after you.
When the man fell over he hurt himself.
When the dog swam to the shore it shook itself.
When the people went to the party they enjoyed themselves.
When we put on our costumes, we admired ourselves.
3 Practise these examples in groups.

LESSON FOUR

Objective
The children will practise this sentence pattern:
When Susa fell off the chair, she hurt herself.

Method
1 Tell the children to mime the following:
Fall off a chair.
Pretend to fall in the river.
Pretend to cut open a watermelon and cut your hand.
2 Ask questions after each mime, e.g: What happened when Jula fell off the chair? Children must answer: When Julia fell off the chair, she hurt herself.

LESSON FIVE (Lesson Suggestion 1C)

Objective
The children will practise the new sentence pattern using a substitution table.

Preparation
Write the following substitution table on the blackboard.

When	PETA	looked in the	MIRROR	HE	saw	HIMSELF.
	SARA		PHOTOGRAPH	SHE		HERSELF.
	WE		WATER	WE		OURSELVES.
	THEY		POOL	THEY		THEMSELVES.
	THE PIG		RIVER	IT		ITSELF.

Note
Leave the table on the board for next week's revision lesson.

ORAL EXPRESSION

LESSON ONE

Objective
The children will be able to tell a story about a picture.

Preparation
Give out *Pupil's Book 1* to each child (page 38, Written Composition).

Method
1 Tell the children to study the robbery picture on page 38.
2 Ask the children to tell you what is happening in this picture, e.g: Who are the robbers? Why are they robbing the bank? How are they going to escape? Will they get caught? What are they planning to do with the money?

Note
Encourage the children to be imaginative. They could bring in ideas not shown in the picture, e.g: the police.

LESSON TWO

Objective
The children will be able to ask questions to obtain information.

Method
1 Pretend to be someone important. Give only one clue, e.g: I am a famous PNG sportsman.
2 The children must ask questions to which you can answer only 'yes' or 'no'.
3 The children must keep asking questions until they guess the right person.
4 The person who guesses correctly will then pretend to be someone else who is well-known, e.g:
T: I am a famous PNG sportsman.
C: Are you a runner?
T: No.
C: Are you from the Central Province?
T: Yes.
etc.

LESSON THREE

Objective
The children will be able to greet each other and say goodbye politely.

Method

1 Teacher will write the following lists on the blackboard.

[GREETINGS]	[FAREWELLS]
Hello, Good Morning, Good afternoon, How are you? Good Evening.	Goodbye, Goodnight, See you again, See you later, It was nice seeing you.

2 Choose two pupils to act out a meeting. Pupils must greet each other politely using one of the phrases listed on the blackboard, hold a short conversation, then end the conversation with a farewell.

For Example

1st Pupil: Good morning Anis. How are you?
2nd Pupil: Hello Mary. I'm very well thank you.
1st P: Is your mother still in hospital?
2nd P: No, she's home again now and feeling much better.
1st P: That's good news. I must go now or I'll be late for school.
2nd P: It was good to see you. Goodbye!
1st P: Goodbye!

WRITTEN SENTENCES

Note

Teach only FIVE of the six lessons.

LESSON ONE (Lesson Suggestion 7)

Objective

The children will be able to choose the correct form of the verb to fit in a sentence.

Preparation

Give out *Pupil's Book 1* to each child (page 35, Lesson 1).

Method

1 Work out several examples orally with the class. Point out the words which show whether the verb needs to be past, present or future, e.g: tomorrow – future (will eat), am – present (reading), yesterday – past (bought).

2 When the children understand how to do this work, tell them to write down answers in their exercise books.

Answers

1 run or ran	4 looked	7 seen	10 gave
2 will eat	5 sank or sinks	8 drank	
3 went	6 reading	9 bought	

LESSON TWO (Lesson Suggestion 8)

Objective

The children will be able to choose the correctly spelled word from two similar sounding words (homonyms).

Preparation

Give out *Pupil's Book 1* to each child (page 35, Lesson 2).

Method
Follow Lesson Suggestion 8.

Answers

1 boar	4 tide	7 cell	10 sore
2 lessen	5 buy	8 bear	
3 piece	6 bury	9 mist	

LESSON THREE

Objective
The children will be able to write suitable questions for given answers and suitable answers to given questions.

Preparation
Give out *Pupil's Book 1* to each child (page 36, Lesson 3).

Method
1 Read the instructions to the class.
2 Ask for questions to match the answers given.
3 Look at number 6. Now ask for answers. Do the exercise orally before you ask the children to write down the answers.

Possible Answers
1 'Did you take my pen, Kila?' asked John.
2 'Have you seen Pipi?' asked Ella.
3 'Are you going to the market today, Herea?' asked Maria.
4 'Kessie, will you do my work for me today?' Bena asked.
5 'Are you good at Mathematics, Sarei?' asked Pita.
6 'No, I won't take Kia with me,' said Uncle.
7 'No, you can't come, Konio,' said Thomas.
8 'No, I'm not going to the river, Lai,' said Herea.
9 'No, I didn't take your bicycle, Sevese,' said Lukas.
10 'No, I haven't been busy,' said Toku.

LESSON FOUR (Lesson Suggestion 12)

Objective
The children will be able to change sentences from the past to the present tense.

Preparation
Give out *Pupil's Book 1* to each child (page 36, Lesson 4).

Method
Follow Lesson Suggestion 12. (Concentrate on past and present, not future.)

Answers
1 We are going to the singsing at Rebiamul.
2 They are going fishing in my canoe.
3 Father is catching a large lobster.
4 The women are preparing some taro for the men to take with them.
5 I am sweeping the kitchen floor.
6 Ria is helping father build a new house.
7 Mother is learning how to speak English.
8 Rawali is playing football with the High School boys.
9 They are filling the sacks with coffee beans.
10 They are picking many tea leaves at Warawau plantation.

LESSON FIVE (Lesson Suggestion 13)

Objective
The children will be able to put in the correct punctuation.

Preparation
Give out *Pupil's Book 1* to each child (page 37, Lesson 5).

Method
1 Revise the use of punctuation marks given at the beginning of the lesson. Give examples (see Lesson Suggestion 13).
2 Either write the story on the blackboard, and ask the children to correct the punctuation as you write, or ask the children to write the story correctly in their exercise books.

Answer
A few miles out of Lae is a small business called 'The Hatchery'. A man called Pela owns this business. Can you guess what this project is? Yes, it's a poultry farm. Pela rears chickens and sells them to people in town and in nearby villages.
One day a car stopped outside 'The Hatchery' and a man got out. 'Can I help you, Sir?' asked Pela.
'Yes', said the man. 'I am having a party and I need some chickens.'
'How many would you like?' asked Pela.
'I'd like two dozen', said the man.
'All right, if you drive your car round the side of the building, we'll load them into the back of it.'

LESSON SIX

Objective
The children will be able to think of suitable naming words to go in the spaces.

Preparation
Give out *Pupil's Book 1* for each child (page 37, Lesson 6).

Method
1 Read out instructions and ask for examples of naming words for things in the classroom. Do the exercise orally before you ask the children to write down their answers.

Possible Answers
1 ship/boat funnels
2 cup/plate/glass/mirror.
3 gate paddock/field
4 plane/aeroplane/helicopter
5 sea waves
6 bait line water/sea/river
7 boat/canoe spear water/sea/river

WRITTEN COMPOSITION

LESSON ONE

Objective
The children will be able to remember details from a picture and write about them.

Preparation
Give out *Pupil's Book 1* to each child (page 38, Lesson 1).

Method
1 Instruct children to study the picture very carefully, looking at details, e.g: the sign, the clock, the people, their clothes, etc.
2 Then ask the children to close their books.
3 Now read out each question slowly, allowing plenty of time for the pupils to write down their answers. They need not write complete sentences.

Answers
1 at twenty minutes past twelve
2 two
3 a truck and a car
4 two
5 shorts and shirts and scarves around their mouths and noses
6 a bag cach
7 they looked around them and ran
8 no, only two
9 a woman holding a baby
10 the car's number was T — 311; one man wore a dark shirt.

Follow-Up
Turn back to the illustration. Read out the answers for the children to mark their own. Discuss the answers, while looking at the picture. The children may have other suggestions for question 10.

LESSON TWO

Objective
The children will be able to describe a picture.

Preparation
Give out *Pupil's Book 1* to each child (page 39, Lesson 2).

Method
1 Ask the children for oral descriptions of the two pictures. Who is in each picture? What are they wearing? What are they carrying? Do they have any ornaments? etc.

Possible Answers
The Old Man
This man has a beard. He is dressed in both traditional and modern clothes. He is wearing a jacket and carrying an umbrella. He has on a feather head-dress and is wearing a kina shell around his neck. He is carrying an axe.
The Young Girl
This young girl is wearing a skirt made from grass. She is also wearing traditional ornaments round her neck and arms, and in her ears. She is sitting down.

SPELLING

LESSON ONE (Lesson Suggestion 22)

Objective
The children will learn to spell this week's words.

Preparation
Give out *Pupil's Book 1* to each child (page 39, Spelling List).

LESSON TWO

Select from Exercises A–E, or give a spelling test and dictation (Lesson Suggestion 25).

Preparation
Give out *Pupil's Book 1* to each child (pages 39–40).

Exercise A (Lesson Suggestion 29)

Answers

1 expect	3 envelope	5 feast
2 register	4 east	

Exercise B

Answers

bow and arrow	hammer and nails
hand and foot	shoes and socks
salt and pepper	lime and betel-nut

Exercise C

Answers

1 y	4 c	7 i	10 t (tea)
2 l	5 u	8 o (oh!)	
3 b	6 r	9 p (pea)	

Exercise D

Answers

1 outrigger	4 net	7 bait
2 spear	5 line	8 trawler
3 hook	6 sinker	

Exercise E

Answers

a broom	c enough	e seat
b chief	d why	

HANDWRITING (Lesson Suggestion 33)

Preparation
Give out *Pupil's Book 1* to each child (pages 41–2).

READING

INTRODUCTION (Lesson Suggestion 34)

Objective
The children will be able to understand the background to the story and the meaning of new words. They will read the story silently.

Preparation
Give out *Reader 1* (pages 14–16), '*The Letters*' (Part 1).

Method
1 Talk about old things which are rare and therefore valuable (worth a lot of money). Remind children of the story '*The Carving*' and how you discussed the value of old artifacts. Some stamps are also very valuable, especially if they are old and rare.
2 Follow Lesson Suggestion 34B.

LESSON ONE (Lesson Suggestion 34C)

Objective
Children will be able to answer questions to show that they understand the story.

Preparation
Give out *Reader 1* (pages 14–16) and *Pupil's Book 1* (page 42, Lesson 1).

Answers
1 It was the dry season and the dust made Ania's father cough.
2 The family could only visit their father at weekends because they could only afford the bus fares once a week.
3 The doctor gave Ania two kina so that she could come back the next day to see her father.
4 Ania could not open the box so she dropped a stone on it until the lid sprang open.
5 The box was full of old letters.
6 Ania's father had to go to hospital because he was sick.
7 He told her about the box so that if he died, his family would have some money.
8 The doctor gave Ania the money because he knew she did not have enough to come and see her father every day.
9 It was a black metal box.
10 Ania felt disappointed because she thought the letters were worthless.

LESSON TWO

Exercise A

Objective
The children will be able to understand written directions.

Preparation
Give out *Pupil's Book 1* (page 43, Lesson 2, Exercise A).

Method
1 Read the directions.
2 Ask the questions for children to answer orally.

Note
Make sure the children understand these words in the instructions.

sandpaper: paper covered with sand, used by painters for smoothing rough surfaces.
apply: to put on (paint)
thoroughly: really well
coat: (of paint) one layer of paint; i.e. when you paint a surface once

mineral turps: special cleaning fluid which can remove paint from paint brushes
contents: what is inside the tin
primer: a type of paint that is always used first on an unpainted surface
undercoat: a type of paint that is used after the primer
supergloss: a type of paint that is used for the last coat. Gloss means 'shine'
sealer: is a special type of waterproof paint

Answers

1 You must clean the surface by removing grease, dust, dirt and rust. Then you smooth it with sandpaper.
2 You must stir the paint thoroughly before you use it.
3 Use mineral turps to clean the brushes.
4 It will take about 72 hours, or three days. (3 coats × 24 hours)
5 You would need two tins of paint this size. (one tin covers 3 to 3.5 square metres)
6 primer undercoat gloss

LESSON THREE

Exercise B

Objective

The children will be able to obtain information by reading a notice.

Preparation

Give out *Pupil's Book 1* to each child (page 43, Lesson 2, Exercises B & C).

Method

1 Ask a child to read the notice aloud.
2 Read out the paragraph on page 44, choosing different children to fit in the right words.
3 If there is time, children can write the paragraph in their exercise books.

Answers

flight delayed two two Goroka weather take-off two Goroka

Exercise C

Objective

The children will be able to follow instructions.

Method

1 Read the introduction.
2 Very slowly read the instructions aloud to the class. Explain that the dashes beside each answer tell you the number of letters in the answer. (e.g: four dashes means a four-letter word)
3 Children must write the answers in their exercise books.

Answers

hand handle candle can cannot not note notes votes

LESSON FOUR (Lesson Suggestion 39)

Objective

The children will be able to read for enjoyment.

Preparation

Gather together reading material suitable for the children in your class.

LESSON FIVE – Poetry (Lesson Suggestion 40)

Objective
The children will be able to listen to a poem and think about what it means.

Preparation
Give out *Pupil's Book 1* to each child (page 45) '*The Mango Tree*'.

Possible Answers
1 The mango tree is an old tree so it would probably have been there before the road was made.
2 The tree likes the children because they stop it being lonely and it feels happy to give them its fruit.
3 The tree felt proud because it was able to make the children happy.
4 It feels sad and lonely because fewer children visit it and it knows that soon it will die.

LISTENING 5

LESSON ONE

Objective
The children will be able to remember 'key' words on re-telling a story.

Method
1 Select a short story.
2 Mark 'key' words which are important for the sense of the story. Read the story aloud and write each 'key' word on the blackboard as you say it, asking the children to remember these words.
3 Rub the 'key' words off the blackboard.
4 Now read the story again, this time pausing when you come to a 'key' word. The children must tell you what the missing word is.
e.g: Read this story to the class and write the underlined words on the blackboard: It was a **cloudy** day in Selep, one of those **rainy** season days when the sky looked like an old, grey, unwashed blanket.
Then rub off the words and read the story again, asking the children to say the missing words:
It was a . . . day in Selep, one of those . . . season days when the . . . looked like an old, grey, . . . blanket.

LESSON TWO

Objective
The children will listen carefully to hear which word in each group does not rhyme with the others.

Preparation
Write the following lists of words on the blackboard:
1 ball wall fall call
2 boy toy joy pie
3 truck back luck suck
4 see say me be
5 dog dig big pig
6 lot hot pot it

Method

1 Read out the words in number 1. Explain that they all 'rhyme' because the last part of each word sounds the same.
2 Now read out number 2 and ask the children to listen for the word which doesn't rhyme, i.e: in which the last part *doesn't* sound the same – 'pie'.
3 After doing several examples orally, ask the children to write down the two words that don't rhyme.

Answers

2 pie
3 back
4 say
5 dog
6 hit

TALKING

LESSON ONE (Lesson Suggestion 1)

Objective

The children will practise last week's sentence pattern:
When Waru looked in the mirror he saw himself.

Method

1 Use the substitution table on the blackboard and revise this work with the class.

LESSON TWO

Objective

The children will practise a sentence pattern they already know:
Who did you see when you went to the market?

Method

1 T: Who did you see when you went home last night?
C: I saw . . .
2 Other examples to ask: Who did you see when you went to town? Who did you see when you went to the pictures?
3 Introduce: Who came into the room before the bell rang?
Who went swimming after school?
Who saw the town before the earthquake?
4 Encourage children to ask similar questions and give answers.

LESSON THREE

Objective

The children will be able to use a new sentence pattern:
Who did they buy the peanuts for? They bought them for themselves.

Preparation

Set up a 'pretend' Tradestore in the classroom. Children buy goods. Teacher be the storekeeper. Later on, give a child a turn.

Method

1 T: Yes, what would you like?
C: I'd like a biro please.
T: There you are. Who is the biro for?
C: It's for me.

T: You bought it for yourself?
T: Who did you buy it for?
C: I bought it for myself.
T: (To the class) Who did he buy it for?
Class: He bought it for himself.

2 Choose other children to be in the shop.
Teacher ask the questions, e.g: Who did you buy the rice for?
I bought it for myself.
3 Choose children in the class to ask questions of the customer who bought something at the shop.

LESSON FOUR

Objective
The children will practise this sentence pattern:
Who did they buy the bananas for? They bought them for themselves.

Method
1 Give other examples of this sentence pattern, e.g:
Who did he make the canoe for? He made it for himself.
Who did she knit the jumper for? She knitted it for herself.
Who did she bake the cake for? She baked it for herself.
Who did they build the house for? They built it for themselves.
Who did we buy the food for? We bought it for ourselves.
2 Choose pupils to say a pattern after you, then make up one for themselves.

LESSON FIVE (Lesson Suggestion 1C)

Objective
The children will revise the new sentence pattern using a substitution table.

Preparation
Write the following substitution table on the blackboard.

Who did	THEY	BUY	the	FOOD	for?	THEY	BOUGHT	it for	THEMSELVES.
	WE			MILK		WE			OURSELVES
	SHE	SEW		DRESS		SHE	SEWED		HERSELF
	HE	CATCH		FISH		HE	CAUGHT		HIMSELF
	YOU	PAINT		PICTURE		I	PAINTED		MYSELF
	THEY	SING		SONG		THEY	SANG		THEMSELVES

Method
Follow Lesson Suggestion 1C.

Note
Leave the table on the board for next week's revision lesson.

ORAL EXPRESSION

LESSON ONE

Objective
The children will be able to ask for things in a polite way.

Method

1 Explain the difference between 'demanding' and 'asking politely', e.g:
I want a fish — demanding
May I have a fish please? — asking politely
2 Explain that it is important to ask for things politely, or people are offended, or think you are rude.
3 Choose two pupils to act out a realistic situation asking for something, e.g:
T: Jon, you are the villager. Lukas, you are the Diddiman. Now, the villager is going to ask the Diddiman how to make a strong pig sty.
Villager: Please will you show me how to make a strong pig sty, Mr Diddiman?
Diddiman: Yes, of course, Jon. Come over here and I'll show you.
4 Divide children into pairs and have each partner ask the other for something. Walk around the classroom listening and helping.

LESSON TWO

Objective

The children will be able to introduce people to each other.

Method

1 Choose two pupils and introduce one to the other, e.g:
T: Kila, I'd like you to meet Keli. He's from Daru. Keli, this is Kila, our Head Prefect.
2 Kila can then introduce Keli to other members of the class. Class member should say 'Hello Keli', or 'Pleased to meet you Keli' or 'How do you do Keli', or something similar.
3 Now teach a more formal meeting, e.g: A pupil introducing his father to his teacher.
C: Father, I'd like to meet my teacher Mr Garuwa. Mr Garuwa, this is my father, Mr Mea.
T: How do you do Mr Mea. It's nice to meet you.
Mr Mea: Hello Mr Garuwa, my son has told me what a good teacher you are.
4 Divide the children into threes and ask them to act out the same meeting.

LESSON THREE

Objective

The children will be able to apologize about something and excuse themselves.

Method

1 Act out examples with a child in front of the class, e.g:
A situation which requires an apology (saying sorry)
T: (Bumping into student) Oh, I'm terribly sorry, I didn't meant to bump into you.
2 Suggest other situations when someone has to apologise, e.g:
Stepping on someone's foot by accident.
Breaking a friend's spear by accident.
Knocking over a pot of water.
Breaking a clay pot.
3 Suggest the type of apology to give in these situations, e.g:
Oh I'm sorry, I didn't see your foot there.

I'm very sorry that I broke your spear. I didn't mean to.
I'm sorry for spilling that water. It was an accident.
I'm very sorry for breaking that pot.
4 Divide children into groups and get them to act out these situations.

WRITTEN SENTENCES

Note
Teach only FIVE of the six lessons.

LESSON ONE (Lesson Suggestion 21)

Objective
The children will be able to write telegrams.

Preparation
Give out *Pupil's Book 1* to each child (page 46, Lesson 1).

Method
1 Read the instructions and discuss the example given. (See also Lesson Suggestion 21.)
2 Work out telegrams 1 and 2 orally with the class before you ask them to write any down. Don't expect the children to do all 5.

Possible Answers
1 Dad sick. Come quick. Raka.
2 Please send K50 urgently. Raka.
3 Vegetables arriving PMV Chings store Saturday. Raka.
4 Kema imprisoned two months for stealing. Raka.
5 Congratulations on S.C. pass. Raka.

LESSON TWO

Objective
Children will be able to complete sentences using the correct phrase.

Preparation
Give out *Pupil's Book 1* to each child (page 46, Lesson 2).

Method
1 Explain the instruction. Read out all the phrases. Explain any of the phrases the children might not understand:
looked after (took care of)
sold out (all sold; no more left)
by mistake (not an purpose)
cheer up (be happy)
lost his balance (slipped or wobbled)
she didn't mind (didn't worry or complain)
made up his mind (decided)
scratched his head (made a sign which showed that he didn't understand; that he was puzzled)
2 Do the lesson orally first, asking children to select the correct phrases to complete each sentence.

Answers

1 lost his balance
2 looked after
3 in a hurry
4 all over
5 she didn't mind
6 scratched his head
7 cheer up
8 sold up
9 made up his mind
10 by mistake

LESSON THREE (Lesson Suggestion 6)

Objective
The children will be able to complete the sentences.

Preparation
Give out *Pupil's Book 1* to each child (page 47, Lesson 3).

Method
Follow Lesson Suggestion 6.

Possible Answers
1 They'll have to fix that tyre before they can sell the car.
2 Who's going to the market this afternoon?
3 After I light the fire, I will help you carry the water.
4 Will you help me collect some firewood? Yes, I will.
5 Before I went to school, I washed in the river.
6 When are you going to feed the pigs?
7 Have you seen that baby cassowary? No, I haven't.
8 I can't play football with you because I have to clean the school yard.
9 Can you play corner ball? Yes, I can.
10 Did you rememeber to do your homework? No, I didn't.

LESSON FOUR (Lesson Suggestion 2)

Objective
The children will be able to write answers to questions about pictures.

Preparation
Give out *Pupil's Book 1* to each child (page 47, Lesson 4).

Method
Follow Lesson Suggestion 2.

Possible Answers
1 Mother is ironing her dress.
2 Tom went into the bush to sleep.
3 The women are cutting the grass.
4 The man is taking medicine because he is sick.
5 The cowboys are trying to catch the cattle.
6 The boys went fishing in their canoe.
7 Maria is cutting down a pawpaw.
8 Elia is chopping down a tree.
9 The dog is eating some tinned fish.
10 Joseph is buying some rice.

LESSON FIVE (Lesson Suggestion 2)

Objective
The children will be able to match descriptions with pictures.

Preparation
Give out *Pupil's Book 1* to each child (page 49, Lesson 5).

Method
1 Explain the instructions.
2 Ask children to match the descriptions with the pictures orally.

Answers
1 Pori caught the small one.
2 Kipi caught the one with big fins.
3 Vagi caught the one with the long tail.
4 Dilo caught the big one.
5 Biga caught the one with shripes.

LESSON SIX

Objective
The children will practise using adverbs (words which tell us how, when and where).

Preparation
Give out *Pupil's Book 1* to each child (page 49, Lesson 6).

Method
1 Read the instructions and the examples given.

Possible Answers
He ran very quickly.
Put it down there.
Before you go to school you must wash.
The two children played happily with the new toy.
We will go swimming now.
They looked everywhere for the missing woman.

WRITTEN COMPOSITION

LESSON ONE (Lesson Suggestion 17)

Objective
The children will be able to set out a letter.

Preparation
Give out *Pupil's Book 1* to each child (page 50, Lesson 1).

Method
1 Explain the importance of letter-writing. (See Lesson Suggestion 17.)
2 Read the instructions and discuss with the children how to set out a letter.
3 After discussing the two examples given, tell children to write their letter.
4 Check that the letters are set out correctly.

LESSON TWO

Objective
The children will be able to see the mistakes in a picture.

Preparation
Give out *Pupil's Book 1* for each child (page 51, Lesson 2).

Method

1 Discuss the picture thoroughly with the children. If you live in a rural area and do not see many cars or trucks, you may have to tell the children what the mistakes are.)

Possible Answers

1 Too many passengers in the truck.
2 People should not be standing up in the back of the truck in case they fall.
3 The back part of the truck should not be down. People should not be sitting on it in case they fall onto the road.
4 The driver should not be drinking.
5 People should not sit on top of the driver's cabin as the driver will not be able to see clearly.
6 The woman's bilum should not be hanging over the side of the truck. It should be inside the truck.
7 Animals should not be allowed loose on the back of the truck with so many people. They could get excited and cause an accident.

SPELLING

LESSON ONE (Lesson Suggestion 22)

Objective

The children will learn to spell this week's words.

Preparation

Give out *Pupil's Book 1* to each child (page 52, Spelling List).

LESSON TWO

Select from Exercises A–E. (Some of these exercises could be given as homework.)

Preparation

Give out *Pupil's Book 1* to each child (pages 52–3).

Exercise A (Lesson Suggestion 29)

Answers

1 waved
2 explore
3 brave
4 save
5 explanation

Exercise B

Answers

blouse shirt jeans dress sandals overcoat socks shoes

Exercise C (Lesson Suggestion 28)

Possible Answers

1 drain paint stain chain main pain pair
2 main pond pair pain cold heat
3 pain pair pest pill
4 main pair pain tail
5 pair paint
6 petrol pedestrian
7 pain pair pail

Exercise D

Answers
office letters stamps register parcel weighed

Exercise E

Answers

2 escape	4 shelter	6 manager	8 melt	10 knob
3 blade	5 soccer	7 unload	9 selfish	

HANDWRITING (Lesson Suggestion 33)

Preparation
Give out *Pupil's Book 1* to each child (pages 54–5).

Note
Point out to the children that the 'w' joins onto the 'i' from the top of the letter.

READING

INTRODUCTION (Lesson Suggestion 34)

Objective
The children will be able to understand the background to the story and the meaning of new words. They will read the story silently.

Preparation
Give out *Reader 1* to each child (pages 17–20), *'The Letters!'* Part 2.

Method
1 Introduce the story. Remind children about what happened in last week's story. Ask what they think will happen next?
2 Follow Lesson Suggestion 34B.

LESSON ONE (Lesson Suggestion 34)

Objective
Children will be able to answer comprehension questions to show that they understood the story.

Preparation
Give out *Reader 1* and *Pupil's Book 1* (page 55, Lesson 1) to each child.

Answers
1 Ania's family didn't like John because he was lazy and always out of work.
2 The letters were from penfriends from different countries.
3 John tried to steal the letters.
4 Ania decided to ask the doctor about the letters.
5 The stamps were valuable because they were old and rare.
6 John was a mean, dishonest person because he tried to steal from his own relatives.

7 Ania's mother would be astonished and feel very pleased when she found out about the value of the stamps.
8 It would be wise to keep some of the money in the bank and use the rest to buy the things they needed.
9 Ania and her family would probably not want to see John again because he tried to cheat them. John would probably be too ashamed to see them again.
10 They did not want to go back to the village because they had no land, no house and no friends there.

LESSON TWO

Objective
The children will be able to arrange the sentences in the correct order.

Preparation
Give out *Pupil's Book 1* to each child (page 55, Lesson 2, Exercise A).

Method
1 Read the instructions.
2 Read the mixed-up sentences and ask the class which sentence comes first.
3 Now which sentence follows on from there, and so on till it is finished.

Answers
Cousin John arrived soon after Ania had opened the black box. Mother invited him to stay and eat. John looked at the envelopes and seemed to find them very interesting. The next day when Ania arrived home from school she saw someone inside her house.
It was John. When he saw Ania he ran off.
Ania decided to take the letters to the hospital and ask the kind doctor about them.
The doctor gave the stamps to Sari to examine.
Sari told Ania that the stamps were worth nearly two thousand Kina.

LESSON THREE

Objective
The children will be able to answers questions about a passage.

Preparation
Give out *Pupil's Book 1* to each child (page 56, Exercise B).

Method
1 Do the first one with the children.

Answers
1 John looked at each letter, one by one. If he were not interested in them, he would not bother to examine each one so carefully.
2 very surprised
3 They probably live in a simple village house. It has no furniture and people would sit on the mat to eat.

LESSON FOUR

Objective
The children will be able to choose the word that is out of place in a sentence, and replace it with the correct word.

Preparation
Give out *Pupil's Book 1* to each child (page 56, Exercise C).

Method
1 Read the instructions.
2 Do the first one with the children. Explain that *footpath* is wrong because a plane would not be there; it would be on a *runway* or *airstrip*.
3 Read each sentence. Class must tell you which is the wrong word, and what that word should be.

Answers

	Wrong words	**Right words**
1	footpath	runway/airstip
2	calm	rough
3	enjoyed	disliked/hated
4	empty	crowded
5	stole	banked/deposited

LESSON FIVE (Lesson Suggestion 39)

Objective
Children will be able to read for enjoyment.

Preparation
Give out a choice of reading material.

LISTENING 6

LESSON ONE

Objective
The children will listen carefully to hear what is said without looking at the speaker.

Note
Children hear better if they can watch the person who is talking, as they rely on looking at lip movement to help their understanding. This exercise is to encourage children to listen carefully even when they cannot see the speaker.

Method
1 Choose a game, e.g: Messages. Give the class a message, e.g: Will you take all the Library books to Room 3 at half past ten.
2 Turn your back on the class so they cannot see your face, and then say the message.
3 Turn around and face the class. Choose a pupil to come out the front.
4 That pupil must turn her back to the class and repeat the message.
5 Teacher then chooses another pupil to come out and face the class and repeat the same message.
6 Class to decide whether the message was correct.
7 Choose a pupil to start the game again by giving a new message.

LESSON TWO

Objective
The children will be able to remember names of people.

Method

1 Choose six children to come to the front of the room.
2 Tell the children that they must all make up new names for themselves. Give them a few minutes to think up a new name.
3 Now ask the six children to say their new names clearly to the rest of the class.
4 Point to one of the six children and the rest of the class has to remember his or her new name.
5 At the end of the game, you can choose six other children to come out and think up new names.

TALKING

LESSON ONE (Lesson Suggestion 1C)

Objective

The children will practise last week's sentence pattern:
Who did they buy the peanuts for? They bought them for themselves.

Method

1 Use the substitution table that is still written on the blackboard from last week and revise it thoroughly.

LESSON TWO

Objective

The children will practise a sentence pattern they already know:
What did he say? He said he ...
What did he tell us? He told us that he ...

Method

1 Ask a child to come out the front and tell the class about his favourite food.
2 T: What did he tell us?
C: He told us that he likes mangoes.
3 Choose another child to tell the class about her favourite game.
T: What did she say?
C: She say that she likes playing cricket.
4 Divide the class into groups. One person in the group must tell the others something. The group leader asks: What did she tell us? She chooses someone in the group to answer.

LESSON THREE

Objective

The children will be able to use a new sentence pattern:
Did he build that house for himself? No, he built it for his brother.

Method

1 Look for something hand-made in the classroom. Ask questions, e.g:
Q: Namo, did you make that bilum for yourself?
A: No, I made it for my sister.
Q: (To the class) Did she make it for herself?
C: No, she made it for her sister.

2 Divide the class into groups. Each child in the group pretends to have something he has made. He tells the others what it is. Group leader starts by asking a question about it, e.g: Alang, did you draw that picture for yourself? A: Yes, I did.

LESSON FOUR

Objective
The children will practise this sentence pattern:
Did she make that skirt for herself? Yes, she did.

Method
1 Tell the children to draw a picture of something they know how make, e.g: a drum, a canoe, a garden, a cake, a bow and arrow, a spear, a mat, a basket, cooked food. etc.
2 Choose someone in the class to hold up his paper. Choose another person to ask a question about the picture, e.g:
Q: Akis, did you make that spear for yourself?
A: Yes, I did.
3 After several examples, divide into groups. Each person in the group asks the next person about his picture, using the same sentence pattern.

LESSON FIVE (Lesson Suggestion 1C)

Objective
The children will be able to revise Lessons Three and Four using a substitution table.

Preparation
Write the following substitution table on the blackboard. If possible, leave it there till next week.

Did	HE	build	that	house	for	HIMSELF?	Yes,	HE	did.
	SHE	make		scarf		HERSELF?		SHE	
	THEY			canoe		THEMSELVES		THEY	
	YOU			drum		YOURSELF		I	
	SHE	cook		food		HERSELF	No,	SHE	didn't.
	WE					OURSELVES?		WE	
	YOU			kaukau		YOURSELF		I	

ORAL EXPRESSION

LESSON ONE

Objective
The children will be able to carry on a telephone conversation.

Note
See Grade 6 Syllabus (pages 121–7) on how to make a telephone call.

Method
1 Write a plan on the blackboard like this:
Caller: Say hello. Ask for person to speak to.
Say who you are.
Say why you are calling.
Say goodbye.

2 Divide the class into pairs. One person is the caller, the other answers him. (Each person to use a cardboard telephone or stick as a receiver.)
e.g: Caller: Hello, may I speak to Mary please?
Answer: Just a minute please and I'll get her.
Hello, this is Mary speaking.
Caller: Hello Mary, this is Elizabeth. Can you come to eat at our house tonight?
Answer: I'd love to, Elizabeth. What time should I come?
Caller: Oh, about seven o'clock will be fine!
Answer: Good. I'll see you then. Goodbye!
Caller: Goodbye!

3 Each pair of children will make up their own conversations. The teacher will walk around the classroom listening and giving help.

LESSON TWO

Objective

The children will know how to answer the telephone politely.

Note

Point out that when answering the telephone, you should always be polite, give your name or the business you work for. You should then give the caller the information he wants. Always end a call politely and never hang up (the receiver) without saying anything.

Method

Write the example on the blackboard.

Example

(Ring, ring) Good morning, Bena's Service Station.
Caller: Hello, could I speak to the manager please?
Answer: I'm sorry but Mr Kimoko is not here at the moment.
Caller: I see. Could you please give him a message to ring Mr Nipa at number 42-3196, urgently, as soon as he gets in.
Answer: Yes, of course Mr Nipa, I'll do that for you.
Caller: Thank you. Goodbye.
Answer: Goodbye.

1 Now, choose a pupil to be the caller. You be the person who answers the phone and do the example together.
2 Divide the class into pairs. They must do the example together and then make up other examples.

LESSON THREE

Objective

The children will practise holding a telephone conversation.

Method

1 Teacher remind the children of the things they have learned in the last two lessons about answering calls.
2 Divide the class into pairs with their telephones and tell them to make up telephone conversations about the following topics (write these on the blackboard):

1 Ringing an ambulance after an accident
2 Ordering goods from a store
3 Ringing the police to report a theft
4 Ringing the N.B.C. to request a record
5 Ringing the airport to ask when a plane is arriving

WRITTEN SENTENCES

Note
Teach only FIVE of the six lessons.

LESSON ONE

Objective
The children will be able to choose the most suitable word to fit in a sentence.

Preparation
Give out *Pupil's Book 1* to each child (page 57, Lesson 1).

Method
1 Read out the instructions and then the list of words. Explain any difficult words.
2 Read out several examples, asking children for the correct answers.
3 Then ask the children to write their answers.

Answers

1 tired	4 crashed	7 puncture	10 bothered
2 delicious	5 personality	8 switch	
3 voyage	6 explore	9 loose	

LESSON TWO (Lesson Suggestion 13D)

Objective
The children will be able to use quotation marks.

Preparation
Give out *Pupil's Book 1* to each child (page 57, Lesson 2).

Method
1 Write down the first example on the blackboard, putting in the quotation marks. Discuss why you put them where you did.

Answers
1 'Hey you! What do you think you're doing?' shouted the policeman.
2 The girl called to her brother, 'Peter, come and help me. I'm stuck!'
3 'Well', said the spider to himself, 'There goes my tasty meal!'
4 'Can I help you, young lady?' the storekeeper asked.
5 'I would like a can of tomato soup', said the girl. 'And a kilo of rice too, please.'
6 'Where are you going today Mother?' asked the small boy.
7 'I can't find my shoe!' Ila exclaimed. 'Tom, have you taken it?'
8 'No!' cried the child. 'I won't eat it! I won't!'
9 'Somebody has stolen food from the gardens', said Raro sternly.
10 'I haven't seen it', said Hano shaking his head. 'Perhaps it's just disappeared.'

LESSON THREE (Lesson Suggestion 6)

Objective
The children will be able to write correct answers to questions.

Preparation
Give out *Pupil's Book 1* to each child (page 58, Lesson 3).

Method
Follow Lesson Suggestion 6.

Possible Answers

1 We buy newspapers so that we can read about what is happening in our country and in the rest of the world.
2 We heard music on the radio last night.
3 I wasn't at the singsing last night because I hurt my leg.
4 Yes. I think we should have three days in the weekend and only work four days a week.
5 I did a lot of work in the gardens yesterday. First I repaired the fence and then I planted kaukau.
6 I am not helping with the gardening because I have malaria.
7 No, I haven't seen Hano anywhere.
8 I didn't finish my homework because I had to help my father fix his outrigger
9 I cooked and ate the flying fox that I caught yesterday.
10 Yes, I have been fishing today.

LESSON FOUR (Lesson Suggestion 7)

Objective
The children will be able to choose the correct form of the verb to fit in a sentence.

Preparation
Give out *Pupil's Book 1* to each child (page 58, Lesson 4).

Method
Follow Lesson Suggestion 2.

Answers

1 go	4 came	7 teaching	10 bought
2 thinks	5 seen	8 built	
3 find	6 caught	9 wore	

LESSON FIVE (Lesson Suggestion 8)

Objective
The children will be able to choose the correct word from two similar sounding words to fit in a sentence.

Preparation
Give out *Pupil's Book 1* to each child (page 58, Lesson 5).

Method
Follow Lesson Suggestion 8.

Answers

1 till	4 unless	7 after	10 saw
2 whichever	5 when	8 beside	
3 as	6 which	9 know	

LESSON SIX

Objective
The children will be able to choose the most suitable adverb to fit in a sentence.

Preparation
Give out *Pupil's Book 1* to each child (page 59, Lesson 6).

Method
1 Read the instructions and then work out several examples orally with the class.

Answers

1 anxiously	4 nearly	7 bravely	10 everywhere
2 silently	5 neatly	8 carefully	
3 impatiently	6 early	9 there	

WRITTEN COMPOSITION

LESSON ONE

Objective
The children will be able to write direct speech suitable for cartoon pictures.

Preparation
Give out *Pupil's Book 1* to each child (page 60, Lesson 1).

Method
1 Discuss what is happening in the pictures with the class.
2 Ask children to suggest what the two boys are saying in each picture.

Possible Answers
1 There's a wild pig! See if you can hit him.
2 Ah, you missed it Kelema! There goes our dinner.
3 Look out behind you! A snake!
4 Well, we can't eat this for dinner either, can we!
5 Oh look! A little cuscus! Got him!
6 I'm going to keep him as a pet.

LESSON TWO

Objective
The children will be able to learn that each paragraph in a story contains one main idea.

Preparation
Give out *Pupil's Book 1* to each child (page 61, Lesson 2).

Method
1 Read the introduction to this lesson.
2 Read the story about 'Growing Rubber'.
3 Point out the main idea of each paragraph which is written in heavy print. Explain that the remainder of the paragraph *expands* this idea.
4 Now read out the next four paragraphs about Papua New Guinea.
5 Ask children for a suitable title for this story, e.g: Papua New Guinea – A Developing Country; Changes in Papua New Guinea, etc.
6 What is the main idea in each paragraph? Discuss this carefully with the children.
7 Now children finish the sentences, telling the main ideas of each paragraph.

Answers
Paragraph 1: Today, Papua New Guinea can be described as a developing country.

Paragraph 2: Until about fifty years ago the way of life hardly changed over the years.
Paragraph 3: The old way of life changed because the Europeans introduced many new things.
Paragraph 4: Countries become 'developing' countries when they come in contact with people from a more complicated way of life.

SPELLING

LESSON ONE (Lesson Suggestion 22)

Objective
The children learn to spell this week's words.

Preparation
Give out *Pupil's Book 1* to each child (page 62, Spelling List).

LESSON TWO

Select from Exercises A–E. (Some of these exercises could be given as homework.)

Preparation
Give out *Pupil's Book 1* to each child (pages 62–3).

Exercise A (Lesson Suggestion 29)

Answers

1 underneath
2 instead
3 until
4 instructions
5 untidy

Exercise B

Answers
Testing in pairs.

Exercise C

Answers

1 cave
2 excellent
3 brave
4 exercise
5 waved

Exercise D (Lesson Suggestion 23)

Possible Answers
post – tent – take – each – hand – draw – wind – drop –

Exercise E

Possible Answers

1 took hook book cook crook
2 beef see meet seen deer
3 goat coat float soap
4 beach teach peach reach
5 thief brief relief
6 brain main pain drain stain
7 pour your flour sour hour
8 condition dictation election

HANDWRITING (Lesson Suggestion 33)

Preparation
Give out *Pupil's Book 1* to each child (page 63).

Note
That letter 'a' has an upstroke when starting a word.

READING

INTRODUCTION (Lesson Suggestion 34)

Objective
The children will be able to understand the background to the story, and the meanings of new words. They will read the story silently.

Preparation
Give out *Reader 1* (pages 21–3), *'Machele and the Heron's leg'*.

Method
1 Introduce the story. Discuss the picture on page 21 of the Reader. Are these people from Papua New Guinea? How do you know? Explain to the children that this story is about an African chief and his cook. What is a Heron? Explain that it is a large white bird found in Africa, found around rivers and lakes where it catches fish. It can stand on one leg with the other folded up underneath its body.
2 Follow Lesson Suggestion 34.

LESSON ONE (Lesson Suggestion 34C)

Objective
Children will be able to answer comprehension questions to show that they understand the story.

Preparation
Give out *Reader 1* (pages 21–3) and *Pupil's Book 1* (page 64, Lesson 1).

Answers
1 best of Africa
2 he was in love with one of his servants
3 herons only had one leg
4 pleased
5 never did she made lots of trouble for him.
6 Machele gave the heron's leg to Moshe because he was in love with her.
7 He felt nervous and worried about what the chief would say.
8 The chief liked Machele and didn't want to make trouble for him so he said nothing about the missing leg.
9 The chief did not want to lose his good cook. He knew that if he fired him, one of his friends would immediately hire him as their cook.
10 They wanted him to fire Machele so they would be able to employ him.

LESSON TWO

Objective
The children will be able to find the word that does not belong to a group.

Preparation
Give out *Pupil's Book 1* to each child (page 64, Lesson 2, Exercises A & B).

Exercise A

Answers
1 pig (all the others are birds)
2 hands (all the others belong to birds)
3 burned (all the others are ways of preparing food)
4 servant (all the others are leaders)

Exercise B

Answers
fresh, young; smiling, black; white, shining; sweetest; old

LESSON THREE

Objective
The children will be able to use the Emergency Section of the Telephone Directory.

Preparation
Give out *Pupil's Book 1* to each child (page 65–6, Exercise C).

Method
1 If you have a Telephone Directory, show the class where you can find this page in the book.
2 Read the introduction to this lesson and the examples given.
3 Work out the first problem together, as a class.
Which service are you going to require?
Which town will you look under?
What number will you ring?
4 Ask the children to work out the next ones for themselves and give you the answer orally. Encourage children to explain how they found that number.

Answers
1 You would ring the Fire Station at Mt Hagen – phone 52 1311
2 You would ring the ambulance at Lae – phone 42 1211
3 You would ring Civil Defence at Rabaul – phone 92 1746
4 You would ring the Electricity Commission at Madang – phone 82 2122
5 You would ring the Police at Wewak – phone 86 2222
6 You would ring the Kimbe Hospital – phone 93 5142
7 The answer to this question should be similar to number 5.
They would live near Lorengau and be ringing the police about something, e.g: stolen goods.
8 This answer would also be similar to number 5. They would live near Alotau and be ringing the Police about a crime.

LESSON FOUR (Lesson Suggestion 39)

Objective
The children will be able to read for enjoyment.

LESSON FIVE

Objective
The children will be able to play Reading Games.

Preparation
Give out *Reading Games for Grade 6* to each child (pages 14–16, Unit 6).

Method
Choose games for children to play.

OR POETRY (Lesson Suggestion 40)

Objective
The children will be able to listen to a poem and think about what it is saying.

Preparation
Give out *Pupil's Book 1* to each child (page 67) '*Golden Arms*'.

Answers
1 The poem is about dawn, first thing in the morning, just as the sun rises.
2 The poet is talking about rain.
3 Because the sun has not reached the valley below to bring it light.
4 It brightens up the world below and wakes up all the living things in the valley.

LISTENING 7

LESSON ONE

Objective
The children will be able to put sentences into the right order.

Method
1 Read out a short paragraph to the class (no more than five short sentences.)
2 Tell the children that the sentences are in the wrong order, so the story does not make sense. Ask the children to re-arrange the sentences so that the story does make sense, e.g:
Read the following story:
Eight fish were caught. The boys pushed the canoe into the water. They went home and cooked them. They paddled out to the reef.
T: Which sentence should come first?
C: The boys pushed the canoe into the water.
T: Which sentence comes next?
C: They paddled out to the reef.
T: Next?
C: Eight fish were caught.
T: Last?
C: They went home and cooked them.
3 You could write these sentences on the blackboard in the correct order. Then give another example if there is time.

LESSON TWO

Objective
The children will be able to listen carefully and name sounds around them.

Method
1 Choose a place to listen. (This could be in the classroom; outside the classroom; down by the river; by the sea; by the road.)
2 Tell the children to sit quietly and listen. What sounds can they hear?
3 Children must answer in good sentences, e.g:
(Beside the road) I can hear someone walking along the road. I can hear a truck coming. I can hear a car horn. etc.

TALKING

LESSON ONE (Lesson Suggestion 1C)

Objective
The children will practise last week's sentence pattern:
Did he build that house for himself?
Yes, he did. No, he built it for his brother.

Method
Use the substitution table that is still written on the blackboard from last week. Revise it thoroughly.

LESSON TWO

Objective
The children will practise a sentence pattern they already know:
What will you do *when* the bell rings?
What will you do *after* school?
What will you do *before* you eat dinner?

Method
1 T: What will you do after school today?
C: I will go home.
T: What will you do before you come to school tomorrow?
C: I will wash in the river.
2 Write the following sentence beginnings on the blackboard:
What will you do when . . .?
What will you do after . . .?
What will you do before . . .?
3 In groups, children will practise this pattern by completing the sentences.
4 Teacher walk around listening to each group.

LESSON THREE

Objective
The children will be able to use a new sentence pattern:
What did he do?
He poured water on himself. He drew a picture of himself. He told you something about himelf.

Preparation
Have the following things ready: water, paint, mud, sand, etc.

Method

1 Give some water to a child and ask him to spill it on his foot.
Say to the class: He spilt some water on his foot.
T: What did he do?
C: He spilt some water on his foot.
T: Who did he spill some water on?
C: He spilt some water on himself.

2 Do another example, this time using paint.
T: Who did Josef and Lan put some paint on?
C: They put some paint on themselves.

3 Now tell the class something about yourself, e.g: I am 24 years old and I come from Manus Island. I am married and have one child.
T: I told you something about myself. What did I do?
C: You told us something about yourself.
T: Lari, tell us something about yourself.
C: I like playing football.
T: What did he do?
C: He told us something about himself.
T: Maria told us something about yourself, etc.

LESSON FOUR

Objective

The children practise this sentence pattern:
What did she do?
She poured water on herself. She drew a picture of herself. She told you something about herself.

Method

1 Tell one group to write a few sentences on paper about themselves.
Tell another group to draw a picture of themselves.
Tell another group to decorate themselves using paint or mud.
Tell another group to go outside and pick flowers. They must bring these back into the classroom and decorate themselves with the flowers and leaves.

2 Point to the first group.
T: You wrote something about yourselves. What did you do?
C: We wrote something about ourselves.
Point to the second group.
T: You drew pictures of yourselves. What did you do?
C: We drew pictures of ourselves.
Point to the third group.
T: You put paint on yourselves. What did you do?
C: We put paint on ourselves.
Point to the fourth group.
T: You decorated yourselves with flowers. What did you do?
C: We decorated ourselves with flowers.

LESSON FIVE (Lesson Suggestion 1C)

Objective

The children will revise Lessons Three and Four using a substitution table.

Preparation

Write the following on the blackboard.

What did	SHE	do?		SHE	poured water on	HERSELF.
	HE			HE	mud	HIMSELF
	THEY			THEY	drew pictures of	THEMSELVES.
	WE			WE		OURSELVES
	I			I	a	MYSELF
	HE	tell	US?	HE	told us something about	HIMSELF.
	SHE			SHE	told us something about	HERSELF.
	THEY			THEY		THEMSELVES.

Note
Leave the substitution table on the blackboard for Lesson One next week.

ORAL EXPRESSION

LESSON ONE

Objective
The children will be able to make accurate oral descriptions.

Method
1 Describe a place which everyone knows well.
2 Children have to guess which place you are describing.
3 Divide the class into groups. One person in each group must describe a place for the others to guess.
4 Each person in the group must have a turn at describing a place, e.g: their home, their village, the tradestore, singsing place.

LESSON TWO

Objective
The children will be able to describe differences (contrasts).

Method
1 Write a list of pairs on the blackboard, e.g:
  A Haus Tambaran and village house
  B Bus and bicycle
  C Dog and cat
  D Mango tree and a coconut tree
  E A football match and a basketball match
2 Describe the differences between the first two:
  T: A Haus Tambaran is s sacred place where only men are allowed. It has a very high roof and has secret things inside. However, a village house has only a low roof and anyone is allowed inside it.
3 Then choose pupils to describe differences between the other pairs. Encourage them to use contrasting words like **but** or **however**.

LESSON THREE

Objective
The children will be able to describe different types of boats.

Method
1 Study the picture about Sea Transport in *Pupil's Book 1* page 73.
2 Choose pupils to describe the different boats in the picture, i.e: ocean liner, cargo ship, speed boat, yacht, tanker, ferry.

3 Ask pupils to make contrasts between two of these vessels, e.g:
Cargo ships and ocean liners are both very large but the liner carries only passengers while the cargo ship carried only cargo.
4 Encourage pupils to make contrasts between: an ocean liner and a ferry; a speed boat and a yacht; a tanker and a cargo ship; a speed boat and a tug boat.

WRITTEN SENTENCES

LESSON ONE (Lesson Suggestion 10)

Objective
The children will be able to change words into the short form (contractions).

Preparation
Give out *Pupil's Book 1* to each child (page 68, Lesson 1).

Method
Follow Lesson Suggestion 10.

Answers

1	Where's	I'm	6 won't	I'm
2	isn't	can't	7 It's	isn't
3	They'll	they're	8 mustn't	
4	That's	you're	9 We're	it's
5	He'll		10 Aren't	it's

LESSON TWO (Lesson Suggestion 6)

Objective
The children will be able to complete sentences using phrases which explain **how, when, where** or **why**.

Preparation
Give out *Pupil's Book 1* to each child (page 68, Lesson 2).

Possible Answers
1 ... in the new garden down by the river.
2 ... next August.
3 ... by plane.
4 ... to catch the large fish.
5 ... in traditional costume.
6 During the wet season ...
7 ... to the market ...
8 ... so that his grandson will know the traditional methods.
9 ... to catch the dangerous driver.
10 Because the weather in Port Moresby was very hot, ...

LESSON THREE

Objective
The children will be able to join two sentences using joining words.

Preparation

Give out *Pupil's Book 1* to each child (page 69, Lesson 3).

Answers

1 That is the man who stole my axe.
2 Maria lost her money when she was going to market.
3 Kemo's pig died because he forgot to feed it.
4 The child looked so sad that I asked her what was wrong.
5 I sang a song while I mended the fishing nets.
6 The girl caught a crab so she took it to her mother.
7 Warea heard screams as he passed Timon's house.
8 This is Garawai village where I was born.
9 I was travelling in a PMV when it crashed into a car.
10 The girl ran to the Aid Post but the medical orderly was not there.

LESSON FOUR (Lesson Suggestion 2)

Objective

The children will be able to complete sentences about a picture.

Preparation

Give out *Pupil's Book 1* to each child (page 69, Lesson 4).

Possible Answers

1 broken and ruined
2 blown down
3 frightened and upset
4 had broken in places leaving large holes.
5 smashed to pieces.
6 with rubbish made by the storm.
7 under the house where they were safe from the storm.

LESSON FIVE

Objective

The children will be able to choose the correct word to complete the sentences.

Preparation

Give out *Pupil's Book 1* to each child (page 70, Lesson 5).

Method

1 Read the instruction and discuss the first sentence before you ask the children to write down their answers. Explain the meanings of **before** and **after**:
After I wash my hands, I eat my dinner.
I wash my hands before I eat my dinner.
After I get some bait, I go fishing.
Before I go fishing, I get some bait.

Answers

1 after	4 before	7 after
2 before	5 after	8 before
3 before	6 before	

WRITTEN COMPOSITION

LESSON ONE

Objective
The children will be able to write accurate descriptions.

Preparation
Give out *Pupil's Book 1* to each child (page 70, Lesson 1).

Method
1 Read introduction to lesson.
2 Ask the children: If you were describing me to someone, what would you say about me?
Refer to questions: What does the person look like? About how old is he? What job does he do? etc.

Follow-Up
Choose children to read their descriptions to the rest of the class.
The class must guess who the child is describing.

LESSON TWO (Lesson Suggestion 17)

Objective
The children will be able to write a business letter.

Preparation
Give out *Pupil's Book 1* to each child (page 71, Lesson 2).

Method
1 Read through the lesson with the class, then ask them to write Iga's second letter.
2 Encourage the children to make a plan about what they are going to say, e.g:
a Received parcel of sporting goods.
b One cricket ball missing.
c Please send another ball as soon as possible.
The letter should be set as it is in the sample letter.

Possible Answers

Dear Sir,

I have just received the parcel of sporting goods which I ordered for the school two weeks ago. However, you have sent only three cricket balls instead of the four I ordered and paid for.

I would be grateful if you would forward one more ball as soon as possible.

Yours faithfully,
Iga Pau
Captain
Guba Cricket Team

Follow-Up
Read through pupils' letters, checking that setting out is correct and content is relevant.

SPELLING

LESSON ONE (Lesson Suggestion 22)

Objective
The children will learn to spell this week's words.

Preparation
Give out *Pupil's Book 1* to each child (page 72, Spelling List).

LESSON TWO

Select from Exercises A–E. (Some of these exercises could be set as homework.)

Preparation
Give out *Pupil's Book 1* to each child (pages 72–4).

Exercise A (Lesson Suggestion 29)

Answers

1 knife
2 condition
3 constable
4 contest
5 consider

Exercise B

Answers
cargo ship, tug boat, yacht, tanker, ferry

Exercise C

Answers

1 cent sent
2 blue blew
3 saw sore/soar
4 would wood
5 tied tide
6 male mail
7 meat meet

Exercise D (Lesson Suggestion 27)

Answers

1 faint paint saint train
2 age cage page rage wage
3 file mile pile tile while
4 band hand land sand stand
5 bind find kind mind wind

Exercise E

Answers

1 plain
2 male
3 weight
4 meet
5 wood

HANDWRITING (Lesson Suggestion 33)

Preparation
Give out *Pupil's Book 1* to each child (pages 74–5).

Note
Remind the children to look carefully to see how 'oo' is joined together.

READING

INTRODUCTION (Lesson Suggestion 34)

Objective
The children will understand the background to the story, and the meaning of new words. They will read the story silently.

Preparation
Give out *Reader 1* to each child (pages 24–7), *'The Mark of the Borowei'*. Discuss how people use legends and myths to explain things which cannot be explained in any other way. This story is about a man who knows that some people will believe anything they are told.

Method
1 Introduce the story.
2 Follow Lesson Suggestion 34B.

LESSON ONE (Lesson Suggestion 34C)

Objective
The children will be able to answer questions to show that they understand the story.

Preparation
Give out *Reader 1* (pages 24–7) and *Pupil's Book 1* (page 75, Lesson 1), *'The Mark of the Borowei'*.

Answers
1 Togai's wife screamed because she saw a huge footprint in the ground and became frightened because it was so large.
2 Totone said the Borowei was very big and fierce. It had strong claws that could tear a man to pieces and it had a big mouth with huge teeth. He said it was very dangerous. It also had four large eyes which could see in the dark.
3 She didn't like him because he was lazy, but she knew he was clever about some things.
4 She thought it strange that there was only one footprint. How did the Borowei walk with only one foot.
5 The men decided to trap the Borowei.
6 The branches had been pushed in and the food had gone but there was no Borowei.
7 Togai's wife woke all the women in the village and they went to the Borowei trap with their torches.
8 Togai's wife guessed Totone was the Borowei because she knew he was lazy and he was the one who suggested that the mark was left by a

Borowei. He was the only one who could describe such a beast.
9 The footprint was made by pushing the thick end of the stick into the ground and using the thin end to make the four smaller marks.
10 Totone ran away and never went back to that village.

LESSON TWO

Objective
The children will be able to tell the difference between fact and opinion.

Preparation
Give out *Pupil's Book 1* to each child (pages 75–6, Lesson 2).

Method
1 Read the instructions and the examples given.
2 Ask the children to write 'fact' or 'opinion' for statements 1–10.

Answers

1 opinion	4 opinion	7 fact	10 fact
2 opinion	5 fact	8 opinion	
3 fact	6 fact	9 fact	

LESSON THREE

Objective
The children will be able to tell which headlines are fact and which are opinion.

Preparation
Give out *Pupil's Book 1* to each child (page 77, Exercise B). Find some old newspapers and pass them around the class.

Method
1 Look at the old newspapers. Ask pupils to read out some of the news headlines. They must decide whether they are fact or opinion.
2 Read the headlines on page 77. Discuss whether they are fact or opinion.

Answers
1 Port Moresby dock men are 'slowest' — opinion
2 Killed in accident — fact
3 Magani beat Tigers 20–13 — fact
4 Vandals should be sent home — opinion
5 Licence Law alters — fact

LESSON FOUR

Objective
The children will be able to read for enjoyment.

Preparation
Give out *Supplementary Reader 1* to each child (pages 2–4).

Method
1 Children read '*The Boy Who Wanted to See the Sea*'.

LESSON FIVE

Objective
The children will be able to do reading games.

Preparation
Give out *Reading Games for Grade 6* to each child (pages 16–19).

Method
Choose some games for the children to play.

OR POETRY (Lesson Suggestion 40)

Preparation
Give out *Pupil's Book 1* to each child (page 78), '*Tapura Spring*'.

Answers
1 time
2 very quickly
3 dry cloudy thunderstorm
4 make him do something

LISTENING 8

LESSON ONE

Objective
The children will be able to hear differences between vowel sounds which are rather similar. (Remember, vowel sounds are a, e, i, o, u, and combinations of these letters, like ie, ou, ea.)

Preparation
Make a wall chart of words or sounds which the children often get mixed up, e.g:

hair here
bear beer
stare steer
air ear
rare rear

poor pure
duty dirty
heart hurt
cap cup

(You can add to this list all year.)

Method
1 Read down the list. The children repeat after you.
2 Read across the list. The children repeat after you.
3 Read one word and ask the children to write it down or point to the word you have read.

LESSON TWO

Objective
The children will be able to listen for stress in a word, and will learn to say the words correctly.

Preparation
Write a list of words from a story in *Reader 1* (page 4) or from the Grade 6 vocabulary list (page 85 of the English syllabus).
Divide each word into its syllables, and underline the syllable you stress when you say the word, e.g:

<u>grum</u>/bling
<u>gloo</u>/my
<u>hus</u>/band

<u>pro</u>/per/ly
<u>hun</u>/ting
i/<u>mme</u>/diate/ly

<u>co</u>/co/nut
en/<u>or</u>/mous
im/<u>poss</u>/i/ble

Method

1 Write the words on the blackboard without marking the syllables or the stress.
2 Remind the children that words can be broken up into parts (syllables). Show this by marking the first three words:
grum/bling gloo/my hus/band
3 Then read through the list slowly and ask the children: How many syllables are there in 'properly'? and so on. Say each word clearly but naturally. When the children answer correctly, mark the syllables on the blackboard.
4 Then say each word again and ask the children to repeat it after you. Make sure they stress the correct syllables. Mark the stress on the blackboard as you say each one.

TALKING

LESSON ONE (Lesson Suggestion 1C)

Objective

The children will practise last week's sentence pattern: What did he do?
He poured water on himself.
He drew a picture of himself.
He told you something about himself.

Method

1 Use the substitution table that is still on the blackboard from last week. Revise this work with the class.

LESSON TWO

Objective

The children will practise a sentence pattern they already know:
What does he need? He needs a comb.
What will be need? He'll need some bait and a fishing line.

Method

1 Say to the children: Tom is going fishing. What will he need?
Children answer: He'll need some bait and a fishing line.
Say to the children: I've just washed my hair. What do I need?
Children answer: You need a towel and a comb.
2 Continue to ask similar questions for the children to answer, e.g:
I'm going to bake a cake. What do I need?
She's going to make a dress. What does she need?
He's going to have a party. What does he need?
They're going to go shopping. What do they need?
We're going to make a mumu. What do we need?

LESSON THREE

Objective

The children will be able to use a new sentence pattern:
What did he buy himself? He bought himself a shirt.

Method

1 Tell the class to write the name of something that you can buy at a shop, on a piece of paper. Point to a child. She holds up her paper for all to see.
T: What did she buy herself?
C: She bought herself some chewing gum.
Point to another child and repeat the question.

2 Tell the children to write the name of one item of cooked food, e.g: taro, on the back of the same piece of paper. Point to a child. He holds us his paper for all to read.
T: What did Kara cook himself for lunch?
C: Kara cooked himself some taro for his lunch.
Point to other children and ask the same question.

LESSON FOUR

Objective

The children will practise this sentence pattern:
What did they cook themselves for dinner? They cooked themselves some fish.

Method

1 T: I went to the shop and bought myself some tobacco. What did I buy myself?
C: You bought yourself some tobacco.
T: What did you buy yourself? (Pointing to a girl)
C: I bought myself a torch.
T: What did she buy herself?
C: She bought herself a torch.

2 Divide children into groups to practise this sentence pattern.

LESSON FIVE (Lesson Suggestion 1C)

Objective

The children will practise the new sentence pattern using a substitution table.

Preparation

Write the following substitution pattern on the blackboard (remember to leave it there until next week):

What did	HE	buy	HIMSELF?	HE	bought	HIMSELF	A SHIRT.
	SHE		HERSELF?	SHE		HERSELF	COAT.
	THEY		THEMSELVES?	THEY		THEMSELVES	BUSINESS.
	I		MYSELF?	I		MYSELF	RADIO.
	WE		OURSELVES?	WE		OURSELVES	SOME FOOD.

ORAL EXPRESSION

LESSON ONE

Objective

The children will be able to form and express opinions.

Preparation

Give out *Pupil's Book 1* to each child (page 88, Exercise B).

Method

1 Discuss the two different opinions given by Peter and the manager.
2 Now ask whether the children think that running your own business is better than working for someone else. Encourage children to give their opinions on this topic, e.g:
YES: You can be your own boss: You make more money. You do what you want to.
NO: You have to be there all the time. You have a lot of worries. If things go wrong, you get blamed. You have too much responsibility.
3 Other topics for discussion could be:
Should educated people return to the village?
How should old people in the village be treated?
If someone steals vegetables from your garden, how should they be punished?

LESSON TWO

Objective

The children will be able to argue effectively.

Method

1 Tell the children that they must always give reasons for what they say in a debate (discussion).
2 When a debate is held, some people give opinions 'for' something, while others give opinions 'against' something, e.g:
Topic: Should educated young people return to the village?
Opinion FOR: Yes, (reason) because they should use their knowledge to benefit the village.
Opinion AGAINST: No, (reason) because educated people are needed to work in towns and for the Government, to benefit our country.
3 Organize a class debate. Divide the class in half. One half must be FOR, the other half AGAINST. Give them a topic to debate.

LESSON THREE

Objective

The children will be able to make logical connections between words.

Method

1 Start this activity by saying: Water reminds me of fish.
2 Then point to a child and he must make a connection with that statement, e.g: Fish reminds me of food.
3 That child must then point to another child. He might say: Food reminds me of pigs.
4 And so on, until everyone in the class has a turn.

WRITTEN SENTENCES

LESSON ONE (Lesson Suggestion 5)

Objective

The children will be able to use 'self' pronouns.

Preparation
Give out *Pupil's Book 1* to each child (page 79, Lesson 1).

Method
1 Read introduction and work out some examples orally.

Answers

1 himself	4 herself	7 He's dressing himself.
2 yourself	5 He's washing himself.	8 I'm drying myself.
3 itself	6 She's looking at herself.	9 It's scratching itself.

LESSON TWO

Objective
The children will be able to sort jumbled words into the correct order to make sentences.

Preparation
Give out *Pupil's Book 1* to each child (page 80, Lesson 2).

Method
1 Read through the words in the first example. Read the answer. Point out that each sentence starts with the word with the capital letter.
2 Read through the jumbled words several times before trying to arrange them in the correct order.

Answers
2 Some of the Grade Six boys brought their guitars to school to start a band.
3 The old man chased the pig out of his garden.
4 The children found some silver coins buried under the ground.
5 Our school visited the crocodile farm at Moitaka, near Port Moresby.
6 Everyone wore traditional dress last Sunday at the singsing.
7 Two hundred pigs were killed at Mt Hagen at the exchange ceremony.
8 Kana speared a large red emperor fish from his canoe.
9 Lakei shot a Bird of Paradise with his bow and arrow.
10 Port Moresby is the capital of Papua New Guinea.

LESSON THREE (Lesson Suggestion 9)

Objective
The children will be able to use apostrophes.

Preparation
Give out *Pupil's Book 1* to each child (page 80, Lesson 3).

Method
1 Read introduction and examples.
2 REMEMBER: — to put the apostrophe before the 's' (one boy's)
— to put the apostrophe after the 's' (more than one boys')

Answers

1 boys' shorts	5 boat's engine	9 farmers' crops
2 pig's tusks	6 plants' leaves	10 school's football team
3 girl's decoration	7 girls' father	
4 teachers' books	8 bird's song	

LESSON FOUR (Lesson Suggestion 2)

Objective
The children will be able to answer questions about illustrations.

Preparation
Give out *Pupil's Book 1* to each child (page 81, Lesson 4).

Answers
2 Mother is buying (vegetable or fruit) at the market.
3 Carmel is making the bed.
4 The children went to the pictures last night.
5 It took one hour to cook the fowl.
6 Father has been working on his canoe for three weeks.
7 Loa's favourite sport is swimming.
8 Una is taking the truck to town.
9 Wida has malaria/Wida is sick.
10 The soup tastes delicious.

LESSON FIVE (Lesson Suggestion 13)

Objective
The children will be able to use quotation marks, exclamation marks and question marks.

Preparation
Give out *Pupil's Book 1* to each child (page 83, Lesson 5).

Answers
1 'Where are you going John?' Kano asked.
2 'Stop!' cried the policeman. 'I want to talk to you!'
3 'How much is this dress, Lili?' asked the shopkeeper.
4 'Wait for me!' cried Timothy in alarm. 'I want to come too!'
5 'I can't decide which one to choose', said Koi scratching his head. 'Which one do you like best?'
6 'Come quickly!' called the boy. 'My brother is being swept out to sea.'
7 Where are you going for the holidays, Tom?' asked his friend. OR 'Where are you going for the holidays?' Tom asked his friend.
8 'I did not enjoy that film,' said Kea, shaking his head. 'Did you?'
9 'Stop it!' screamed Sali, who hated being tickled.
10 'Where's my bow and arrow? Has anyone seen it?' asked Raru.

WRITTEN COMPOSITION

LESSON ONE

Objective
The children will be able to finish writing a play.

Preparation
Give out *Pupil's Book 1* to each child (page 83, Lesson 1).

Method
1 Read the introduction.

2 Divide the class into groups of about six pupils. Tell them to read the play and then discuss how it could end. Remind them that they need to include two more characters.
3 Wander round the classroom, listening to each group. If they do not have many ideas, ask them questions like: How could the Bird of Paradise help Man? What could the snake do for man?
4 When each group has discussed a possible ending, one person from each group is chosen to write it down, while the others all help.

Follow-Up
Children should be given time during this week (perhaps during an Expressive Arts lesson) to put on this play, each group using their own ending.

LESSON TWO (Lesson Suggestion 20)

Objective
The children will be ble to fill in different types of forms.

Preparation
Give out *Pupil's Book 1* to each child (page 84, Lesson 2).

Method
1 Read the lesson carefully with the children.
2 Copy the form onto the blackboard. Fill it in, asking one of the children in your class to supply the details.

Sample Answer
SURNAME: Gemo FIRST NAMES: Elizabeth, Pia
DATE OF BIRTH: 29.10.58 AGE: 12 PLACE OF BIRTH: Ogelbeng, W.H.P.
ADDRESS: C/- Catholic Mission Ogelbeng. W.H.P.
QUALIFICATIONS: Grade 6
PRESENT OCCUPATION: Student

Follow-Up
It is important that the children have experience in filling in a variety of forms. Collect as many different forms as possible for the children to fill in.

SPELLING

LESSON ONE (Lesson Suggestion 22)

Objective
The children will be able to spell this week's words.

Preparation
Give out *Pupil's Book 1* to each child (page 85, Spelling List).

LESSON TWO (Lesson Suggestion 25)

Select from Exercises A–E, or give a spelling test and dictation.

Preparation
Give out *Pupil's Book 1* to each child (pages 85–6).

Exercise A (Lesson Suggestion 29)

Answers

1 beard
2 beach
3 sour
4 sound
5 south

Exercise B

Possible Answers

1 A helicopter was used to rescue people in the flooded area.
2 The plane landed on the runway.
3 A large areoplane flew over our village yesterday.
4 The pilot flew the plane over the mountains.
5 The man in the control tower told the pilot that he could land his plane now.
6 The men loaded the cargo into the plane.
7 The plane is in the hangar being fixed.
8 There are many different types of aircraft.

Exercise C

Answers

a decide
b accept
c wreck
d arrange
e shallow
f save
g instructions
h pedestrian
i register

Exercise D (Lesson Suggestion 27)

Answers

1 bald banjo beach boast bucket
2 tale teeth title top tune
3 seen show single soap suitable

HANDWRITING (Lesson Suggestion 33)

Preparation

Give out *Pupil's Book 1* to each child (page 86).

Note

Remind childen to put quotation marks in the right places.

READING

INTRODUCTION (Lesson Suggestion 34)

Objective

The children will be able to understand the background to the story, and the meaning of new words. They will read the story silently.

Preparation

Give out *Reader 1* (pages 28–31), *'Kemuse and the Strike'*.

Method

1 Introduce the story. Talk about people who leave the village to work in towns. What type of jobs do they do there? Most pupils will know of someone working in a town somewhere. Discuss 'going on strike'. This is when workers decide to stop work because they are unhappy about something (often their wages). They stay 'on strike' until an agreement is reached.
2 Follow Lesson Suggestion 34B.

LESSON ONE (Lesson Suggestion 34C)

Objective

Children will be able to answer questions to show that they understand the story.

Preparation

Give out *Reader 1* (pages 28–31) and *Pupil's Book 1* (page 87, Lesson 1).

Answers

1 Kemuse got the job at the sawmill because he looked strong and someone had left the job that morning
2 He helped put the planks of wood into different piles according to their size. Sometimes he helped unload logs off trucks.
3 Peter was always complaining.
4 Peter suggested that the men go on strike because they had two kina less in their pay that week.
5 Kemuse suggested that they ask the manager to explain why they were given less money.
6 They got two kina less because the week before they were overpaid by two kina.
7 They felt angry and could not understand why they were given less money.
8 The men believed Kemuse because they didn't want to make trouble over nothing.
9 Kemuse was an honest and reasonable person.
10 grumbled — complained; angry — furious; sack you — fire you; stop work — go on strike; error — mistake; puncture — flat tyre; happy — pleased; not easy — difficult; wages — pay.

LESSON TWO

Objective

The children will be able to think carefully about what they read.

Preparation

Give out *Pupil's Book 1* to each child (page 87, Lesson 2, Exercise A).

Method

1 Read through the sentences and questions, answering them orally.

Answers

1 Yes, the manager was fair to say that, because he knew that Peter was a lazy and dishonest person. However he probably would have said the same thing to any of the other workers if they were late for work.
2 He could be telling the truth or he could be telling a lie.
Yes, the manager was right to tell him not to be late again, in case he was late all the time.

3 Peter's bag was bigger than Kemuse's.
He found a plank of timber that was cut into small pieces.
No, Peter lied about the wood.
4 The manager made him pay for the plank of timber he cut up because it was not scrap timber.
5 Once he arrived half an hour late and the manager told him to be on time in future.
6 If I were the manager, I would call the men together and explain that they were overpaid the week before by mistake. Because of this, they received a dollar less this week.

LESSON THREE (Lesson Suggestion 36)

Objective
The children will be able to see both sides of an argument.

Preparation
Give out *Pupil's Book 1* to each child (page 88, Exercise B).

Method
1 Read introduction to the lesson.
2 Discuss with the children arguments 'for' and 'against' running a business.
3 Children write down their opinions.

Answers
FOR: Yes, it would be good to run your own business, because then you could be the boss and do as you please and earn more money.
AGAINST: No, it would be better to work for someone else because then you would have less responsibility. You would not have to worry so much or work so hard. If you don't like a job you can leave it and get another one.

LESSON FOUR (Lesson Suggestion 35)

Objective
The children will be able to work out the meanings of words from context clues.

Preparation
Give out *Pupil's Book 1* to each child (page 88, Exercise C).

Method
1 Read the introduction.
2 Work out several examples with the class.

Answers
1 complaining means to grumble and be unhappy about something
2 protested means he argued with someone
3 increase means more than usual
4 adjustment means change
overpayment means they were paid too much

LESSON FIVE (Lesson Suggestion 39)

Objective
Children will be able to read for enjoyment.

OR POETRY (Lesson Suggestion 40)

Preparation
Give out *Pupil's Book 1* to each child (page 89), *'The Sunset'*.

Answers
1 The poet is saying that everything rests at sunset after the day's work.
2 comforted peaceful
3 red yellow orange purple
4 The whole world is covered by a pink light at sunset.

LISTENING 9

LESSON ONE

Objective
The children will be able to listen for words which rhyme.

Preparation
Write on the blackboard a long list of words which rhyme.

For Example

able	table	away	play
act	fact	axe	backs
after	laughter	bad	sad
age	page	band	hand
air	hair	beach	each
all	fall	bed	red
along	song	below	toe
black	track	blood	flood
bread	said	brick	kick
canoe	shoe	chair	care

Method
1 Read out pairs of rhyming words from your list and ask the children to repeat the words after you.
2 Then read one word and ask the children to say a new word which rhymes, e.g:
T: book
C: took, look, hook, cook
3 Then make up some sentences with rhyming words. Ask the children to say just the rhyming words, e.g:
T: I hit my head and went to bed.
C: head, bed

LESSON TWO

Objective
The children will be able to listen for stressed words in a sentence.

Method
1 Remind the children that if you *stress* a word in a sentence, it means that that word is the most important in the sentence. It affects the meaning of a sentence.
Write these examples on the blackboard:
You ate my banana stresses *who* ate the banana

You *ate* my banana stresses *what happened* to the banana
You ate *my* banana stresses *whose* banana you ate
You ate my *banana* stresses *what* you ate

2 Read the following sentences slowly, stressing the underlined word. First ask the children to say which word you stressed. Then ask them to say whether this word stresses: who, what happened, whose, or what.
I wore her dress (I/who)
I wore her dress (wore/what happened)
I wore her dress (her/whose)
I wore her dress (dress/what)
Do the same with other sentences, like:
He broke my bicycle.

TALKING

LESSON ONE (Lesson Suggestion 1C)

Objective
The children will practise last week's sentence pattern:
What did he buy himself? He bought himself a shirt.

Method
1 Use the substitution table that is still on the blackboard from last week. Revise it thoroughly.

LESSON TWO

Objective
The children will practise a sentence pattern they already know:
Why does he *need* some wood? He needs wood to make a fire.
He has a new shirt. He doesn't *need* another one.

Method
1 Draw the following pictures quickly on the blackboard: fish, tools, matches, firewood, salt, sugar, money. Point to one of the pictures and say: Why does Joe need some matches?
C: He needs matches to light the fire.
T: Why does Maria need some salt?
C: She needs salt to put in the food.
2 Encourage children to think up their own examples when they work in their groups.

LESSON THREE

Objective
The children will be able to use a new sentence pattern:
Did anyone help Malu to carry the box? No, he carried it himself.

Method
1 Give tasks to several children, e.g: Lua clean the blackboard; Raka, carry the chair to the corner; Malu sweep the floor; Kevau and Sere collect the books.
2 Wait until they finish these tasks.
T: Nobody helped Lua to clean the blackboard. He cleaned it by himself.

Did anyone help Lua to clean the blackboard?
C: No, he cleaned it by himself.
T: Did anyone help Raka to carry the chair?
C: No, she carried it by herself.
T: Did anyone help Malu sweep the floor?
C: No, she swept it by herself.
T: Did anyone help Kevau and Sere collect the books?
C: No, they collected them by themselves.
3 Ask children for similar examples.

LESSON FOUR

Objective
The children will practise this sentence pattern:
Did anyone help Malu carry the box? No, he carried it himself.

Method
1 T: Awa, clean the blackboard.
T: He isn't working with other children. He's working by himself. Is he working with other children?
C: No, he's working by himself.
T: Is Sevese reading with other children?
C: No, he's reading by himself.
T: Grade 5 children are working in their gardens. Are they working with anyone else?
C: No, they're working by themselves.
2 T: Did anyone help Susan write that story?
C: No, she wrote it by herself.
T: Did anyone help Dagu plant that corn?
C: No, he planted it by himself.
3 Ask children for similar examples.
4 Divide the class into groups to practise this pattern.

LESSON FIVE (Lesson Suggestion 1C)

Objective
The children will practise the new sentence pattern by using a substitution table.

Preparation
Write the following substitution table on the blackboard. If possible, leave it there until next week.

Did anyone help	LUA	carry that	BED?	No,	HE	carried it by	HIMSELF.
	BENA		BOX?				
	MARGRIT		BILUM?		SHE		HERSELF.
	THE PARENTS	make that	FIRE?		THEY	made it by	THEMSELVES.

Is	UNA	working with anyone else?	No,	SHE'S	working by	HERSELF.
	BINI	reading		HE'S		HIMSELF.
	DIKA					

Are	THE TEACHERS	going?	They're going	THEMSELVES.
	THE CHILDREN			
	WE		We're	OURSELVES.

ORAL EXPRESSION

LESSON ONE

Objective
The children will be able to tell the time using the correct phrases.

Preparation
Children can make cardboard clocks during an Expressive Arts lesson. Otherwise, you should have a large clock for the class to see.

Method
1 Set your clock and ask the children: What's the time?
2 The children must reply: The time is one o'clock. Or It's one o'clock. Other phrases that should be used are: a quarter to, a quarter past, half past, ten minutes to, twenty past, etc.
3 If the children have their own clocks, the teacher will give a time, e.g: The time is ten past five. The children must make that time on their clocks. Then the teacher will ask: What's the time? The class must answer: The time is ten past five.

LESSON TWO

Objective
The children will be able to make up sentences in a word game.

Preparation
Divide the children into groups of about six pupils.

Method
1 One child says a sentence.
2 The next pupil in the group must use the last word of that sentence in a sentence of his own, e.g:
1st C: Young people should learn traditional skills *today*.
2nd C: *Today* I am going into *hospital*.
3rd C: We waited at the *hospital* to see the *doctor*.
4th C: I would like to become a *doctor* when I finish *school*.
3 Teacher should walk around the room listening to each group.

LESSON THREE

Objective
The children will be able to discuss a given topic.

Method
1 Begin a discussion on some ways in which your school could help the local community.
2 Encourage the children to think of special areas of the community where help is needed, or things which need improvement. How could your school help?

Note
If there are some good ideas for things the class really could do, arrange for a group of children to discuss them with the Head Teacher.

WRITTEN SENTENCES

Note
Teach only FIVE of the six lessons.

LESSON ONE

Objective
The children will be able to use the plural form of reflexive pronouns ('self' pronouns).

Preparation
Give out *Pupil's Book 1* to each child (page 90, Lesson 1).

Method
1 Read introduction to lesson, giving examples.
2 Ask the children to write the answers in their exercise books.

Answers
1 ourselves 2 themselves 3 yourselves 4 themselves
They're scratching themselves.
We're dressing ourselves.
They're looking at themselves.
It's licking itself.

LESSON TWO

Objective
The children will be able to use 'self' pronouns correctly.

Preparation
Give out *Pupil's Book 1* to each child (page 91, Lesson 2).

Answers
1 He hurt himself.
2 She burned herself.
3 They injured themselves.
4 We made ourselves sick.
5 It licked itself clean.

LESSON THREE

Objective
The children will be able to use prepositions correctly.

Preparation
Give out *Pupil's Book 1* to each child (page 91, Lesson 3).

Method
Do a few examples orally, before you ask the children to write down answers.

Answers

1 to	1 off
2 at	2 for
3 in	3 of
4 to	4 off
5 at	5 of, for

LESSON FOUR (Lesson Suggestion 2)

Objective
The children will be able to write suitable sentences to match pictures.

Preparation
Give out *Pupil's Book 1* to each child (page 92, Lesson 4).

Possible Answers
1 'You tripped me over on purpose, you great bully! I'll teach you a lesson you won't forget in a hurry.'
2 'A snake! I've got no weapon. Perhaps if I keep very still, it won't attack me.'
3 'Oh my son! That car has hit you! Oh my beloved son!'
4 'The winner of the Grand Quiz Show is Michael Kome. Michael, here is your prize money.'
5 'There it goes! That dynamite will blast the cliff to pieces.'
6 'Oh no! I've been seen. Just when I was nearly over the fence.'

LESSON FIVE (Lesson Suggestion 6)

Objective
The children will be able to complete the questions and write good answers to them.

Preparation
Give out *Pupil's Book 1* to each child (page 93, Lesson 5).

Possible Answers
1 When are you going to hospital?
I'm going on Wednesday.
2 Which way is it to Burimi village?
It's about a kilometer further down that road.
3 How much was that pumpkin?
It was one kina.
4 Why doesn't he buy himself a truck?
He doesn't have enough money.
5 What does he want to do when he leaves school?
He wants to be a teacher.
6 When did that tree fall down?
It fell down during the storm.
7 How does Sara feel now?
She feels much better.
8 Why aren't you at school today?
I am feeling sick.

LESSON SIX (Lesson Suggestion 6)

Objective
The children will be able to complete the sentences correctly.

Preparation
Give out *Pupil's Book 1* to each child (page 93, Lesson 6).

Answers
1 his
2 his
3 its
4 her
5 her
6 their

WRITTEN COMPOSITION

LESSON ONE (Lesson Suggestion 17)

Objective
The children will be able to write a business letter.

Preparation
Give out *Pupil's Book 1* to each child (page 93, Lesson 1).

Method
1 Read lesson introduction and discuss with the class.
2 Discuss what you would say in the letter.

Possible Answer

Bula Community School,
Morobe Province.

4th May, 1982

The Superintendent,
Angau Memorial Hospital,
Lae.

Dear Sir,

I am the leader of a special school project to help our local community. I would like to send a group of students to your hospital to help with any work that needs doing.

We could help with things like cutting grass, gardening, repairing broken furniture, scrubbing floors and walls, or perhaps reading stories to younger patients.

Please let me know if this would be helpful, and on which day you would like us to come. Would you like us to bring tools or other equipment with us when we come?

Yours faithfully,
Galang Akis.

LESSON TWO (Lesson Suggestion 20)

Objective
The children will be able to fill in a bank form.

Preparation
Give out *Pupil's Book 1* to each child (page 95, Lesson 2).

Method
1 Study the deposit slip with the children. Discuss the information that has been written in.
2 Explain the meanings of the headings, e.g: Branch, Name, etc.
3 Explain what a withdrawal slip is used for. Discuss what needs to be filled in.
4 Children copy the numbers shown on the withdrawal slip into their exercise books, and fill in the details next to the numbers. *Do not allow children to write their answers in their pupil's book.*

SPELLING

LESSON ONE (Lesson Suggestion 22)

Objective
The children will learn to spell this week's words.

Preparation
Give out *Pupil's Book 1* to each child (page 96, Spelling List).

LESSON TWO

Select from Exercises A–E.

Preparation
Give out *Pupil's Book 1* to each child (pages 96–7).

Exercise A (Lesson Suggestion 29)

Answers
1 employ
2 employer
3 employee
4 employment
5 relation

Exercise B

Answers
mallet screw-driver hammer pliers spanner saw

Exercise C (Lesson Suggestion 28)

Possible Answers
1 pear meat treat meals cream peace
2 meat meals month merry mend
3 meals cream stand month merry peace
4 meals cream peace
5 meat meals
6 meals month
7 meals

Exercise D (Lesson Suggestion 27)

Answers
stand step sting stove stretch stuck style
1 drama dream drive drown drum
2 flag flea flown flung fly

Exercise E

Answers
below/above tall/short mend/break leave/arrive
wrong/right worst/best dirty/clean north/south
cheap/expensive clever/stupid deep/shallow sweet/sour

HANDWRITING (Lesson Suggestion 33)

Preparation
Give out *Pupil's Book 1* to each child (page 98).

READING

INTRODUCTION (Lesson Suggestion 34)

Objective
The children will be able to understand the background of the story, and the meaning of new words. They will read the story silently.

Preparation
Give out *Reader 1* to each child (pages 32–34), *'The Hermit and the Rajah's Crown'*.

Method
1 Explain that this story is set in India. (Find it on the atlas.) Say a few things about the country: jungle, tigers and elephants, type of clothes worn, type of food eaten there, etc. Discuss these new words: Rajah — like an Indian King; Hermit — someone who lives on his own, away from other people; Crown — a hat made from gold and precious stones worn by kings and queens.
2 Follow Lesson Suggestion 34B.

LESSON ONE (Lesson Suggestion 34C)

Objective
The children will be able to answer questions to show that they understand the story.

Preparation
Give out *Reader 1* (pages 32–4) and *Pupil's Book 1* to each child (page 98, Lesson 1).

Answers
1 The tiger and the snake could not get out of the hole because it was too deep for them to climb out.
2 The hermit tossed down a length of creeper and pulled out the animals one at a time.
3 The snake told the hermit that if ever he was in trouble, he was to think hard of the snake and he would come to his aid.
4 The tiger killed the Rajah's son.
5 The jeweller realized immediately that the crown belonged to the Rajah's son.
6 The Rajah probably felt hopeful that there was news of his missing son.
7 The Rajah wanted to ask the hermit where he had got the crown and what he knew about his missing son.
8 No, the Rajah did not believe the hermit's story because he did not believe that tigers could talk.
9 The hermit felt sorry that he had come to town. He thought he would be punished for something he had not done.
10 The snake helped the hermit get out. The snake helped the hermit to please the Rajah by saving the Rajah's daughter from illness.

LESSON TWO (Lesson Suggestion 35)

Objective
The children will be able to work out the meanings of new words by using context clues.

Preparation
Give out *Pupil's Book 1* to each child (page 99, Lesson 2, Exercises A & B).

Exercise A

Method
Read the sentences out loud and discuss the meaning of the words in heavy print.

Answers
1 slithered — slid along (the way a snake moves on its belly)
hermit — a person who lives alone, away from other people
cure — to make well again

Exercise B

Answers
Bride Price 'Wrong' — opinion
Two killed in fight — fact
Thieves raid club — fact
Cold Air — fact
24 guilty over riot — fact

LESSON THREE

Objective
The children will be able to use the Table of Contents found at the front of a book.

Preparation
Give out *Pupil's Book 1* to each child (pages 100–101, Exercise C). Show one or two books containing a Table of Contents (e.g: *Reader 1*) to the class.

Method
1 Introduce the lesson by explaining that a Table of Contents lists what is in a book and helps you find the part you want. Study the Contents page of the Telephone Directory on page 101.
2 Talk about the meanings of difficult words listed at the bottom of that page.
3 Work out the answers to the questions orally with the class, e.g:
Q: Which words tells us how much something will cost?
A: Charges.
Q: Can you find a heading which uses this word?
A: Telephone Call Charges on page 19.

Answers
1 Telephone Call Charges on page 19.
2 Telegrams by Telephone on page 4.
3 Emergency Numbers on page 2.
4 How to Call on page 18.
5 Postal information on page 25.
6 Telegram Rates on page 4.

LESSON FOUR

Objective
The children will be able to do reading games.

Preparation
Give out *Reading Games for Grade 6* to each child (page 22, Unit 9).

Method
Choose one of these games for the children to do. (See *Reading Games for Grade 6 Teacher's Notes* for the answers.)

LESSON FIVE (Lesson Suggestion 39)

Objective
The children will be able to read for enjoyment.

Preparation
Give out varied reading material for children to read.

OR POETRY (Lesson Suggestion 40)

Preparation
Give out *Pupil's Book 1* to each child (page 102) Poetry.

Answers
1 It is cool in the evening because the sun has gone down.
2 'Casting' means throwing.
3 The village men will go fishing tonight.
4 The weather may not be fine tomorrow night.

LISTENING 10

LESSON ONE

Objective
The children will be able to listen for stressed words in a sentence.

Method
1 Quickly go over Lesson 2 for Unit 9, reminding children that you can stress who, what, whose, and what happened, in a sentence.
2 Explain that you can also stress *how* things are done and *when* things are done, e.g:
I travelled by bus yesterday. (how)
They will sail quickly tomorrow (when)
3 Read the following sentences, stressing the underlined word. Ask the children which word you stressed and whether this tells when or how, e.g:
You ate slowly tonight. (how)
They sang loudly yesterday. (when)
You must work hard today. (how)
4 Now give the children harder examples, asking them to say whether the stressed words mean who, what happened, how, when or whose, e.g:
You must kill that pig today (when)
Don't run so fast (how)
You must stand, not sit. (what happened)

He is the one who bought a car. (who)
That long piece of rope is mine (whose)

LESSON TWO

Objective
The children will be able to concentrate, listen carefully and remember what they hear.

Preparation
Write several messages on separate pieces of paper, e.g:
Take this money and buy four bananas, one tin of fish, two packets of matches and a newspaper at the tradestore.
Tell Gima, Tuk, Kave and Dika's brother to meet me at the market.

Method
1 Divide the class into groups of about six children.
2 Give one message to the first child in each group. That child reads the message to herself (she *must not* let the others see it). Then she whispers it to the second child. He listens carefully, and whispers it to the third child, and so on. The last child says the message out loud and compares it with the message on the piece of paper.
3 Then ask someone in each group to make up their own message, and try again.

TALKING

LESSON ONE (Lesson Suggestion 1C)

Objective
The children will practise last week's sentence pattern:
Did anyone help Malu to carry the box? No, he carried it by himself.

Method
1 Use the substitution table on the blackboard. Revise it.

LESSON TWO

Objective
The children will practise a sentence pattern they already know:
Can you go swimming now? Yes, I can.
No, I can't, because I have to collect firewood.

Method
1 Point to a child and say: Can you eat your lunch now?
C: No, I can't because it's not lunch-time.
Choose other children and ask them questions, e.g:
T: Can you fix that chair now?
Can you read that book now?
Can you tell me the time?
Can you hear that bird whistling?
Can you see that boy running?
Can you run fast?

2 Divide class into groups and tell them to practise this sentence pattern using questions and answers.

LESSON THREE

Objective
The children will be able to use a new sentence pattern:
Can you make a kundu by yourself? Yes, I can.

Method
1 Ask a pupil to lift a chair. When she has finished ask the class:
T: Can Kati lift the chair by herself?
C: Yes, she can.
T: Can she lift the cupboard by herself?
C: No, she can't.
T: Can you make a canoe by yourself?
C: No, I can't.
T: Can Vele dig in the garden by himself?
C: Yes, he can.
2 Ask: Who can make a spear by himself?
C: Tamu can.
T: Who can make a basket by herself?
C: I can.
T: Who can lift this table by himself?
C: I can.
3 Divide children into groups to practise this pattern.

LESSON FOUR

Objective
The children will practise this sentence pattern:
What can you do by yourself? I can work in the garden by myself.

Method
1 Talk about things children can do alone.
T: What can you do by yourself?
C: I can paddle a canoe by myself.
I can play by myself.
I can do my homework by myself.
2 Give instructions that children cannot do alone.
T: Lift that table please.
C: I can't lift it by myself.
T: Why didn't you lift that table?
C: I couldn't lift it by myself.
3 Practise in groups.

LESSON FIVE (Lesson Suggestion 1C)

Objective
The children will practise the new sentence pattern using a substitution table.

Preparation
Write the following substitution table on the blackboard. Remember to leave it there until next week.

Can	YOU	make a	BASKET	by	YOURSELF	Yes,	I	can.
	SHE		BILUM		HERSELF		SHE	
	HE		CANOE		HIMSELF		HE	
	THEY		GARDEN		THEMSELVES		THEY	

Who can	MAKE	a	KUNDU	by	HIMSELF?	I	CAN.
			DRESS		HERSELF?		
	READ		BOOK				
	WRITE		LETTER			I	CAN'T.
	DRIVE		CAR				

What can	YOU	do by	YOURSELF?	I	can work	GARDEN	by	MYSELF.
	SHE		HERSELF	SHE	in the	HOUSE		HERSELF.
	THEY		THEMSELVES	THEY		FACTORY		THEMSELVES.
	WE		OURSELVES	WE	plant kaukau			OURSELVES.

ORAL EXPRESSION

LESSON ONE

Objective
The children will practise using their imagination.

Method
1 Turn to page 105 in *Pupil's Book 1*. Read the story to the children.
2 Tell the children to imagine they are one of the robbers. Choose different pupils to say why they planned the robbery, how they planned it and what went wrong. How did the police find them? How did they feel when they were caught?
3 Mime the robbery, choosing two pupils to be the robbers and another to be the policeman. Use classroom furniture as buildings and the police car, etc.

LESSON TWO

Objective
The children will be able to use their imagination to think up an alibi.

Note
Explain that an alibi is something which proves that you were somewhere else when a crime was committed, therefore you are not guilty of that crime.

Method
1 Remind children of the previous lesson about the robbery.
2 Choose two children as suspects for the robbery the night before. These two children are sent outside to think up an alibi. They have to convince the rest of the class that they were together somewhere on that night, so they could not possibly have committed that crime.
3 After five minutes, one of the robbers is brought inside and the class ask him questions about his activities on the night of the robbery, e.g:
Q: Where were you on Wednesday night?
A: I went fishing.
Q: Did anyone go with you?
A: Yes, Gari (the boy outside.)
Q: How many fish did you catch?

A: Four.
Q: Where did you go fishing?
A: Where the river joins the sea.
Q: Was there a moon?
A: No, it was cloudy.

4 The other boy is then brought inside and pupils ask him the same questions. If his answers are not the same, then they do not have a good alibi so everyone knows that they are lying. If their answers are exactly the same you know they have a good alibi.

LESSON THREE

Objective
The children will be able to give instructions.

Preparation
Bring to class something which requires instructions before it can be used, e.g: hurricane lamp, cassette radio, etc.

Method
1 Show the radio to the children. Tell them that before they use this radio they must know how to operate it. Give the class instructions, e.g: First make sure you put new batteries in here. Next you turn the 'on-off' switch to 'on'. Then you must turn this knob, called a 'tuner', until you find a radio station. You turn the volume knob to control the sound level. When you have finished listening, you turn the 'on-off' switch to 'off'.
2 Now ask the class to think up instructions for doing something which they know about, e.g: making a spear; making a bamboo jew's harp; lighting a fire; making sago; making sacsac roofing; making a bilum; making a kite; making a mumu, etc.
3 After the children have thought about this for a while, ask someone to come out the front and give instructions to the rest of the class. Encourage the use of words like: first, next, then, after that, finally.

WRITTEN SENTENCES

LESSON ONE (Lesson Suggestion 7)

Objective
The children will be able to choose the correct form of a verb.

Preparation
Give out *Pupil's Book 1* to each child (page 103, Lesson 1).

Answers

1 scored	4 bought	7 reading	10 seen
2 gave	5 coming	8 ate	
3 went	6 said	9 gone	

LESSON TWO (Lesson Suggestion 11)

Objective
The children will be able to change sentences from singular to plural, and from plural to singular.

Preparation
Give out *Pupil's Book 1* to each child (page 103, Lesson 2).

Method
Follow Lesson Suggestion 11, stressing point 4.

Answers
Changing from singular to plural.
1 The boys washed their dirty feet.
2 The girls cleaned their teeth.
3 The children ran quickly into the sea.
4 Why weren't they at school today?
5 The women were sitting under some trees weaving baskets.

Changing from plural to singular.
6 The man was very tired after his long walk.
7 She told me she does the gardening every day.
8 The worker collected his pay every Friday.
9 The sheep drank water from the river. (Note: sheep is the same, whether singular or plural.)
10 The girl sheltered from the rain under the huge tree.

LESSON THREE (Lesson Suggestion 1)

Objective
The children will practise writing a sentence pattern.

Preparation
Give out *Pupil's Book 1* to each child (page 104, Lesson 3).

Method
1 Do all this work orally with the class first before writing any answers.

Possible Answers
1 How long have you been at school?
I've been at school for six years.
2 How long have we been waiting for him?
We've been waiting for him for an hour.
3 How long has she been at High School?
She's been at High School for two years.
4 How long has he been in Wewak?
He's been in Wewak for two months.
5 How long have they been married?
They've been married for six months.

LESSON FOUR (Lesson Suggestion 1)

Objective
The children will practise writing a sentence pattern.

Preparation
Give out *Pupil's Book 1* to each child (page 104, Lesson 4).

Method
As for Lesson 3.

Answers
1 Are you sure they will find that plant?
Yes, I'm sure they will.

2 Are you sure he will pass his exam?
Yes, I'm sure he will.
3 Are you sure she will see her mother?
Yes, I'm sure she will.
4 Are you sure we will catch some fish?
Yes, I'm sure we will.
5 Are you sure the dog will eat that meat?
Yes, I'm sure it will.

LESSON FIVE (Lesson Suggestion 1)

Objective
The children will practise writing a sentence pattern.

Preparation
Give out *Pupil's Book 1* to each child (page 104, Lesson 5).

Answers
1 Are you sure they won't find that money?
Yes, I'm sure they won't.
2 Are you sure he won't beat his wife?
Yes, I'm sure he won't.
3 Are you sure they won't burn that rubbish?
Yes, I'm sure they won't.
4 Are you sure it won't sting my eyes?
Yes, I'm sure it won't.
5 Are you sure she won't break that mirror?
Yes, I'm sure she won't.

WRITTEN COMPOSITION

LESSON ONE (Lesson Suggestion 19)

Objective
The children will be able to write a report.

Preparation
Give out *Pupil's Book 1* to each child (page 105, Lesson 1).

Method
1 Read through the lesson.
2 Read Constable Vagi's report and ask the class to finish each sentence orally.
3 If there is time, tell the children to write the full report in their exercise books.

Possible Answers
. . . when I noticed that the window of a tradestore was open.
Then I saw two men climb out of the window.
They were carrying torches and heavy bags.
I got quietly out of the car and crept towards them.
Just as they were about to run off into the bush, I switched on my torch and shone it in their faces.
Shortly after, the other patrol car arrived and Constable Bundu helped me to arrest the two men and take them to the police station.

Follow-Up
Ask children to read out their reports to the rest of the class.

LESSON TWO (Lesson Suggestion 17)

Objective
The children will be able to write a letter in reply to an invitation.

Preparation
Give out *Pupil's Book 1* to each child (page 106, Lesson 2).

Method
1 Read the letter of invitation.
2 Read through the points to be mentioned in the reply and discuss these with the class.
3 Then ask the children to write the letter to Sera in their exercise books.

Model Answer

Kilam Community School,
Lae,
Morobe Province.

12th April 19. .

Dear Sera,

Thank you and your parents for the kind invitation to come and stay in the holidays. My parents say I can come and I will be able to stay for ten days. I will be coming on 24th April by PMV which arrives at Kundiawa at about 4.30 p.m.

I am really excited about coming as I have never been to the Highlands before. I am also looking forward to seeing you and your family again.

love,
Denipa.

SPELLING

LESSON ONE (Lesson Suggestion 22)

Objective
The children will learn to spell this week's words.

Preparation
Give out *Pupil's Book 1* to each child (page 107, Spelling List).

LESSON TWO

Select from Exercises A–E.

Preparation
Give out *Pupil's Book 1* to each child (pages 107–8).

Exercise A (Lesson Suggestion 29)

Answers

1 deserve
2 despair
3 describe
4 enough
5 cough

Exercise C

Answers

without
football
headache
grandmother
cupboard
lifetime

Exercise D (Lesson Suggestion 23)

Possible Answers

rain – rainfall rainy rains raining rained
see – seeing saw sees seen
cry – cried crying cries
run – ran running runs runner
have – has having had
look – looking looked looks
took – take taking taken takes
hear – heard hearing hears
lose – lost loser losing loses

Exercise E (Lesson Suggestion 30)

Answers

1 unhealthy
2 unhappy
3 unlock
4 unwrap
5 unfit

HANDWRITING (Lesson Suggestion 33)

Preparation
Give out *Pupil's Book 1* to each child (page 108).

READING

INTRODUCTION (Lesson Suggestion 34)

Objective
The children will be able to understand the background to the story, and the meaning of new words. They will read the story silently.

Preparation
Give out *Reader 1* to each child (pages 35–8), '*Kamapua*'.

Method
1 This story is 'fiction', which means it is not true. Ask the children if they know any stories about people having magic powers.
2 Follow Lesson Suggestion 34B.

LESSON ONE (Lesson Suggestion 34C)

Objective
Children will be able to answer questions to show that they understand the story.

Preparation
Give out *Reader 1* (pages 35–8) and *Pupil's Book 1* to each child (page 109, Lesson 1).

Answers
1 The villagers were puzzled and frightened because they knew strange things were happening. The wind whistled loudly but the tree branches did not move. The sea roared with the crashing of great waves but it was calm.
2 The chief's wife gave birth to a pig.
3 An old woman on the other side of the island looked after the girl and her baby pig.
4 The old woman warned Kamapua that if he ate too much he would lose his magic powers until he became hungry again.
5 He changed into a bird, a fish, a leaf, a boy and a giant pig.
6 Kamapua stole fowls from his father.
7 The chief left two very fat, cooked fowls at the edge of the village because he knew Kamapua liked food.
8 He ate too much and lost his magic powers.
9 Kamapua changed himself into a giant pig when the chief came to kill him.
10 He learned not to eat too much.

LESSON TWO (Lesson Suggestion 35)

Objective
The children will be able to work out the meaning of a word from its context.

Preparation
Give out *Reader 1* (pages 35–8) and *Pupil's Book 1* to each child (page 109, Lesson 2).

Method
1 Work out some examples together, e.g: Find 'glaring' in the first paragraph. Read the sentence: The sky was black and the moon hung like a big, red, angry eye, glaring down at the world below. Ask: What does 'glaring' mean? If John scribbled on a library book, I would glare at him.
Answer: Glaring means looking angrily at something or someone.

Answers
warning — notice about danger
explored — travelled around to get to know
property — land (or things) owned by someone
advice — an opinion given by someone about what to do
approaching — coming towards
preparations — things came to get ready for something

LESSON THREE

Objective
The children will be able to read a notice and understand what it says.

Preparation
Give out *Pupil's Book 1* to each child (page 110, Exercise B).

Answers

1 The fete will be held at Kububu Community School.
2 A fete is like a fair or carnival.
3 It will be held on Saturday, May 24th.
4 It will begin at 1.00 p.m.
5 No, it will not be finished at 4 o'clock because the mumu will be ready then.
6 It will cost 80 toea.
7 The children will be able to play games, have races, join in the lolly scramble, and watch the traditional dancing.
8 The adults will be able to see traditional dancing, stalls and an art display.

LESSON FOUR (Lesson Suggestion 37)

Objective

The children will be able to follow directions.

Preparation

Give out *Pupil's Book 1* to each child (page 111, Exercise C).

Method

1 Discuss the instructions with the children.
2 Tell the children to quickly copy the picture into their books.
3 Now ask them to follow the instructions.

Answer

LESSON FIVE

Objective

The children will be able to do reading games.

Preparation

Give out *Reading Games for Grade 6* (page 23, Unit 10).

Method

Choose games for the children to play.

OR POETRY (Lesson Suggestion 40)

Preparation
Give out *Pupil's Book 1* to each child (page 111), *'A Book'*.

Answers

1 The book could tell a lot if it could speak. It does speak to us in a way, when we read it. But when the book is closed, and sitting on the shelf, it cannot be read so cannot tell anyone the stories inside it.
2 When a person opens a book and starts to read it, she can learn many new things, and read about other parts of the world.

TERM TWO

WEEKLY UNITS OF WORK: LISTENING

Unit 11 1 Following instructions: Game
2 Choosing the word that does not belong

Unit 12 1 Filling in details on a map by listening to instructions
2 Listening to a guest speaker

Unit 13 1 Choosing the word that does not belong because it has a different sound
2 Listening to the order in which things happen in a story

Unit 14 1 Remembering the main idea and important details of a story
2 Work out who someone is from their description

Unit 15 1 Listening carefully to hear the correct word
2 Listening carefully to hear which word was used in a sentence

Unit 16 1 Re-telling a conversation
2 Interpreting the meanings of certain actions

Unit 17 1 Thinking of the right word from its description
2 Listening carefully to directions

Unit 18 1 Remembering a list of things in the correct order
2 Completing two-line jingles with a rhyming word

Unit 19 1 Listening to a message and then passing it on to someone
2 Following instructions

Unit 20 1 Listening carefully to hear the correct word
2 Listening carefully to hear the correct word in a sentence

WEEKLY UNITS OF WORK: TALKING

Unit 11 Revision of work from the last week of Term 1.
Revision: I need some rice but I don't need any meat.
New sentence pattern: Can Manarangi get into that drawer? No, he's too big to get into that drawer.

Unit 12 Revision of last week's work
Revision: We need some more pencils. We need another pencil.
New sentence pattern: Can this boy reach the top of the door? Yes, he's tall enough to reach the top of the door.

Unit 13 Revision of last week's work
Revision: This shirt needs washing. This one doesn't need washing.
New sentence pattern: Can you lift the table? No, it's too heavy for me to lift.

Unit 14 Revision of last week's work
Revision: Where's your mother gone? She's gone to the garden.
New sentence pattern: Can Tunde wear this shirt? Yes, it's big enough for him to wear.

Unit 15 Revision of last week's work
Revision: He lost his pen so he had to buy a new one.
New sentence pattern: Here's a good book for you to read.

Unit 16 Revision of last week's work
Revision: I can't come now. I have to chop the wood.
New sentence pattern: It's bad for you to steal. It's good for you to eat protein.

Unit 17 Revision of last week's work
Revision: I need new batteries so I'll have to go to the store.
New sentence pattern: He's going to draw it again. There's no need for him to draw it again.

Unit 18 Revision of last week's work
Revision: If you want to light a fire, you have to collect firewood.
New sentence pattern: Did they start the game before their friends arrived? No, they waited for them to arrive.

Unit 19 Revision of last week's work
Revision: He sharpened his pencil before he wrote his name.
New sentence pattern: How long have you been sitting here? We've been sitting here since eight o'clock.

Unit 20 Revision of last week's work
Revision: How long has he been standing? He's been standing for five minutes.
New sentence pattern: Are you sure they will come? Yes, I know they will come.

WEEKLY UNITS OF WORK: ORAL EXPRESSION

Unit 11
1 Passing on telephone messages
2 Remembering a list of items
3 Using sequence signals

Unit 12
1 Asking questions
2 Asking questions
3 Discussion (raising money)

Unit 13
1 Giving instructions
2 Discussion (organizing a school project)
3 Telling a story (sequence pictures)

Unit 14
1 Class Discussion (about a show)
2 Remembering a list of things and events
3 Telling about personal experiences

Unit 15
1 Discussion (how to improve the school)
2 Telling a story from a picture
3 Holding an interview

Unit 16
1 Discussion (singsing)
2 Making contrasts
3 Asking questions

Unit 17
1 Personal talks
2 Asking for information
3 Interrupting politely

Unit 18
1 Personal talks
2 Expanding a story
3 Thanking guest speakers

Unit 19
1 Giving explanations
2 Expressing personal opinions
3 Emphasising a point strongly

Unit 20
1 Talking about a picture
2 Giving directions
3 Asking questions to find out information

WEEKLY UNITS OF WORK: WRITTEN SENTENCES

Unit 11
1 Substituting one word for a group of words
2 Using new words in sentences (optional)
3 Making telegrams
4 Reflexive pronouns
5 Using reflexive pronouns after 'for'
6 Prepositions

Unit 12 1 Apostrophes (to show possessive)
2 Choosing the correct word (optional)
3 Joining words
4 Choosing the correct form of the verb
5 Reported speech
6 Prepositions

Unit 13 1 Changing from present to past tense
2 Apostrophes (showing possessive)
3 Punctuation
4 Completing sentences about pictures
5 Completing questions (optional)
6 Descriptions

Unit 14 1 Writing sentences about a picture
2 Choosing the correct word to fit the context
3 Writing answers to questions
4 Finding the sentence that is out of context
5 Writing questions

Unit 15 1 Writing sentences about a picture
2 Using adjectives
3 Answering questions
4 Changing from present to past tense (optional)
5 Answering questions
6 Choosing the best adjectives

Unit 16 1 Writing sentences about a picture
2 Joining sentences
3 Using apostrophes
4 Answering questions about a picture
5 Writing questions

Unit 17 1 Writing sentences about a picture
2 Completing sentences
3 Answering questions about a picture
4 Completing sentences using adverbial phrases (optional)
5 Writing answers

Unit 18 1 Writing sentences about a picture
2 Answering questions (about Vocational Schools)
3 Changing from past to present tense
4 Completing sentences
5 Answering questions

Unit 19 1 Writing good sentences about a picture
2 Choosing the correct form of the verb
3 Answering questions about a picture
4 Using quotation marks correctly
5 Answering questions

Unit 20 1 Writing good sentences about a picture
2 Finding suitable words for sentences
3 Completing sentences
4 Answering questions
5 Writing a diary

WEEKLY UNITS OF WORK: WRITTEN COMPOSITION

Unit 11 1 Writing an imaginative story
2 Writing a telephone conversation

Unit 12 1 Addressing envelopes
2 Writing about an interview

Unit 13 1 Writing an ending to a story
2 Writing a story about sequence pictures

Unit 14 1 Making a plan of a story
2 Writing a paragraph

Unit 15 1 Writing a description
2 Writing an interview

Unit 16 1 Writing a story about a set of sequence pictures
2 Planning a business letter

Unit 17 1 Planning a business letter
2 Writing a story about sequence pictures

Unit 18 1 Writing an imaginative story
2 Replying to a business letter

Unit 19 1 Writing a composition
2 Writing an imaginative story

Unit 20 1 Writing personal opinions
2 Following written directions

WEEKLY UNITS OF WORK: SPELLING

Unit 11 circle cigarette circus city (soft 'c')
joke broke choke poke ('oke' group)
Family Group: Games
Written Exercises A–E

Unit 12 diary diamond diagram diameter ('dia' group)
believe chief relief thief ('ie' group)
Family Group: Church
Written Exercises A–E

Unit 13 electric electrician electricity electrical ('electric' group)
parachute paragraph parallel parade ('para' group)
Family Group: Relatives
Written Exercises A–E

Unit 14 faint against trail mail ('ai' group)
completely quickly suddenly anxiously ('ly' group)
Family Group: The Show
Written Exercises A–E

Unit 15 pearl learned earth earned ('ea' group)
teach rear Easter clean ('ea' group)
Family Group: Work Parade
Written Exercises A–E

Unit 16 grass grabbed ground growl ('gr' group)
condition relation station plantation ('ion' group)
Family Group: The Singsing
Written Exercises A–E

Unit 17 flew flute float flour ('fl' group)
ground found sound around ('ou' group)
Family Group: Athletics Day
Written Exercises A–D

Unit 18 ticket pocket picked click ('ck' group)
giant trial diamond diary ('ia' group)
Family Group: Vocational School
Written Exercises A–E

Unit 20 team stream peanut please ('ea' group)
agree between freeze breed ('ee' group)
Family Group: The Village
Written Exercises A–E

WEEKLY UNITS OF WORK: HANDWRITING

Unit 11 Practise letter combinations 'sn' and zy'
Copy model passage about Bread

Unit 12 Practise letter combinations 'ich' and 'ell'
Copy model passage about Wealth

Unit 13 Practise letter combinations 'pro' and 'veg'.
Copy model passage about Oil Palm

Unit 14 Practise letter combinations 'ic' and 'no'.
Copy model passage about Crocodiles

Unit 15 Practise letter combinations 'an' and 'rp'
Copy model passage about Salt

Unit 16 Practise letter combinations 'os' and 'ff'
Copy model passage of direct speech

Unit 17 Practise letter combinations 'af' and 'ex'.
Copy model passage about the Bush

Unit 18 Practise writing numbers 1–10
Copy model passage of direct speech

Unit 19 Practise letter combinations 'sn' and 'ly'
Copy model letter

Unit 20 Practise letter combinations 'ju' and 'os'
Copy model passage about Jackson's Airport

WEEKLY UNITS OF WORK: READING

Unit 11
1 Reader: *'Coming to the Town'*
2 Comprehension
3 Context clues
4 Writing a letter/Word meanings from picture clues
5 Reading Games
6 Supplementary Reader or Poetry

Unit 12
1 Reader: *'The Pie Stall'*
2 Comprehension
3 Comprehension
4 Reading exercise
5 Reading Games
6 Reading for enjoyment or Poetry

Unit 13
1 Reader: *'The Black Cloud and the Old Woman'*
2 Comprehension
3 Reading exercises
4 Comprehension
5 Reading Games
6 Supplementary Reader or Poetry

Unit 14
1 Reader: *'Eruption'*
2 Comprehension
3 Comprehension exercise
4 Reading Games
5 Supplementary Reader
6 Poetry

Unit 15
1 Reader: *'One Thing After Another'*
2 Comprehension
3 Telephone Directory — Post Offices
4 Interpreting a weather forecast
5 Comprehension exercise
6 Reading for enjoyment or Poetry

Unit 16 1 Reader: *'Lost, Stolen or Strayed'*
2 Comprehension
3 Reading exercise
4 Context clues
5 Reading Games
6 Reading for enjoyment or Poetry

Unit 17 1 Reader: *'Idajojo the Giant'*
2 Comprehension
3 Reading exercise
4 Finding the odd word
5 Supplementary reader
6 Reading Games or Poetry

Unit 18 1 Reader: *'It's My Life'* (Part 1)
2 Comprehension
3 Telephone Directory — Postage
4 Reading directions
5 Reading for enjoyment or Poetry
6 Reading Games

Unit 19 1 Reader: *'It's My Life'* (Part 2)
2 Comprehension
3 Comprehension exercise
4 Comprehension exercise
5 Supplementary Reader or Poetry
6 Reading Games

Unit 20 1 Reader: *'The Boar-Killer'*
2 Comprehension
3 Comprehension exercise
4 Table of Contents
5 Reading for enjoyment or Poetry
6 Reading Games

LISTENING 11

LESSON ONE

Objective
The children will listen carefully and follow instructions correctly.

Method
1 Call out instructions which the children can follow while sitting at their desks. If you say 'You must . . .', the children must do as you say. If you *don't* say 'You must . . .', or if you say something else instead, the children must *not* follow your instructions, e.g:
T: You *must* stand up. (children do it)
T: Sit down. (children *don't* do it)
T: You must close your eyes. (children do it)
T: You can open your eyes. (children *don't* to it)

LESSON TWO

Objective
The children will listen carefully and pick out the word which does not fit in each list. This is practice at listening in order to classify things.

Method
Read out these lists of words and ask the children to write down the word which does not fit in each list.
1 plate cup dish chalk bowl (chalk — not used for eating with)
2 plane sail airstrip pilot helicopter (sail — not connected with airports)
3 trawler canoe lakatoi car cargo ship (car — not connected with sea transport)
4 shirt shoes shorts curtain dress (curtain — not connected with clothes)
5 letter parcel book stamp envelope (book — not connected with the post office)
6 hook line bait ball spear (ball — not connected with fishing equipment)

Note
These lists are taken from the spelling lessons covered this term. They are a good opportunity for revision.

TALKING

LESSON ONE (Lesson Suggestion 1C)

Objective
The children will practise the sentence pattern they learned in week 10 of Term 1:
Can you make a kundu by yourself? Yes, I can.

Preparation
Write the substitution table from Term 1, Unit 10, Talking Lesson Five on the blackboard.

Method
Follow Lesson Suggestion 1C.

LESSON TWO

Objective
The children will practise a sentence pattern they already know:
I need some rice but I don't need any meat.

Method
1 Point to the blackboard and pick up some chalk. Say: I need a duster but I don't need any chalk.
2 Point to a child and say: You need a pencil but you don't need any paper.
3 Ask children to think up other examples, e.g:
I need a shirt but I don't need a coat.
I need a drink but I don't need any food.
I need a rest but I don't need any sleep.
I need some fruit but I don't need any vegetables.
4 Divide children into groups to practise this sentence pattern.

LESSON THREE

Objective
The children will be able to use a new sentence pattern:
Can Manarangi get into that drawer? No, he's too big to get into the drawer.

Method
1 Ask a pupil to come to the front of the class and say: Tokome is very small. Ask him to reach the top of the cupboard. Say to the class:
T: He's too small to reach the top of the cupboard. Can he reach the top of the cupboard?
C: No, he's too small to reach the top of the cupboard.
T: Can Manarangi get into that drawer?
C: No, he's too big to get into that drawer.
2 Show the children a picture of an old woman and say:
T: Can this old woman do the gardening?
C: No, she's too old to do the gardening.
T: Can this sick woman do the washing?
C: No, she's too sick to do the washing.
3 Divide class into groups to practise this pattern.

LESSON FOUR

Objective
The children practise this sentence pattern:
Can Meli reach that shelf? No, she's too small to reach the shelf.

Method
1 Take the children outside. Ask them to do things, e.g:
T: Kame, can you reach that branch?
C: No, I'm too short to reach that branch.
T: Kope, can you touch the roof?
C: No, I'm too small to touch the roof.
T: Sali, can you fit in that hole?
C: No, I'm too big to fit in that hole.

T: Sela, can you climb through that pipe?
C: No, I'm too big to climb through that pipe.

2 Ask children to find partners. Each partner must ask the other to do something and they give an answer.

LESSON FIVE (Lesson Suggestion 1C)

Objective
The children will practise the new sentence pattern using a substitution table.

Preparation
Write the following substitution table on the blackboard:

Can	SUSI	fit in that	CUPBOARD?	No,	SHE'S	too big to fit ......
	JON		BOX		HE'S	
	KARL		BASKET			
	JOSEPH	reach that	PAWPAW?	No, he's too small to reach		
	PENI		MANGO?			
	AKE		BRANCH:			

Note
Remember to leave this table on the blackboard for Talking Lesson 1 next week.

ORAL EXPRESSION

LESSON ONE

Objective
The children will be able to pass on a telephone message accurately.

Method
1 Divide children into groups of three people: a caller, the person who answers the call, and the person who is given the message.

2 Each group must act out a call. Teacher act an example with two children first, e.g:
Caller: Hello, this is Josie here. Is Mele there?
Answer: No, I'm sorry, Mele's out tonight.
Caller: Do you know when she'll be home?
Answer: Not till quite late. She's gone to a party.
Caller: Well, could you ask her to meet me at the post office at about 10.30 tomorrow?
Answer: All right, I'll tell her.
Caller: Thanks. Oh, and tell her to be early if she can. Bye!
Answer: Goodbye!

3 Person who answered the phone turns to third person and gives her the message, e.g:
Josie rang last night when you were out. She wants you to meet her at the post office at about 10.30 tomorrow. She said you should come early, if you can.

4 The third person then tells the other two what she must do, e.g:
Mele wants me to meet her at the post office . . . etc.

5 Now tell the groups to act out a similar situation.

LESSON TWO

Objective
The children will be able to tell a story, remembering a list of things.

Method
1 Divide the class into four groups.
2 The leader of the first group begins: I went to the trade store and bought a knife.
3 The next child in that group says: I went to the trade store and bought a knife and a T-shirt.
4 Continue in this way, with each child adding one thing, until everyone in that group has a turn. Other teams must listen for mistakes in repeating the list of things.
5 The next group then has a turn. Variations of this game could be:
I went to the market and bought . . .
I went to the beach and I saw . . .

LESSON THREE

Objective
The children will be able to use sequence signals when talking about what they did.

Method
1 Write the following sequence signals on the blackboard: firstly, secondly, thirdly, then, next, also, finally.
2 Next write the following topics on the blackboard:
On my way home from school . . .
During the holidays . . .
Last year . . .
3 Give an example of how to use the sequence signals with one of the topics, e.g:
Last year I had a very busy time. Firstly, I had to help my father build a new house after school. Then I had to sell vegetables at the market every Saturday. I also had to visit my sister in hospital every Sunday until she came home again.
4 Now divide the class into four groups. Choose a child from each group to start making up a story. The other children in the group must add to the story, using the sequence signals on the blackboard, e.g:
First child: Yesterday I did the washing. Firstly I collected up all the dirty clothes. Second child: Then I went down to the river, etc.

WRITTEN SENTENCES

Note
Remember, you will teach only FIVE of the six Written Sentences lessons in the *Using English* books. Choose one lesson each week for homework, or for fast workers.

LESSON ONE

Objective
The children will be able to replace a group of words with one word which means the same.

Preparation
Give out *Pupil's Book 1* to each child (page 112, Lesson 1).

Method
1 Read the words in heavy print. Ask: can you think of one word that means this?
Work out several examples with the children before you ask them to write down their answers.

Answers

1 notice	4 plantation	7 deserve	10 soup
2 parcel	5 instruments	8 screw-driver	
3 passenger	6 sour	9 geckos	

LESSON TWO

Objective
The children will be able to use words in sentences to show their meanings.

Preparation
Give out *Pupil's Book 1* to each child (page 112, Lesson 2).

Method
Read the example and give several more. Discuss the meaning of the words. If children find this lesson difficult, then do it orally with the class.

Note
These words have all been covered in earlier Pacific Series Work.

Possible Answers
1 Your punishment for being late will be to stay after school and sweep the room.
2 We can use these hermit crabs as bait on our fishing lines.
3 The audience clapped for ten minutes after the play was over.
4 The men unloaded the cargo from the plane.
5 The children jumped in the puddles, splashing muddy water all over their clothes.
6 The dishonest shopkeeper gave the child the wrong change.
7 The new bed was very soft to lie on.
8 The box contained fruit and vegetables.
9 The trousers were too loose for James so they kept falling down.
10 If you lose that money you will not be able to go home by PMV.

LESSON THREE (Lesson Suggestion 21)

Objective
The children will practise writing telegrams including only the main points.

Preparation
Give out *Pupil's Book 1* to each child (page 113, Lesson 3).

Possible Answers
1 Mother sick. Meet her today's plane Lae airport. Take her to hospital. Kele.
2 Pots arriving your village on 21st by Tom's truck. Mea.
3 Arriving Mini Sunday. Staying 1 week. Meet me at airstrip. Bili.
4 Send exhaust pipe Mitsubishi Colt 1000. Charge my account Colting Motors. Urgent. Kila.

LESSON FOUR (Lesson Suggestion 5)

Objective
The children will practise using 'self' pronouns in sentences.

Preparation
Give out *Pupil's Book 1* to each child (page 113, Lesson 4).

Answers

1 myself	4 themselves	7 itself
2 yourself	5 herself	8 yourself
3 himself	6 ourselves	

LESSON FIVE (Lesson Suggestion 5)

Objective
The children will be able to use the word 'for' before a 'self' pronoun.

Preparation
Give out *Pupil's Book 1* to each child (page 113, Lesson 5).

Answers

1 themselves	3 ourselves	5 myself
2 himself	4 herself	

LESSON SIX

Objective
The children will be able to use prepositions.

Preparation
Give out *Pupil's Book 1* to each child (page 114, Lesson 6).

Method
Give some examples of the use of prepositions, using things in the classroom, e.g: The cupboard is *near* the door.

Answers
(any of the following are correct)

1 beneath/beside/in/near/against	4 above/over
2 against	5 around/on/down
3 with/beside/near/among	

WRITTEN COMPOSITION

LESSON ONE

Objective
The children will be able to write a descriptive passage.

Preparation
1 Give out *Pupil's Book 1* to each child (page 114, Lesson 1).
2 If possible, show children a spider and its web, or show them a photograph from a magazine. Discuss this after studying it carefully with the class.

Method

1 Now read the lesson introduction and ask the children the questions.
2 Read the words written in the spider's web and encourage the children to use these when writing their story.

Follow-Up

Choose children to read their descriptions to the rest of the class.

LESSON TWO

Objective

Children will imagine a telephone conversation, and write it down.

Preparation

Give out *Pupil's Book 1* to each child (page 114, Lesson 2).

Method

1 Read the introduction and the beginning of the telephone conversation to the children.
2 Finish the conversation orally, asking the children for ideas. Then ask them to write down the conversation.

Possible Answers

You: I found Mother very upset. She was crying.
Father: What was wrong with her?
You: Your friend Gebo came to our house this afternoon and asked Mother for money.
Father: That good-for-nothing Gebo!
You: That's not all, Dad. He threw things everywhere. The house was in an awful mess when I got home. And he found Mum's food money and took it!
Father: What? Go home to your mother immediately and tell her not to worry. I'm going to get the police!

Extra Work

Children who finish this work quickly could then write telephone conversations between the following people:
a Raka Bunang and the police.
b Raka Bunang and the thief, Gebo.
c The police and Raka Bunang's wife.

SPELLING

LESSON ONE (Lesson Suggestion 22)

Objective

The children will learn to spell this week's words.

Preparation

Give out *Pupil's Book 1* to each child (page 115, Spelling List).

LESSON TWO

Select from Exercises A–E.

Preparation

Give out *Pupil's Book 1* to each child (pages 115–17).

Exercise A (Lesson Suggestion 29)

Answers

1 broke
2 cigarette
3 football
4 poke
5 joke

Exercise B (Lesson Suggestion 27)

Method

Read instructions A to D to the children. Make sure they understand the example.

Answers

1 labour (leader ledge left length) light locust lunch
2 passage (pearl pencil people pest) piano pounce punch
3 sail sharp sly smooth soup squeal (still storm strike)

Exercise C (Lesson Suggestion 23)

Answers

1 play
2 talk
3 short
4 think
5 eat
6 push
7 travel
8 carry

Exercise D (Lesson Suggestion 30)

Answers

forehead disagree approve lead mis

Exercise E (Lesson Suggestion 23)

Possible Answers

tent	twin	near	runs	send	dent	
mend	door	roof	find	dish	hill	lead
time	each	have	east	tall	lean	neat

HANDWRITING (Lesson Suggestion 33)

Preparation

Give out *Pupil's Book 1* to each child (pages 117–18).

READING

INTRODUCTION (Lesson Suggestion 34)

Objective

The children will be able to understand the background to the story, and the meaning of new words. They will read the story silently.

Preparation

Give out *Reader 1* to each child (pages 39–42), *'Coming to The Town'*.

Method

1 Introduce the story. Discuss the problems people face when moving from the village to live in a town. Things to discuss would be housing, food, work, money, traffic. Point out how different the two life-styles are.
2 Follow Lesson Suggestion 34B.

LESSON ONE (Lesson Suggestion 34C)

Objective

Children will be able to answer questions to show that they understand the story.

Preparation

Give out *Pupil's Book 1* (pages 39–42) and *Pupil's Book 1* (pages 118, Lesson 1) to each child.

Answers

1 Tanye thought that life in town should be very exciting, so he and his wife went to live there.
2 They found that Duna did not live there any more because he was in jail.
3 Tanye heard that they were knocking down the warehouse that day as they were going to build a new supermarket there.
4 Tanye saw a large yellow crane swing a heavy metal ball into the wall of the warehouse.
5 Flora packed up their things and left when she saw the workmen coming.
6 Flora and Tanye probably felt very frightened and lonely.
7 He probably felt very unhappy as he thought his wife and child were still inside the building.
8 He felt happy and relieved.
9 He probably thought that she had done the best thing.
10 They probably felt very glad to be back home.

LESSON TWO (Lesson Suggestion 35)

Objective

The children will be able to work out the meaning of new words from context clues.

Preparation

Give out *Pupil's Book 1* to each child (page 119, Lesson 2, Exercise A).

Answers

1 afford means to have enough money to buy something
2 enjoy means to like doing something
3 peered means looked closely at something
4 possessions are things that belong to you
5 collapsed means fallen down
6 deserted means that no one uses it anymore; abandoned

LESSON THREE (Lesson Suggestion 17)

Note

Choose either Exercise B or Exercise C for this lesson.

Objective

Children will be able to write a letter.

Preparation
Give out *Pupil's Book 1* to each child (page 119, Exercise B).

Model Answer

Dear Duna,

I hope you are out of jail and have a job and somewhere to live. Flora and I did go to the town. We went to your address and found that you were in prison. We had no money and nowhere to stay, so we lived in a deserted warehouse. Flora was very unhappy there and missed life in the village.

One day I heard they were pulling down the warehouse. I got there just as the building collapsed. I thought that Flora and the baby were still inside, but they had left the building in time and were safe.

Shortly after that we flew back to the village. We are very happy to be home where it is so peaceful. It is good to be with our relatives and friends once more. Now we realize how well off we are in the village.

We hope that you are well and that you will come back to the village one day.

Your friend,
Tanye

OR EXERCISE C (Lesson Suggestion 35)

Objective
The children will be able to work out the meaning of words by looking at picture clues.

Preparation
Give out *Pupil's Book 1* to each child (page 119, Exercise C).

Answers
1 aggressive means angry and violent
2 preferred means liked one better than the other
3 resembled means looked the same
4 swerve means to change direction very quickly
5 visibility means ability to see clearly

LESSON FOUR

Objective
The children will be able to play Reading Games.

Preparation
Give out *Reading Games for Grade 6* to each child (pages 26–8).

Method
Choose some of the games for the children to play.

LESSON FIVE

Objective
The children will be able to read for enjoyment.

Preparation
Give out *Supplementary Reader 1* to each child.

Method
Let the children choose a story to read quietly to themselves.

OR POETRY (Lesson Suggestion 40)

Preparation
Give out *Pupil's Book 1* to each child (page 121), *'Jungle'*.

Note
Ask the children to tell you what they can remember about walking in the jungle.

Answers
1 The poet notices that even though the leaves cover the jungle floor, the ground is still hard.
2 He hears the whistling and singing of birds in the tree tops.
3 It is dark in the jungle because the trees prevent the sunlight coming through.
4 The 'bed' of the jungle means the ground.

LISTENING 12

LESSON ONE

Objective
The children will listen to instructions and fill in details on a map.

Preparation
Ask the children to open their *Pupil's Book 1* at page 124 and study the map.

Method
Read out the following instructions and ask the children to answer the questions. Read each set of instructions twice, slowly and clearly.
Q: Walk up Market Street to Rata St. Turn right. What is the second building on the left?
A: Steamies.
Q: What is next door to Steamies?
A: The bank.
Q: Cross Market St. to the Post Office and walk past Ching's. Where are you now?
A: At the car park.
Q: Cross the road from the car park. What can you buy in this shop?
A: Dresses.
Q: Walk back towards Market St. What is on the corner of Rata St. and Market St.?
A: The Picture Theatre.

Note
This is good practise for this week's Written Sentences Lesson 6.

LESSON TWO

Objective
The children will listen to a guest speaker.

Preparation
Ask someone in the village to come into class and tell the children a story, describe a trip they have made, or the work that they do.

Method
Encourage the children to listen carefully, concentrate and ask questions when the speaker has finished. When the speaker goes home, ask the children to tell you about what he or she said.

TALKING

LESSON ONE (Lesson Suggestion 1C)

Objective
The children will practise last week's sentence pattern:
Can Manarangi get into that drawer? No, he's too big to get into that drawer.

Method
Use the substitution table that is still on the blackboard from last week. Revise it thoroughly.

LESSON TWO

Objective
The children will practise a sentence pattern they already know:
We need some more pencils. We need another pencil.

Method
1 T: Now we shall do some painting. We need some more brushes. What else do we need?
C: We need some more food.
C: We need some more paints.
T: Carmel, what do you need?
C: I need another piece of paper.
2 T: Now we shall do some gardening. We need some more seeds. What else do we need?
C: We need some more tools.
C: We need some more plants.
T: Jon, what do you need?
C: I need another tool.

LESSON THREE (Lesson Suggestion 1A & B)

Objective
The children will be able to use a new sentence pattern:
Can this boy reach the top of the door? Yes, he's tall enough to reach the top of the door.

Method
T: This boy can lift the table. He's strong enough to lift the table. Is he strong enough to lift the table?
C: Yes, he's strong enough to lift the table.
T: Can Boaru reach the top of the door?
C: No, he isn't tall enough to reach it.

T: Can Arua lift that table?
C: No, she isn't strong enough to lift it.
2 Divide children into groups to practise this pattern.

LESSON FOUR

Objective

The children will practise this sentence pattern:
Can Sere go to the Doctor? No, he isn't sick enough to go to the doctor.

Method

1 Give more examples:
T: Can Pele go to High School?
C: No, he isn't old enough to go to High School.
T: Can Maru buy that car?
C: No, he's not rich enough to buy that car.
T: Can Dura read that book?
C: No, he isn't clever enough to read that book.
T: Can Umpit push that truck?
C: No, he isn't strong enough to push it.
2 Children practise these examples in groups.

LESSON FIVE (Lesson Suggestion 1C)

Objective

The children will practise the new sentence pattern using a substitution table.

Preparation

Write the following substitution table on the blackboard:

Is	HE STRONG	enough to	LIFT	that	TABLE?
	SHE TALL		REACH		BRANCH?
	BILI		FIT IN	that	BOX
	MARA				CUPBOARD?
					BAG
					DESK

Yes,	HE'S	strong enough to	LIFT	it.
	SHE'S			

No,	HE'S	tall not tall enough to small	REACH FIT IN	it.

Can	UMPIT	push that	TRUCK?	No,	HE'S	not strong	PUSH	it.
	KALA		TRACTOR?					
	GUAN	lift					LIFT	
	SERA		LOG?		SHE'S			

Note

Leave this table on the blackboard for Talking Lesson 1 next week.

ORAL EXPRESSION

LESSON ONE

Objective
The children will be able to ask questions to find out information.

Method

1 Stage a Press Conference. Choose several pupils to be the Press (newspaper reporters) who must ask the questions. Then the teacher will pretend to be some well-known local person, e.g: a councillor or village headman. The Press must ask you questions to find out all about you, e.g: Interviewing a well known long distance runner.
Q: When did you first become interested in running?
Do you spend a lot of time training?
Why do you have to train so hard?
Do you have to be careful about your weight? Why?
Have you run overseas?

2 Act out several different Press Conferences, using different pupils each time.

LESSON TWO

Objective
The children will be able to ask questions to find out about something.

Method

1 A child stands in front of the class and says she has found something, without saying what it is. The rest of the class must question her to find out what it is. Then they must question her to find out where and how she found it.

2 When the class has guessed what the thing is, another child has a turn out the front.
Suggest lost items like: a library book, an umbrella, a shell necklace, one kina.

LESSON THREE

Objective
The children will be able to talk about ideas for raising money.

Note
This lesson should be done after reading this week's story from *Reader 1, 'The Pie Stall'*.

Method

1 Discuss with the class ways in which the children could start a small business like in the story. Encourage children to think up their own ideas. Suggestions:

a sew clothes and sell them at a stall
b start up a school handcraft shop to sell things made during expressive arts
c hold a school lunch one day a week to sell food made during cooking class
d sell produce from school gardens at the market

2 Discuss what they could use the money for, e.g: a cassette recorder, a film projector, sporting equipment, books for the library, etc.

WRITTEN SENTENCES

Note
Teach only FIVE of the six lessons.

LESSON ONE (Lesson Suggestion 9)

Objective
The children will be able to shorten sentences by using apostrophes.

Preparation
Give out *Pupil's Book 1* to each child (page 122, Lesson 1).

Answers
1 Mele's sister came first in today's spelling test.
2 Remi's pig ruined my father's garden.
3 The men's hats were blown off by the wind.
4 The canoe's sails were torn by the cyclone's strong winds.
5 Lala's sisters went to the show with Raka's brothers.
6 The egg's yolk is very good food for us.
7 The hen's legs were still moving even though the hen's head had been cut off.
8 Kune's teacher showed the students how to build a piggery.
9 Kolo's dog got his leg caught in Dobi's cuscus trap.
10 The crocodile's teeth are very valuable and make attractive necklaces for women.

LESSON TWO

Objective
The children will be able to choose the correct word to fit in a sentence.

Prepartion
Give out *Pupil's Book 1* to each child (page 122, Lesson 2).

Answers

1 hard	4 longest	7 best	10 happier
2 prettier	5 smaller	8 longer	
3 sweeter	6 biggest/loudest	9 faster	

Method
1 Remind the children of how to use comparative and superlative adjectives (i.e. -er, -est) by giving examples:
I am *tall* (describes *one* person)
You are *taller* than I am (describes *one* of *two* people)
She is the *tallest* in the class (describes *one* of *more than two* people).
2 Ask the children to give other examples. Discuss them with the class before you ask the children to write the answers to questions 1–10.

LESSON THREE

Objective
The children will be able to use the correct joining word to link sentences.

Preparation
Give out *Pupil's Book 1* to each child (page 123, Lesson 3).

Answers

1 after/when	4 although	7 while/when	10 since/because
2 when	5 because/since	8 before	
3 so	6 during	9 so	

LESSON FOUR (Lesson Suggestion 7)

Objective

The children will be able to choose the correct form of the verb to fit in a sentence.

Preparation

Give out *Pupil's Book 1* to each child (page 123, Leson 4).

Answers

1 saw	4 seeing	7 think	10 thought
2 sight	5 sees	8 thoughtless	
3 seen	6 thinks	9 thinking	

LESSON FIVE

Objective

The children will be able to set out a play as if it were a story, using direct speech.

Answers

1 'Can I play corner ball too?' asked Susan.
'No you can't, Susan. Go away!' cried Lettie.
'Why can't I?' Susan asked.
'Because you can't even throw the ball properly!' Lettie sneered.
'Let her play with us, Lettie', said Hannah. 'Come on Susan, I'll teach you how to play.'
'Hey, that's my new pocket knife you've got!' cried Pele.
'It is not', said Kali. 'It's mine!'
'Where did you get it?' demanded Pele.
'My father bought it for me at the tradestore yesterday', Kali replied.
'You're a liar, Kali', said Pele angrily. 'You stole that knife from my desk when I was out of the room!'

Note

Encourage children to use other words as well as 'said', e.g: cried, replied, sneered, demanded, asked.

LESSON SIX

Objective

The children will practise reading a map and using prepositions correctly.

Preparation

Give out *Pupil's Book 1* to each child (page 124, Lesson 6).

Answers

1 opposite	4 near/by	7 by/near	10 at
2 between	5 in front of	8 on/opposite	
3 next to	6 beside/behind	9 between	

WRITTEN COMPOSITION

LESSON ONE (Lesson Suggestion 18)

Objective
The children will be able to address envelopes.

Answers

1 The Chairman,
Tusbab Board of Management,
P.O. Box 453,
Madang,
MADANG PROVINCE.

2 The Director,
Management Services Division,
National Broadcasting
Commission,
P.O. Box 1359,
Boroko,
NATIONAL CAPITAL PROVINCE.

3 The Secretary,
Young Women's Christian
Association,
P.O. Box 1338,
Boroko,
NATIONAL CAPITAL PROVINCE.

4 The Manager,
Burns Shipping,
P.O. Box 862,
Lae,
MOROBE PROVINCE.

LESSON TWO

Objective
The children will be able to hold an interview.

Preparation
Give out *Pupil's Book 1* to each child (page 126, Lesson 2).

Method
1 Read the introduction and discuss possible answers to these questions.
2 Stage a 'pretend' interview. Teacher be the interviewer. Choose a child to be the person interviewed. Ask the student the questions listed.
3 Now children write down their version of the interview ending.

Possible Answers

Interviewer: Which countries did you visit?
Student: I visited America, Canada, England, Malaysia, Australia and New Zealand.
Interviewer: Which of these countries did you like best?
Student: Well, that's a difficult question to answer. I enjoyed them all. Each country was so different from Papua New Guinea.
Interviewer: How long were you away for, Galang?
Student: The trip took nearly four months.
Interviewer: Did anyone go with you?
Student: Yes, my uncle, who is a teacher, came with me.
Interviewer: Did you do or see anything particularly interesting on your trip that you'd like to tell the listeners about?
Student: I did many interesting things but probably the one I found most exciting was skiing on snow in New Zealand. I never saw snow until then.

Continue the interview in this way until all the questions have been answered.

Follow-Up
Read out the best interview with the pupil who wrote it. This could be done during a Talking or an Oral Expression lesson.

SPELLING

LESSON ONE (Lesson Suggestion 22)

Objective
The children will be able to spell this week's words.

Preparation
Give out *Pupil's Book 1* to each child (page 126, Spelling List).

LESSON TWO (Lesson Suggestion 25)

Select from Exercises A–E, or give a spelling test and dictation.

Preparation
Give out *Pupil's Book 1* to each child (pages 126–7).

Exercise A (Lesson Suggestion 29)

Answers

1 diagram
2 diameter
3 hymns
4 relief
5 believe

Exercise B (Lesson Suggestion 30)

1 hope kind comfort employ mouth
2 thoughtless fearless careless
3 gentleness happiness laziness loneliness
4 miserable capable preferable reliable
5 beautiful successful doubtful painful peaceful

Exercise C (Lesson Suggestion 30)

harmless plant development al rough

Exercise D (Lesson Suggestion 27)

Answers

1 bargain (beach beast best) bounce business
2 (camera catch caution) challenge credit
3 (sandals satellite sausage save) scatter stall
4 parcel pollution (pretend promise protest)

Exercise E (Lesson Suggestion 27)

Method

1 Study the list given.
2 Starting from the front of the room, ask the children to call out their names while you write them on the blackboard. Ask children to say their surname (father's name), followed by their first name.
3 When the list is complete, ask pupils to write down these names in alphabetical order, as shown in the example given.

HANDWRITING (Lesson Suggestion 33)

Preparation
Give out *Pupil's Book 1* to each child (page 128).

READING

INTRODUCTION (Lesson Suggestion 34)

Objective
The children will understand the background to the story, and the meaning of new words. They will read the story silently.

Preparation
Give out *Reader 1* (pages 43–5), '*The Pie Stall*'.

Method
1 Introduce the story. Discuss 'What is a business'. Introduce the following words into the discussion: stall, bargain, on credit, running a business, real businessman. Talk about the kind of business students would like to start when they leave school, e.g: Tradestores, making furniture, selling artifacts, growing vegetables, etc.
2 Follow Lesson Suggestion 34B.

LESSON ONE (Lesson Suggestion 34)

Objective
The children will be able to answer questions to show that they understand the story.

Preparation
Give out *Reader 1* (pages 43–5) and *Pupil's Book 1* (page 128, Lesson 1) to each child.

Answers
1 They saw children running out of the school gate at lunch time to buy their lunches at the nearest shop.
2 They needed pies, a sign and a table.
3 The truck had a flat tyre.
4 Sevese told the manager that he had agreed to deliver the pies every day at a quarter to twelve and he had not kept his side of the bargain. He then added that they could easily get their pies from another bakery.
5 The boys made two toea profit on each pie.
6 They collected K6.00 on the first day. They made K1.20 profit.
7 The boys took the cold pies back to the Bakery some time after half past one.
8 on credit – means that you take something without paying for it but you must pay for it later
9 bargain – this means a deal; two people agree on certain terms
10 leaned – means propped up or rested against something

LESSON TWO

Objective
The children will be able to answer questions about a story.

Preparation
Give out *Pupil's Book 1* to each child (page 129, Lesson 2).

Exercise A

Method
Read the stories aloud and discuss them with the children. You may have to explain what the clutch and the gears are for in a car.

Answers
1 Rea's sister had two hats. Tia had the most hats.
2 He planted three fruit trees.
3 He put the gears into first position.
He sat down in the driver's seat.
To start the engine.
4 It was its natural colour.
Pia and Maria.
He painted his rock green.
She was busy mixing the paints.

Exercise B

Method
1 Read the sentences in the order they are written in the *Pupil's Book*.
2 Ask the children: What must have been the first thing Maria did? When did she forget about the fire? What happened next? and so on.
3 Then ask the children to write down the sentences in the correct order.

Answers
Maria lit a cooking fire close to her house, then went to see her neighbour. She soon forgot about the cooking fire, as she and her neighbour talked together. Suddenly they heard someone shout 'Fire! Fire!' Maria jumped up and ran outside. The roof of the house had caught fire. Everyone ran to get buckets of water to put out the fire.

LESSON THREE (Lesson Suggestion 3)

Objective
The children will be able to find the wrong word and replace it with the correct one.

Preparation
Give out *Pupil's Book 1* to each child (page 130, Exercise C).

Answers
1 hungry is wrong. It should be full/happy/content.
2 calm is wrong. It should be rough.
3 tear is wrong. It should be read.
4 danced is wrong. It should be slept/rested.
5 fish is wrong. It should be vegetables.

LESSON FOUR

Objective
The children will be able to play reading games.

Preparation
Give out *Reading Games for Grade 6* to each child (pages 28–30, Unit 12).

Method
1 Choose games for the children to play.
2 Discuss answers with the class.

LESSON FIVE (Lesson Suggestion 39)

Objective
The children will read for enjoyment.

Preparation
Select varied reading materials for the children to read.

OR POETRY (Lesson Suggestion 40)

Preparation
Give out *Pupil's Book 1* to each child (page 130), '*Blindness*'.

Method
1 Talk about what it would be like to be blind.
2 Follow Suggestion 40.

Answers
1 'Like a prisoner guarded by darkness' – if you were blind, then darkness would be like a prison to you because you would never be able to escape from it.
2 He would be able to hear the dog panting, growling, whining or barking.
He would be able to smell that it was a dog.
He would be able to feel the fur and know how big it was.
He might feel its rough tongue licking his arm.

Note
'environment' means place or surroundings.

LISTENING 13

LESSON ONE

Objective
The children will be able to listen carefully and pick out the word in each list which does not begin with the same sound as the others.

Method
1 Read the first list and stress the word in brackets. Explain that this word does not fit in the list because it sounds different from the others: harm, hard, harbour, (heavy).
2 Read each list slowly, twice. Ask the children to say the word which does not sound the same as the others (that is the one in brackets.)
accident accept (announce) account

decide deceive declare delay (damage)
wrong write (trap) wrap
explain explore (accept) exercise
until (into) untidy under
knife knock (mice) knot
describe despair destroy (repair)

Note
These words are taken from spelling lessons covered this term. This is a good opportunity for revision. Remind the children that: knife, knock, knot are *written* 'kn' but you *say* 'n'. Wrong, write, wrap, are *written* 'wr' but you *say* 'r'.

LESSON TWO

Objective
The children will be able to concentrate, listen to a story and notice the order in which things happen.

Method
1 Turn to *Pupil's Book 1* (page 108). Read the Handwriting passage slowly and clearly to the children. Read it again.
2 Ask the children: What happens first? What happens next? Then what happens? and so on.
A: Amos shouts to Esi. A big dog stands between them and the way home. Amos holds Esi's arm and tells her to keep still. The dog growls. They hear a high-pitched whistle. The dog runs off into the forest.

TALKING

LESSON ONE (Lesson Suggestion 1C)

Objective
The children will practise last week's sentence pattern:
Can this boy reach the top of the door? Yes, he's tall enough to reach it.

Method
1 Use the substitution table that is still on the blackboard. Revise it thoroughly.

LESSON TWO

Objective
The children will practise a sentence pattern they already know:
This shirt needs washing. This one doesn't need washing.

Method
1 Show the children two towels (or shirts, trousers, etc.)
T: This towel needs washing. This one doesn't need washing. What's wrong with this towel?
C: It's dirty. It needs washing.
T: What about this one?
C: It's clean. It doesn't need washing.
2 Give children other examples to practise:
His hair needs combing. Hers doesn't need combing.

His face needs washing. His doesn't need washing.
Her hands need washing. His don't need washing.

3 Children practise these examples in groups.

LESSON THREE (Lesson Suggestion 1B)

Objective

The children will be able to use a new sentence pattern:
Can you lift the table? No, it's too heavy for me to lift.

Method

1 Point to a heavy object and say: This cupboard is very heavy. Try to lift it.
T: I can't lift it. It's too heavy for me to lift. Can you lift the cupboard?
C: No, it's too heavy for me to lift.
T: Can Sere lift the table?
C: No, it's too heavy for her to lift.
T: This ceiling is very high. Can Mary touch it?
C: No, it's too high for her to touch.
T: Can the girls touch the ceiling?
C: No, it's too high for them to touch.

2 Children practise this work in groups.

LESSON FOUR

Objective

The children will practise this sentence pattern:
Can you lift the table? No, it's too heavy for me to lift.

Method

1 Provide more examples for the children to practise saying in their groups, e.g:
T: Can you do this sum?
C: No, it's too difficult to me to do.
T: Can you make this coat?
C: No, it's too hard for me to make.
T: Can you read this book?
C: No, it's too hard for me to read.
T: Can you drive this tractor?
C: No, it's too hard for me to drive.
T: Can you fix this desk?
C: No, it's too hard for me to fix.

LESSON FIVE (Lesson Suggestion 1C)

Objective

The children will practise the new sentence pattern using a substitution table.

Preparation

Write a following substitution table on the blackboard:

Can	YOU	lift this	BOX?	No, it's too heavy for	ME	to lift.
	SHE		TABLE?		HER	
	HE		CUPBOARD?		HIM	
	THEY		TRUCK?		THEM	

Can	YOU	make a	CANOE?	No, it's too hard for	ME	to make.
	HE		DRUM?		HIM	
	SHE		SHIRT?		HER	
	THEY		FEAST?		THEM	
Can	YOU	fix this	DESK?		ME	to fix.
	HE		PEN?		HIM	
	SHE		BELT?		HER	
	THEY		ENGINE?		THEM	

Note
Remember to leave this work on the blackboard for next week.

ORAL EXPRESSION

LESSON ONE

Objective
The children will be able to give instructions about how to do something.

Method
1 Divide the class into groups. Give each group a piece of paper with the name of a job that is familiar to them.
2 The group must work out the best way to do the job. Discuss it with group members and then choose one child from each group to tell the rest of the class how to do it.
Names of jobs could be: sago making, cooking rice, making traditional dyes, making traditional gardening tools, preparing a garden for yams, building a canoe, catching coconut crabs or hermit crabs.

Note
Encourage the children to use sequence signals for this lessons, e.g: first, next, then, after that, finally.

LESSON TWO

Objective
The children will be able to solve problems and organize a school project.

Method
Discuss which of the suggestions made last week in Oral Expression Lesson Three would be the best to raise money for your school. Then discuss how to go about starting such a project, e.g:
First ask the Head teacher and School Committee.
Decide what the money would be used for.
Organize people to make or grow the goods to be sold.
Choose people to be in charge of advertising by using notices, local radio, etc.
Form a committee to be in charge of the project once it gets going.
Decide on a date for the project to begin.

Note
Even if it is not possible for your school to really carry out such a project, you could still discuss how to organize it.

LESSON THREE

Objective
The children will be able to tell a story about sequence pictures.

Preparation
Give out *Pupil's Book 1* to each child (page 132, Lesson 4).

Method
1 Study the sequence pictures on this page without worrying about the words underneath the pictures.
2 Ask the children to talk about what is happening in each picture. You may have to ask lots of questions to get them started, e.g: Why did the truck go off the road? Why did they jump out of the truck? How bad was the damage? Was anyone hurt? etc.
3 Now choose different pupils to be the truck driver, the passenger and the cyclist. Ask each of these people to give the rest of the class their idea of what happened.

WRITTEN SENTENCES

Note
Teach only FIVE of the six lessons.

LESSON ONE (Lesson Suggestion 12)

Objective
The children will be able to change sentences from present to past tense.

Preparation
Give out *Pupil's Book 1* to each child (page 131, Lesson 1).

Answers
1 I *took* the children with me to the market.
2 I hope you *had* a good time at the party.
3 The ground *was* muddy because it *was raining*.
4 The sun *was shining* and the ground *was drying* out. OR The sun *shone* and the ground *dried* out.
5 *That was* one of the worst storms I can remember.
6 There *was* an Agricultural show on *yesterday* and many people from the village *went* to it.
7 I *flew* in the plane to Wewak.
8 I *made* a bilum for my sister.
9 I *polished* this carving to make it shiny.
10 They *were* down at the beach swimming.

LESSON TWO (Lesson Suggestion 9)

Objective
The children will be able to tell whether the sentences are singular or plural by looking at the position of apostrophes.

Preparation
Give out *Pupil's Book 1* to each child (page 131, Lesson 2).

Answers

1 Many wonen (it would have been woman's it it were only one.)
2 One bird
3 Many pigs
4 One country
5 One man
6 Many boys
7 One girl
8 One plane
9 Many teachers
10 One library

LESSON THREE (Lesson Suggestion 13)

Objective

The children will practise using the correct punctuation.

Preparation

Give out *Pupil's Book 1* to each child (page 131, Lesson 3).

Answers

1 'Help! Help!' cried the drowning child.
2 'Where is my new shirt?' asked Tonu.
3 'I'll come with you to Mendi', said the hitch-hiker.
4 'We've forgotten to bring Wara's torch with us!'
5 Kepa's dog followed Lia to Yip's store.
6 'I haven't taken your pen!' shouted Henao.
7 'Stop!' shouted the policeman.
8 'Where are you taking that pig?' asked Father.
9 'Why don't you carry that pot on your head?' suggested Mother.
10 'Don't do that!' shouted the old woman angrily.

LESSON FOUR (Lesson Suggestion 2)

Objective

The children will be able to write suitable sentences to match sequence pictures.

Preparation

Give out *Pupil's Book 1* to each child (page 132, Lesson 4).

Possible Answers

1 'Watch out! You nearly ran me off the road! Crazy driver!'
2 'We're too close to the edge of the road! Watch out Lemi!'
3 'Jump out quick! We're gong over!'
4 'Are you two all right? You were lucky you weren't killed.'
5 'The truck is in an awful mess. Do you think it can be repaired?'
6 'The truck has to be towed to a garage in town to be fixed.'

LESSON FIVE

Objective

The children will be able to write good questions.

Preparation

Give out *Pupil's Book 1* to each child (page 133, Lesson 5).

Possible Answers

1 Where have you put my grass knife?
2 Who has seen my pencil?
3 Why have you cut your hair so short?

4 What did you do with that shell?
5 Where is the teacher?
6 Who did that drawing on the blackboard?
7 Why did you throw that book at me?
8 Where did you go this morning?
9 How did you work out that problem?
10 How is she getting to the hospital?

Note
You could help the children by telling them to make all their questions about one topic, e.g: Relatives (using words from this week's Family Group).

LESSON SIX

Objective
The children will be able to use adjectives to describe feelings.

Preparation
Give out *Pupil's Book 1* to each child (page 133, Lesson 6).

Method
1 Discuss the boy's expressions. Ask the children to suggest words to describe his feelings. Write a list on the blackboard.

Answers
1 The boy feels pleased/happy/excited.
2 The boy feels content/pleased with himself.
3 The boy feels angry/cross/furious.
4 The boy feels surprised/amazed/frightened.
5 The boy feels tired/sleepy/weary/bored.
6 The boy feels unhappy/sad/sick/miserable.

WRITTEN COMPOSITION

LESSON ONE (Lesson Suggestion 2)

Objective
The children will be able to write a story about a set of sequence pictures.

Preparation
Give out *Pupil's Book 1* to each child (page 134, Lesson 1).

Model Answers
Nipa planted the mango in the ground behind his house. The next morning, he was surprised to see a huge mango tree growing exactly where he had planted the fruit. Everyone came to eat the ripe fruit from the tree. Now the people were content, and because of the magic mango tree they were never hungry again.

LESSON TWO (Lesson Suggestion 2)

Objective
The children will be able to write a story about sequence pictures.

Preparation
Give out *Pupil's Book 1* to each child (page 135, Lesson 2).

Model Answer

The children went to the airport to see off their friend Rea who was flying back to Rabaul.
Suddenly they noticed a plane about to land on the runway. It was on fire. The plane landed safely. The children could see the flames and smoke coming out of the plane.
A few minutes later, two fire engines raced out onto the runway with their sirens screaming.
The fire engines turned hoses onto the fire. They also helped the passengers leave the plane by sliding down an escape chute. The passengers were very frightened by this accident. Their friends at the terminal comforted them.

SPELLING

LESSON ONE (Lesson Suggestion 22)

Objective

Children will learn to spell this week's words.

Preparation

Give out *Pupil's Book 1* to each child (page 137, Spelling List).

LESSON TWO

Select from Exercises A–E.

Preparation

Give out *Pupil's Book 1* to each child (pages 137–8).

Exercise A (Lesson Suggestion 29)

Answers

1 electrician electric
2 electricity
3 grandfather
4 cousins
5 niece

Exercise B

Answers

overflow – The rainstorm lasted long enough to make the watertank overflow.
overload – You must not overload that small plane.
overlook – I will overlook your bad manners this time.
overtake – You must not overtake a car unless you can see ahead.
overturn – The truck crashed through the fence and then overturned.

Exercise C (Lesson Suggestion 27)

Answers

1 charge cheat check cheese children chopping church
2 wheat wheel when whether which while why
3 stack star stay stew stick story stuff

Exercise D (Lesson Suggestion 30)

Answers

disapprove — I disapprove of you going to the party alone.
disagree — I disagree with you about that.
disappear — Don't tell him there's work to be done or he will disappear.
dishonest — Don't let your dishonest cousin see that money.

Exercise E (Lesson Suggestion 31)

Answers

Clues Across
1 Butterfly
6 Bandits
7 Fortune
11 Giggle
12 Territory

Clues Down
1 Breadfruit
2 Timber
3 Earn
4 Famine
5 Yams
8 Tiger
9 Night
10 Every

HANDWRITING (Lesson Suggestion 33)

Preparation
Give out *Pupil's Book 1* to each child (page 139).

READING

INTRODUCTION (Lesson Suggestion 34)

Objective
The children will understand the background to the story, and the meaning of new words. They will read the story silently.

Preparation
Give out *Reader 1* to each child (pages 46–8), *'The Black Cloud and the Old Woman'*.

Method
1 Introduce the story. Talk about having good manners and thinking of other people, not just ourselves. Talk about greed, how some people are always wanting more.
2 Follow Lesson Suggestion 34B.

LESSON ONE (Lesson Suggestion 34C)

Objective
Children will be able to answer questions about the story to show that they understand it.

Preparation
Give out *Reader 1* (pages 46–8) and *Pupil's Book 1* to each child (page 140, Lesson 1).

Answers

1 good natured/young
2 firewood
3 crack
4 beautiful girl
5 thank
6 carrying a heavy load
7 thoughtless

Possible Answers

8 The old woman gave Tapas the coconut because she wanted to give him a gift, for being kind to her.
9 Iakob wanted a coconut so that it would change into a beautiful girl.
10 Iakob hit the crocodile with his paddle and it fell out of his canoe and swam away.

LESSON TWO (Lesson Suggestion 35)

Objective

The children will be able to work out the meanings of new words by using picture clues.

Preparation

Give out *Pupil's Book 1* to each child (page 141, Lesson 2, Exercises A & B).

Exercise A

Answers

idly means lazily
diagram means a drawing or a plan of something
horrified means very shocked and frightened
elaborate means complicated or highly decorated

Exercise B

Objective

The children will be able to understand the main points in a passage.

Answers

1 b the stall was too crowded.
2 c they were afraid of sharks.

LESSON THREE

Objective

The children will be able to answer questions about a story to show that they understand it.

Preparation

Give out *Pupil's Book 1* to each child (page 142, Exercise C).

Answers

1 Food must be kept cool or it will go bad very quickly.
2 Food must be covered so that insects and rats cannot get to it.
3 The smell attracts flies to meat and fish.
4 Maggots hatch from flies' eggs.
5 Salt should not be stored in times becaust it will make the tin rust.
6 Salt could be kept in a plastic big or container or in a bottle with a lid on it.
7 Put it in another covered container and use it as soon as possible.

8 Meat and fish should be kept in plastic bags if they are sold at the market. This will keep away the flies and people will be able to see what it is without having to touch it. If you cannot get plastic then it should be wrapped up well in newspaper or kept in a covered container.

LESSON FOUR

Objective
The children will be able to play reading games.

Preparation
Give out *Reading Games for Grade 6* to each child (pages 30–2, Unit 13).

Method
1 Choose games for the children to play.
2 Mark the work done with the children using the *Reading Games Teacher's Notes*.

LESSON FIVE (Lesson Suggestion 39)

Objective
Children will read for enjoyment.

Preparation
Give out *Supplementary Reader 1* to each child.

Method
Let the children choose a story to read.

OR POETRY (Lesson Suggestion 40)

Preparation
Give out *Pupil's Book 1* to each child (page 143), *'My Country'*.

Possible Answers
The noise of a plane flying overhead; the buzzing of bees around flowers; the noise of the wind blowing in the trees; birds singing; crickets chirping; frogs croaking.

LISTENING 14

LESSON ONE

Objective
The children will listen carefully to a story and remember the main idea and the most important details.

Method
1 Read this story out loud, slowly and clearly:
People have lived in Papua New Guinea for at least ten thousand years. The earliest people here lived by hunting animals, gathering fruits, roots and leaves for food. They hunted tree kangaroos, wallabies, possums, bandicoots and rats, as well as reptiles, birds and fish. They used simple tools made of wood and stone.

2 Ask the children to tell you the main idea of the story.
Answer: The story is about the earliest people who lived in PNG.
3 Read the story again. Tell the children to listen carefully and remember as many details as they can.
4 Ask questions about the details in the story:
Q: Does the story tell you exactly how long people have been living in PNG?
A: No, it doesn't.
Q: How long does it say they have been here?
A: It says they have been here for at least ten thousand years.
Q: How did the earliest people live?
Q: What animals did they hunt?
Q: What were their tools made of? etc.

LESSON TWO

Objective
The children will listen carefully to a description of a person and work out who it is.

Method
1 Describe one of the children in the class, or one of the teachers. It must be someone everyone knows, e.g:
This person is tall and slim. She lives on the other side of the village. She has just had a baby. Sometimes she brings her baby to school. She wears gold ear-rings.
The children must guess who this person is.
2 In groups, each child must describe someone and the others must guess who it is. If the others cannot guess who it is, the describer must give more clues about that person.

TALKING

LESSON ONE (Lesson Suggestion 1C)

Objective
The children will practise last week's sentence pattern:
Can you lift the table? No, it's too heavy for me to lift.

Method
Use the substitution table that is still on the blackboard. Revise it thoroughly.

LESSON TWO

Objective
The children will practise a sentence pattern they already know:
Where's your mother gone? She's gone to the garden.

Method
1 Point to a child and say: Go outside and pick a leaf.
2 Then point to another child and say: Where's Pora gone?
A: He's gone outside to pick a leaf.
3 Point to another child and ask: Where's your father gone?
A: He's gone fishing/hunting.

Q: Where's your sister gone?
A: She's gone to school.
Q: Where's your uncle gone?
A: He's gone to work.

4 Children practise this sentence pattern in groups.

LESSON THREE

Objective
The children will be able to use a new sentence pattern:
Can Tunde wear this shirt? Yes, it's big enough for him to wear.

Method
1 Hold up a small shirt.
T: Tunde can't wear this shirt. It's too small for him to wear.
T: Can Tunde wear this shirt?
C: No, it's too small for him to wear.

2 Hold up a bigger shirt.
T: Devi can wear this shirt. It's big enough for him to wear.
T: Can Devi wear this shirt?
C: Yes, it's big enough for him to wear.
T: Can you do this sum in your head: 564 × 321?
C: No, it's too hard for us to do in our head.
T: Can you do this one: 3 × 5?
C: Yes, it's easy enough for us to do.
T: Can we eat these bananas?
C: Yes, they're ripe enough for us to eat.

3 Children practise this sentence pattern in groups.

LESSON FOUR

Objective
The children will practise this sentence pattern:
Can Tunde wear this shirt? No, it's too small for him to wear.

Method
1 Provide more examples for the children to practise in their groups, e.g:
Can you read this writing?
Yes, it's big enough for us to read.
Can you wear these shoes?
Yes, they're big enough for me to wear.

2 Use this pattern to revise other tenses, e.g:
T: Did you go swimming yesterday?
C: No, it wasn't hot enough for us to go swimming.
T: Will you eat those mangoes tomorrow?
C: No, they won't be ripe enough for us to eat.

LESSON FIVE (Lesson Suggestion 1C)

Objective
The children will practise the new sentence pattern using a substitution table.

Preparation
Write the following substitution table on the blackboard:

Can	YOU	wear this	SHIRT?	No, it's too	BIG	for	ME	to wear.
	SHE		DRESS		SMALL		HER	
	HE		COAT				HIM	

Can	I	eat this	PAWPAW?	No, it's not ripe enough to eat.
	YOU		PINEAPPLE	
	SHE		MANGO	
	HE		BANANA	

Did	YOU	go	SWIMMING	YESTERDAY?	No, it wasn't hot enough.
	HE		FISHING	LAST WEEK?	
	SHE		SHOPPING		
	THEY			on Monday?	

Note
Remember to leave this work on the blackboard for next week's revision.

ORAL EXPRESSION

LESSON ONE

Objective
The children will be able to carry on a class discussion about a show, e.g: Highland Show, Port Moresby Show.

Preparation
If possible, collect pictures about a show and display these for the class to see.

Method
1 Introduce the lesson by referring to the pictures (if possible) or by talking about a Show.
2 Encourage children in the class who have been to a show to talk about it. Ask questions like: What type of show was it? Were there many people there? What type of things were on display? Were there any tourists there? What things could you buy there?
3 If no one in your class has ever been to a Show then change the topic to suit your class, e.g: a singsing, a Moka exchange ceremony, etc.

LESSON TWO

Objective
The children will be able to remember a list of things and events.

Method
1 Divide the class into four teams. The leader of the first team begins a sequence story, e.g: I went to the show and I saw some baby crocodiles . . .
The next child says: I went to the show and saw some baby crocodiles and a cassowary . . .
The next child says: I went to the show and saw some baby crocodiles, a cassowary and . . .
Continue in this way right through the team, each child repeating the things already mentioned and adding something else.
2 Other teams listen for mistakes.
3 The next team then has a turn, and so on.

LESSON THREE

Objective
The children will be able to tell about their experiences.

Method
1 If you have read this week's story, '*Eruption*', the class will have heard Uncle Damien's exciting story of how Matupit erupted. Ask the class if they remember any similar exciting experiences, e.g: while out hunting, fishing, tribal fighting, etc.
2 Ask the child to come to the front of the class. After he has told his story ask the rest of the class to ask him questions.

WRITTEN SENTENCES

LESSON ONE (Lesson Suggestion 2)

Objective
The children will be able to write good sentences about a picture.

Preparation
Give out *Pupil's Book 2* to each child (page 4, Lesson 1).

Possible Answers
(Children to write 10 sentences like these)
1 The mudmen from Asaro danced around wearing their frightening masks.
2 A young man flew over the arena on a hang glider which made everyone stare.
3 The young children enjoyed riding on the ponies.

LESSON TWO

Objective
The children will be able to choose the correct word to fit in the context.

Preparation
Give out *Pupil's Book 2* to to each child (page 5, Lesson 2).

Answers

1 some, from	4 were, made, came	7 took, worn	10 were, see
2 could, from	5 bought, with	8 decorated, opened	
3 made, called	6 wore, made	9 ate, between	

LESSON THREE (Lesson Suggestion 2)

Objective
The children will be able to write good answers to questions about a picture.

Preparation
Give out *Pupil's Book 2* to each child (page 5, Lesson 3).

Possible Answers
1 There were hundreds of people at the show.
2 A tourist is a person on holiday from another country.
3 You would find animals, farm machinery and crops in the agricultural exhibition.

4 You could buy hot dogs and ice creams at the show.
5 There were baskets, pots, tapa cloth, masks, ceremonial axes, necklaces and kina shells on sale.
6 The Police were on duty at the show, in case there was any trouble.
7 I liked seeing so many different things and so many different people at the show.
8 I saw a man flying through the sky on a big kite called a hang glider. I have never seen one of these before.
9 A huge crocodile frightened me when it snapped its great jaws.
10 A hot dog is a sausage placed between two pieces of bread.

LESSON FOUR (Lesson Suggestion 3)

Objective
The children will be able to find the sentence which is out of context.

Preparation
Give out *Pupil's Book 2* to each child (page 6, Lesson 4).

Answers
A The horse galloped across the field. (not about ships and cargo)
B It was a very interesting book. (not about the marriage feast)

LESSON FIVE

Objective
The children will be able to write questions for the answers given.

Preparation
Give out *Pupil's Book 2* to each child (page 6, Lesson 5).

Method
1 Read the example given.
2 Now read through the other answers and encourage the children to give questions for each.

Answers
1 Who did she spill food on?
2 Who did the baby tip water all over?
3 Who did they spill paint on?
4 Who did he build the house for?
5 Who did they build the new canoe for?
6 Who did she buy the bilum for?
7 Who did he write a story about?
8 Who did he tell you something about?
9 Who was Ared laughing at?
10 Who was she very cross with?

WRITTEN COMPOSITION

LESSON ONE (Lesson Suggestion 14B)

Objective
The children will be able to write a story from a plan.

Preparation
Give out *Pupil's Book 2* to each child (page 6, Lesson 1).

Method
1 Read through the lesson with the class.
2 Divide the class into four groups. Ask each group to work out one paragraph of the story.
3 Ask one child from each group to read out their paragraph.

LESSON TWO

Objective
The children will be able to write a paragraph about something they did during the last holidays, or last Sunday.

Preparation
Give out *Pupil's Book 2* to each child (page 7, Lesson 2).

Method
1 Talk about the topic with the children. Perhaps tell them what you did.
2 Tell the children to write five sentences about it.
3 When they have finished writing, tell the children to underline all the nouns in their story (that is, all the words for people, places or things).

SPELLING

LESSON ONE (Lesson Suggestion 22)

Objective
The children will learn to spell this week's words.

Preparation
Give out *Pupil's Book 2* to each child (page 7, Spelling List).

LESSON TWO

Select from Exercises A–E.

Preparation
Give out *Pupil's Book 2* to each child (pages 7–9).

Exercise A (Lesson Suggestion 29)

Answers
1 quickly
2 suddenly
3 mail
4 against
5 anxiously

Exercise B

Answers
a pair of jeans
a pair of glasses
a pair of pants
a pair of socks
a pair of gloves
a pair of scissors
a pair of boots
a pair of feet
a pair of hands
a pair of eyes

Exercise C

Answers

1 reply
2 return
3 refill
4 repeat
5 refuse
6 release
7 remove
8 repay
9 repair
10 relay

Exercise D

Method

1 Remind the children of the following rules for changing certain words from singular to plural:
'y' changes to 'ie' when you add an 's'
e.g: army armies, bully bullies, party parties
'f' changes to 'v' when you add 'es'
e.g: calf calves, half halves
'x' must have 'es' added to it
e.g: fox foxes
(There are exceptions to these rules.)
2 Explain that the children have to look at plural words in this exercise and work out the singular.
3 If they find it difficult, make up sentences to help them, e.g:
I have two babies but Maria has only one . . . (what?)
Three men are walking, one . . . (what?) is running.

Answers

baby newspaper man leaf box

Exercise E (Lesson Suggestion 32)

Answers

changing writing making diving moving giving

Possible Answers

John and Ella are changing places in class.
I am writing in my book.
They are making a noise.
They are diving into the pool.
We are moving to a new house.
I am giving you my lunch money.

HANDWRITING (Lesson Suggestion 33)

Preparation

Give out *Pupil's Book 2* to each child (page 9 Writing).

READING

INTRODUCTION (Lesson Suggestion 34)

Objective

The children will be able to understand the background to the story, and the meaning of new words. They will read the story silently.

Preparation
Give out *Reader 2* to each child (pages 4–6), '*Eruption*'.

Method
1 Introduce the story. Talk about 'active' volcanoes in Papua New Guinea, e.g: Mt. Lamington, Matupit etc. What causes an eruption? What happens when a volcano erupts?
2 Follow Lesson Suggestion 34B.

LESSON ONE (Lesson Suggestion 34C)

Objective
Children will be able to answer questions to show that they understand the story.

Preparation
Give out *Reader 2* (pages 4–6) and *Pupil's Book 2* to each child (page 10, Lesson 1).

Answers
1 Uncle Damien went to market in Rabaul with his father to sell some coconuts.
2 His father went to collect some fish.
3 People were woken by the shaking of the earth. Uncle Damien and his father went to market in Rabaul. Uncle Damien walked home while his father went to collect fish. A new volcano appeared on Vulcan Island. A storm blew up in the night. A tidal wave swept up the beach. Some of the villagers set out for Nonga. Matupit erupted. The people reached Nonga and were taken by lifeboat to an ocean liner. The people were landed safely at Kokopo. Uncle Damien's father escaped from Vulcan Island.
5 Uncle Damien has told this story before. The first sentence on page 6 tells us this.
6 He pauses at the exciting parts when the children want to know what happens next. Levi and Teresa were very excited.
7 relieved pleased happy joyful
8 The liner came to take them to safety, away from the erupting volcano.
9 An ocean liner is a very large ship. It cannot go close to shore or it will run aground.
10 Deafening means extremely loud, e.g: The blast from the dynamite was deafening.
Effect means the result of something that was done, e.g: When they finished decorating the hall for the school dance, the effect was bright and colourful.
Tremor means shaking, e.g: We felt the earth tremor which made the house shake.

LESSON TWO

Objective
The children will be able to answer questions correctly.

Preparation
Give out *Pupil's Book 2* to each child (pages 10–11, Exercises A & B).

Exercise A

Answers

1 The price of each article.
2 How much they cost her altogether.
3 K1.42 (i.e: 54 toea for the meat plus 44 toea × 2 for the fish)
4 Add

Exercise B

Answers

1 The committee plans to run bingo nights and raffle a car to raise money for the show.
2 At the moment the show committee has K300.
3 They will need thousands of kina for the show.
4 The 'feature' of the show will be the four hour exhibition on the final night of Filipino arts and dancing by the Philippines community in Goroka.
5 The 'Bird Man' will probably be a man flying on a hang glider. A stunt motor cyclist is a man who does tricks on a motor cycle.

LESSON THREE

Objective
The children will be able to play Reading Games.

Preparation
Give out *Reading Games for Grade 6* to each child (pages 32–5, Unit 14).

Method

1 Choose games from these pages for the children to do.
2 Mark children's work using *Teacher's Notes* (pages 42–4).

LESSON FOUR

Objective
The children will be able to read from a supplementary reader.

Preparation
Give out *Supplementary Reader 2* to each child.

Method
Let the children choose a story to read quietly to themselves.

LESSON FIVE — POETRY (Lesson Suggestion 40)

Objective
The children will be able to listen to a poem and understand what the poet is saying.

Preparation
Give out *Pupil's Book 2* to each child (page 12).

Answers

1 The poet is thanking his mother and father, and uncle and aunty.
2 The poet may have received pigs, yams, sago or many other goods.
3 He will give gifts back to his relatives.
4 (This answer will depend on the area in which you live.)

LISTENING 15

LESSON ONE

Objective
The children will listen carefully to hear the correct word.

Preparation
Write these words on the blackboard before the lesson. Set them out like this, in three columns.

1 chains	chained	change	5 sort	short	shorts
2 choose	shoes	chose	6 beat	bit	bits
3 they	there	tear	7 leave	left	live
4 serves	service	serve	8 bird	bed	bad

Method
1 Call out the number and then say one of the three words, e.g: Number 1 change. (Say the word very clearly.)
2 The children must write down the word you have said.
3 Go through all the numbers, calling out one word from each. When you have finished, spell out the correct answers. Children can mark their own work.

Note
Leave the lists of words on the blackboard for the next lesson.

LESSON TWO

Objective
The children will listen carefully to hear the correct word.

Preparation
Use the same blackboard work as for Lesson One above.

Method
1 Tell the pupils that you are going to use one word from each number in a sentence. They must write down the word that you have used, e.g:
T: Number 1: I chained the dog to the fence so it could not get away.
Answer: chained
2 After each sentence, choose someone in the class to give his answer. Everyone mark their work. If necessary, repeat the sentence.

TALKING

LESSON ONE (Lesson Suggestion 1C)

Objective
The children will practise last week's sentence pattern:
Can Tunde wear this shirt? Yes, it's big enough for him to wear.

Method
1 Use the substitution table that is still on the blackboard. Revise it.

LESSON TWO

Objective
The children will practise a sentence pattern they already know:
He lost his pen so he had to buy a new one.

Method
1 T: Pita broke his bow. He had to make a new one. What happened to Pita's bow?
C: Pita broke his bow so he had to make a new one.
2 T: Letti lost her comb so she had to buy a new one. (Class repeat.)
T: Galang stole that spear so he had to return it. (Class repeat.)
T: James lost his pen. What did he do?
C: James lost his pen so he had to buy a new one.
3 Children practise these in groups.

LESSON THREE

Objective
The children will be able to use a new sentence pattern:
Here's a good book for you to read.

Method
1 Ask the class to draw a picture of a house. Then say: Who needs a pencil?
C: I do.
T: Here's a pencil for you to write with. Who else needs a pencil?
C: Kepa does.
T: Here's a pencil for him to write with. Who wants a good book to read?
C: I do.
T: Here's a good book for you to read. She wants some pictures to cut out. Here are some pictures for her to cut out.

LESSON FOUR

Objective
The children will be able to practise this sentence pattern:
Here's a good book for you to read.

Method
1 Give something to a child and say: Here's a pen for you to write with.
2 In groups, tell each child to give something to someone else in their group and say what it's for, e.g:
Here's a cup for you to drink with.
Here's a knife for you to cut with.
Here's a pair of scissors for you to cut with.
Here's a ball for you to play with.
Here's a rope for you to skip with.
Here's a guitar for you to play.
Here's a book for you to read.
Here's a picture for you to copy.
Here's a rubber for you to borrow. etc.

LESSON FIVE (Lesson Suggestion 1C)

Objective
The children will practise the new sentence pattern using a substitution table.

Preparation
Write the following substitution table on the blackboard:

Here's a	CUP	for	YOU	to	DRINK	with.
	KNIFE		HER		CUT	
	BALL		THEM		PLAY	
	ROPE				SKIP	
	GAME					
	GUITAR		US		SING	
	BOOK				READ	
	PICTURE				DRAW	
an	UMBRELLA		HIM		USE	
	KINA				SPEND	

Note
Leave this on the blackboard for revision next week.

ORAL EXPRESSION

LESSON ONE

Objective
The children will be able to hold a class discussion.

Method
1 Turn to page 13 in *Pupil's Book 2* and discuss what the children are doing in this picture to improve their school. Then ask: How could we improve our school?
2 Children could suggest some of the things shown in the picture, but should be encouraged to come up with ideas of their own, e.g: We should plant more trees for shade around the oval.

LESSON TWO

Objective
The children will be able to tell a story from a picture.

Preparation
Show the children an interesting picture on any topic.

Method
1 Look at the picture and tell the class that you want each group to think up a story to tell the rest of the class about the picture.
2 Divide the class into four groups.
3 When each group has thought up an interesting story, one person from each group tells it to the rest of the class.

LESSON THREE

Objective
The children will be able to hold an interview.

Note
This lesson should be taken after Lesson 2, pages 16–17, has been completed.

Method

1 Choose two pupils to conduct an interview. (They will be the person who wrote the interview and another pupil of his choice.)
2 After several interviews have been carried out, discuss with the class, which was the best and why.

WRITTEN SENTENCES

Note
Teach only FIVE of the six lessons.

LESSON ONE (Lesson Suggestion 2)

Objective
The children will be able to write good sentences about a picture.

Preparation
Give out *Pupil's Book 2* to each child (page 13, Lesson 1).

Possible Answers
(Children must write ten sentences similar to these)
1 A boy is feeding scraps to the pigs.
2 The boys are cutting the grass with sharp knives.
3 Some of the boys are repairing the hole in the roof.

LESSON TWO

Objective
The children will be able to use descriptive words (adjectives) to make sentences more interesting.

Preparation
Give out *Pupil's Book 2* to each child (page 14, Lesson 2).

Method
1 Remind the children that adjectives are descriptive words. They tell you *what* something or someone is like.
2 Work out some examples with the class showing where to put the adjectives.

Answers
1 filthy pig sty
2 long grass
3 traditional designs
4 younger girls
5 hungry pigs
6 leaky roof
7 white coral
8 noisy tractor
9 playing field
10 Christmas holidays

LESSON THREE (Lesson Suggestion 2)

Objective
The children will be able to answer questions about a picture.

Preparation
Give out *Pupil's Book 2* to each child (page 14, Lesson 3).

Answers

1 The strong fence is to keep the pigs inside the sty so they won't damage the gardens.
2 The boys are repairing the roof because it is leaking.
3 They could be using sacsac or many other different materials depending on the area in which they live.
4 The boys are painting designs on the building to make it look more attractive.
5 The tractor is pulling the trailer with all the gardening tools on it.
6 It could be used for cutting the grass on the playing field, for carrying loads of weeds, firewood, vegetables, building materials and many other things.
7 The pigs are given scraps from the cook house to eat.
8 This is probably a coastal school because the buildings are built up off the ground to keep them cool and there are coconut palms growing here.
9 There is a lot of work to be done at school because everyone was away for the Christmas holidays.
10 (Many answers are possible for this question.)

LESSON FOUR (Lesson Suggestion 12)

Objective

The children will be able to change the sentences from present to past tense.

Preparation

Give out *Pupil's Book 2* to each child (page 14, Lesson 4).

Answers

2 The grass was cut by some grade five boys.
3 The designs made the building look more attractive.
4 The girls were weeding the vegetable gardens.
5 The pigs were eating scraps from the cookhouse.
6 The grade six boys were repairing the roof.
7 The boys were collecting coral from the beach to put on the path.
8 A teacher was showing a student how to drive the tractor.
9 The tractor was used for cutting the grass on the field.
10 Everyone was helping to clean up the school after the holidays.

LESSON FIVE (Lesson Suggestion 1B)

Objective

The children will be able to answer questions using known sentence patterns.

Preparation

Give out *Pupil's Book 2* to each child (page 15, Lesson 5).

Possible Answers

1 She bought herself a dress.
2 They cooked themselves some rice.
3 She made herself a basket.
4 She made herself a skirt.
5 He carved himself a table.
6 He weaved himself a sleeping mat.
7 We caught ourselves some fish.
8 They made themselves aprons.

LESSON SIX

Objective
The children will be able to choose the most suitable adjective to fit in the space.

Preparation
Give out *Pupil's Book 3* to each child (page 15, Lesson 6).

Answers

1 naughty	6 rough
2 muddy/slipping	7 sore
3 untidy	8 tired
4 shiny	9 wise
5 steep	10 slippery/muddy

WRITTEN COMPOSITION

LESSON ONE (Lesson Suggestion 16C)

Objective
The children will be able to write a description.

Preparation
Give out *Pupil's Book 2* to each child (page 16, Lesson 1).

Method
1 Children must describe only *one* of the following: Kundu drum, garamut drum, dog's tooth necklace, Hagen ceremonial axe, mounted kina shell used in moka, Sepik basket hook. Discuss the things with the children. Read suggestions a-c.

Note
If children have been brought up in a town and do no know about any of these things, then you should tell them about each item and then get them to write a description of one of them.

LESSON TWO

Objective
The children will be able to write an interview.

Preparation
Give out *Pupil's Book 2* to each child (page 17, Lesson 2).

Method
1 Read lesson introduction and the newspaper report. Discuss with the class. Read the questions listed.
2 Tell the children to study the newspaper report to answer the questions. Base the interview on the questions listed.

Follow-Up
Stage a mock interview using pupils' answers.

SPELLING

LESSON ONE (Lesson Suggestion 22)

Objective
The children will learn to spell this week's words.

Preparation
Give out *Pupil's Book 2* to each child (page 17, Spelling List).

LESSON TWO

Select from Exercises A–E.

Preparation
Give out *Pupil's Book 2* to each child (pages 17–18).

Exercise A

Answers
teach clean learned earth
True statements: b We learned how to build a pig sty.
d Compost makes the earth better for growing plants.

Exercise B

Answers
beach reach preach tear clear bear tea real steal neat meat defeat lean mean etc.

Exercise C

Answers

1 spider	2 spear	3 spoon	4 spade	5 speed
6 crab	7 crane	8 creek	9 crowd	10 crew

Exercise D (Lesson Suggestion 27)

Answers
captain certain change circus club completely crushed customer

Exercise E (Lesson Suggestion 30)

Answers
impossible — not able to be done
unkind — rather cruel
discover — to find out
return — to come back

HANDWRITING (Lesson Suggestion 33)

Preparation
Give out *Pupil's Book 2* to each child (pages 19–20).

Note

Children may have difficulty with joining 'rp' in the fluency exercise. Do this example on the blackboard before they write the lesson. Point out the difficult areas.

READING

INTRODUCTION (Lesson Suggestion 34)

Objective

The children will be able to understand the background to the story, and the meaning of new words. They will read the story silently.

Preparation

Give out *Pupil's Book 2* to each child (pages 7–10), *'One Thing After Another'*.

Method

1 Introduce the story. Talk about cars, trucks, motor bikes. Say how these things help us get from one place to another. However, they must be looked after or they will not work properly.
2 Follow Lesson Suggestion 34B.

LESSON ONE (Lesson Suggestion 34C)

Objective

Children will be able to answer questions to show that they understand the story.

Preparation

Give out *Reader 2* (pages 7–10) and *Pupil's Book 2* to each child (page 20, Lesson 1).

Answers

1 First the motorbike wouldn't start because the clutch cable snapped.
The motorbike was not repaired in time for them to get home.
The truck had a flat tyre.
Dewi missed the bus when she ran over to see Ketut.
The bike ran out of petrol.
2 The person talking stresses 'now', which suggests that other things have already gone wrong.
3 It happened on a Friday night.
4 Fried noddles, fried vegetables and soup.
5 Klungkung is on the island of Bali.
6 'Trudged' means walking tiredly. 'Musicians' are people who make music.
7 The play was held in the temple at Nyoman's village. It started at eleven o'clock and ended at three o'clock.
8 early — late
light — dark
pulling — pushing
stopped — started
day — night
9 He was still awake because he was worried about them because they were late coming home.
10 They laughed because so many silly things had gone wrong that it was really quite funny.

LESSON TWO

Exercise A

Objective
The children will be able to obtain information from a given page of the Telephone Directory.

Preparation
Give out *Pupil's Book 2* to each child (pages 20–22, Lesson 2, Exercise A).

Method
Read out instructions a–e at the top of the page. Make sure the children understand them.

Answers
1 Badili Baimuru Baiyer River Balimo Banz Bereina Bogia Boroko Buambub Buin Buka Bulolo Bundi Bwagaoia
2 Alotau
3 A Telegraph Office
4 Yes, he would receive it quickly as telegrams are delivered to addresses within one kilometre radius of the Telegraph Office and Daru is only a small island.
5 Bundi/Alexishafen/Bogia

Exercise B

Objective
The children will be able to interpret a weather forecast.

Preparation
Give out *Pupil's Book 2* to each child (page 22, Exercise B).

Method
1 Discuss the meanings of 'weather' words at the beginning of the lesson. Make sure children understand them.
2 Examine the weather report together to find answers to the questions.

Answers
1 Along the North coast of the mainland and over the northern islands.
2 In the afternoon and in the evening
3 In the Highland valleys
4 It tells the highest temperature for that day at that place.
5 It tells the lowest temperature for that day at that place.
6 It tells how much rain has fallen in that place — measured in millimetres.
7 Misima (86.0)
8 Lae had no rain.
9 Wewak and Misima (32)
10 Breezes

Exercise C

Objective
The children will be able to answer questions about a passage.

Preparation
Give out *Pupil's Book 2* to each child (page 23, Exercise C).

Method

1 Read through stories 1–3.
2 Ask children to choose the correct answers from those given, and explain why the others are incorrect.

Answers

1 c Gema is of medium build and dark.
2 a Pep caught the biggest fish.
3 b Gari has no brothers.

OR POETRY (Lesson Suggestion 40)

Preparation

Give out *Pupil's Book 2* to each child (page 24), *'Boys and Girls'*.

Answers

1 basketball hopscotch soccer swimming marbles
2 The girls were swimming.
3 (Pupil's personal choice.)
4 'To show off' means the boys were trying to impress the girls by doing smart things.

LESSON THREE (Lesson Suggestion 39)

Objective

The children will be able to read for enjoyment.

Method

1 Give children a variety of reading matter, or give out *Supplementary Reader 2* to each pupil.
2 Children read quietly to themselves. Help children with any difficult words.

LISTENING 16

LESSON ONE

Objective

The children will be able to report conversations.

Method

1 Choose two people to come to the front of the class. Tell them to have a conversation about something, e.g:
Mary: Did you see Pem's house burn down last night?
Kila: No, I didn't. I was out fishing until quite late, so I missed it.
2 Next choose another child to come out the front to report that conversation, e.g:
Mary asked Kila if he had seen Pem's house burn down last night.
Kila said that he hadn't because he was fishing till quite late.
3 In groups, the leader chooses people to have a conversation and then someone else to report it.
4 Teacher listens in to each group giving help where needed.

LESSON TWO

Objective

The children will practise understanding what people feel, from their actions.

Method

1 People often show how they feel by their actions, rather than by words. Explain this to the class, e.g: when a person is angry or worried he often frowns.
2 Choose children to show the way they feel with actions and not words, e.g:
scratching their head and frowning (trying to think of something)
yawning (feeling tired)
sighing (feeling fed-up or frustrated)
moaning (in pain)
crying (being sad or upset)
screaming (frightened by something)
shrugging their shoulders (meaning 'I don't know')
kiss (showing affection)
patting someone on the shoulder (showing sympathy)
shaking hands (when making a deal)
winking (when playing a joke on someone)
3 The rest of the class must guess how the person miming feels from his actions.

TALKING

LESSON ONE (Lesson Suggestion 1C)

Objective

The children will practise last week's sentence pattern:
Here's a good book for you to read.

Method

1 Use the substitution table which is still on the blackboard. Revise it.

LESSON TWO

Objective

The children will practise a sentence pattern they already know:
I can't come now. I have to chop the wood.

Method

1 Let's all go to the market now! We can't go now. We have to do our school work.
T: Tia, why don't you go for a swim now?
C: I can't go now. I have to do my lessons.
T: Petra, why don't you eat your lunch now?
C: I can't eat it now. I have to do my work.
2 Children practise this sentence pattern in groups.

LESSON THREE

Objective

The children will be able to use a new sentence pattern:
It's bad for you to steal. It's good for you to eat plenty of protein.

Method

1 People who eat green fruit get sick. It's had for you to eat green fruit. Should you eat green fruit?
 C: No, it's bad for you to eat green fruit.
 T: Should you eat Cheezepops every day for lunch?
 C: No, it's bad for you to eat Cheezepops for lunch.

2 T: People who read books do better in English. It's good for you to read books. Should you read books?
 C: Yes, it's good for me to read books.
 T: Should you eat ripe fruit?
 C: Yes, it's good for you to eat ripe fruit.

LESSON FOUR

Objective

The children will practise this pattern:
It's bad for you to steal. It's good for you to eat plenty of protein.

Method

1 Divide the class in half. One half must think up things that are good for you, while the other half must think up things that are bad for you.

2 Ask the children from one half to see how many things they have thought of. They must use the new sentence pattern for their answers, e.g:
Things that are bad for you: sweets ice-blocks green fruit smoking lolly water
It's bad for you to eat sweets.
Things that are good for you: green vegetables beans protein books oranges education
It's good for you to eat oranges.

LESSON FIVE (Lesson Suggestion 1C)

Objective

The children will practise the new sentence pattern using a substitution table.

Preparation

Write the following substitution table on the blackboard:

It's bad for you to eat	SWEETS.	
	GREEN FRUIT.	
	SMOKE CIGARETTES.	
	ICE-BLOCKS.	
drink	LOLLY WATER.	
It's good for you to eat	GREEN	vegetables.
	FRUIT.	
	BEANS	
	PROTEIN	
read books.		
have education.		
learn to DRIVE.		
SWIM.		

Note

Remember to leave this substitution table on the blackboard for next week. week.

ORAL EXPRESSION

LESSON ONE

Objective
The children will be able to hold a class discussion.

Method
1 Discuss the picture on page 25 in *Pupil's Book 2*.
Has anyone been to a singsing like the one in the picture? (Children in Highland areas will know all about this topic. If your school is in another area, choose a special occasion or festival known to your children, to talk about.)
2 What happens at a singsing? How long does it last? Do people decorate themselves? How? What do the women and children do?

LESSON TWO

Objective
The children will be able to make contrasts between things.

Method
Study the picture on page 25 in *Pupil's Book 2* again. Choose pupils to describe the traditional dress and decoration shown in this picture. How does this Highland costume differ from the traditional dress in your area? (If you live in a Highland area you would ask: How does our traditional costume and body decoration differ from other areas?)

Note
When making contrasts, we use words like but, however, e.g: In the Highlands the men make head-dresses from Bird of Paradise feathers, however in coastal areas they cannot get many of these feathers.

LESSON THREE

Objective
The children will be able to ask good questions about a given topic.

Method
1 Teacher will write a list of topics currently being studied in your class in all subjects, e.g: reptiles; fishing methods in PNG; the Government today.
2 Divide the class into four groups.
3 Give the children ten minutes to write out a list of questions based on the topics written on the blackboard.
4 The leader from one group will then ask a question and the people from the next group must give the correct answer. If they get it correct, they get a point. That group then asks the next group a question and so on until all the questions have been asked.
5 The winning group is the one with the most points. The teacher must decide whether or not the answers are correct.

Note
Remind children to ask questions beginning with: why, what, where, and how.

WRITTEN SENTENCES

LESSON ONE (Lesson Suggestion 2)

Objective
The children will be able to write six good sentences about a picture.

Preparation
Give out *Pupil's Book 2* to each child (page 25, Lesson 1).

Possible Answers
1 The men are beating their kundus or drums.
2 The women are preparing the food.
3 Some of the dancers are carrying ceremonial spears.
4 The children are dancing too.
5 These feather head-dresses are kept for special occasions.
6 There is a pig tied to a stake.
7 The men are carrying a pig to be cooked in the feast.

LESSON TWO

Objective
The children will be able to link sentences by using suitable joining word.

Preparation
Give out *Pupil's Book 2* to each child (page 26, Lesson 2).

Answers

1 while	4 after	7 until	10 where/because
2 before	5 because/but	8 but	
3 so	6 when/before	9 as	

LESSON THREE (Lesson Suggestion 9)

Objective
The children will be able to use apostrophes to show that something belongs to someone.

Preparation
Give out *Pupil's Book 2* to each child (page 26, Lesson 3).

Answers

1 pig's feet	3 men's legs	5 girls' faces	7 men's bark skirts
2 women's bilums	4 pigs' squeals	6 dancers' head-dresses	8 dancer's spears

LESSON FOUR (Lesson Suggestion 2)

Objective
The children will be able to answer questions about the picture on page 25.

Preparation
Give out *Pupil's Book 2* to each child (page 26, Lesson 4).

Possible Answers
1 The women are preparing the food for the feast.
2 There will be bananas, sweet corn, kaukau and other vegetables. There will also be pig meat.

3 The pigs are tied to stakes ready to be killed and cooked for the feast.
4 The children are having their own singsing.
5 The dancers are decorated with paint and feathers.
6 I can see ceremonial spears, a knife and an axe.
7 The people are wearing the traditional Highland costume. The village, houses are low and round.
8 exciting colourful noisy busy

LESSON FIVE (Lesson Suggestion 5)

Objective
The children will practise writing sentence patterns containing reflexive pronouns (himself, herself, yourself).

Preparation
Give out *Pupil's Book 2* to each child (page 27, Lesson 5).

Answers
1 Can you make a canoe by yourself?
2 Can he lift that log by himself?
3 Can he make a head-dress by himself?
4 Can she weave a basket by herself?
5 Can you carry that heavy bilum by yourself?

WRITTEN COMPOSITION

LESSON ONE (Lesson Suggestion 16B)

Objective
The children will be able to write a story about a set of sequence pictures.

Preparation
Give out *Pupil's Book 2* to each child (page 28–29, Lesson 1).

Model Answer
One morning Koru and Pita set out in their canoe to go diving. They took their spears and a basket with them.

When they reached the best place, they both dived into the water to search for crayfish. Koru saw one and speared it.

He picked up his spear and the crayfish, and swam back to the canoe. He put the crayfish in the basket. They caught many crayfish this way.

Koru was just returning from the canoe when he saw Pita waving to him. His foot was caught in a calm shell and he could not get free.

Koru swam quickly back to the canoe for his knife. He dived under again and swam straight towards his friend.

Quickly Koru opened the clam shell and Pita swam to the surface. He felt as if his lungs were bursting. He gulped in a big mouthful of air and hung onto the canoe while he caught his breath. Pita thanked Koru for saving his life.

Note
Tell the children that this is not a true story: clams shells do not really trap divers' legs.

LESSON TWO

Objective
The children will be able to plan a business letter before writing it.

Preparation
Give out *Pupil's Book 2* to each child (page 29, Lesson 2).

Method
Read out the lesson introduction and go over the plan of the letter.

Model Answer

Afore Community School,
Afore Patrol Post.
Northern Province.

3rd May, 19. .

Local Government Councillor,
Afore Patrol Post.
Northern Province.

Dear Mr Perembo,

I am writing to ask if our school could possibly borrow your tractors. We need it to help clear the bush land at the back of the school to make a football field.

A Grade Six boy at our school can drive a tractor. His father taught him when he worked for an Agricultural Station in Popondetta. He would be the only student allowed to drive the tractor. He would be under the supervision of a teacher.

The father of another of our students works on a nearby cardamom plantation as a mechanic. He has offered to supply fuel and to look after the tractor while we have it. We will need it for only one or two days.

Please let us know if the council will lend us the tractor and we will arrange to collect it from you when convenient.

Yours faithfully,
(name of student)

SPELLING

LESSON ONE (Lesson Suggestion 22)

Objective
The children will learn to spell this week's words.

Preparation
Give out *Pupil's Book 2* to each child (page 30, Spelling List).

LESSON TWO

Select from Exercises A–E, or give a spelling and dictation test on words learned over the past four weeks.

Preparation
Give out *Pupil's Book 2* to each child (pages 30–1).

Exercise A (Lesson Suggestion 29)

Answers
station relation plantation grass growl grabbed

Exercise B

Answers
shallow — deep
usual — unusual/extraordinary
thick — thin
real — unreal/imaginary
interesting — uninteresting/dull
lucky — unlucky

Exercise C (Lesson Suggestion 27)

Answers
1 stared stirred stood stretched
2 trail tribe trouble truth

Exercise D (Lesson Suggestion 27)

Answers
MAIPU, Alfred
MARIOSU, Nason
MIRIA, Lohia
MOI, Hunter
NOVULU, Hikari
OGERA, Gali
PES, Nombi
RAI, Kana

Exercise E (Lesson Suggestion 28)

Possible Answers
1 porch paddle poor prize port pencil porter
2 snore store more floor game name
3 sore order for story storm
4 porter poor
5 porch port porter
6 sore poor prod door
7 port poor

HANDWRITING (Lesson Suggestion 33)

Preparation
Give out *Pupil's Book 2* to each child (page 32).

READING

INTRODUCTION (Lesson Suggestion 34)

Objective
The children will be able to understand the background to the story, and the meaning of new words. They will read the story silently.

Preparation

Give out *Reader 2* to each child (pages 11–14), *'Lost, Stolen or Strayed?'*.

Method

1 Introduce the story. Talk about superstitions, good luck charms and magic. What do the children think about these things? Ask them to tell you stories about these things.
2 Follow Lesson Suggestion 34B.

LESSON ONE (Lesson Suggestion 34C)

Objective

Children will be able to answer questions about a story to show they understand it.

Preparation

Give out *Reader 2* (pages 11–14) and *Pupil's Book 2* to each child (page 33, Lesson 1).

Answers

1 Lina was in Port Moresby because she was a member of the Papua New Guinea team for the South Pacific Games.
2 Vinnie went to the Games once before.
3 She hung it over the back of her chair at the dance.
4 Vinnie did not actually agree with Lina by saying 'Yes' or 'I know'. Instead she says, 'Do you really think so?', which tells us that Vinnie probably doesn't think so.
5 . . . it was too heavy and hot to wear while she was dancing.
6 Lina was younger than Vinnie.
7 At the Opening Parade, the competitors marched around the stadium.
8 She felt pleased that she didn't need a good luck charm to win the race. She won it because she ran fast, and not because she had good luck.
9 excited nervous horrified worried pleased
10 I felt very nervous when I sat the exam.
There were nine competitors in the race.
It was a race to see who could reach the trees first.
The competitors walked up to the starting line.

LESSON TWO

Objective

The children will be able to choose the correct word to fit in a sentence.

Preparation

Give out *Pupil's Book 2* to each child (page 33, Lesson 2, Exercise A).

Answers

1 shed	4 weave	7 costumes	10 escaped
2 distant	5 sharp	8 strike	
3 cage	6 crowd	9 rare	

Note

If there is time, ask the children to use some of the other words in sentences.

LESSON THREE (Lesson Suggestion 35)

Objective

The children will be able to work out word meanings from the context in which they are used.

Preparation
Give out *Pupil's Book 2* to each child (page 34, Exercise B).

Answers
a 1 To increase means to give more.
  2 Extra means more than usual.
  3 Terms are conditions.
b 1 Gloomy means unhappy.
  2 A bargain is something which is good value because it is being sold cheaply.
  3 A loan is money lent which has to be paid back later.

LESSON FOUR

Objective
The children will be able to play Reading Games.

Preparation
Give out *Reading Games for Grade 6* to each child (pages 37–40, Unit 16).

Method
1 Choose games for the children to play.
2 Teacher mark this lesson from *Teacher's Notes* (pages 47–9).

LESSON FIVE (Lesson Suggestion 39)

Objective
The children will be able to read for pleasure.

Preparation
Give out a variety of reading material for the children to choose from.

OR POETRY (Lesson Suggestion 40)

Preparation
Give out *Pupil's Book 2* to each child (page 35).

Note
If children do not know a song or chant from their district, choose another poem to read to the class.

LISTENING 17

LESSON ONE

Objective
The children will practise working out a word from clues.

Method
1 Choose something simple to describe to the class, e.g: I am thinking of something man-made with four legs, that you sit on.
  A: Chair.
2 After several examples, the class could be divided into groups. Each person in the group must say a riddle while the others have to guess the answer.

Other examples:
I am thinking of something I use to write on the blackboard. (chalk)
I am thinking of a word that tells how you feel when you have worked hard all day. (tired)
I am thinking of a word that means you have good manners. (polite)
I am thinking of something I do with my mouth when I feel happy. (smile)

LESSON TWO

Objective
The children will be able to listen carefully to directions.

Method
1 This game is called 'Master and Robot'. (Explain that a robot is a mechanical person which obeys instructions from its master.)
2 One child is chosen as Master and another as Robot.
3 The Master must give the Robot instructions which he must obey, e.g: Walk over to the window nearest the door and tap it gently five times with your left hand. Now go over to the book shelf and take out the third book from the left off the bottom shelf. Bring the book to me.
4 If the Robot doesn't obey the instructions exactly as instructed by the Master, then the class must all shout out 'Boooo!'
5 Then choose someone from the class to say what he did wrong. Then a new Master and Robot are chosen.

Note
This lesson can be fun for the children, particularly if you show them how a Robot moves, i.e: very stiffly and slowly, in a jerking manner.

TALKING

LESSON ONE (Lesson Suggestion 1C)

Objective
The children will practise last week's sentence pattern:
It's bad for you to steal. It's good for you to eat plenty of protein.

Method
1 Use the substitution table that is still on the blackboard. Revise it.

LESSON TWO

Objective
The children will practise a sentence pattern they already know:
I need new batteries so I'll have to go to the store.

Method
1 Hold up a transistor radio and say: This radio doesn't go. It needs new batteries so I'll have to go to the store. Why doesn't it go?
C: Because it needs new batteries.
T: So what will I have to do?
C: You'll have to go to the store.
2 Say different examples for the children to repeat after you.
I need some medicine so I'll have to go to the Aid Post.

I need some sugar so I'll have to go to the tradestore.
I need some water so I'll have to go to the river.
I need some vegetables so I'll have to go to the gardens.
I need some money so I'll have to go to the bank.

LESSON THREE

Objective

The children will be able to use a new sentence pattern:
He's going to draw it again. There's no need for him to draw it again.

Method

1 Write this sum on the board 5 + 4 = ? Ask the class to do it. Check to see that everyone got it right.
T: Who got it wrong?
C: Pandum did.
T: Pandum must do it again.
T: Nason, did you get it right?
C: Yes, I did.
T: There's no need for you to do it again.
Say to the class:
T: Nason got it right. There's no need for him to do it again. Must he do it again?
C: No, there's no need for him to do it again.
2 Tell the class to think up other examples and practise them in groups.

LESSON FOUR

Objective

The children will practise this sentence pattern:
He's going to draw it again. There's no need for him to draw it again.

Method

1 Write some examples on the blackboard:
Monday is a holiday. There's no need for us to come to school.
We've finished our work. There's no need for us to do any homework.
She's made a dress. There's no need for her to make a skirt.
He's fixed your bike. There's no need to buy another one.
We've got enough money to buy that car. There's no need to borrow any more.
2 Children practise saying these in groups.

LESSON FIVE (Lesson Suggestion 1C)

Objective

The children will practise the new sentence pattern using a substitution table.

Preparation

Write the following substitution table on the blackboard:

Tomorrow is Saturday. There's no need for us to	COME TO SCHOOL. PACK OUR LUNCH. GET UP EARLY. DO ANY HOMEWORK.
It's going to be fine today. There's no need for us to	WEAR A RAINCOAT. TAKE AN UMBRELLA.

The house is finished. There's no need for us to CUT ANY MORE TIMBER.
WEAVE ANY MORE BAMBOO WALLS.
MAKE ANY MORE THATCHING.

Our gardens are ready. There's no need for us to do any more DIGGING.
PLANTING
WATERING
FENCING.

Note
Leave this work on the blackboard for next week.

ORAL EXPRESSION

LESSON ONE

Objective
The children will be able to talk about their own experiences.

Method
1 Study the picture on page 36 in *Pupil's book 2*.
2 Discuss the events being held at this sports day.
3 Ask children to talk about their own experiences at a school sports day, e.g: which races they won, found difficult, enjoyed the most.
4 Discuss the rules for each event, e.g: an egg-and-spoon race — this is a race where each person must hold a spoon with an egg balanced in it. She must go as fast as she can without dropping the egg. If the egg falls, she must stop to pick it up. The first across the finishing line wins.

LESSON TWO

Objective
The children will learn how to ask for information politely.

Method
1 This lesson will teach children how to ask for information from a stranger, e.g: asking directions or the time.
2 Choose two students to act out a situation, e.g:
Student: Excuse me, can you tell me how to reach the Aid Post from here?
Stranger: Yes, you just follow the track along by the river to the next village. You will find the Aid Post at the back of the village, by the waterfall.
Student: Thank you very much.
3 Put the class into pairs. Each pair must think up a situation and then act it out. Remind them to use the words 'excuse me', 'please', 'thank you'.

LESSON THREE

Objective
The children will be able to interrupt a speaker politely.

Method
1 This lesson will teach children to interrupt a speaker to get information. Often, if we do not understand something a speaker is saying, it is better to

interrupt at once before he continues talking. Children should learn to interrupt by saying things like:
I'm sorry to interrupt, but . . .
I'm sorry, I didn't quite understand. Could you repeat that?
Excuse me. Could you explain that again?

2 Encourage children to do this during lessons (i.e: interrupt the Teacher) if they do not fully understand what is said.
3 You could choose several pupils to interrupt while you pretend to take a lesson. The rest of class listen to see if they do it correctly.

WRITTEN SENTENCES

LESSON ONE (Lesson Suggestion 2)

Objective
The childnen will be able to write ten good sentences about a picture.

Preparation
Give out *Pupil's Book 2* to each child (page 36, Lesson 1).

Possible Answers
1 Many parents turned up to watch their children on Athletics Day.
2 The girls giggled when they tried to run in the three-legged race.
3 The Grade Six boys were busy the week before, preparing the jumping pits.
4 The children were very thirsty by mid-day.
5 Jon easily won the egg-and-spoon race.

LESSON TWO

Objective
The children will be able to complete the sentences by studying the picture.

Preparation
Give out *Pupil's Book 2* to each child (page 36, Lesson 2).

Answers

1 first	3 last/fifth	5 egg pick it up	7 relay
2 third	4 second	6 the three-legged race	8 archery

LESSON THREE (Lesson Suggestion 2)

Objective
The children will be able to answer questions based on a picture.

Preparation
Give out *Pupil's Book 2* to each child (page 37, Lesson 3).

Answers
1 Jon won the egg-and-spoon race.
2 Geo was last.
3 The teachers helped to organize the events.
4 A relay race is a long race for teams of runners. One runner has to pass on a stick to the next runner in his team who passes it to the next runner, and so on until they reach the finishing line.
5 There were ten events.

6 For the three-legged race, two children must stand close together with their arms around each other. They tie their inside legs together with a scarf and then run together as fast as possible.
7 (Different answers possible.)
8 The gun is used for starting the races.

LESSON FOUR

Objective
The children will be able to complete sentences using phrases which describe *how, where* or *why* something happened.

Preparation
Give out *Pupil's Book 2* to each child (page 37, Lesson 4).

Possible Answers
1 Rumin ran very fast in the hundred metres race.
2 The Athletics Day was held at the . . . Community School.
3 . . . because he ran too fast.
4 . . . because they were entering the three-legged race.
5 . . . because it had been a long tiring day.
6 . . . because he won the egg-and-spoon race.
7 . . . because they had worked hard too.
8 . . . at the edge of the sports field to watch.
9 . . . because it was a great success.
10 . . . because they enjoyed themselves and liked having their parents watching them.

LESSON FIVE (Lesson Suggestion 1B)

Objective
The children will be able to complete answers using a known language pattern.

Preparation
Give out *Pupil's Book 2* to each child (page 38, Lesson 5).

Answers
1 No, I'm too short to reach that branch.
2 No, I'm too weak to lift this box.
3 No, I'm too young to drive a car.
4 No, I'm too tired to come to the party tonight.
5 No, she's too lazy to finish the work.
6 No, it's too difficult for me to understand.
7 No, it's too low for him to crawl under.
8 No, it's too fast for us to swim in.
9 No, there's too much for us/me to eat.
10 No, there's too many for us/me to carry.

WRITTEN COMPOSITION

LESSON ONE (Lesson Suggestion 17)

Objective
The children will be able to plan a business letter and set it out correctly.

Preparation
Give out *Pupil's Book 2* to each child (page 38, Lesson 1).

Method
1 Read through the introduction and study the letter heading.

Model Answer

Bogia Community School,
Madang,
Madang Province.

3rd June, 19. .

The Health Extension Officer,
Bogia Aid Post,
Bogia.

Dear Sir,

I am a leader of a group from our school working on a special project to help our local community.

Our group would like to help with any jobs that need doing at the Aid Post. We thought we could help with things like cutting grass, gardening, making new mats and doing repairs to the building.

If you think this is a good idea, please let us know when you would like us to come and what you would like us to bring. We do have tools and spades that we could bring with us.

Yours faithfully,
(Student's name)

Note
If possible, you could choose the best letter to send to your local Aid Post. Such a community aid project could be carried out by a group of your students. Discuss this with your head teacher if you would like to try it.

LESSON TWO (Lesson Suggestion 16B)

Objective
The children will be able to write a story about sequence pictures.

Preparation
Give out *Pupil's Book 2* to each child (page 39, Lesson 2).

Model Answers
1 One day Kel and Rima decided to go swimming. They dived off the rocks into the water.
2 Suddenly they saw a big black fin in the water ahead. 'Shark! Look out!' Kel shouted to Rima.
3 They both swam for their lives, back to the rocks. As the two boys scrambled onto the rocks, they heard laughter behind them.
4 They turned around to see Kane in the water. He was chuckling to himself and holding a piece of bark, tied to a stick, which looked just like a shark's fin. The boys were very cross with Kane.

SPELLING

LESSON ONE (Lesson Suggestion 22)

Objective
The children will learn to spell this week's words.

Preparation
Give out *Pupil's Book 2* to each child (page 40, Spelling List).

LESSON TWO

Select from Exercises A–E.

Preparation
Give out *Pupil's Book 2* to each children (pages 40–1).

Exercise A (Lesson Suggestion 29)

Answers
sound around sound found ground

Exercise B (Lesson Suggestion 23)

Answers
works – Jon never works on Saturday mornings.
worker – He is a very hard worker.
working – Mother is always working too hard.
worked – They worked hard to put out the fire.
workshop – The mechanic took the motorbike into his workshop.

Exercise C (Lesson Suggestion 30)

Answers
Meanest toughest smallest
He is the meanest person I know.
Buy the toughest rope you can find.
I chose the smallest puppy to be my pet.
excitement improvement argument
The crowd cheered with excitement during the football match.
The new library is a great improvement for the school.
slowly softly loudly
We climbed slowly up the steep hill.
He whistled softly while he worked.
She shouted loudly to scare the birds from the garden.

Exericse D

Answers
1 suddenly
2 trail
3 against
4 growl
5 float

HANDWRITING (Lesson Suggestion 33)

Preparation
Give out *Pupil's Book 2* to each child (page 42).

READING

INTRODUCTION (Lesson Suggestion 34)

Objective
The children will be able to understand the background to the story, and the meaning of new words. They will read the story silently.

Preparation
Give out *Reader 2* to each child (pages 15–17), *'Idajojo the Giant'*.

Method
1 Introduce the story. Talk about people who are disabled in some way, e.g: some people are blind, deaf or dumb. Others, because of some accident or disease, cannot walk or use their hands. How do such people get on in the village? Do you know of anyone like that in your village? Does anyone ever help this person? Do you ever help this person? Explain that this story is a legend about a man who has no hands or feet.
2 Follow Lesson Suggestion 34B.

LESSON ONE (Lesson Suggestion 34C)

Objective
Children will be able to answer questions to show that they understand the story.

Preparation
Give out *Reader 2* (pages 15–17) and *Pupil's Book 2* to each child (page 42, Lesson 1).

Answers
1 Waidudu was alone because his brothers went off to their gardens.
2 Idajojo lent Waidudu his hands and feet so he could climb the coconut tree to throw him down some coconuts.
3 Waidudu was not used to walking, and the giants feet were too big for him. It took him a while to get used to them.
4 The huge hands felt like blocks of stone on his thin weak arms. They didn't seem to understand what he wanted them to do. His feet felt the same.
5 Some people do not like being in high places. They get dizzy, especially if they look down. Waidudu was not used to high places and he did not like the feeling. (Personal opinion about how children felt when they first climbed a high tree.)
6 Idajojo had no feet to run away on and no hands to fight with, so he knew he was trapped.
7 The first time he 'demanded' his feet and hands back, he knew Waidudu was too frightened to refuse. The next time he 'begged' for them back because he knew that this time Waidudu was not frightened because his brothers were coming.

8 Idajojo only thought of himself, never about other people.
cruel impatient greedy strong
9 disobey – Karu was too frightened to disobey his father.
pale – His face turned pale when he saw a huge snake close by.
gobbled – She was so hungry she gobbled all her dinner in a few minutes.
10 screamed call out demanded ordered growled

LESSON TWO

Objective
The children will be able to fit the most suitable phrases into the spaces.

Preparation
Give out *Pupil's Book 2* to each child (page 43, Lesson 2, Exercise A).

Method
1 Discuss the meaning of the phrases with the class.

Answers
1 keep an eye on (watch)
2 carry out (do)
3 before long
4 took no notice
5 to our surprise
6 any longer
7 leaped to his feet
8 for a moment

LESSON THREE

Objective
The children will be able to find the odd word out.

Preparation
Give out *Pupil's Book 2* to each child (page 43, Exercise B).

Answers
1 'house' does not belong because all the others are things given to people
2 'spoon' does not belong because food is cooked in all the others
3 'listened' does not belong because all the others are to do with talking
4 'sat' does not belong because all the others are active things
5 'rubber' does not belong because all the others are for drawing
6 'song' does not belong because all the others are musical instruments.
7 'valley' does not belong because all the others rise up high
8 'dinner' does not belong because all the others are furniture

LESSON FOUR (Lesson Suggestion 39)

Objective
The children will be able to read for pleasure.

Preparation
Give out *Supplementary Reader 2* to each child.

LESSON FIVE

Objective
The children will be able to do Reading Games.

Preparation
Give out *Pupil's Book 2* to each child (page 44), *'The Changing Times'*.

Method
1 Choose games from Unit 17 for the children to do.
2 Mark the work using *Teacher's Notes* (pages 50–2).

OR POETRY (Lesson Suggestion 40)

Preparation
Give out *Pupil's Book 2* to each child (page 44) '*The Changing Times*'.

Answers
1 The poet is old because he sees his old way of life changing.
2 Many new things have come into the village like trucks, tradestores and missions. Young people are exchanging the old traditional ways for new foreign ways.
3 Many village people now wear European clothing. Instead of tapa, they wear modern cloth.
4 Journeys to longer take weeks or months. Most Patrol Posts have air strips and many people travel quickly from one place to another by plane, or PMV trucks. Sometimes they travel by river, using canoes with outboard motors.
5 Village agriculture has changed because many villagers now grow cash crops to sell. They grow more different types of vegetables than before and use modern tools and fertilizers.

Note
'Intruding' means thrusting itself on, spoiling, or getting in the way of something.

LISTENING 18

LESSON ONE

Objective
The children will be able to listen carefully so that they can remember a list of things in the correct order.

Method
1 Start the game by listing three or four parts of the body.
2 Then choose a child who must stand up and touch each part of the body in the order in which you have said them, e.g: chin, knee, eyes, hair.
3 If the child points to these parts of the body in the correct order, then it is his turn to list four other parts. He chooses someone to point to them in the correct order. If he gets them wrong, the rest of the class must all call out 'Booo!'
4 This game can be made more difficult by naming more parts or by being more specific, e.g: the right ear, the left knee, the back of your head, the heel of your foot, etc.

LESSON TWO

Objective
The children will be able to complete two-line jingles.

Method

1 Give several examples:
 Yes of course,
 I'll ride on a . . . (horse)
 If you get mud on your dress
 It will be in a quite a . . . (mess)
2 The children must think of the rhyming word to end the jingle.
3 Divide the class into groups. Give children time to think up their own easy jingles. Someone else in the group must guess the rhyming word.

Note

Tell children that the easiest way to think up a jingle is to think of two words that rhyme, e.g: look/book. Next think of a sentence to put them in, e.g: I opened my desk to look, for my missing library . . . (book)
Other examples:
I didn't know what to do, when I lost my new brown . . . (shoe)
I got the teacher's broom, and decided to sweep the . . . (room)
I got up and started to walk, then tripped on a piece of . . . (chalk)

TALKING

LESSON ONE (Lesson Suggestion 1C)

Objective

The children will practise last week's sentence pattern:
He's going to draw it again. There's no need to draw it again.
The house is finished. There's no need to cut any more timber.

Method

1 Use the substitution table on the blackboard to revise the pattern.

LESSON TWO

Objective

The children will practise a sentence pattern they already know:
If you want to light a fire, you have to collect firewood.

Method

1 T: If we felt cold, how could we get warm?
 C: We could light a fire.
 T: If you want to light a fire, you have to collect firewood. (Class repeat.)
2 T: If you want to get better, you have to go to the hospital. (Class repeat.)
 T: If you want to be a teacher, you have to work hard at school. (Class repeat.)
 T: If you want to make a garden, you have to clear the bush.
3 Divide class into groups. Children must think of similar examples.

LESSON THREE

Objective

The children will be able to use a new sentence pattern:
Did they start the game before their friends arrived? No, they waited for them to arrive.

Method

1 T: This morning you didn't come into the classroom before I arrived. You waited for me to arrive. What did you do?
C: We waited for you to arrive.
T: Take out your English books. Now, I'll tell you what to do. I didn't tell you before you took your books out. I waited for you to take your books out. What did I do?
C: You waited for us to take our books out.
T: Did we go to assembly before the bell rang?
C: No, we waited for the bell to ring.
T: Did the Headmaster leave before the PMV came?
C: No, he waited for the PMV to come.
T: Did you set out before the rain stopped?
C: No, we waited for the rain to stop.

LESSON FOUR

Objective

The children will practise the new sentence pattern:
Did they start the game before their friends arrived? No, they waited for them to arrive.

Method

1 Children practise saying these examples in groups:
Did they start eating before their father arrived? No, they waited for him to arrive.
Did they start the meeting before the chairman arrived? No, they waited for him to arrive.
Did you start school before I arrived? No, we waited for you to arrive.
2 Use other examples from Lesson 3.

LESSON FIVE (Lesson Suggestion 1C)

Objective

The children will practise the new sentence pattern using a substitution table.

Preparation

Write the following substitution table on the blackboard:

Did they start the	RACE GAME LESSON PLAY	before	JON PITA MR. GAU MARIA GALANG	arrived?
go out	FISHING HUNTING SWIMMING DIVING		THE PARENTS	

No, they waited for	HIM HER THEM	to arrive.

Note

Remember to leave this table on the blackboard for next week's revision.

ORAL EXPRESSION

LESSON ONE

Objective
The children will be able to talk about what they want to do when they leave school.

Preparation
Give out *Pupil's Book 2* to each child (page 45).

Method
1 Discuss the skills being taught in the picture on page 45. Why are the students learning these skills?
2 Divide the class into groups.
3 Pupils in each group must tell the others what she would like to do when she leaves school. Children must say why they want to do this, and where they would do it, e.g: I would like to become a community nurse and then return to this area to look after sick people in local villages.

LESSON TWO

Objective
The children will be able to expand a story by using their imagination.

Method
1 Suggest two characters and an event, e.g: a doctor, a child and an accident. Or, a policeman, a thief and a chase.
2 Divide the class into groups. The first child in each group starts a story. The next child continues. Each child should try to make the story exciting, e.g:
1st child: One day a child was sitting by his house with nothing to do . . .
2nd child: Then he saw his father's knife lying by the step.
3rd child: He picked it up and decided to cut some bamboo.
4th child: He was cutting the bamboo when the knife slipped and cut into his leg, etc.

LESSON THREE

Objective
The children will be able to thank guest speakers or visitors to the school.

Method
1 Tell the children that when a person comes to school to give a talk to the class it is good manners to clap hands after he has finished talking and then for someone to thank him for coming and giving the talk.
2 Give an example: Pretend we have just had a visit from our local Medical Orderly who gave a talk about what to do if you or a friend is bitten by a snake. Pita was chosen to say thank you. He would say something like this: 'On behalf of Grade Six, I would like to thank you very much or coming along to our school today to give us your interesting talk. I know we have all learned something from it and we hope you will be able to come again some time.' Everyone claps hands.
3 Children practise similar thank you speeches in groups.

WRITTEN SENTENCES

LESSON ONE (Lesson Suggestion 2)

Objective
The children will be able to write ten good sentences about a picture.

Preparation
Give out *Pupil's Book 2* to each child (page 45, Lesson 1).

Possible Answers
1 ... develop many skills which will be useful in the village.
2 ... baskets and bilums in the traditional style.
3 ... make pots using the coil method.
4 ... how to make large fish traps.
5 ... make a canoe.
6 ... have learned many skills.

LESSON TWO

Objective
The children will be able to answer questions about Vocational Schools and what is learned there.

Preparation
1 Give out *Pupil's Book 2* to each child (page 45, Lesson 2).
2 If there is a Vocational School nearby, arrange a visit there during this week. If not, arrange for someone who has been to one to come and tell the class about it. Otherwise, find out about it from your head teacher so you can discuss it with your class.

Possible Answers
1 It is a school which teaches you skills which you can use in the village.
2 Things like woodwork, traditional arts, sewing, cooking, furniture-making and weaving are taught.
3 Tapa cloth is made from bark from the paper Mulberry tree.
4 The pots are made of clay.
5 (Children's answers.)
6 You could make baskets from coconut palm leaves and cane.
7 They would probably use bamboo and kunda vine.
8 Bilums and string bags are made of bush string.
9 (Any reasonable length of time.)
10 Furniture-making is a modern skill. You could set up a furniture-making business using bush materials like kunda and bamboo.

LESSON THREE (Lesson Suggestion 12)

Objective
The children will be able to change sentences from the past tense to present tense.

Preparation
Give out *Pupil's Book 2* to each child (page 46, Lesson 3).

Answers
2 The boys are making a canoe which they will use for fishing.
3 Some of the village women are teaching the girls how to make bilums.

4 Mr Koipa comes every week to show the boys how to make fish traps.
5 Some of the boys are making furniture for the classrooms.
6 The children are learning to make pots using the coil method.
7 The teacher is showing the girls how to paint colourful designs on the tapa cloth.
8 The boy is using a traditional stone adze to make a drum.
9 Maria is making a colourful design for screen printing.
10 Aileen and Budoia are learning how to beat designs into sheets of copper using nails and small hammers.

LESSON FOUR (Lesson Suggestion 6)

Objective
The children will be able to complete the sentences.

Preparation
Give out *Pupil's Book 2* to each child (page 47, Lesson 4).

Answers
1 Traditional fish nets
2 furniture.
3 bilums.
4 drying plates and saucepans after they are washed.
5 Koipa
6 make bilums
7 they could make their own clothes.
8 they can build them in the village.
9 they are not forgotten.
10 tapa.

LESSON FIVE

Objective
The children will be able to answer questions using known sentence patterns.

Preparation
Give out *Pupil's Book 2* to each child (page 47, Lesson 5).

Answers
1 Yes, she is clever enough to do the difficult exercises.
2 Yes, our team is fast enough to win the race.
3 Yes, those books are small enough to fit on the shelf.
4 Yes, it is strong enough to sit on.
5 Yes, the wood is dry enough to burn easily.
6 Yes, it is shallow enough for us to cross.
7 Yes, it is big enough for all of us.
8 Yes, they are ripe enough for picking.
9 Yes, it is close enough for us to see.
10 Yes, it's cheap enough for me to buy.

WRITTEN COMPOSITION

LESSON ONE (Lesson Suggestion 16A)

Objective
The children will be able to write an imaginative story.

Preparation

Give out *Pupil's Book 2* to each child (page 48, Lesson 1).

Model Answer

The owner of a coffee plantation decided to sell his plantation to a mining company. However, he said that he wanted the money in cash. The company arranged for a truck to carry the money to the place where the man lived. Soon after the truck left Arawa, it turned a sharp corner to find a big log blocking the road. The driver and the armed guard with him got out of the truck and walked over to the log. Just then six men jumped up from behind the log. They screamed at the two men and threw rocks at them. One of the bandits grabbed the driver and made him unlock the door at the back of the truck where the money was kept. One man pointed his gun at the driver while the other bandits quickly unloaded all the money into their own truck.

When they had done this, one of the bandits took the keys from the driver. Then they all climbed into their truck and drove off with the money.

Follow-Up

Read some of the stories to the rest of the class.

LESSON TWO (Lesson Suggestion 17)

Objective

The children will be able to reply to a business lètter.

Preparation

Give out *Pupil's Book 2* to each child (page 48, Lesson 2).

Method

1 Read out some of the letters written last week to the Health Extension Officer.
2 Read the lesson.
3 Discuss the reply, following the plan given. Then ask the children to write the letter.

Model Answer

Bogia Aid Post,
Bogia.

6th June, 19. .

Dear . . . ,

Thank you for your letter offering to help with jobs at the Aid Post. We will be very pleased to have any help which you and your friends can give.

The most urgent jobs that need doing at the moment are weeding the gardens and cutting the grass.

We are short of tools, so please bring grass knives with you.

Is Wednesday afternoon a good time for you to come? We will expect you about one o'clock.

Many thanks,
Your sincerely,
(Mr . . . .)

SPELLING

LESSON ONE (Lesson Suggestion 22)

Objective
The children will learn to spell this week's words.

Preparation
Give out *Pupil's Book 2* to each child (page 48, Spelling List).

LESSON TWO

Select from Exercises A–E.

Preparation
Give out *Pupil's Book 2* to each child (pages 48–9).

Exercise A

Possible Answers
1 You have to buy a ticket to go on the bus.
2 He put his money in his trouser pocket.
3 They picked a basket full of mangoes.
4 They heard the door click as it opened.

Exercise B (Lesson Suggestion 8)

Answers

1 pour, paw	3 whole, hole	5 won, one
2 piece	4 past, passed	

Exercise C (Lesson Suggestion 23)

Answers
RANge SOLDiers giANT cLICK POTter

Exercise D (Lesson Suggestion 9)

Answers
can't shouldn't couldn't isn't wasn't I'm haven't

Exercise E

Answers
diary trial giant diamond

HANDWRITING (Lesson Suggestion 33)

Preparation
Give out *Pupil's Book 2* to each child (page 50).

Note
Write the numbers on the blackboard before class begin the lesson.

READING

INTRODUCTION (Lesson Suggestion 34)

Objective
The children will be able to understand the background to the story, and the meaning of new words. They will read the story silently.

Preparation
Give out *Reader 2* to each child (pages 18–20), *'It's My Life!'* (Part 1).

Method
1 Introduce the story. Discuss traditional and modern cures for illnesses. Should we learn to use modern medical cures or continue to use traditional medicines? Ask the children what they think. Point out that many traditional cures are still of value for some illnesses.
2 Follow Lesson Suggestion 34B.

LESSON ONE (Lesson Suggestion 34C)

Objective
Children will be able to answer questions to show that they understand the story.

Preparation
Give out *Reader 2* (pages 18–20) and *Pupil's Book 2* to each child (page 51, Lesson 1).

Answers
1 Asemo decided to take Garaso to hospital because the witch doctor could not cure her. He thought the doctors at the hospital might be able to.
2 The stretcher was made from two long bamboo poles with a blanket tied between them.
3 Lusi and her family felt nervous at the hospital because they did not know whether to trust the strangers who were looking after their mother.
4 During the week at the hospital, Lusi watched the nurses work, chatted to her mother and bought fruit from the market for her.
5 Hetty advised Asemo to grow corn and green vegetables in his garden as well as sweet potato.
6 'Improved' means got better.
7 Asemo did not want his daughter to leave the village to become a nurse.
8 The correct answer could be either: Yes, he has being fair, as girls should stay on in the village to do their work. Or: No, he was not fair, as Lusi should be given a chance to become a nurse to help her people. If I were her father I would . . .
9 They lived in a small thatched hut in the Highlands. It was quite a long way to the nearest town and the roads were narrow and bumpy.
10 Lotuwa thought it would be a good idea. Namuri frowned, which suggests that he did not agree with the idea.

LESSON TWO

Objective
The children will be able to find out information about postage by understanding how to use a section from the Telephone Directory.

Preparation

Give out *Pupil's Book 2* to each child (page 52, Lesson 2, Exercise A).

Method

1 Read through the lesson carefully with the class. Explain that 'zones' means different areas in the world.
2 Explain how to find out what zone a country is in by looking at the lists of countries. To find out the cost of a letter or parcel, you look at the bottom table and find the right zone.
3 Work out some examples together.

Answers

1 15t	4 25t	7 Japan	10 Zone 5
2 30t	5 K3.00	8 35t	
3 75t	6 letter	9 3t	

LESSON THREE

Objective

The children will be able to read directions on a packet and understand what they mean.

Preparation

Give out *Pupil's Book 2* to each pupil (page 53, Exercise B).

Method

1 Read the directions out loud and discuss the answers with the class before you ask them to write anything.

Answers

1 into the soil
2 after planting
3 tomatoes
4 Use it between each layer of compost material and cover it with soil.
5 Mix it with one part of sulphate of potash.

LESSON FOUR (Lesson Suggestion 39)

Objective

The children will read for enjoyment.

Method

Provide material for children to read for enjoyment.

LESSON FIVE — POETRY (Lesson Suggestion 40)

Preparation

Give out *Pupil's Book 2* to each child (page 54), '*The Seeds*' and '*The Tiny Plant*'.

Answers

1 It is smooth and black and oval in shape.
2 He is a lover of nature.
3 sunshine and rain
4 soil

LISTENING 19

LESSON ONE

Objective
The children will be able to listen carefully to a message and then pass it on to someone else.

Preparation
Write imaginary 'gossip' stones on several slips of paper (suggestions below).

Method
1 This game is called 'Gossip'. Divide the class into groups. Give each group leader a slip of paper with a bit of gossip written on it, e.g: Mr and Mrs Garahu had an argument. He said he drank only a little bit of beer and lots of coconut milk. She said he drank too much beer and the coconut milk was really rum.
2 The leader must read his piece of 'gossip' and then whisper it to the next person in his group. Then that person whispers it to the next person and so on, until it comes back to the leader again. The leader tells everyone what was whispered to him by the last person. Then he opens his paper and reads out what the real 'gossip' said. (You will find that in most cases the 'gossip' will change quite a bit by the time it gets back to the leader.)

LESSON TWO

Objective
The children will be able to listen carefully and follow instructions.

Method
1 Read out each instruction twice, slowly. The children must do what you say.
T: Write the words 'from', 'with' and 'at' on your paper.
T: Write in alphabetical order these words: 'hat', 'red', 'ball'.
T: Draw one small circle inside a larger circle.
T: It is now ten o'clock. What time will it be in one hour and ten minutes?
2 Make sure you read these instructions slowly and clearly. When finished, read out the instructions again and write the answers on the board for the children to mark theirs from.

TALKING

LESSON ONE (Lesson Suggestion 1C)

Objective
The children will practise last week's sentence pattern:
Did they start the game before their friends arrived? No, they waited for them to arrive.

LESSON TWO

Objective
The children will practise a sentence pattern they already know:
He sharpened his pencil *before* he wrote his name.

Method

1 T: I sharpened this pencil *before* I wrote my name. What did you do when you went home last night, Pele? Did you play straight away?
C: No, I did my homework before I went out to play.

2 In groups, children must think of similar examples:
I cleaned my teeth before I came to school.
I ate my breakfast before I came to school.
I washed myself before I came to school.
I lit the fire before I came to school.
I swept the floor before I came to school.
I did my homework before I went to bed.
I washed the plates before I went to bed.
I read a book before I went to bed.
I listened to my father before I went to bed.
I listened to my brother playing the guitar before I went to bed.

LESSON THREE

Objective

The children will be able to use a new sentence pattern:
How long have you been sitting here? We've been sitting here since eight o'clock.

Method

1 T: I started teaching you at 8 o'clock this morning. Now it's 9 o'clock. I'm still teaching you. I've been teaching you since 8 o'clock. How long have I been teaching you?
C: You've been teaching us since 8 o'clock.
T: When did you start sitting at your desks?
C: We started sitting here at 8 o'clock.
T: How long has Kabu been sitting at his desk?
C: He's been sitting there since 8 o'clock.

2 Talk about outside situations:
T: Kunop started doing the washing at 7 o'clock. How long has she been doing the washing?
C: She's been doing the washing since 7 o'clock.

LESSON FOUR

Objective

The children will practise this sentence pattern:
How long have you been sitting there? We've been sitting here since 8 o'clock.

Method

1 Give further examples:
How long has Thomas been cutting the grass? He's been cutting the grass since 10 o'clock.
How long have you been reading that book? I've been reading this book since January.
How long have you been making that canoe? I've been making it since March of last year.
How long has she been teaching? She's been teaching since 1980.

2 Children practise saying these in their groups.

LESSON FIVE (Lesson Suggestion 1C)

Objective
The children will practise the new sentence pattern using a substitition table.

Preparation
Write the following substitution table on the blackboard before the lesson:

	GUAN		SWEEPING THE FLOOR?		
	MANU		PAINTING THE WALLS?		7 O'CLOCK.
	GERA		READING THAT BOOK?		3 O'CLOCK.
	PEGGI		COOKING THE MEAL?		
Hong long has	SALI	been	CLEANING THE HOUSE?	Since	9 O'CLOCK.
	LUKAS		FIXING THE TRUCK?		JANUARY.
	MICHAEL		MAKING THAT DRUM?		ARPIL.
	NAGOSI		LOOKING AFTER HER MOTHER?		APRIL.

Note
Leave this table on the blackboard until next week.

ORAL EXPRESSION

LESSON ONE

Objective
The children will be able to give confident and accurate explanations.

Method
1 Turn to Written Composition Lesson One on page 57 in *Pupil's Book 2*.
2 Choose pupils to talk about one of those topics to the rest of the class.

Note
This lesson should be done before the Written Composition Lesson One.

LESSON TWO

Objective
The children will be able to express their own opinions.

Method
1 Write the following (or similar) topics on the blackboard:
What extra subjects should be taught in school?
What things would you change if you were the Prime Minister of this country?
Should people be allowed to chew betel-nut at work?
2 Choose a chairman and six people to form a panel. Put them at the front of the room so they are facing the class.
3 The chairman reads out one of the questions on the blackboard and asks the panel what they think about it. Each person on the panel should give his own opinion.
4 When each person has given his opinion, the chairman then asks if anyone in the class has a different opinion.
5 The chairman then asks another question.

Note

Explain the need to give *reasons* for your opinion, e.g: I think we should learn First Aid at school *because* then we would be able to treat minor injuries ourselves.

LESSON THREE

Objective

The children will be able to emphasize a point strongly.

Method

1 Last year, the children learned phrases like 'I know', 'I think' and 'definitely'. When people say 'I know' or 'definitely', it means that they are sure about something. When someone says 'I think', it means they are not really sure. Revise this work with the class.

2 Ask children questions about local events and village life. They should reply using the right amount of emphasis depending on whether they are sure or not about the answer they give, e.g:
Q: Who will win the next election?
A: I think Mrs Obi will win.
Q: Which food is better for you, lolly water or milk?
A: Milk is definitely better for you.
Q: Which is the biggest town in Enga?
A: I know that Wabag is the biggest town.

WRITTEN SENTENCES

LESSON ONE (Lesson Suggestion 2)

Objective

The children will be able to write good sentences about a picture.

Preparation

Give out *Pupil's Book 2* to each child (page 55, Lesson 1).

Possible Answers

1 Some boys are diving for crayfish.
2 The fisherman is pulling in his net.
3 The wreckage of a plane lies on the ocean floor.
4 One diver is trying to chase a shark away from his friend.
5 There are lots of fish swimming on the reef.

LESSON TWO

Objective

The children will be able to choose the correct form of a verb to fit in the sentences.

Preparation

Give out *Pupil's Book 2* to each child (page 55, Lesson 2).

Answers

1 diving
2 starting
3 caught
4 shining
5 waiting
6 pulling
7 chased swam
8 were
9 has
10 grows

LESSON THREE (Lesson Suggestion 2)

Objective
The children will be able to answer questions about a picture.

Preparation
Give out *Pupil's Book 2* to each child (page 56, Lesson 3).

Answers
1 They were pulling in their nets because they were full of fish.
2 They were diving for crayfish.
3 The weather is fine but it is raining in the distance.
4 It is not safe to go diving alone in case you get into trouble and no one else is there to help you.
5 One boy is being chased by a shark and he has no spear to protect himself. His friend is chasing away the shark with his spear.
6 An octopus has eight tentacles.
7 Its engine stopped and it crashed into the sea. (Many other answers possible.)
8 A school of fish.

LESSON FOUR (Lesson Suggestion 13D)

Objective
The children will be able to use quotation marks correctly.

Preparation
Give out *Pupil's Book 2* to each child (page 56, Lesson 4).

Method
Remind the children of the correct way to use quotation marks.

Answers
'Well, if they come near me I shall sting them with my tail', said the stingray crossly.
'And if they come near me, I shall grab them with one of my long tentacles', said the octopus. 'They'll never escape from me.'
'Ah, don't worry everyone', sneered the shark. 'They'll take one look at my sharp teeth and then swim off for their lives. Ha! Ha!'
'Well, I'm going to hide under a rock if they come diving for me', said the lobster. 'If they try to catch me I shall nip them on the nose with my claws.'
'Scatter! Scatter! The fishermen are here!' warned the little whitebait, darting through the seaweed.

LESSON FIVE

Objective
The children will be able to answer questions using phrases revised in oral expression.

Preparation
Give out *Pupil's Book 2* to each child (page 57, Lesson 5).

Possible Answers
1 Yes, I think it will rain tomorrow.
2 Yes, I know the shop is shut.
3 Yes, I hope I will be able to come tomorrow.
4 No, I don't know how many people live in my village.

5 No, I don't know why my friends are late today.
6 No, I don't think the teacher has gone home yet.
7 Yes, I hope so.
8 I hope not.
9 I hope not.

WRITTEN COMPOSITION

LESSON ONE (Lesson Suggestion 16A)

Objective
The children will be able to write a composition.

Preparation
Give out *Pupil's Book 2* to each child (page 57, Lesson 1).

Method
1 Discuss the three topics listed. If some of your children have grown up in the town, ask children who have come from villages to tell the others about these topics.

Follow-Up
Read a selection of the children's stories, describing different methods.

LESSON TWO

Objective
The children will be able to write an imaginative story.

Preparation
Give out *Pupil's Book 2* to each child (page 57, Lesson 2).

Method
1 Read through the lesson with the children.
2 You could dramatize the crash to make it more exciting. Read through the list of words and use these in sentences about the crash, e.g: Suddenly there was a *frightening roar* from the engine, followed by a loud *explosion*. The *worried* pilot looked out the window to see the engine on fire.

SPELLING

LESSON ONE (Lesson Suggestion 22)

Objective
The children will learn to spell this week's words.

Preparation
Give out *Pupil's Book 2* to each child (page 58, Spelling List).

LESSON TWO

Select from Exercises A–E.

Preparation
Give out *Pupil's Book 2* to each child (pages 58–9).

Exercise A (Lesson Suggestion 29)

Answers

1 advice	3 admit	5 about
2 admired	4 shout	

Exercise B

Answers
1 To have a high opinion of someone
2 An opinion about the best way to do something
3 To confess
4 Where you live

Exercise C (Lesson Suggestion 30)

Answers

1 encouragement	3 useless	5 arrangements
2 enjoyable	4 lonely	

Exercise D (Lesson Suggestion 30)

Answers
(Many answers are possible.)
repeat remind relief retire release reply
previous pretend prepare prefix prefer
depend decide demand deliver depart
discover disturb distance distress
restore reserve rescue respect respond

Exercise E (Lesson Suggestion 26)

Possible Answers
– paint – trail – light – trout – tools – stand – diary – years – sleep –

HANDWRITING (Lesson Suggestion 33)

Preparation
Give out *Pupil's Book 2* to each child (page 60).

Note
Remind children to set out the letter heading exactly as shown in the example.

READING

INTRODUCTION (Lesson Suggestion 34)

Objective
The children will understand background to the story, and the meaning of new words. They will read the story silently.

Preparation

Give out *Pupil's Book 2* to each child (pages 21–2). *'It's My Life!'* (Part 2).

Method

1 Introduce the story. Remind children about Part 1 of this story. Do they think Lusi will become a nurse? Should she go against her father's wishes. What would they do in her place?
2 Follow Lesson Suggestion 34B.

LESSON ONE (Lesson Suggestion 34C)

Objective

Children will be able to answer questions to show that they understand the story.

Preparation

Give out *Pupil's Book 2* to each child (page 61, Lesson 1) and *Reader 2* (pages 21–2).

Answers

1 Namuri said that Lusi would have to stay to work in the garden and carry all the firewood because their mother wasn't strong enough. He was also worried that they might not get a bride price for her if she married some one from another clan.
2 Namuri was very angry when his sister suggested that he carry the firewood, because he thought that was woman's work. He might do it later if there was no one else.
3 Asemo was worried that if Lusi went away she would forget about the village and the traditions of their people.
4 (Personal opinion) e.g: Yes, Lusi was right to train as a nurse, so that she could return to her village and help the sick people there.
5 Lusi stayed at a nurses' hostel.
6 In their spare time, the nurses had to go to school and learn about the human body and the diseases which attacked it.
Lusi had to learn English so she could understand the lessons.
7 Some work was dirty, often sad and always tiring. She hated seeing people suffer and worried about babies who were not properly looked after by their mothers.
8 Garoso was probably thinking that she had given her opinion, now it was up to Asemo to decide what his daughter should do. Namuri was hoping that Lusi would have to stay in the village. Lotuwa was hoping that father would say that Lusi could go.
9 Garoso smiles about what Asemo says because it is not completely truthful.
10 interrupted patients protect

LESSON THREE

Objective

The children will be able to answer questions about a story.

Preparation

Give out *Pupil's Book 2* to each child (page 62, Lesson 2, Exercise A).

Answers

A approximately — about
looking — searching
make — build

gathering — collecting
on the move — travelling

B1 Someone who travels from place to place looking for food
2 Because they prefer to travel around
3 The cassowary
4 The crocodile
5 The women gather things to eat.

LESSON FOUR

Objective
The children will be able to answer questions about a passage.

Preparation
Give out *Pupil's Book 2* to each child (page 62, Exercise B).

Answers
1 He has a damp, cold nose if he is healthy.
2 He wags his tail when he is happy.
3 Some can be trained to help the Police. Huskies pull sleds for eskimoes. They also help man hunt animals.
4 In Canada
5 If a dog is unhappy, he drops his tail between his legs.

LESSON FIVE

Objective
The children will be able to read for pleasure.

Preparation
Give out *Supplementary Reader 2* to each child.

OR POETRY (Lesson Suggestion 40)

Preparation
Give out *Pupil's Book 2* to each child (page 63).

Answers
1 They go fishing in the morning.
2 The sea is very calm.
3 The dolphins usually jump out of the water when they say this chant.
4 (Personal opinion)

LESSON SIX

Objective
The children will be able to do Reading Games.

Preparation
Give out *Reading Games for Grade 6* to each child (page 45–8, Unit 9).

Method
1 Choose games for the children to play.
2 Mark their work using *Teacher's Notes* (pages 55–7).

LISTENING 20

LESSON ONE

Objective
The children will listen carefully to hear the correct word.

Preparation
Write these words on the blackboard before the lesson. Set them out like this, in three columns.

1 coast	cost	toast	5 his	is	its
2 cheap	sheep	seep	6 attend	entered	attended
3 thought	taught	fought	7 show	saw	shore
4 heard	head	hair	8 close	class	grass

Method
1 Call out the number and then say one of the three words, e.g: Number 1 toast.
2 The children must write down the word you have said.
3 Go through all the numbers, calling out one word from each. When you have finished, spell out the correct answers. Children can mark their own work.

Note
If you have room on your blackboard, leave this work here for the next Listening Lesson 2.

LESSON TWO

Objective
The children will listen carefully to hear the correct word.

Preparation
Use the same blackboard work as for Lesson 1.

Method
1 Tell the class that you are going to use a word from each line in a sentence. They must write down the word you say on a piece of paper, e.g:
Number 1: My new shoes cost K32.
Answer: cost
2 After each sentence, choose someone to give his answer. Discuss whether it is right. Children mark their own work.

TALKING

LESSON ONE (Lesson Suggestion 1C)

Objective
The children will practise last week's sentence pattern:
How long have you been sitting there? We've been sitting here since 8 o'clock.

LESSON TWO

Objective

The children will practise a sentence pattern they already know:
How long has he been standing? He's been standing for five minutes.

Method

1 Give examples:
How long has she been saying her tables? She's been saying her tables for five minutes.
How long have you been sitting there? I've been sitting here for ten minutes.
How long have you been listening to the radio? We've been listening to the radio for an hour.
How long have you been playing this game? We've been playing this game for half an hour.

2 Ask the children to make up other examples.

LESSON THREE

Objective

The children will be able to use a new sentence pattern:
Are you sure they will come? Yes, I know they will come.

Method

1 T: I know I'll go home after school. (This means that I am sure that this will happen.)
T: Will it get dark tonight?
C: Yes, it will.
T: Are you sure?
C: Yes, you know it will get dark tonight.
T: Yes, I know it will.
T: Will the sun rise tomorrow morning?
C: Yes, it will.
T: Are you sure it will?
C: Yes, I know it will.

2 Children practise this pattern in groups.

LESSON FOUR

Objective

The children will be able to use the negative form of this sentence pattern:
Are you sure they won't come? Yes, I know they won't.

Method

1 T: Will the sun shine at 12 o'clock tonight?
C: No, it won't. I know it won't.
T: Are you sure it won't?
C: Yes, we know it won't.
T: Will the women go to the gardens at 4 o'clock tomorrow morning?
C: No, they won't.
T: Are you sure they won't?
C: Yes, we know they won't.

2 In groups, children will practise other examples:
Will it snow tomorrow?
Will we all go to the moon tomorrow?
Will we all run 100 kilometres tomorrow?

Will the village dogs attack us today?
Will the pigs all die tonight?
Will we all still be at this school in another ten years?

LESSON FIVE (Lesson Suggestion 1C)

Objective
The children will practise the new sentence pattern using a substitution table.

Preparation
Write the following table on the blackboard before starting the lesson:

Are you sure	THEY	will come	TO STAY?
	HE		GO HOME?
	SHE		HELP US?
	WE		BE ALLOWED?
			WIN THE GAME?
			RUN THE RACE?

Yes, I know	THEY	will	COME.
	HE		GO HOME.
	SHE		HELP US.
	WE		BE ALLOWED.
			WIN.
			RUN.

Are you sure	THEY	won't	SEE	us?	Yes, I know	THEY	won't
	HE		BEAT			HE	
	SHE		FIGHT			SHE	
			SHOOT				

ORAL EXPRESSION

LESSON ONE

Objective
The children will be able to talk about a picture.

Method
1 Turn to the picture on page 64 in *Pupil's Book 2*. Ask: How is this village different from yours? Is it similar to yours?
2 Then ask: How could your village be improved? Encourage children to give their own ideas. If they cannot think of their own ideas, turn back to pages 6–7 which give ideas for keeping the village clean. Encourage them to think of other ideas, e.g: forming co-operatives; buying a village truck; building a special community house; making a playing field for village children, etc.

LESSON TWO

Objective
The children will be able to give directions on how to reach a certain place.

Preparation
Copy the picture on page 68 in *Pupil's Book 2* onto the blackboard before this lesson.

Method

1 Choose one child to tell another how to reach one of the houses, e.g: Kabum, pretend you are at Heni's house. Tell Hana how you would go from there to get to Guba's house.
2 Hana must follow Kabum's directions, using a stick to point to the map on the blackboard.

LESSON THREE

Objective

The children will be able to ask questions to find out information.

Method

1 Most children will already know how to play the game 'I Spy'. A child starts by saying: I spy with my little eye, something starting with 'g'. Instead of the rest of the class just guessing, they must ask questions like: Is it outside? Is it large? Is it something you eat? The child must answer 'yes' or 'no' to these questions, until someone guesses the correct word. Then she has a turn.
2 If no one can guess the right word, the teacher can ask the child to give a clue, e.g: it's something we use in the garden.

WRITTEN SENTENCES

LESSON ONE (Lesson Suggestion 2)

Objective

The children will be able to write good sentences about a picture.

Preparation

Give out *Pupil's Book 2* to each child (page 64, Lesson 1).

Possible Answers

1 The village men are busily mending the holes in their fishing nets.
2 The truck was delivered some building materials for Rama's new house.
3 The children are on the beach collecting pretty shells to sell to tourists.
4 The small children are playing with a ball from the tradestore.
5 Some women are weeding their small gardens.

LESSON TWO

Objective

The children will be able to think of suitable words to put in sentences.

Preparation

Give out *Pupil's Book 2* to each child (page 64, Lesson 2).

Answers

1 working	4 selling	7 helping, make	10 digging, looking/ searching
2 mending/fixing	5 sweepng	8 collecting	
3 playing	6 helping, build	9 carrying	

LESSON THREE (Lesson Suggestion 6)

Objective
The children will be able to complete sentences.

Preparation
Give out *Pupil's Book 2* to each child (page 65, Lesson 3).

Possible Answers
1 ... to dig up vegetables for dinner.
2 ... in the centre of the village.
3 ... after she cleaned her house.
4 ... by climbing up the palm and throwing them down to the ground.
5 ... to take to the market to sell.
6 ... dry wood ...
7 ... outside her house.
8 ... because Rama needed wood for his house.

LESSON FOUR (Lesson Suggestion 1)

Objective
The children will be able to answer questions using known sentence patterns.

Preparation
Give out *Pupil's Book 2* to each child (page 65, Lesson 4).

Method
Read the example. Explain that the children have to make up a description for the person in each sentence.

Answers
1 The boy with the spear is going fishing.
2 The girl with the new dress is getting married tomorrow.
3 The men with the tools are helping to build the church.
4 The girl with the books goes to the Vocational Centre.
5 That child with red hair got lost in the bush.
6 I gave the spear to the oldest boy.
7 I gave the axe to the man with the long beard.
8 I gave the basket to the woman wearing the red dress.
9 I gave the football to the child with long hair.
10 I gave the dress to the girl who was very sick.

LESSON FIVE

Objective
The children will be able to write a diary.

Preparation
Give out *Pupil's Book 2* to each child (page 66, Lesson 5).

Method
1 Read the sample diary to the children.
2 Talk about what the children did last week.
3 Ask them to write a diary telling what they did last week. Tell them to set it out as in the sample diary.

Follow-Up
Collect children's work to be marked.

WRITTEN COMPOSITION

LESSON ONE

Objective
The children will be able to give their own opinion about something.

Preparation
Give out *Pupil's Book 2* to each child (page 67, Lesson 1).

Method
1 Read the introduction and study the illustrations.
2 Hold a brief discussion about the advantages and disadvantages of having a four day school week.
3 Tell children to write down their opinion. (Remind them to use words like 'I think' and 'I believe' when giving their opinions.)

LESSON TWO

Objective
The children will be able to follow written directions.

Preparation
Give out *Pupil's Book 2* to each child (page 68, Lesson 2).

Method
1 Study the picture.
2 Work out the answer to the first question with the children.
3 Then ask the children to write answers to the other questions.

Answers
1 Kika's house
2 Guba's house
3 Sisia's house is by the bend in the river near Pipi's house and behind Heni's house.
4 Go down the hill past Kika's house. Cross the bridge and then go straight past Pipi's house. Carry on and you will find Heni's house by the coconut palms.
5 Walk down hill to the river. Cross the river to Heni's house in the canoe. Then walk past the coconut palms to Kore's house.

SPELLING

LESSONE ONE (Lesson Suggestion 22)

Objective
The children will be able to spell this week's words.

Preparation
Give out *Pupil's Book 2* to each child (page 68, Spelling List).

LESSON TWO

Select from Exercises A–E, or give a spelling and dictation test on the last month's spelling work.

Preparation
Give out *Pupil's Book 2* to each child (pages 68–70).

Exercise A (Lesson Suggestion 29)

Answers
1 please
2 team
3 stream
4 peanut
5 breed

Exercise B (Lesson Suggestion 23)

Possible Answers
took look brook crook hook cook stood
ill hill fill fall wall pill kill mill still pull tall

Exercise C (Lesson Suggestion 32d)

Answers
noisily – The children ran inside noisily.
sleepily – Harry yawned sleepily.
luckily – Luckily the window was open and Tom could climb out.
angrily – Father shouted angrily at me.
hungrily – The child ate her dinner hungrily.
easily – Ben was able to lift the log off the road quite easily.

Exercise D

Answers
ninety thirty one thousand thirteen twelve eleven

Exercise E (Lesson Suggestion 31)

Answers

Clues across:
1 cold
3 won
6 ordinary

Clues down:
1 crowd
2 do
4 ant
5 school
7 nine

HANDWRITING (Lesson Suggestion 33)

Preparation
Give out *Pupil's Book 2* to each child (pages 20–1).

READING

INTRODUCTION (Lesson Suggestion 34)

Objective
The children will understand the background to the story, and the meaning of new words. They will read the story silently.

Preparation
Give out *Reader 2* to each child (pages 23–6), *'The Boar-Killer'*.

Method
1 Introduce the story. Discuss hunting wild boar. Ask if any of the boys have hunted for boar with their fathers. Ask them to tell the class about it. What weapon was used to kill the boar? How did they get it home?
2 Follow Lesson Suggestion 34B.

LESSON ONE (Lesson Suggestion 34C)

Objective
Children will be able to answer questions to show that they understand the story.

Preparation
Give out *Reader 2* (pages 23–6) and *Pupil's Book 2* to each child (page 71, Lesson 1).

Answers
1 They moved to get away from the fierce boar that lived near the village and killed the villagers.
2 She crept into a secret cave and lived there.
3 At night when the boar was asleep, she went out into the gardens to collect food.
4 The 'cruel enemy' is the fierce boar.
5 It was part of his plan to kill the boar.
6 The boar followed his shadow, which fell on the ground beside the platform.
7 They made him their leader because he was wise and clever enough to kill the huge boar.
8 rushed, fled, raced
waded
crept
9 We met Uncle Ranu in town by accident, on a day when we didn't expect to see him there.
He tried to grab hold of the vine, but it was out of reach.
10 (Personal opinion) e.g: I would go straight back to the place where my house and gardens were and start rebuilding.

LESSON TWO

Objective
The children will be able to answer questions about a story.

Preparation
Give out *Pupil's Book 2* to each child (page 72, Lesson 2, Exercise A).

Answers
1 gloomy
2 swooped
3 the noise of the bats swooping around; a cough
4 cautiously
5 astonishment

LESSON THREE

Objective
The children will be able to find out a bit about a book by studying the Table of Contents.

Preparation
Give out *Pupil's Book 2* to each child (page 72, Exercise B). Show children some books with a Table of Contents in the front.

Answers
1 Chapters 1, 3, 4, 5
2 Papua New Guinea
3 Chapters 6, 7, 8, 9, 10
4 Chapter 2
5 Chapter 4
6 Chapter 3
7 Plane, car or truck, boat or trading vessel
8 flight, driving
9 Hanuabada
10 Chapter 5 (or personal choice)
Title: A Journey through Papua New Guinea

LESSON FOUR (Lesson Suggestion 39)

Objective
The children will be able to read for enjoyment.

Method
1 Give children a wide range of reading material. Allow them to choose.

OR POETRY (Lesson Suggestion 40)

Preparation
Give out *Pupil's Book 2* to each child (page 73), '*The Highlands Highway*'.

Answers
1 tea, coffee, pyrethrum
2 coconuts, fish, betel-nut, lime (i.e: not found in the Highlands)
3 It is more expensive to transport goods by plane.
4 cabbages, sweet corn, carrots, taro, pineapples. These things grow well in the cool Highlands climate. It is too cold to grow pineapples or coconuts there. Fish are caught on the coast.

LESSON FIVE

Objective
The children will be able to play Reading Games.

Preparation
Give out *Reading Games for Grade 6* (pages 48–51, Unit 20).

Method
1 Choose games for the children to play.
2 Mark this work from *Teacher's Notes* (pages 57–9).

TERM THREE

UNITS OF WEEKLY WORK: LISTENING

Unit 21
1 Choosing the word that doesn't belong (Meaning)
2 Choosing the word that doesn't belong (Spelling)

Unit 22
1 Distinguishing between fact and opinion
2 Choosing the word that doesn't belong (Meaning or Spelling)

Unit 23
1 Telling whether a phrase means 'who', 'when' or 'why'
2 Detecting wrong details

Unit 24
1 Finding wrong details in a story
2 Drawing conclusions about a story

Unit 25
1 Listening to hear the correct word
2 Listening to hear the correct word in a sentence

Unit 26
1 Deciding whether something is true or false
2 Deciding whether a story is true or make-believe

Unit 27
1 Listening to obtain information
2 Recognizing sentences and phrases

Unit 28
1 Listening to follow directions
2 'Hearing' the words that don't rhyme

Unit 29
1 Identifying the speaker without looking at him
2 Remembering people by their number

Unit 30
1 Recognizing vowel sounds
2 'Hearing' the correct word

UNITS OF WEEKLY WORK: TALKING

Unit 21
Revision of last week's work
Revision: I know what he said. I know where he hid the money.
New sentence pattern: Do you know who it is? Yes, I know who it is. No, I don't know who it is.

Unit 22
Revision of last week's work
Revision: I know who built this school. Do you know who built this school?
New sentence pattern: Do you think it will rain tomorrow? Yes, I think it will. No, I don't think it will.

Unit 23
Revision of last week's work
Revision: Will you go fishing on Tuesday? No, I won't go fishing on Tuesday.
New sentence pattern: Do you think he'll win the race? I don't know. I hope so. I hope not.

Unit 24
Revision of last week's work
Revision: While Bato was cleaning the board, Foru was sweeping the room.
New sentence pattern: He's going to sweep the floor.

Unit 25
Revision of last week's work
Revision: We've been here since eight o'clock.
New sentence pattern: Do you think it's going to rain. Yes, I do. No, I don't.

Unit 26
Revision of last week's work
Revision: He has opened the door.
New sentence pattern: A large, deadly spider is under the table.

Unit 27 Revision of last week's work
Revision: I can't lock the door. She's already locked it.
New sentence pattern: Which box is empty? The box on the table is empty.

Unit 28 Revision of last week's work
Revision: Have you ever been to Rabaul? No, I've never been to Rabaul.
New sentence pattern: Take this to the old man in the tradestore. Which old man? The old man with the beard.

Unit 29 Revision of last week's work
Revision: Have you tidied your desks yet? We haven't tidied our desks yet.
New sentence pattern: Which boy is ill? The one who's holding his stomach.

Unit 30 Revision of last week's work
Revision: Have you finished writing? No, I'm still writing.
New sentence pattern: Who is he? He's the man I saw yesterday.
Revision

UNITS OF WEEKLY WORK: ORAL EXPRESSION

Unit 21
1 Talking about a picture (In the Town)
2 Comparing two pictures
3 Giving descriptions

Unit 22
1 Talking about a picture (The Airport)
2 Describing a journey
3 Solving a problem

Unit 23
1 Giving accurate instructions
2 Making up an interesting story
3 Telling the time

Unit 24
1 Talking about a picture (The Gumi Race)
2 Re-telling a story
3 Preparing talks

Unit 25
Talking about a picture (Preparing a Mumu)
2 Giving instructions (using sequence signals)
3 Giving a prepared talk

Unit 26
1 Asking questions to find out information
2 Thinking carefully about a picture
3 Giving a description

Unit 27
1 Making contrasts
2 Giving directions
3 Giving instructions

Unit 28
1 Word association game
2 Making polite requests
3 Greeting one another politely and ending a conversation

Unit 29
1 Introducing people to one another
2 Making apologies
3 Forming and expressing personal opinions

Unit 30
1 Remembering a list of things in the right order
2 Discussing a set of pictures
3 Using your imagination to tell a story

UNITS OF WEEKLY WORK: WRITTEN SENTENCES

Unit 21 1 Writing sentences about a picture
2 Choosing the correct form of a verb
3 Using apostrophes
4 Answering questions about a picture
5 Answering questions

Unit 22 1 Writing sentences about a picture
2 Changing from plural to singular
3 Answering questions
4 Writing sentences
5 Descriptions

Unit 23 1 Writing sentences about a picture
2 Choosing the correct word (their/there)
3 Punctuation
4 Apostrophes
5 Answering questions

Unit 24 1 Writing sentences about a picture
2 Choosing the correct word
3 Joining sentences
4 Answering questions
5 Answering questions

Unit 25 1 Writing sentences about a picture
2 Choosing the best word
3 Using words in sentences
4 Complete the answers

Unit 26 1 Writing sentences about a picture
2 Joining sentences
3 Drawing conclusions from a picture
4 Writing answers to questions
5 Writing sentences

Unit 27 1 Writing sentences about a picture
2 Finishing sentences
3 Listing reasons
4 Using exclamation marks
5 Choosing the correct form of the verb
6 Using commas

Unit 28 1 Writing good sentences about a picture
2 Changing from singular to plural
3 Taking the main points to make a telegram
4 Answering questions
5 Using 'more' and 'most' correctly

Unit 29 1 Writing sentences about a picture
2 Using correct punctuation
3 Quotation marks
4 Answering questions
5 Choosing the best adverb

Unit 30 1 Writing sentences about a picture
2 Changing direct speech into reported speech
3 Ex A Choosing the correct word
Ex B Writing sentences about pictures
4 Match sentence beginnings with sentence endings
5 Answering questions
6 Joining sentences using 'unless'

UNITS OF WEEKLY WORK: WRITTEN COMPOSITION

Unit 21 1 Listing errors in a picture
2 Writing about a legend

Unit 22 1 Writing a story about a journey
2 Writing a personal letter

Unit 23 1 Expanding notes to make a story
2 Solving a problem

Unit 24 1 Writing a story
2 Writing a legend

Unit 25 1 Writing a story about old ways
2 Writing a story about how food is prepared

Unit 26 1 Writing a business letter
2 Writing a story

Unit 27 1 Finding the solution to a problem
2 Taking notes

Unit 28 1 Writing down the main points of a passage
2 Elaborating from notes

Unit 29 1 Writing an imaginative story
2 Writing a report

Unit 30 1 Listing the main points of a story
2 Writing a story from notes

UNITS OF WEEKLY WORK: SPELLING

Unit 21 borrow sorrow tomorrow correct ('rr' group)
remind bind blind unkind ('ind' group)
Family Group: The Town
Spelling Exercises A–E

Unit 22 through threw thread threat ('thr' group)
throat thought thief thumb ('th' group)
Family Group: Airport
Spelling Exercises A–E

Unit 23 frown drown clown brown ('ow' group)
arrow hollow pillow swallow ('ow' group)
Family Group: The Agricultural Station
Spelling Exercises A–E

Unit 24 meal squeal steal real ('ea' group)
hour around loud mountain ('ou' group)
Family Group: The Gumi Race
Spelling Exercises A–E

Unit 25 shine mine line fine ('ine' group)
talk stalk walk chalk ('alk' group)
Family Group: The Mumu
Spelling Exercises A–E or Spelling and Dictation Test

Unit 26 attach attack attempt attention ('att' group)
continent continue control contest ('con' group)
Family Group: The Market
Spelling Exercises A–D

Unit 27 bruised struggled nearby ashore
prefers moment crow fireplace (From Reader)
Family Group: At the River
Spelling Exercises A–E

Unit 28 cyclone sway cautiously steel
shriek scrape overflow upright (From Reader)
Family Group: In the Gardens
Spelling Exercises A–E

Unit 29 firewood generation culture serious
skills moist winked normal (From Reader)
Family Group: Pottery
Spelling Exercises A–D

Unit 30 desperate sensible object thorn
luggage attention packages material (From Reader)
Family Group: Tapa
Spelling Exercises A–E or Spelling and Dictation Test

UNITS OF WEEKLY WORK: HANDWRITING

Unit 21 Practise letter combinations 'tt' and 'bs'
Copy model passage about Lighting Fires.

Unit 22 Practise letter combinations 'in' and 'vy'
Copy model passage about the Cassowary.

Unit 23 Practise letter combinations 'ng' and 'mp'
Copy model passage about the Snake

Unit 24 Practise letter combinations 'ch' and 'ew'
Copy model passage about Sago.

Unit 25 Practise letter combinations 'kn' and 'rs'
Copy model passage.

Unit 26 Practise letter combinations 'go' and 'ha'
Copy model passage about Buffalo.

Unit 27 Copy model passage about the Sepik River.

Unit 28 Copy model passage about the Highland Drought.

Unit 29 Copy model passage using direct speech.

Unit 30 Copy model passage about Fijian Fire-walkers.

UNITS OF WEEKLY WORK: READING

Unit 21
1 Reader: '*Freda in Sydney*'
2 Comprehension
3 Reading exercise – Comprehension
4 Reading exercise – Choosing the correct answer
5 Reading Games
6 Reading for enjoyment or Poetry

Unit 22
1 Reader: '*The Rescuers*' (Part 1)
2 Comprehension
3 Reading exercise – Comprehension
4 Reading exercise – Table of Contents
5 Supplementary Reader or Poetry
6 Reading Games

Unit 23
1 Reader: '*The Rescuers*' (Part 2)
2 Comprehension
3 Reading exercise – Comprehension
4 Reading exercise – Writing conclusions
5 Supplementary Reader 2 or Poetry
6 Reading Games

Unit 24 1 Reader: '*The Good Companions*' (Part 1)
2 Comprehension
3 Reading exercise — Comprehension
4 Poetry
5 Reading for enjoyment
6 Reading Games

Unit 25 1 Reader: '*The Good Companions*' (Part 2)
2 Comprehension
3 Reading exercise — Matching sentences with pictures
4 Reading exercise — Comprehension
5 Supplementary Reader 2 or Poetry
6 Reading Games

Unit 26 1 Reader: '*The Talking Bananas*'
2 Comprehension
3 Reading exercise — Comprehension
4 Reading exercise
5 Supplementary Reader 2 or Poetry
6 Reading Games

Unit 27 1 Reader: '*The Frog's Husband*'
2 Comprehension
3 Reading Exercise Following Directions
4 Arranging sequence pictures in correct order
5 Supplementary Reader or Poetry
6 Reading Games

Unit 28 1 Reader: '*Cyclone Hannah*'
2 Comprehension
3 Choosing the correct answers
4 Writing down the main points
5 Reading for enjoyment or Poetry
6 Reading Games

Unit 29 1 Reader: '*Maratsaip*'
2 Comprehension
3 Understanding abbreviations
4 Finding irrelevant sentences
5 Choosing the correct word or Poetry
6 Reading Games

Unit 30 1 Reader: '*The Red Suitcase*'
2 Comprehension
3 Skimming to find main points
4 Telling fact from opinion
5 Supplementary Readers
6 Reading Games

LISTENING 21

LESSON ONE (Lesson Suggestion 3)

Objective
The children will be able to select the word that does not belong.

Preparation
Write some lists of things on the board, e.g:
1 taro yam kaukau *cabbage* (not a root crop)
2 bilum suitcase paper bag *tapa cloth* (not a bag)
3 taxi PMV *boat* truck (not road transport)
4 snake crocodile lizard *possum* (not a reptile)

Method
1 The children must decide which word does not belong to the rest of the group and write it down. They must be able to say *why* it does not belong. (Use examples which the children know and understand.)
2 In groups, the leader must think of four things. One must be out of place. Someone in the group must say which word does not belong and be able to tell the leader why it doesn't belong. Then that person must think up a list.

LESSON TWO (Lesson Suggestion 3)

Objective
The children will be able to select the word that does not belong because of its *spelling*.

Preparation
Write these words on the blackboard: (Note: the underlined words are to show the *Teacher* which is the different word. Do not underline them when you write them down.)
ticket pocket <u>thread</u> picked (not a 'ck' word)
advice admire admit <u>shout</u> (not an 'ad' word)
<u>freeze</u> remind bind unkind (not an 'ind' word)
<u>faint</u> ground found sound (not an 'ound' word)
giant trial diary <u>growl</u> (not an 'ia' word)
condition <u>diamond</u> relation station (not an 'ion' word)

Method
Tell the children to study these words carefully. Three of the words are similar but one is different. They must write down the word that does not belong, e.g: *ground, found* and *sound* all end in 'ound' therefore *faint* is the word that doesn't belong.

TALKING

LESSON ONE (Lesson Suggestion 1C)

Objective
The children will practise the sentence pattern they learned in Week 20, Term 2.
Are you sure they will come? Yes, I know they will, come.

Method
Write the substitution table from Week 20, Term 2, on the board, and revise it with the children.

LESSON TWO

Objective
The children will practise a sentence pattern they already know:
I know what he said. I know where he hid the money.

Method
1 Explain that when you are very certain about something you use the word 'know'.
2 T: I heard what Tau said about the plan. I *know* what he said.
Give someone a piece of chalk and tell him to hide it somewhere.
T: Who knows where Kila hid the chalk?
C: I know where he hid it!
T: Does everyone know where he hid it?
C: Yes, we know where he hid it.
3 In groups, children practise this pattern.

LESSON THREE (Lesson Suggestion 1B)

Objective
The children will be able to use a new sentence pattern:
Do you know who it is? Yes, I know who it is. No, I don't know who it is.

Method
1 Show pictures of people or things.
T: Do you know who this is?
C: Yes, we know who it is. It's the Prime Minister.
T: Do you know who this is?
C: No, we don't know who it is.
T: It's Prince Charles.
T: Do you know where this man comes from?
C: Yes, he comes from the Trobriand Islands.
T: Do you know where this man comes from?
C: No, we don't.
T: Where do you think he might come from?
C: I think he might come from China.
T: What do you think might be in this parcel?
C: I think it might be a book.
T: I know it is a book, because I wrapped it up.

Note
Tell the children to use 'think' if they are not sure about something.

LESSON FOUR

Objective
The children will practise this sentence pattern:
Do you know who it is? Yes, I know who it is. No, I don't know who it is.

Method
1 Give each group leader a picture magazine. The leader must point to the pictures inside the magazine and ask the rest of the group: 'Do you know

who this is?' or 'Do you know what this is' (or a similar question starting with 'Do you know . . .') The other children must answer.

2 Walk around the room listening to each group to make sure they are saying the sentence pattern correctly.

LESSON FIVE (Lesson Suggestion 1C)

Objective
The children will practise the new sentence pattern using a substitution table.

Preparation
Write the following substitution table on the blackboard:

Do you know	WHO	this is?	Yes, I know	WHO IT IS.
			No, I don't know	WHO IT IS.
	WHAT			WHAT
	HOW THIS WORKS?			HOW IT WORKS
	WHAT TIME IT IS?			WHAT TIME IT IS
	WHERE HE WENT?			WHERE HE WENT
	HOW MUCH IT COSTS?			HOW MUCH IT COSTS
	WHERE IT IS?			WHERE IT IS
	WHY SHE'S SICK?			WHY SHE'S SICK

Who do you think	TOOK IT?	I think	SAMI TOOK IT.
	SAW THEM.		JILL SAW THEM
	BOUGHT IT?		KALA BOUGHT IT
	ATE IT?		ATE IT
	STOLE IT?		STOLE IT

Note
Remember to leave this substitution table on the blackboard.

ORAL EXPRESSION

LESSON ONE

Objective
The children will be able to talk about a picture.

Method
1 Study the picture on page 75 in *Pupil's Book 2*.
2 Ask if anyone in the class has been to a town like the one in the picture. Explain everything in the picture for those children who have not been to a town, e.g: why people must use footpaths.
3 Ask children who have been to a town to tell the others about it. How did they feel with so much traffic around them?

LESSON TWO

Objective
The children will be able to see differences in two similar pictures.

Method
1 Look at the picture on page 78 in *Pupil's Book 2*.

2 Ask how this picture is different from the one on page 75. Explain that this picture has been changed to show what mustn't be done in a city.
3 Ask the children to tell you all the things that are wrong in this picture and say *why* they are wrong.

Note
City children will have no difficulty with this exercise. If you fully explained the picture in Lesson One to rural children, then they should also be able to spot the mistakes. It is important that rural children are aware of dangers in the city. They should have some knowledge of traffic laws and rules that apply in a town so they are prepared if they visit one.

LESSON THREE

Objective
The children will be able to give descriptions.

Preparation
Give out *Pupil's Book 2* to each child (page 80, Exercise D).

Method
1 Read out the riddles in this exercise and ask children for the answers.
2 Now tell them to turn to the Spelling and Family Lists on page 79. Tell children to choose a word from here and give clues like in Exercise D so the rest of the class can guess which word it is, e.g:
I start with 'b' and rhyme with 'kind'. I cannot see. Answer: Blind.
I have two words. I am a place where cars and trucks must visit or they will not go. Answer: Petrol Station.

WRITTEN SENTENCES

LESSON ONE (Lesson Suggestion 2)

Objective
The children will be able to write good sentences about a picture.

Preparation
Give out *Pupil's Book 2* to each child (page 75, Lesson 2).

Note
This picture was discussed during Oral Expression Lesson One, so children should be able to write about it.

Possible Answers
1 The policeman is stopping the traffic so the people can cross the road.
2 The bus driver is fixing a flat tyre.
3 A PMV truck is filling up with petrol at the Petrol Station.
4 Many children are lining up to go the the pictures.

LESSON TWO (Lesson Suggestion 7)

Objective
The children will be able to write the correct form of the verb to fit in the sentences.

Preparation
Give out *Pupil's Book 2* to each child (page 75, Lesson 2).

Answers

1 crossed	3 waiting	5 parked	7 going, broken
2 selling	4 directing	6 going	8 advertises, sticking

LESSON THREE (Lesson Suggestion 9)

Objective
The children will be able to put apostrophes in the correct places.

Preparation
Give out *Pupil's Book 2* to each child (page 76, Lesson 3).

Answers

1 old man's carved table	5 bus's tyre
2 police car's siren	6 officer's helmet
3 child's ice-cream	7 town's roads
4 shop's windows	8 taxi's sign

LESSON FOUR (Lesson Suggestion 2)

Objective
The children will be able to answer questions about a picture.

Preparation
Give out *Pupil's Book 2* to each child (page 76, Lesson 4).

Possible Answers
1 The policeman is directing the traffic.
2 A pedestrian crossing is a place where people are allowed to cross the road.
3 No, it is not safe for people to walk in the road (unless they are on a pedestrian crossing) because a car might hit them.
4 All vehicles must keep to the left side of the road so that they do not bump into each other.
5 The people are waiting in line to buy tickets.
6 They are called footpaths or pavements.

LESSON FIVE

Objective
The children will be able to answer questions using sentence patterns they already know.

Possible Answers
1 The girls with flowers in their hair are making tapa cloth.
2 The black dog dug up your garden.
3 The youngest baby had a bad cough.
4 The house on top of the hill belongs to Hamo.
5 This land belongs to Umbuga clan.
6 I gave more tapa cloth to the girls with flowers in their hair.
7 I beat the black dog for digging up your garden.
8 I gave the cough medicine to the youngest baby.
9 I bought this shirt from Steamships.
10 I live in the house on top of the hill.

WRITTEN COMPOSITION

LESSON ONE

Objective
The children will be able to notice mistakes in a picture and say why they are wrong.

Preparation
Give out *Pupil's Book 2* to each child (page 78, Lesson 1).

Method
1 This lesson was discussed for Oral Expression, Lesson 2.

Possible Answers
1 People in town should cross the road only on a pedestrian crossing.
2 Children should never play with a ball on a busy street in case they get hit by a car.
3 Rubbish should be put in rubbish bins and not thrown on the street because it makes the town dirty.
4 People should never smoke near a petrol station because petrol can explode if it is set alight.
5 A car is going down a one way street in the wrong direction. The sign tells you that you can drive only the way in which it is pointing.
6 The cars are driving too fast in the main street.
7 The young boy is crossing the road in front of the school bus. This is dangerous because he cannot see the cars coming behind the bus.
8 Cars must stop to give way to pedestrians walking on the crossing.
9 The little girl should stand on the footpath to eat her ice-cream, not in the road.
10 The children should *walk*, not run, across the pedestrian crossing, in case they trip over.

LESSON TWO

Objective
The children will be able to write a story or legend they have heard.

Preparation
Give out *Pupil's Book 2* to each child (page 79, Lesson 2).

Method
1 Read the introduction to the lesson.
2 If the children do not know of a legend, ask them to write about a legend they have read about in their readers, e.g: *The Boar-Killer*.

SPELLING

LESSON ONE (Lesson Suggestion 22)

Objective
The children will learn to spell this week's words.

Preparation
Give out *Pupil's Book 2* to each child (page 79, Spelling List).

LESSON TWO

Select from Exercises A–E.

Preparation
Give out *Pupil's Book 2* to each child (pages 79–80).

Exercise A (Lesson Suggestion 29)

Answers

1 blind	3 correct	5 bind
2 remind	4 borrow	

Exercise B

Possible Answers
daybreak today forgot cargo cowboy penknife
cupboard sunset notebook necklace firelight moonlight daylight
Then children must use five of their words in sentences.

Exercise C (Lesson Suggestion 30)

Possible Answers
1 pretend – He tried to pretend to be brave.
2 unkind – She was very unkind to the child and would not give him a drink.
3 mistake – He made a spelling mistake in his story.
4 discover – They did not discover where the thief was hiding.

Exercise D

Answers

1 basket	3 shoe	5 baby
2 trousers	4 grass	

Exercise E

Possible Answers
GARDENING – tools, spade, fork, fertilizer, manure, compost, vegetables, fruit, roots, weeds, digging, planting, crops, soil, ground, fences, plants, pests, etc.
FISHING – canoes, nets, spears, line, hook, sinker, bait, diving, fish, reef, boat, trawler, outboard motor, fisherman, etc.

HANDWRITING (Lesson Suggestion 33)

Preparation
Give out *Pupil's Book 2* to each child (page 81).

READING

INTRODUCTION (Lesson Suggestion 34)

Objective
The children will be able to understand the background to the story, and the meaning of new words. They will read the story silently.

Preparation
Give out *Reader 2* to each child (pages 27–30), *'Freda in Sydney'*.

Method
1 Introduce the story. Discuss travelling by plane. Who has flown in a plane? Ask these children to tell the others what it was like. Explain how a big city in Australia is very different from a city in PNG. There are many more people, houses, shops, buildings, traffic, etc. Show some magazine photographs, if you have any suitable ones.
2 Follow Lesson Suggestion 34B.

LESSON ONE (Lesson Suggestion 34C)

Objective
Children will be able to answer questions to show that they understand the story.

Preparation
Give out *Reader 2* (pages 27–30) and *Pupil's Book 2* to each child (page 82, Lesson 1).

Answers
1 Freda worked in a Bank in Bulolo.
2 She was one of eight people chosen to study banks in Australia.
3 All three at once.
4 They were all rather nervous about Freda going such a long way to a strange country.
5 Freda worked in a bank. She was chosen to join a group going to Sydney. She said goodbye to her family. The group went by plane from Port Moresby to Sydney. Freda rode on an escalator for the first time. Helen Mason showed the group around Sydney. Freda got separated from her friends. She travelled on the underground train and was frightened. She went home by bus.
6 They saw the Sydney Harbour bridge and the Sydney Opera House.
7 Sydney was so different from home. The people were all in such a hurry, pushing past and not speaking or smiling.
8 When the train went through the tunnel it made a very loud noise, like an earthquake, and the earth shook.
9 aeroplane, ferry, train, bus
truck, car, bicycle
10 skyscrapers occasionally escalator

LESSON TWO

Objective
The children will be able to answer questions about a passage they have read.

Preparation
Give out *Pupil's Book 2* to each child (page 82, Lesson 2, Exercise A).

Method
Read through each story and discuss it with the children before you ask them to write answers to the questions.

Answers
1 She was sick on Friday.
2 The table, the bed, and the bench were painted red.
3 Heno had eleven visitors.
4 a gourd filled with lime
  b a piece of cooked kaukau wrapped up in a banana leaf
  c necklace of bright beads
  d axe head
  e tobacco leaves rolled up in newspaper

LESSON THREE

Objective
The children will be able to choose the correct answer from several choices.

Preparation
Give out *Pupil's Book 2* to each child (page 83, Exercise B).

Answers
1 terrified
2 exhausted
3 The sun was high in the sky at midday.
4 Hemi chopped the wood and I cleaned the fowl at the same time

LESSON FOUR

Objective
The children will be able to play Reading Games.

Preparation
Give out *Reading Games for Grade Six* to each child (pages 52–54, Unit 21).

Method
1 Choose games for the children to do.
2 Mark their work using *Teacher's Notes* (pages 60–62).

LESSON FIVE (Lesson Suggestion 39)

Objective
The children will read for enjoyment.

Method
1 Give out a choice of reading matter for the children.

OR POETRY (Lesson Suggestion 40)

Preparation
Give out *Pupil's Book 2* to each child (page 84) *'The Parked Cars'*.

Answers
1 They are parked in the morning.
2 They work all day.
3 Because they worked all day.

LISTENING 22

LESSON ONE (Lesson Suggestion 36)

Objective
The children will be able to tell the difference between true and false statements.

Preparation
Get each child to write TRUE on one side of a piece of paper, and FALSE on the other side. The words must be quite big so they can be seen from the back of the room.

Method
1 Choose a child to come out to the front of the room to make a statement. (It must be something *true* — something which can be proved — or something false), e.g:
Wewak is the capital of Papua New Guinea. (false)
My father's name is Matua. (true)
2 After the child has said her statement, the rest of the class must hold up their cards to say whether they think what she said was true or false. She tells them the answer.
3 The teacher then chooses someone else to come to the front. He must say something true or false. Encourage children to talk about things they have studied at school, e.g: a spider has eight legs (true).

LESSON TWO (Lesson Suggestion 3)

Objective
The children will be able to choose the word that does not belong to the group.

Method
1 Explain that sometimes the word does not belong because it does not have the right meaning, and sometimes because it does not have the right spelling, e.g:
uncle, cousin, *teacher*, mother (not a member of a family)
chief, thief, *achieve*, relief (doesn't end in 'ief')
2 Read the lists below slowly to the class. Ask them to put their hands up if they know which word does not belong, and why.
A parachute, paragraph, parallel, *burial* (the others begin with 'para')
B joke, broke, *bike*, poke (the others have 'oke' in them)
C football, baseball, *athletics*, soccer (all the others are ball games)
D tough, rough, *reef*, enough (the others have 'ough' in them)
E station, relation, *lotion*, plantation (the others have 'ation' in them)
F shout, cry, *whisper*, scream (the others are loud)
G *advice*, correct, right, true (does not mean true)

TALKING

LESSON ONE (Lesson Suggestion 1C)

Objective
The children will practise last week's sentence pattern:
Do you know who it is? Yes, I know who it is. No, I don't know who it is.

Method

1 Use the substitution table that is still on the blackboard and revise it thoroughly with the class.

LESSON TWO

Objective

The children will practise a sentence pattern they already know:
I know who built this school. Do you know who built this school?

Method

1 T: I know how to make a spear. Do you know how to make a spear Kerua?
C: Yes, I do.
2 In groups, the leader starts off by saying to the next person: 'I know how to make an adze. Do you know how to make one, Sila?' The next child says, 'No, I don't. I know how to make a dress. Do you know how to make one, Kem?' And so on around the group until everyone has a turn.

LESSON THREE

Objective

The children will be able to use a new sentence pattern:
Do you think it will rain tomorrow? Yes, I think it will. No, I don't think it will.

Method

1 T: The plane usually comes on Tuesday. Do you think it will land tomorrow?
C: Yes, I think it will.
T: Do you think it will rain this afternoon?
C: Yes, I think it will.
T: The PMV has broken down. Do you think it will leave tomorrow?
C: No, I don't think it will.
T: Do you think that Bari is the best student?
C: No, I don't think he is.
2 In groups children must think of questions to ask each other starting with 'Do you think . . .

LESSON FOUR

Objective

The children will practise this sentence pattern:
Do you think we will go to Daru next week? I don't think so.

Method

1 Ask questions as in Lesson Three, starting with 'Do you think . . .?' Children this time must answer 'I don't think so'.
T: Do you think it's going to be fine this afternoon?
C: I don't think so.
T: Do you think you'll pass your exams?
C: I think so.
2 Further practise in groups.

LESSON FIVE (Lesson Suggestion 1C)

Objective

The children will practise the new sentence pattern using a substitution table.

Preparation

Write the following substitution table on the blackboard:

Do you think	IT WILL RAIN TOMORROW? IT WILL BE FINE TOMORROW? THE PMV WILL BE ON TIME? THIS BOW WILL BREAK? THIS PIG WILL DIE? THAT FENCE WILL BE STRONG ENOUGH? WE WILL GO TO THE MARKET TODAY? WE WILL GO SWIMMING AFTER SCHOOL? YOU CAN LIFT THIS TABLE? YOU CAN CARRY THAT LOG?	Yes, I think it will. No, I don't think it will. I don't think so.

Note

Leave this table on the blackboard for next week.

ORAL EXPRESSION

LESSON ONE

Objective

The children will be able to talk about a picture.

Preparation

Give out *Pupil's Book 2* to each child (page 85).

Method

1 Ask the children to tell you about this picture.
2 Explain everything in the picture to the class, describing what its function is, e.g: a wind sock shows the pilots which way the wind is blowing; a hangar is a building where planes are fixed; a runway is like a wide road where planes land and take off; a helicopter is different from a plane – it has a propellor on top, and no wings. It does not need a runway.
3 If any of the children have visited an airport, ask them what they saw. Those who haven't visited one could talk about what they'd like to see, or about planes they have seen flying.

Follow-Up

Children could make model planes or a model airport during an Expressive Arts lesson.

LESSON TWO

Objective

The children will be able to talk about a journey they have made.

Method

1 Choose pupils to describe a journey they have made. The rest of the class must ask questions about it, e.g: How long did it take? Were you frightened? What interesting things happened?

LESSON THREE

Objective

The children will be able to think about a problem and decide how they would solve it.

Note
This lesson is to be done *after* reading this week's story, '*The Rescuers*'.

Method
1 How did the children in this story solve the problem of:
a) reaching the crashed plane; b) carrying the injured pilot; c) being able to see in the dark?
2 Think up realistic problems which the children in your class could at some time be faced with, e.g:
What would you do if you got lost in the bush? . . . were bitten by a snake? . . . your boat capsized at sea? . . . your house caught fire? . . . you started to cough up blood?
3 Encourage the children to think up sensible answers to these (and similar) questions. Discuss their ideas with the rest of the class.

WRITTEN SENTENCES

LESSON ONE (Lesson Suggestion 2)

Objective
The children will be able to write good sentences about a picture.

Preparation
Give out *Pupil's Book 2* to each child (page 85, Lesson 1).

Note
Do this lesson *after* Oral Expression Lesson One.

Possible Answers
1 The wind sock shows the pilots and the man in the Control Tower which way the wind is blowing.
2 The pilots keep in radio contact with the men in the control tower.
3 A fire engine is always ready at the airport in case there is a crash landing or some other accident.
4 The passengers are boarding the Fokker Friendship.
5 The men are pumping fuel from the petrol tanker into the plane.
6 All aircraft must take off from the runway.
7 Planes stay inside hangars when they are being mended.
8 The people are waving to their friends from the passenger terminal.
9 A man is driving the luggage to the plane.
10 The aircraft engineers are fixing a broken plane in one of the hangars.

LESSON TWO (Lesson Suggestion 11)

Objective
The children will be able to change the sentences from plural to singular.

Answers
1 The plane has landed on the runway.
2 The fire engine is in the fire station.
3 The passenger is boarding the aeroplane.
4 The porter is loading the suitcase into the luggage compartment.
5 The plane in the hangar is being mended by an aircraft engineer.
6 The helicopter is landing at the airport.
7 The plane's propeller is turning very fast.

8 The man in the control tower tells the pilot when it is safe to land and take off.
9 The petrol tanker is refuelling the aeroplane before it takes off again.
10 The person is walking up the steps to the plane.

LESSON THREE

Objective
The children will be able to answer questions about the airport.

Preparation
Give out *Pupil's Book 2* to each child (pages 85–6, Lesson 3).

Possible Answers
1 The steps are next to the plane so the passengers can climb up to the plane.
2 The petrol tanker fills the plane with fuel for the journey.
3 The cargo men are driving the luggage to the plane.
4 The wind sock shows the pilots which way the wind is blowng.
5 The planes are mended inside the hangars.
6 An airport terminal is where the passengers buy their tickets and wait for their plane to leave. People also go there to meet friends who are arriving on a plane.
7 The men who work in the control tower are called Air Traffic Controllers. They talk to the pilots by radio, and tell them when to land and take off.
8 A helicopter has one propellor on top. It does not need to take off and land on a runway. All it needs is a helipad or a clear space on the ground in which to land.

LESSON FOUR

Objective
The children will be able to write good sentences using words given.

Preparation
Give out *Pupil's Book 2* to each child (page 86, Lesson 4).

Possible Answers
1 The Traffic Controllers in the control tower talk to the pilots by radio.
2 There are many people waiting in the terminal for plane to leave.
3 You have to buy your plane tickets at the terminal building.
4 The luggage is loaded aboard the plane.
5 The aircraft made a smooth landing on the runway.
6 The aeroplane lifts up its wheels when it had left the runway and is flying in the air.
7 The plane's engines turn the propellors which make the plane fly through the air.
8 The fire engines are ready at the airport in case a plane catches fire.

LESSON FIVE

Objective
The children will be able to describe what the children in the picture are wearing.

Preparation
Give out *Pupil's Book 2* to each child (page 87, Lesson 5).

Answers

1 Karu is the boy in traditional costume wearing the head-dress.
2 Raka is the boy wearing the policeman's helmet.
3 Anis is the boy wearing the long trousers and T-shirt.
4 Galang is the boy wearing the shorts and an SP T-shirt.
5 Angon is the boy wearing the Highland tunget or traditional apron and bark belt.

WRITTEN COMPOSITION

LESSON ONE

Objective
The children will be able to write a story about a journey they have made.

Preparation
Give out *Pupil's Book 2* to each child (page 87, Lesson 1).

Method
1 Choose pupils to describe their journey. If some children have not been on any interesting journeys, ask them to describe the walk to the next village or the nearest mission station.

Note
The Family Groups on pages 58, 79, 88, 106 and 124 may have some helpful words for the children to use.

LESSON TWO (Lesson Suggestion 17)

Objective
The children will be able to write a personal letter.

Preparation
Give out *Pupil's Book 2* to each child (page 87, Lesson 2).

Method
1 Read the introduction to the lesson.
2 Suggest that pupils make a plan of all the things they are going to mention in their letter, e.g:
   a went hunting with uncle
   b learned to make bow and stone-tipped arrows
   c shot a possum with them
   d cousin taught me how to ride his bicycle
   e want to save up and buy one
   f he showed me how to play jew's harp
   g he made me one from bamboo and vine
   h feel happy, but miss the family
   i will see them soon

Follow-Up
Read out some of the letters when they are finished.

SPELLING

LESSON ONE (Lesson Suggestion 22)

Objective
The children will learn to spell this week's words.

Preparation
Give out *Pupil's Book 2* to each child (page 88, Spelling List).

LESSON TWO

Select from Exercises A–E.

Preparation
Give out *Pupil's Book 2* to each child (pages 88–9).

Exercise A (Lesson Suggestion 29)

Answers

1 tomorrow	3 unkind	5 thief
2 thread	4 threat	

Exercise B (Lesson Suggestion 8)

Answers

1 threw	3 though	5 wear
2 thread	4 thumb	

Exercise C (Lesson Suggestion 23)

Possible Answers
pit bet net bad den mat made team beat

Note
This could be made into a contest by giving pupils a time limit. At the end of a given time, the pupils count the number of words to see who got the most. Check the winner's work to ensure that she has not written the same word twice.

Exercise D

Answers
tables glasses brushes books matches branches shoes wishes

Exercise E

Preparation
Bring a lot of small stones and shells to the lesson. (Beads, seeds or coins would do instead.)

Method
1 Read instructions. Make sure the children understand the rules.
2 Divide class into pairs. If there is not an even number of pupils, one group can have three players.

3 Give each pair six small stones and two shells or flat stones.
4 Show children what 'tossing' means. When you think the children fully understand how to play the game, they may start. Walk around the classroom, making sure that children are playing correctly and checking their answers are correct.

Answers to Harder Examples

11 high – low, in – out, above – below, shallow – deep, outside – inside, wise – foolish/stupid
30 boxes, stitches, grass/grasses, tables, girls, churches
44 sand
51 cat, cow, cuscus, cassowary
53 buses, itches, ditches, dishes, wishes
59 one hundred, one thousand, one million

HANDWRITING (Lesson Suggestion 33)

Preparation

Give out *Pupil's Book 2* to each child (page 89).

READING

INTRODUCTION (Lesson Suggestion 34)

Objective

The children will be able to understand the background to the story, and the meaning of new words. They will read the story silently.

Preparation

Give out *Reader 2* to each child (pages 31–4), '*The Rescuers*' (Part 1).

Method

1 Introduce the story. Discuss what to if you find someone in trouble. Talk about using your initiative (making decisions about what to do) in difficult situations. If you and your friend are out chopping wood when suddenly your friend chops his leg, what would you do? (A: Stop the bleeding by putting something over the wound and then tie a piece of cloth around it).
2 Follow Lesson Suggestion 34B.

LESSON ONE (Lesson Suggestion 34C)

Objective

The children will be able to answer questions to show that they understand the story.

Preparation

Give out *Pupil's Book 2* to each child (page 92, Lesson 1) and *Reader 2* (pages 31–4).

Answers

1 The boys were late home from school because they were on work parade.
2 Dark clouds were gathering which meant it was going to rain soon.

3 Kemo told Timon that he was the fastest runner, which made Timon feel important.
4 If the plane was on fire, it would explode when the fire reached the petrol tank.
5 The body of the plane lay with its tail and one wing broken off. The broken wing was burned to ashes.
6 They used a dry branch for a torch.
7 They could not cross the river at the same place on the way back because it had flooded and now it was too deep to wade through.
8 Kemo was always the one to give instructions. He was able to make quick decisions about what to do in difficult situations.
9 They watched the plane fly until it was out of sight.
They managed to lift the heavy log with much difficulty.
10 They made a stretcher from branches and vines.

LESSON TWO

Objective
The children will be able to answer questions about a story.

Preparation
Give out *Pupil's Book 2* to each child (page 92, Lesson 2, Exercise A).

Method
Read out the story, or ask one of the pupils to read it.

Answers
1 national
2 Men called 'banderilleros' make the bull angry by chasing it round the ring.
3 They tire the bull and make it weak.
4 The matador carries a red cloak and then a sword.
5 He pushes the sword into the bull's neck.

LESSON THREE

Objective
The children will be able to find things in a newspaper.

Preparation
Give out *Pupil's Book 2* to each child (page 93, Exercise B).

Answers
1 Births on page 16
2 Lost Property on page 16
3 Motorcycles for Sale on page 12
4 Dogs, Cats and Pets on page 10
5 Musical Instruments on page 10
6 Cars for Sale on pages 11–12
7 Situations Vacant on pages 8–10
8 Theatres on page 15

LESSON FOUR (Lesson Suggestion 39)

Objective
The children will be able to read for enjoyment.

Preparation
Give out *Supplementary Reader 2* to each child.

OR POETRY (Lesson Suggestion 40)

Preparation
Give out *Pupil's Book 2* to each child (page 94), *'First Time in Jackson's Airport'*.

Answers
1 He says it's like a big iron bird.
2 Voices coming through the walls. (loudspeakers)
Serving drinks in a big iron box (drink machine)
3 lonely
4 Personal opinion

LESSON FIVE

Objective
The children will be able to play Reading Games.

Preparation
Give out *Reading Games for Grade 6* (pages 62–4, Unit 22).

LISTENING 23

LESSON ONE

Objective
The children will be able to say whether a phrase tells 'who', 'when' or 'why'.

Method
1 Read out the list of phrases to the children. They must decide whether the phrase answers the questions 'who?', 'when?' or 'why?', e.g:
the children (who)
because it was raining (why)
after dark (when)
a short time later (when)
because he felt sick (why)
the parents and teachers (who)
at midnight (when)
because I felt hungry (why)
the village people (who)
later (when)
because he was angry (why)
next week (when)
last year (when)
2 Check the answers with the class.
3 If the children find this difficult, use the phrases in sentences, e.g: The children jumped into the water. (*Who* jumped into the water?) I came inside because it was raining. (*Why* did I come inside?)

LESSON TWO

Objective
The children will practise listening and watching carefully.

Method
1 Play the game: Follow Me.
Explain to the children that you will give a command and do an action. If you

do what you *command*, the children must do it too, e.g:
T *says*: Point to the door.
T *does*: point to the door.
C: must point to the door.
However, if you *say* one thing and *do* something *different*, the children must *not* do this action or they will be out of the game, e.g:
T *says*: Touch your head.
T *does*: point to the roof.
C: must do nothing.

2 Once you have played this game several times with the class, pupils can play in groups with the leaders giving directions.

TALKING

LESSON ONE (Lesson Suggestion 1C)

Objective
The children will practise last week's sentence pattern:
Do you think it will rain tomorrow? Yes, I think it will. No, I don't think it will. I don't think so.

Method
Use the substitution table that is still on the blackboard, and revise it thoroughly.

LESSON TWO

Objective
The children will practise a sentence pattern they already know:
Will you go fishing on Tuesday? No. I won't go fishing on Tuesday.

Method
1 T: Will we go swimming on Sunday?
C: No, we won't go swimming on Sunday.
T: Will we go hunting on Monday?
C: No, we won't go hunting on Monday.
T: Will we go to town on Wednesday?
C: No, we won't.

2 In groups, children must practise this sentence pattern and answer.

LESSON THREE

Objective
The children will be able to use a new sentence pattern:
Do you think he'll win the race? I don't know. I hope so. I hope not.

Method
1 T: I wonder whether we'll win the football tomorrow. I don't know. I hope so.
T: Do you think we will win?
C: I don't know. I hope so.
T: Do you think you will get all your maths right this morning?
C: I don't know. I hope so.
T: Do you think all your written sentences are correct?

C: I don't know. I hope so.
2 T: I wonder if it will rain this afternoon? I don't know. I hope not.
T: Do you think it will rain?
C: I don't know. I hope not.
T: Do you think we will lose the football match next week?
C: I don't know. I hope not.

LESSON FOUR

Objective
The children will practise this sentence pattern:
Do you think he'll win the race? I don't know. I hope so. I don't know. I hope not.

Preparation
Write the following questions on the blackboard.
Do you think our school will burn down one day?
Do you think a cyclone will come next week?
Do you think we'll win the football match?
Do you think there'll be an earthquake?
Do you think we'll visit Kagua school next term?
Do you think we'll go diving after school?
Do you think you'll pass your exams?

Method
In groups, one person must choose a question. He asks the person next to him who must answer either 'I don't know. I hope so.' or 'I don't know. I hope not.'

LESSON FIVE (Lesson Suggestion 1C)

Objective
The children will practise the new sentence pattern using a substitution table.

Preparation
Copy this substitution table on the blackboard:

Do you think	WE'LL WIN THE MATCH?	I don't know. I hope so.
	WE'LL PASS THE TEST?	
	YOU'LL WIN THE RACE?	
	YOU'LL BUY THAT SHIRT?	
	YOU'LL FIX THAT RADIO?	
	YOU'LL GO TO UNIVERSITY?	
	THERE'LL BE A STORM?	I don't know. I hope not.
	WE'LL ALL GET SICK?	
	HE'S GOT MALARIA?	
	THAT PLANT IS POISONOUS?	
	THAT BOY WAS DROWNED?	
	IT'S GOING TO RAIN?	

Note
Leave the table on the blackboard for next week's revision lesson.

ORAL EXPRESSION

LESSON ONE

Objective
The children will be able to give accurate instructions on how to do something.

Method
1 Base this lesson on a topic already studied during an agricultural lesson.
2 Choose pupils to give instructions to the rest of the class on how to look after various animals, e.g: poultry, cattle or pigs (what you must give them to eat; where you should keep them, etc).
3 You could then ask for suggestions on how to improve conditions for village animals, e.g: pigs, hens, dogs.

LESSON TWO

Objective
The children will be able to make up an interesting story from a given beginning.

Method
1 Turn to Exercise B on page 102. Read out A. Ask: Who can finish this story? Then read B and ask someone to finish that.
2 Divide the class into groups. Give each group a beginning sentence and the group must suggest how to make it into a story. One person in the group can write it down quickly.
Beginning sentences could be like this:
Tim ran quickly to the water's edge when he heard the shout . . .
The cyclone hit the village suddenly with no warning at all . . .
I was chopping down the tree when my axe slipped and . . .
The village head man decided to call a meeting . . .
3 When each group has finished, one person from each group reads out their story to the rest of the class.

LESSON THREE

Objective
The children will practise telling the time correctly.

Method
1 Divide the class into groups.
2 Each group should have a model clock. (This could be made during an Expressive Arts lesson.) One person makes a time and chooses someone in the group to say what the time is.
3 The clock is then given to that pupil. He makes a time and asks someone else in the group what the time is. This is done till everyone has had a turn.

Note
You could write the following on the blackboard: midday, midnight, noon, half-past, quarter past, twelve o'clock, ten minutes past, etc.

WRITTEN SENTENCES

LESSON ONE (Lesson Suggestion 2)

Objective
The children will be able to write good sentences about a picture.

Preparation
Give out *Pupil's Book 2* to each pupil (page 95, Lesson 1).

Possible Answers
1 The boys are loading the sacks onto the back of the truck.
2 Kera is feeding the fish in the pond.
3 The tractor is ploughing the field ready for planting.
4 The boys are fixing the broken fence.
5 One of the boys is feeding grain to the hens.

LESSON TWO (Lesson Suggestion 8)

Objective
The children will be able to use the correct word in the sentences.

Preparation
Give out *Pupil's Book 2* to each child (page 96, Lesson 2).

Answers

1 their, there	4 there, their	7 their
2 their, their	5 their	8 there
3 there	6 their	

LESSON THREE (Lesson Suggestion 13)

Objective
The children will be able to punctuate the sentences correctly.

Preparation
Give out *Pupil's Book 2* to each child (page 96, Lesson 3).

Answers
1 'Will you teach me to drive the tractor next, please Sir?' Tom asked Mr Awagasi.
2 'I'm going to help the other students chop down some of the large pine trees today', Kapo told his friend.
3 'We keep pigs, cattle, horses, hens, fish and a few turkeys on our Agricultural Station', said the lecturer.
4 'Will you show me how to ride a horse?' asked Anis.
5 'Today we're going to learn about crop rotation', said Mr Scott.
6 'I'm going to start my own cattle project in my village when I finish my training', said Francis.
7 'I will have to feed this small calf from a bottle because its mother won't feed it', explained Mr Asi.
8 'We will all work in the gardens today', said Mr Sam. 'On Monday we will dig the vegetables and on Tuesday take them to market.'

LESSON FOUR (Lesson Suggestion 9)

Objective
The children will be able to use apostrophes correctly.

Preparation
Give out *Pupil's Book 2* to each child (page 97, Lesson 4).

Possible Answers
1 The cow's tail was covered in mud.
2 The horse's mane was very long.
3 The hen's eggs were still warm.
4 The cow's calf ran across the field.
5 The tractor's wheels are stuck in the ditch.
6 The pigs' sty was always dirty.
7 The man's axe was sharp.
8 The paddock's fence needed mending.
9 The bull's horns (or bulls' horns) were long and dangerous.
10 The hens' house was cleared out yesterday.

LESSON FIVE

Objective
The children will be able to answer questions using a sentence pattern they already know.

Preparation
Give out *Pupil's Book 2* to each child (page 97, Lesson 5).

Possible Answers
1 I saw the old woman who broke her leg.
2 I gave it to the little child who had a sore hand.
3 I met my friend Lusi who went to school with me.
4 I helped the woman who fell over.
5 I took my brother who is on holiday with me.
6 I hit that stupid man who is always stealing fruit.
7 I sat next to Mr Amawa who always sits in the same seat.
8 I waved goodbye to Theresa who was going to Lae.

WRITTEN COMPOSITION

LESSON ONE (Lesson Suggestion 14B)

Objective
The children will be able to write a story from notes.

Preparation
Give out *Pupil's Book 2* to each child (page 97, Lesson 1).

Model Answer
A car turned the corner, travelling very fast. It slowed down when the driver saw a child run onto the road. The driver beeped his horn as the small boy crashed his football into the middle of the road. Then the car swerved as the

driver jammed on the brakes to miss hitting the child. Next the car skidded onto the footpath and stopped.

The child was unhurt and safe, but very frightened. The driver got out of the car and told the child to be more careful next time.

LESSON TWO

Objective
The children will practise solving a problem.

Preparation
Give out *Pupil's Book 2* to each child (page 98, Lesson 2).

Method
Read the passage out loud. Discuss the questions orally before you ask the children to write anything.

A Arag and Umpit could use the vine to tie the pig's legs to the branches. The boys could then put the branches over their shoulders and drag the pig along the ground behind them.

B They could tie the pig's legs together, put one of the branches between its legs, and carry the branch on their shoulders, one boy at each end. (However, the pig may be too heavy for this method.)

SPELLING

LESSON ONE (Lesson Suggestion 22)

Objective
The children will be able to spell this week's words.

Preparation
Give out *Pupil's Book 2* to each child (page 98, Spelling List.)

LESSON TWO

Select from Exercises A–E.

Preparation
Give out *Pupil's Book 2* to each child (pages 98–9).

Exercise A (Lesson Suggestion 29)

Answers

1 arrow
2 swallow
3 hollow
4 clown
5 frown

Exercise B

Answers

1 forest
2 cattle

Exercise C (Lesson Suggestion 30)

Possible Answers

midday — We eat our lunch at midday.
middle — I woke in the middle of the night.

overboard — The sailor fell overboard because he was drunk.
overhead — They saw a large eagle soaring overhead.
overturn — The canoe overturned and they all fell in the water.

Exercise D

Possible Answers

1 Karan arranged the books on the shelves after the lesson.
2 Kewa caught many fish, Pita caught a few, but Kewon caught the least.
3 The electrician arrived to fix the stove.
4 Our clan owns thousands of hectares of land.
5 The author of that book has a good imagination.

Exercise E (Lesson Suggestion 28)

Possible Answers

Section 1 new nation never night naughty nobody nothing
2 driven hollow cattle swallow forest
3 mention attraction lotion action station
Section 4 nation notion navigation
5 nation nearly newest
6 ration motion action lotion
7 nation notion

HANDWRITTING (Lesson Suggestion 33)

Preparation

Give out *Pupil's Book 2* to each child (pages 100–101).

READING

INTRODUCTION (Lesson Suggestion 34)

Objective

The children will be able to understand the background to the story, and the meaning of new words. They will read the story silently.

Preparation

Give out *Reader 2* to each child (pages 35–8), *'The Rescuers'* (Part 2).

Method

1 Remind the class about what happened in the story last week in Part 1. Why did the river rise? How do you think they will cross the river now? What do you think has happened to the little girl?
2 Follow Lesson Suggestion 34B.

LESSON ONE (Lesson Suggestion 34C)

Objective

Children will be able to answer questions about the story to show they understand it.

Preparation
Give out *Reader 2* to each child (pages 35–8) and *Pupil's Book 2* (page 101, Lesson 1).

Answers
1 They used to play on it some years ago when they were younger.
2 Kemo probably spoke sharply because he too was scared, but he knew they mustn't give up.
3 They tied the stretcher to the waists of two of the boys, so they had their hands free to hold on to the bridge.
4 Apu offered to help Kemo carry the stretcher across the bridge because he respected Kemo and wanted to be like him.
5 Kemo did not hesitate to bring the little girl across the bridge after he crossed twice. He was the one to reach down and help Lare when the vine bridge broke. He always did the most dangerous things himself.
6 Apu felt very nervous and relieved that they made it safely across the bridge to the other side. (People often giggle when they are nervous about something.)
7 The vines snapped on the other side of the bridge and the bridge collapsed. The others saved Lare by holding onto Kemo's legs, while he reached down to grab hold of Lare. Then they pulled them both up onto the platform to safety.
8 head, hand, feet, waist, face, eyes, arms, leg
9 separate – They decided to take separate pieces of land for their gardens.
respect – Young people should respect their elders and ask them for advice.
swayed – The skirts of the dancers swayed from side to side as they danced.
10 cried, screamed, called, shouted

LESSON TWO

Objective
The children will be able to understand new words from the context in which they are used.

Preparation
Give out *Pupil's Book 2* to each child (page 102, Lesson 2, Exercise A).

Method
Discuss the story with the children. Ask them questions to make sure that they understand the meaning of the story.

Answers
1 Favourite means the one liked best.
2 Boundary means a line or border showing the end of someone's piece of land.
3 Disguise means to make yourself look different so that you will not be recognized.
4 Misconduct means bad behaviour.

LESSON THREE

Objective
The children will be able to write conclusions (endings) to stories.

Preparation
Give out *Pupil's Book 2* to each child (page 102, Exercise B).

Method
Read through the lesson and discuss possible answers before you ask the children to write their conclusions.

Possible Answers
A The storm reached its full fury.
The storm was the worst one we had ever known.
The storm lasted all night.
B They were ready to go to town on the bus.
They were ready to go to church.
They set out to the picture theatre.

LESSON FOUR

Objective
The children will be able to read for enjoyment.

Preparation
Give out *Supplementary Reader 2* to each child.

OR POETRY (Lesson Suggestion 40)

Preparation
Give out *Pupil's Book 2* to each child (page 103).

Answers
1 No, it is not a job they like doing, but it has to be done.
2 They want their newly cleaned garden to dry; they want their newly beaten tapa cloth to dry; they don't want the weeds to grow quickly and smother the taros.
3 Traditional gardening and harvesting songs are sung to the garden spirits who watch over the gardens and help their crops grow. Different tribes have different songs which they sing to different spirits.

LESSON FIVE

Objective
The children will be able to play Reading Games.

Preparation
Give out *Reading Games for Grade 6* to each child (pages 58–60, Unit 23).

Method
1 Choose games for the children to do.
2 Mark their work using *Teacher's Notes* (pages 65–6).

LISTENING 24

LESSON ONE

Objective
The children will be able to find the wrong detail in a story.

Method

1 Tell the children a short story, but put some wrong detail in it. Children must tell you which part is wrong and be able to say why, e.g:
We won the school sports this year. Mai won the 100 metres sprint while Bonnie won the three-legged race.
Mistake: Bonnie could not have won the three-legged race by herself because she doesn't have three legs.

2 Give children other examples, e.g:
Our water tank broke so we had no water for anything. Mother had to cook kaukau in the fire and we had only coconut milk to drink. When mother called me in for tea, I washed my hands before eating.
Mistake: There was no water so I could not wash my hands.

3 Ask children to work in groups, thinking up examples and putting one wrong detail in their story. You may have to help each group with this.

LESSON TWO

Objective

The children will be able to draw a conclusion about a story they hear.

Method

1 Tell children to listen carefull to this story:
Addi stopped a minute to wipe the sweat from her brow. She listened carefully, hoping to hear the welcome sound of the river. But all was quiet in the bush. She took out her last piece of taro and sat down to eat it. If only she had some water to wash it down with, she thought. With great effort, she staggered to her feet again and reached for her bush knife. She struck out at the dense jungle with it once again. She knew she must hurry as light was fading, and she didn't want to spend a second night alone in the bush.

2 What conclusions can the children draw from this story? Possibilities:
Addi was lost in the bush. (she couldn't find the river)
She had very little food left. ('her last piece of taro')
She was very tired and growing weaker. ('with great effort, she staggered to her feet')
She was cutting her way through the bush.
It was late in the afternoon. ('light was fading')
She had spent one night in the bush. ('didn't want to spend a *second* night . . .')
She was alone.
She had nothing to drink.

TALKING

LESSON ONE (Lesson Suggestion 1C)

Objective

The children will practise last week's sentence pattern:
Do you think he'll win the race? I don't know. I hope so.

Method

Point to the substitution table on the blackboard. Revise it.

LESSON TWO

Objective
The children will practise a sentence pattern they already know:
While Bato was cleaning the board, Foru was sweeping the room.

Method
1 Tell one child to sweep the floor and another to tidy his table. Say: While Kemp was sweeping the floor, Malo was tidying his table.
2 Explain that both activities are going on at the same time, so we start our sentence with 'while'.
T: While I was reading this book, I was eating my lunch.
While I was talking, I was watching that bird.
3 In groups, children give examples to each other.

LESSON THREE

Objective
The children will be able to use a new sentence pattern:
He's going to sweep the floor.

Method
1 T: There are many dark clouds in the sky. It's going to rain. What's going to happen?
C: It's going to rain.
T: (Give a child a broom) What's he going to do?
C: He's going to sweep the floor.
T: (Give a child a duster) What's she going to do?
C: She's going to dust the board.
T: (Give a child a piece of chalk) What's she going to do?
C: She's going to write on the board.
2 In groups, children practise this sentence pattern.

LESSON FOUR

Objective
The children will practise this sentence pattern:
The pig is going to die.

Method
1 Tell the children that we say 'is going to' when something is about to happen.
2 T: That pig cannot stand up. It is very sick. What's going to happen?
C: The pig is going to die.
T: Maria has her bilum full of vegetables. What's she going to do with them?
C: She's going to sell them at the market.
D: Tam has got some soap and a towel. What's he going to do?
C: He's going to wash himself.
2 Ask children think up situations in groups, and use this sentence pattern.

LESSON FIVE (Lesson Suggestion 1C)

Objective
The children will practise the new sentence pattern using a substitution table.

Preparation
Write the following substitution table on the blackboard:

IT'S	going to	FALL OVER.
SHE'S		GO TO BED
THEY'RE		GO TO WORK
WE'RE		FINISH SCHOOL EARLY
I'M		LOOK FOR WORK
HE'S		HUNT FOR WILD PIG

Look at Kip.	He's going to	WASH HIMSELF.
		GO HOME
		DRIVE THE TRUCK
		CUT THE GRASS
		PICK THE FRUIT
		PAINT THE BUILDING

Note
Leave this work on the board for next week.

ORAL EXPRESSION

LESSON ONE

Objective
The children will be able to discuss what is happening in a picture.

Preparation
Give out *Pupil's Book 2* to each child (page 104).

Method
1 Discuss the picture of the Gumi Race with the class.
2 Now choose different children to imagine that they are the children in the race. Ask them questions about the race, e.g: Kila, why didn't you finish the race? How did you feel about that? Tau, why did you and Rubin fall off your tyre? Did you manage to climb on again? Pita, why did you and Ramu decide to enter a canoe instead of a tyre in the race? Do you think it would be more fun on a tyre? Lakei, how did you and Serei feel about winning the race? Was that the first time you won? What was the prize?
3 Children can talk about a race they have been in, or a journey they have made by river or sea.

LESSON TWO

Objective
The children will be able to re-tell a story.

Preparation
Give out *Pupil's Book 2* to each child (page 109, Lesson 2).

Method
1 Read the legend about the Garamut to the class. Then ask a child to re-tell the story in her own words.
2 Now ask the children to tell you a legend they have heard from old people in their village.
3 Find out if anyone knows someone from the village who will come to school to tell a legend to the class.

LESSON THREE

Objective
The children will be able to prepare talks to give to the class.

Method
1 Divide the class into pairs. Tell them that each pair must think of a topic that they would like to talk about to the rest of the class. These should be based on other subjects they are working on at school, e.g: Expressive Arts, Agriculture, etc.
2 Tell them to think about the subject they have chosen. For their prepared talk, each pair should show models (if possible) or draw pictures about their topic.
3 Give the class time to talk about what they will do. Allow them time during other subjects (or when they have finished other lessons) to prepare for this.

Note
Tell the children that they have only one week to prepare for this talk.

WRITTEN SENTENCES

LESSON ONE (Lesson Suggestion 2)

Objective
The children will be able to write good sentences about a picture.

Preparation
Give out *Pupil's Book 2* to each child (page 104, Lesson 1).

Possible Answers
1 The weather was fine for the Gumi race.
2 There were seventeen people in the race.
3 Two people used a raft instead of a tyre.
4 Some of the boys fell off their tyres and some of them lost their paddles.
5 The spectators watched and cheered from the banks of the river.

LESSON TWO

Objective
The children will be able to choose the correct word from the two given.

Preparation
Give out *Pupil's Book 2* to each child (page 104, Lesson 2).

Answers

1 was	4 unable	7 paddle	10 got, 4
2 as	5 first, won	8 hard, right	
3 when	6 watching	9 by	

LESSON THREE

Objective
The children will be able to join sentences using conjunctions (joining words).

Preparation
Give out *Pupil's Book 2* to each child (page 105, Lesson 3).

Answers

1 The river flowed very slowly and it had a lot of bends.
2 Kila could not finish the race because his tyre got caught up in a fallen tree.
3 There was only one canoe entered in the race and it was paddled by Pita and Ramu.
4 Tau and Rubin lost their paddles when/and they fell off their tyre.
5 Number 9 was out of the race because his tyre went down.
6 The boys in number 4 had to get into the water when their tyre caught on a fallen tree.
7 Number 5 needed three boys to paddle it because it was large and very difficult to handle.
8 The crowd cheered when Lakei and Seri crossed the finishing line first.

LESSON FOUR

Objective

The children will be able to answer questions using a sentence pattern they already know.

Preparation

Give out *Pupil's Book 2* to each child (page 105, Lesson 4).

Possible Answers

1 That's the pig that was in the kaukau garden.
2 That's the bird that was in the tree.
3 That's the house that was on fire.
4 That's the car that was following us.
5 That's the village that was the first to have a tradestore.
6 That's the river that was dry last summer.
7 That's the plant that was growing near my house.
8 That's the tree that was creaking in the wind.

LESSON FIVE

Objective

The children will be able to answer questions using a sentence pattern they already know.

Preparation

Give out *Pupil's Book 2* to each child (page 106, Lesson 5).

Answers

1 The blue bag that's on the table is mine.
2 The bicycle that's leaning against the building is mine.
3 The hat that's on top of that coat is mine.
4 The house that's next to the waterfall is mine.
5 The pen that's on the desk is mine.

WRITTEN COMPOSITION

LESSON ONE (Lesson Suggestion 16)

Objective

The children will be able to write a story.

Preparation
Give out *Pupil's Book 2* to each child (page 106, Lesson 1).

Method
1 Read the introduction to the lesson.
2 Read the list of words and phrases, giving their meanings.
3 This lesson is a follow on from Oral Expression, Lesson One, when the children talked about races they'd been in.
4 Children write their story.

LESSON TWO

Objective
The children will be able to write about a legend they have heard.

Preparation
Give out *Pupil's Book 2* to each child (page 106, Lesson 2).

Method
1 This lesson follows on from Oral Expression, Lesson Two for this week.
2 Tell children to write about one of the legends that they heard during this lesson.
3 Write any words the children cannot spell on the blackboard.

SPELLING

LESSON ONE (Lesson Suggestion 22)

Objective
The children will learn to spell this week's words.

Preparation
Give out *Pupil's Book 2* to each child (page 106, Spelling List).

LESSON TWO

Select from Exercises A–E, or give a spelling and dictation test on all words learned over the past four weeks.

Preparation
Give out *Pupil's Book 2* to each child (pages 106–7).

Exercise A (Lesson Suggestion 29)

Answers

1 hour
2 squeal
3 mountain
4 steal
5 loud

Exercise B (Lesson Suggestion 32)

Answers
writing chasing saving smiling coming liking dancing taking

Exercise C (Lesson Suggestion 23)

Answers

turn run turned dove red note nod ton need done reed deter rent deer need

Exercise D

Answers

1 lost
2 none
3 slow
4 finished
5 lost

Exercise E (Lesson Suggestion 27)

Answers

Aitape Angoram Balimo Garaina Kagua Kerema Porgora Wau Wewak

HANDWRITING (Lesson Suggestion 33)

Preparation

Give out *Pupil's Book 2* to each child (page 108).

READING

INTRODUCTION (Lesson Suggestion 34)

Objective

The children will be able to understand the background to the story, and the meaning of new words. They will read the story silently.

Preparation

Give out *Reader 2* to each child (pages 39–42), *'The Good Companions'* (Part 1).

Method

1 Introduce the story. Discuss going into business with someone. The main purpose of this is to make money (a profit). Children could suggest the types of businesses they would like to start when they leave school.
2 Follow Lesson Suggestion 34B.

LESSON ONE (Lesson Suggestion 34C)

Objective

Children will be able to answer questions to show that they understand the story.

Preparation

Give out *Reader 2* (pages 39–42) and *Pupil's Book 2* to each child (page 109, Lesson 1).

Answers

1 Ainui brought five shiny new instruments.
2 They had lessons from one of the older men in the village.
3 They played old favourites, village songs and songs they made up themselves.
4 Sioni felt envious when he watched the others play but he could not afford to buy himself a guitar.
5 You need an old tea chest, a stick and a piece of string to make a bush bass (pronounced 'base').
6 Sioni pretended to be asleep because he did not want to answer the question Kota asked him.
7 They earned K10 every time they played and K60 for the studio recording.
8 instruments, band, play, sing, songs, tunes, strummed, chords, singing, guitar, beat, bush bass, notes, music, musicians, recording
9 home-made
10 The boys had ordinary guitars and the dance band had expensive electric guitars.

LESSON TWO

Objective

The children will be able to answer questions about a story.

Preparation

Give out *Pupil's Book 2* to each child (page 109, Lesson 2).

Method

1 Ask the children to read the legend silently (they have already heard it in Oral Expression, Lesson Two).
2 Discuss the questions and answers with the children.

Answers

1 It is a type of drum.
2 They were used for singsings, marriages, harvesting and friendship feasts.
3 It had a much louder, clearer sound.
4 It sounded louder and clearer, and a wooden drum was easier and quicker to make than a stone drum.

LESSON THREE – POETRY (Lesson Suggestion 40)

Objective

The children will be able to read a poem for enjoyment.

Preparation

Give out *Pupil's Book 2* to each child (page 110).

Answers

1 Coastal people spend a lot of time in canoes, fishing and travelling, so young children learn how to paddle a canoe at a very early age.
2 Big waves and sharks frighten the children.
3 The waves broke and passed the canoe.
4 (Personal opinion) e.g: I would be very frightened, but I would try to hold on to the canoe.

LESSON FOUR (Lesson Suggestion 39)

Objective
The children will be able to read for pleasure.

Preparation
Give out varied reading matter for the children to choose from.

LESSON FIVE

Objective
The children will be able to play Reading Games.

Preparation
Give out *Reading Games for Grade 6* to each child (pages 60–2, Unit 24).

Method
1 Choose games for the children to play.
2 Mark children's work using *Teacher's Notes* (pages 67–9).

LISTENING 25

LESSON ONE

Objective
The children will listen carefully to hear the correct word.

Preparation
Write these words on the blackboard before this lesson. Set them out exactly like this:

1 accept	except	expect	5 Indian	engine	injure
2 machine	mission	machines	6 sewing	showing	shown
3 given	giving	give	7 sties (pig)	skies	sighs
4 seat	set	sit	8 cart	cut	cat

Method
1 Call out the number and then say *one* of the three words, e.g: Number 1 except. (Say the word very clearly.)
2 The children must write down the word you have said.
3 Go through all the numbers, calling out one word from each. When you have finished, call out the correct answers (remember to write them down yourself). Children can mark their own work.

Note
If you have room on your blackboard, leave this work here for Listening Lesson Two.

LESSON TWO

Objective
The children will be able to listen carefully to hear the correct word.

Preparation
Use the same blackboard work as for Lesson One.

Method
1 Choose a word from each number and use it in a sentence. The children

must write down the word they think you have used in that sentence, e.g:
T: Number 1, I expect to get all my spelling right this week.
Answer: expect

2 After each sentence, choose someone to give his answer. Discuss whether it is right. Children mark their own work.

TALKING

LESSON ONE (Lesson Suggestion 1C)

Objective
The children will practise last week's sentence pattern:
It's going to rain this afternoon.

Method
Point to the substitution table on the board. Revise it.

LESSON TWO

Objective
The children will practise a sentence pattern they already know:
We've been here since 8 o'clock.

Method

1 T: How long have we been at school today?
C: We've been here since 8 o'clock.
T: How long have you been coming to school?
C: We've been coming to school since we were small.
T: How long have we been learning English?
C: We've been learning English since Grade One.

2 In groups, the children must first say and then answer the following questions using this sentence pattern:
How long have you been reading this book?
How long have you been drawing this picture?
How long have you lived in your house?
How long have you been coming to this school?
How long have you been in this class?
How long have you been able to swim?

LESSON THREE

Objective
The children will be able to use a new sentence pattern:
Do you think it's going to rain? Yes, I do.

Method

1 T: Do you think it's going to rain?
C: Yes, I do.
T: The sky's very black. I think there's going to be a storm. Do you think there's going to be a storm?
C: Yes, I do.
T: Do you think it's going to be windy?
C: Yes, I do.

2 In groups, children must think up questions to ask each other. They must begin: Do you think it's going to . . .?

LESSON FOUR

Objective
The children will practise this pattern:
Do you think it's going to rain? Yes, I do. No, I don't.

Method
1 T: Do you think you're going to get all your spelling right?
C: Yes, I do.
T: Do you think we're going to get all our work finished by lunch-time?
C: Yes, I do.
T: Do you think it's going to be cold tonight?
C: No, I don't.
T: Do you think it's going to be hot tonight?
C: Yes, I do.
T: Do you think it's going to be windy today?
C: No, I don't.
2 Carry on this work in groups.

LESSON FIVE (Lesson Suggestion 1C)

Objective
The children will practise the new sentence pattern using a substitution table.

Preparation
Write the following substitution table on the blackboard:

Do you think	it's going to	BE WINDY?	Yes, I do.
		BE FINE?	No, I don't.
		BE WET?	
		BE STORMY?	
	we're going to	FINISH OUR WORK?	
		FIX THIS RADIO?	
		LEARN THIS PATTERN?	
		SPEAK GOOD ENGLISH?	
		PASS OUR EXAMS?	
	he's going to	WIN THAT RACE?	
		SMASH THAT WINDOW?	
		BREAK THAT SPEAR?	
		HIT THAT CHILD?	
		THROW THAT STONE?	

Note
Leave this table on the blackboard for next week's Talking Lesson One.

ORAL EXPRESSION

LESSON ONE

Objective
The children will be able to talk about a picture.

Preparation
Give out *Pupil's Book 2* to each child (page 111, Lesson 1).

Method

1 Study the picture which shows village people preparing a mumu.
2 Encourage children to talk about how feasts are prepared in their village. Ask questions like: On which special occasions are feasts held? What jobs are you given to help prepare for the feast? What do the village men do? What do the women do? What do you enjoy most about these feasts? Why?
3 Individual children may remember some special event at a feast they went to. Ask them to tell the class about it.

LESSON TWO

Objective

The children will be able to use sequence signals when giving instructions on how to do something.

Method

1 Write these sequence signals on the blackboard: firstly, secondly, then, next, after that, finally.
2 Give an example of how to use these words when giving instructions, e.g: Fishing with a line can sometimes be difficult. *Firstly* you must make sure that the bait is fixed securely to the hook. *Secondly* you must check that the sinker is heavy enough. *Then* you must make sure that the hook does not get caught up in anything in the boat when you throw it into the water. *Next* you must keep tugging gently on the line to feel whether you have caught a fish. *Finally*, you must keep a good grip on the line when you are pulling in the fish.
3 Divide the class into groups. Tell each group to choose a topic, e.g: making a canoe, weaving a basket, making tapa cloth. One person in the group gives the first instruction using the first sequence signal. The next person continues using the next sequence signal, and so on.

LESSON THREE

Objective

The children will be able to give talks they prepared last week.

Method

1 Choose pairs to come out the front and give the talks they prepared last week (Oral Expression Lesson 3) to the rest of the class.
2 The class can ask each pair questions at the end of their talk.

WRITTEN SENTENCES

LESSON ONE (Lesson Suggestion 2)

Objective

The children will be able to write good sentences about a picture.

Preparation

Give out *Pupil's Book 2* to each child (page 111, Lesson 1).

Possible Answers

1 The men are cutting up the pigs to cook on the mumu.

2 The children are watching the preparations excitedly.
3 A woman is heating stones on a wooden platform over the fire.
4 The women are collecting firewood to heat the stones.

LESSON TWO

Objective
The children will be able to choose the best adjective (describing word) to fit in the sentences.

Preparation
Give out *Pupil's Book 2* to each child (page 112, Lesson 2).

Answers

1 dry	3 hot	5 delicious	7 excited
2 young	4 hungry	6 favourite	8 sharp

LESSON THREE

Objective
The children will be able to use a list of words in good sentences about a feast.

Preparation
Give out *Pupil's Book 2* to each child (page 112, Lesson 3).

Possible Answers
1 Many people gathered to help prepare the mumu.
2 The village children helped by collecting firewood, and stones from the river.
3 The women dug fresh vegetables from the gardens the day before the mumu.
4 The men killed a pig for the special occasion.
5 Everyone had plenty to eat at the feast.
6 The women chattered happily together as they prepared the vegetables.
7 The small children watched the men cutting up the pig.
8 The men put the heated stones on top of the food in the pit.

LESSON FOUR

Objective
The children will be able to finish the answers to questions using a sentence pattern they have learned.

Preparation
Give out *Pupil's Book 2* to each child (page 112, Lesson 4).

Possible Answers
1 . . . bought at the market.
2 . . . belongs to Ope.
3 . . . ate all our pawpaws.
4 . . . Keru caught . . .
5 . . . your brothers caught this morning.
6 . . . is nearly two metres long.
7 . . . plays music all day long.
8 . . . the medicine would make him feel better soon.

WRITTEN COMPOSITION

LESSON ONE (Lesson Suggestion 16)

Objective
The children will be able to write a story telling how something used to be done.

Preparation
Give out *Pupil's Book 2* to each child (page 113, Lesson 1).

Method
1 If children do not know about traditional methods of fire-lighting, discuss the method shown in the Mumu picture on page 111. This shows a man pulling a piece of vine back and forth round a piece of split dry wood till there is a spark. He has soft dry bark and coconut husk close by to catch the flame.
2 Children write their story. (Remind them to use sequence signals.)

Follow-Up
Read out different methods of traditional fire-lighting. (You could take the class outside at some stage for a practical demonstration of each of these methods to see if they really do work.)

LESSON TWO (Lesson Suggestion 16)

Objective
The children will be able to write a short story.

Preparation
Give out *Pupil's Book 2* to each child (page 113, Lesson 2).

Method
1 Read the lesson.
2 Discuss the preparation of everyday food with the class. If there is someone in your class from another province, ask him to tell how food is prepared at his village.
3 Children write their stories.

SPELLING

LESSON ONE (Lesson Suggestion 22)

Objective
The children will learn to spell this week's words.

Preparation
Give out *Pupil's Book 2* to each child (page 113, Spelling List).

LESSON TWO

Select from Exercises A–E.

Preparation
Give out *Pupil's Book 2* to each child (pages 113–14).

Exercise A

Possible Answers

1 The sun will shine when the rain stops.
2 That bag is mine, not yours.
3 Hang those wet clothes on the line to dry.
4 The weather is going to be fine today.
5 You can talk about what you did in the holidays.
6 We watched the cat stalk the bird, then pounce on it and kill it.
7 We walk two kilometres to school every day.
8 The teacher writes on the blackboard with chalk.

Exercise B

Answers

1 shine 3 walk 5 stalk
2 fine 4 talk

Exercise C

Answers

collected, preparation, excited, feast, vegetables, heated, cook

Exercise D (Lesson Suggestion 27)

Answers

collected cook excited feast heated pit preparation vegetables

Exercise E (Lesson Suggestion 30)

Possible Answers

pretend prepare prefix prefer prefect present preserve

HANDWRITING (Lesson Suggestion 33)

Preparation

Give out *Pupil's Book 2* to each child (page 115).

READING

INTRODUCTION (Lesson Suggestion 34)

Objective

The children will be able to understand the background to the story, and the meaning of new words. They will read the story silently.

Preparation

Give out *Reader 2* to each child (pages 42–5), *'The Good Companions'* (Part 2).

Method

1 Introduce the story. Remind the children of what happened last week in Part 1 of the story. Why do you think Sioni did not want to answer the question about money? Do you think the boys have a lot of money by now? What will they do with their money?
2 Follow Lesson Suggestion 34B.

LESSON ONE (Lesson Suggestion 34C)

Objective

Children will be able to answer questions about the story to show they understand it.

Preparation

Give out *Reader 2* (pages 42–5) and *Pupil's Book 2* to each child (page 116, Lesson 1).

Possible Answers

1 Sioni said he was feeling sick when he wasn't. He did not turn up for band practice.
2 He tried to get out of answering the question directly.
3 He had lent the money to his relatives.
4 I will lend you my pencil till you buy yourself a new one.
You can borrow my bicycle to go and visit your aunty in hospital.
5 (Personal opinion)
6 He lent the money to relatives because it is a traditional custom to lend money to your wantoks. He was wrong to do it because it was not his money. His friends were trying to start a business. A business will never work if the people in it give away money to their relatives.
7 The business or co-operative would not be able to continue because they would not be making a profit. The money they earn should be shared among the people in the band. They could use this money to buy new guitars or amplifiers, or other things for the business.
8 They probably kept it in the bank.
9 He probably got some kind of work in Port Moresby.
10 The 'something' was the friendship between all the boys in the band.

LESSON TWO (Lesson Suggestion 15)

Objective

The children will be able to match sentences with pictures.

Preparation

Give out *Pupil's Book 2* to each child (pages 116–18, Lesson 2, Exercise A).

Answers

These European people are sitting at a table, eating with knives and forks.
These Chinese people are sitting on the floor, eating rice with chopsticks.
These Italian people are enjoying a meal of spaghetti.
This woman is washing sago in an old tree trunk.

LESSON THREE

Objective

The children wil be able to answer questions about a story they read.

Preparation
Give out *Pupil's Book 2* to each child (page 118, Lesson 2, Exercise B).

Answers

A The men prepared a cooking pit.
The children helped.
The women helped by digging up vegetables.
Some of the young men killed a pig.
The mumu was left to cook.

B The best title is probably 'Preparing the Mumu'.

C 1 They cut down banana leaves to wrap the food in.
2 They tied it to a stake by one of its legs and then clubbed it to death.
3 The women went to the gardens to get vegetables and bamboo.
4 The mumu was covered with these things to keep the heat in the pit, to cook the food.

LESSON FOUR (Lesson Suggestion 39)

Objective
The children will be able to read for enjoyment.

Preparation
Give out *Supplementary Reader 2* to each child.

OR POETRY (Lesson Suggestion 40)

Preparation
Give out *Pupil's Book 2* to each child (page 119).

Answers

A wealth killing feasting death

B 1 If pigs are stolen, often a pay-back killing is made.
2 Pigs are a sign of wealth. They also give the people meat to eat.
3 They would have no wealth and no meat for their feasts.
4 Pigs can be a nuisance because they ruin gardens and spread hookworm.

LESSON FIVE

Objective
The children will be able to play Reading Games.

Preparation
Give out *Reading Games for Grade 6* (pages 63–5, Unit 25).

Method
Choose games for the children to play.

LISTENING 26

LESSON ONE

Objective
The children will be able to decide whether what they hear is true or false.

Method

1 Tell the children that they will often hear exaggerated accounts of things and events. Therefore they should learn to recognise an exaggeration. Read this story to the children:
I tell you my friends, this provincial government has done *nothing* to help the people at all. They have broken *all* their promises to the people. All their staff do is ride around in fancy cars all day, trying to look important. They spend most of the time spending tax payers money attending cocktail parties. Let me tell you, if I was in power, these things would never happen. (A politician)

2 Discuss the exaggerations in the story:
A The provincial government has no doubt done quite a lot to help the people — he says it has done *nothing* at all.
B They probably haven't broken *all* their promises — sometimes promises are not kept because of problems.
C The staff would not ride around in cars *all* day for nothing.
D They would not spend *most* of their time at cocktail parties — this would happen only occasionally.
E This person is obviously trying to make everyone think bad things about the present government, so they will vote for him in the next election.

LESSON TWO

Objective

The children will be able to tell whether a story is true or make-believe.

Method

1 Many stories are make-believe or not really true. Children should learn to recognise these. Read the following story to the children and ask them whether or not they think it is true:
The head man of a powerful clan was dying. He called a meeting to decide who would become the chief after he died. He called together all the elders of the village and told them that whoever could capture the large eagle on Mt Giluwe would become the next chief.
In the village there lived a youth called Kiapa who badly wanted to become the next chief. He decided to try to catch the eagle. He visited the witchdoctor who lived in some caves nearby and asked for his help. The witchdoctor changed him into a female eagle. Then Kiapa flew up to Mt Giluwe and lured the mighty eagle back down to the village. When he reached the village, Kaipa then changed back into a youth again and caught the eagle.

2 Now discuss whether this story is make-believe or true. Why is it make-believe? (People cannot turn into eagles.) If you have time, read another story and let the children decide whether it is true or false.

TALKING

LESSON ONE (Lesson Suggestion 1C)

Objective

The children will practise last week's sentence pattern:
Do you think it's going to rain? Yes, I do. No, I don't.

Method

Point to the substitution table on the board and revise it.

LESSON TWO

Objective

The children will practise a sentence pattern they already know:
He has opened the door.

Method

1 Choose a child to open the door. Say: Pel has opened the door. What has he done?
  C: He has opened the door.
  T: (Choose a child to lift his chair.) Puk has lifted his chiar. What has he done?
  C: He has lifted his chair.

2 Tell the children to make up sentences in groups, using 'has . . .ed', e.g:
  has opened has finished has listened has lifted.

LESSON THREE (Lesson Suggestion 1)

Objective

The children will be able to use a new sentence pattern:
A large, deadly spider is under the table.

Method

1 This pattern is to teach children to use describing words and phrases.

2 T: I'm holding a short, blunt pencil. What is it?
  C: It's a short, blunt pencil.
  (Hold up a pair of scissors.)
  T: What are these?
  C: Scissors.
  T: Describe them.
  C: They are sharp, shiny scissors.
  T: (Point to a box.) What's that?
  C: It's a large, brown box.

3 On the blackboard write the following:

special words	e.g: beautiful
size	e.g: small
age	e.g: young
shape	e.g: round
colour	e.g: blue

  Teacher explain that when you are describing things, you use adjectives in this order, e.g: I found a beautiful, small, blue flower. (*Not*: I saw a blue, beautiful, small flower.)

LESSON FOUR

Objective

The children will practise this sentence pattern:
Look at that beautiful, large, blue butterfly.

Method

1 Ask children to give at least three adjectives to describe the following things. (Make sure they put them in the correct order.)

a butterfly
a flower
a tree
a river
a spear
a hook
a snake
a shell

LESSON FIVE

Objective
The children will practise the new sentence pattern using a table.

Preparation
Write the following table on the blackboard:

Special Words: clean, dirty, beautiful, shiny, dull, interesting, happy, sad, boring, ugly, wonderful, etc.
Size: little, small, big, large, huge, enormous, short, thin, fat
Age: new, old, young
Colour: white, yellow, green, red, blue, purple, brown, black, orange

Method

1 Ask children to use words from these lists to describe the following: a child, a plant, a book, a fruit, a costume, a house.
2 Make sure children put words they choose in the correct order. They do *not* have to take a word from *every* list for their description. e.g: A dirty, little child.
3 In groups children can do this exercise.

Note
Leave this work on the board for next week.

ORAL EXPRESSION

LESSON ONE

Objective
The children will be able to ask questions to find out information.

Preparation
Send one person from each group outside with a tin, a small box or half a coconut shell. They must quickly find some things outside (e.g: shells, leaves, stones) place them in the container and then return to their group.

Method

1 The child with the container must choose one of the things in his box. He does not let the rest of his group see it but he gives them a clue about the chosen object e.g: It is very hard.
2 The rest of the group must ask questions to find out what it is, e.g: Can you eat it? Is it heavy? Did you find it on a tree? The leader must answer only 'yes' or 'no'.
3 When someone guesses what the object is, the leader passes the container to that person and she must choose a different object, and give the group a clue, e.g: It starts with 'l'. The group must then ask questions to find out what it is.
4 (Encourage children to put interesting things in their containers to make it harder for the children to guess, e.g: a spider, a berry or pod, a flower, a butterfly, beetles, etc.)

LESSON TWO

Objective
The children will be able to think carefully and talk about a picture.

Preparation
Give out *Pupil's Book 2*. Study the market picture on page 121.

Method
1 Ask the class why they think that this picture is of a Highland market and not a coastal market. (Answers as for Written Sentences Lesson Three.)
Ask questions like:
How can we tell the people are Highlanders? (clothes)
What can we tell from the produce they are selling? (Where do those things grow?)
Do you think it is a hot or cold morning? Why? (cold – men hugging themselves)
Does the village in the background tell us anything? (low, round, Highland huts)

LESSON THREE

Objective
The children will be able to describe their local market.

Preparation
Give out *Pupil's Book 2* to each child (page 123, Lesson 5).

Method
1 Tell the children that they must describe their local market.
2 Read through the questions in this lesson and ask the children for answers.
3 Talk about any interesting features of your local market.

WRITTEN SENTENCES

LESSON ONE (Lesson Suggestion 2)

Objective
The children will be able to write good sentences about a picture.

Preparation
Give out *Pupil's Book 2* to each child (page 121, Lesson 1).

Possible Answers
1 There are many different types of fruit on sale at the market.
2 The women carry bunches of bananas on their heads.
3 Many old men go to the market to talk to friends and chew betel-nut.
4 The haus winds are to shelter the goods for sale, in case it rains.
5 Women carry rolled up mats in their bilums, to sit on and display their goods on.

LESSON TWO

Objective
The children will be able to join sentences using conjunctions (joining words).

Preparation
Give out *Pupil's Book 2* to each child (page 122, Lesson 2).

Answers
1 until the rain stopped.
2 ... after they had sold their vegetables.
3 ... because it was too far to walk carrying their heavy loads.
4 ... so he could not buy anything at the market.
5 ... then they are allowed to sell their goods.
6 ... as it is needed to look after the market place.
7 ... and she carried them home in her bilum.
8 ... when they had sold all their vegetables.

LESSON THREE

Objective
The children will be able to draw conclusions from a picture.

Preparation
Give out *Pupil's Book 2* to each child (page 122, Lesson 2).

Note
Do Oral Expression Lesson Two before doing this lesson.

Possible Answers
1 ... the men on the right-hand-side of the picture have their arms crossed because it is cold. It is cold in the Highlands.
2 ... the patterns on the women's bilums are Highland patterns.
3 ... the men and women are wearing traditional Highland costume.
4 ... the village has low, round, Highland houses.
5 ... there are no coconut palms in the picture and no coconuts for sale.
6 ... the men are wearing bamboo ladders for 'omaks' round their necks, which are only worn by Highlanders.
7 ... Bird of Paradise feathers are more often sold in the Highlands than in coastal areas.
8 ... the mountains in the background suggest that this area is hilly.

LESSON FOUR

Objective
The children will be able to write sensible answers to questions about markets.

Preparation
Give out *Pupil's Book 2* to each child (page 122, Lesson 4).

Answers
1 People sell things at the market to get money to buy the goods which they cannot make or grow.
2 Many people working in towns have no gardens of their own. They need to buy all their food from the market, because it costs too much in the shops.
3 There is not enough land for them to have gardens, and they do not have time to look after them.
4 People go to market to see their friends, or just to watch other people.
5 Some councils have freezers which keep meat and fish fresh. Some markets have car parks and toilets and closed-in stalls which can be locked so things can be left there. Some markets have tradestores which sell cold drinks and ice-creams. (Many other possible answers).

6 It is important that there are roads leading to the market-place so that people who live a long way away can bring their heavy produce by truck.
7 coconuts, salt, fish, crayfish
8 tinned meat, salt

LESSON FIVE

Objective
The children will be able to write good sentences about their local market.

Preparation
Give out *Pupil's Book 2* to each child (page 123, Lesson 5).

Note
Do Oral Expression Lesson Three before doing this lesson.

Answers
Answers will depend on where you live. Collect the children's work for marking after the lesson.

WRITTEN COMPOSITION

LESSON ONE

Objective
The chidren will be able to write a business letter.

Preparation
Give out *Pupil's Book 2* to each child (page 123, Lesson 1).

Method
1 Discuss the word list with the children.
2 Tell them to make a plan before they write their letter. Their plan could contain some of the following ideas:
  a build a parking area for trucks and PMVs
  b supply wooden benches for people to sit on
  c buy a freezer to keep fish and meat fresh
  d set up a tradestore to sell cold drinks and ice-creams, as well as other goods
  e install a petrol pump near the car park
  f provide more rubbish bins to keep the market-place cleaner
  g put up notices in the market-place saying 'No spitting of betel-nut' and 'no litter'
  h Haus winds could have iron roofs so less maintenances is required.
  i build more shelter over tables for when it rains
3 When they have made their plan, children write their letter to the council.

Follow-Up
You could choose one of the best letters to post to your local council.

LESSON TWO

Objective
The children will be able to write a factual description.

Preparation
Give out *Pupil's Book 2* to each child (page 124, Lesson 2).

Answers
Children choose one of the following exports to write about:
rubber, coffee, copra, timber, cocoa.
OR They must choose something sold in their local market. They must say how it is grown and prepared for eating and drinking, e.g: breadfruit, coconuts, pitpit, etc.

SPELLING

LESSON ONE (Lesson Suggestion 22)

Objective
The children will learn to spell this week's words.

Preparation
Give out *Pupil's Book 2* to each child (page 124, Spelling List).

LESSON TWO

Select from Exercises A–E.

Preparation
Give out *Pupil's Book 2* to each child (pages 124–5).

Exercise A

Possible Answers
1 In the old days, trading between different clans was very important.
2 People used to exchange food and pots.
3 Today, our country makes many of its own products.
4 We buy machinery and cars from Japan.
5 Women carry vegetables from the gardens in a string bag called a bilum.
6 Trucks and cars transport people to other places.
7 Village people grow produce to sell at the market.
8 Koki market in Port Moresby is always crowded.

Exercise B

Answers
1 attempt attack attach contest continue control continent

Exercise C (Lesson Suggestion 23)

Possible Answers
travel travels traveller travelling travelled
carry carrier carries carried carrying
collect collector collecting collected collects

Exercise D

Answers
ground stream mail/meal bowl coffee trail/trial

Exercise E

Answers
endless energy engine enough enter entry envy

HANDWRITTING (Lesson Suggestion 33)

Preparation
Give out *Pupil's Book 2* to each child (page 126).

READING

INTRODUCTION (Lesson Suggestion 34)

Objective
The children will be able to understand the background to the story, and the meaning of new words. They will read the story silently.

Preparation
Give out *Reader 2* to each child (pages 45–8), '*The Talking Bananas*'.

Method
1 Introduce the story. Discuss myths and legends. How are these stories started? Is there any truth in them? Explain that this story is a legend.
2 Follow Lesson Suggestion 34B.

LESSON ONE (Lesson Suggestion 34C)

Objective
Children will be able to answer questions to show that they understand the story.

Preparation
Give out *Reader 2* (pages 45–8) and *Pupil's Book 2* (page 127, Lesson 1) to each child.

Answers
1 His mother and father had to go on a long fishing trip.
2 The family had an argument with the witch many years ago and she wanted to get revenge. (revenge is pay back)
3 The bananas rubbed their skins together to make a loud squeaking noise.
4 He thought the skins would still rub themselves together to frighten away the witch even though he had eaten the insides.
5 There was silence because the boy had eaten all the bananas.
6 They knew it was the witch when they saw the hole in the boy's side where his liver was cut out. (The witch had threatened to do that one day.)
7 He killed her with his axe.
8 They were both greedy.
9 called, answered, asked, shouted
10 hurried — rushed; leapt — sprang; crept — sneaked

LESSON TWO

Objective
The children will be able to answer questions about a passage they read.

Preparation
Give out *Pupil's Book 2* to each child (page 127, Lesson 2, Exercise A).

Answers
1 meat, fish, eggs, beans, nuts, scum, seaweed
2 beans and nuts
3 Children choose 3 facts, e.g: Beans and nuts contain protein.
4 fish, meat and eggs
5 beans and nuts or seaweed (if you live on the coast)
6 to stay healthy

LESSON THREE

Objective
The children will learn what different types of books are used for.

Preparation
Give out *Pupil's Book 2* to each child (page 128, Exercise B).

Answers

1 dictionary	3 encyclopaedia	5 newspaper	7 manual
2 atlas	4 calendar	6 telephone directory	8 recipe book

LESSON FOUR (Lesson Suggestion 39)

Objective
The children will be able to read for enjoyment.

Preparation
Give out *Supplementary Reader 2* to each child.

OR POETRY (Lesson Suggestion 40)

Preparation
Give out *Pupil's Book 2* to each child (page 129) '*The Old Man*'.

Answers
1 He spends most of his time thinking about the old days and about death.
2 Because he is very old.
3 He knows he is going to die soon.
4 No, he does not sound very happy because he is alone and he knows he is going to die.

LESSON FIVE

Objective
The children will be able to play Reading Games.

Preparation
Give out *Reading Games for Grade 6* to each child (pages 65–8, Unit 26).

Method
1 Choose some of these games for the children to play.
2 Mark their work using *Teacher's Notes* (pages 72–4).

LISTENING 27

LESSON ONE

Objective
The children will be able to listen to obtain information.

Preparation
Give each child a copy of the *PNG School Atlas* (pages 8–9).

Method
1 Ask the children: Which Province am I in? Then very slowly read out a list of places.
2 Children must write down the name of the province where that place is, e.g: Alotau — Milne Bay Province.
3 Allow plenty of time for the children to find the place on the map. Use only well-known places, and say them twice.

For Example
Popondetta — Northern Province
Lae — Morobe Province
Madang — Madang Province
Kerema — Gulf Province
Wewak — East Sepik Province

LESSON TWO

Objective
The children will be able to recognize sentences and phrases.

Preparation
Write the following list on the blackboard:
the last time
The dog barked all night.
in the school library
I helped my father.
every day
I saw it all.
several times
The man was ill.

Method
1 Explain that a *sentence* must make sense on its own. It is a complete statement. A *phrase* is only *part* of a sentence, and does not make sense on its own.
The house is on fire. This is a sentence because it makes sense.
On fire — This is a phrase. It is only *part* of a sentence, not a complete statement — what is on fire?
2 Point to the list on the blackboard. Go through each one with the children asking them whether each one is a phrase or a sentence.

Answers

phrase	phrase
sentence	sentence
phrase	phrase
sentence	sentence

TALKING

LESSON ONE (Lesson Suggestion 1C)

Objective
The children will practise last week's sentence pattern:
A large, deadly spider is under the table.

Method
Point to the substitution table on the board and revise it.

LESSON TWO

Objective
The children will practise a sentence pattern they already know:
I can't lock the door. She's already locked it.

Method
1 Tell a child to lock the door (or shut it). Say: I can't lock (shut) the door. She's already locked (shut) it. Give other examples: I can't ring the bell. He's already rung it.
2 Write the following on the board:
paint the fence   dig the vegetables
clean the board   tell you the news
3 In groups, children must use the above in the same sentence pattern.

LESSON THREE

Objective
The children will be able to use a new sentence pattern:
Which box is empty? The box on the table is empty.

Method
1 Use things in the classroom.
T: Which box is full?
C: The box near the door is full.
T: Which books are in the cupboard?
C: The books with the red covers are in the cupboard.
T: Which boy won the race?
C: The boy from Daru won the race.
T: Which man is going hunting?
C: The man with the spear is going hunting.
2 In groups, the children must practise similar examples.

LESSON FOUR

Objective
The children will practise this sentence pattern:
Which cupboard is full? The cupboard near the door is full.

Method
1 Give more examples of this pattern:
T: Which boy did you give that book to?
C: I gave the book to the very small boy with the funny eye.
T: Which tree did you climb?

C: I climbed the huge breadfruit tree by the track.
T: Which man drove the truck?
C: The man with the red shirt on drove the truck.

2 In groups, children to practise similar examples, this time with short answers, e.g:
Q: Which boy did you give the spade to?
A: The boy from the education office.
Q: Which girl took that paint?
A: The girl with the blue dress.

LESSON FIVE (Lesson Suggestion 1C)

Objective
The children will practise the new sentence pattern using a substitution table.

Preparation
Write the following substitution table on the blackboard:

Which	BOX	is empty?	
	CUPBOARD		
	CUP		
	BASKET		
Which	MAN	is going	HUNTING?
	BOY		SWIMMING
	GIRL		WALKING
Which	CHILD	gave you that	FRUIT?
	MAN		BOOK?
	WOMAN		PIE?

The . . . near the door is empty.
The . . . near the chair is empty.
The . . . by the window.
The . . . under the table.

The . . .	with the spear		HUNTING.
	with the blue shorts	is going	SWIMMING
	with straight hair		WALKING

The	CHILD	wearing	THONGS.
	MAN		BLUE JEANS
	WOMAN		THE STRAW HAT

Note
Remember to leave this substitution table on the blackboard for next week's Talking Lesson One.

ORAL EXPRESSION

LESSON ONE

Objective
The children will be able to make contrasts.

Preparation
Make some cards with the following things printed on them:
a haus tambaran and a village house
a bus and a bicycle

a dog and a cat
a mango tree and a coconut tree
a football match and a basketball match
a harvest dance and a marriage dance

Method

1 Divide the class into groups. Give the group leader several cards. He gives the cards to pupils in his group. Children must describe the two objects printed on the card, pointing out the similarities and differences between them, e.g:
My objects are a church and a house. They both have windows and doors, but a church has a cross. A house has a stove for cooking food but a church doesn't. A church has an altar but a house doesn't, etc.
Encourage children to use contrasting words like 'but' and 'however'.
2 Wander around the room listening to the children's contrasts, giving help where needed.

LESSON TWO

Objective

The children will be able to give accurate directions.

Preparation

Draw a map of the district on the blackboard, showing the main village and all buildings (e.g: schools, churches, Aid Post, council buildings, hospital, etc.).

Method

1 Choose a pupil to give a careful account of how to get to somewhere on the map from the school. Follow the child's directions by pointing to the map with a stick and going where the child says.
2 Choose another child and ask for directions to somewhere else.

LESSON THREE

Objective

The children will be able to give instructions.

Preparation

Write the following topics on the blackboard: making sago, cooking rice, making traditional dyes, preparing a garden, planting yams, preparing a mumu, making a feather head-dress, making a bow and arrows, etc.

Method

1 Divide the class into groups. The group will choose one topic and discuss the best way to do it.
2 After a short discussion time, choose one person from each group to tell the class how to do the task.
3 If there is time, tell each group to look at another topic and do the same with it.

WRITTEN SENTENCES

Note

Teach only FIVE of the six lessons.

LESSON ONE (Lesson Suggestion 2)

Objective
The children will be able to write good sentences about a picture.

Preparation
Give out *Pupil's Book 3* to each child (page 3, Lesson 1).

Possible Answers
1 The children are swinging on vines over the river.
2 The women are washing clothes in the river.
3 A man is skinning a crocodile.
4 Some women are collecting water in bamboo tubes to carry back to their homes.
5 A young boy is trying to spear a fish.

LESSON TWO (Lesson Suggestion 6)

Objective
The children will be able to finish sentences about a picture.

Preparation
Give out *Pupil's Book 3* to each child (page 3, Lesson 2).

Possible Answers
1 ... on vines over the river.
2 ... carrying and storing water.
3 ... bridges.
4 ... it puts germs into the water which make people sick when they drink it.

LESSON THREE

Objective
The children will be able to think up a list of reasons and then write them in a paragraph.

Preparation
Give out *Pupil's Book 3* to each child (page 4, Lesson 3).

Possible Answers
Firstly, a river provides water for drinking, cooking and watering the gardens.
Secondly, villagers can wash their clothes and sago in the river.
Thirdly, they can catch fish to eat from the river.
Lastly, they can wash and swim in the water and travel on it by canoe.

LESSON FOUR

Objective
The children will be able to use exclamation marks.

Preparation
Give out *Pupil's Book 3* to each child (page 4, Lesson 4).

Answers
1 ... alive!'
2 ... Metu!'
3 ... quickly!'
4 ... Yuk!'
5 ... there!'
6 ... Ow!'
7 ... Josephine!'
8 ... Watch out!'

LESSON FIVE (Lesson Suggestion 7)

Objective
The children will be able to choose the correct word to fit each sentence.

Answers

1 Has	3 since	5 before	7 have
2 saw	4 listen	6 ate	8 build

LESSON SIX (Lesson Suggestion 13F)

Objective
The children will be able to use commas.

Preparation
Give out *Pupil's Book 3* to each child (page 5, Lesson 6).

Answers
1 We cross rivers in this country by wading through the shallow parts, by walking across logs or by using vine bridges.
2 We use the river water for drinking, cooking, washing our clothes and our bodies.
3 The young boys from our village catch eels, prawns, tadpoles and small fish in the river.
4 The best known rivers in Papua New Guinea are the Sepik, the Ramu, the Markham and the Fry rivers.
5 Sago palms, nipa palms, mangrove forest and tall cane grasses grow beside these rivers.

WRITTEN COMPOSITION

LESSON ONE

Objective
The children will be able to think of a solution to a problem and write about it.

Preparation
Give out *Pupil's Book 3* to each child (page 6, Lesson 1).

Method
Discuss the picture. Ask for suggestions on how to rescue Mea.

Possible Answer
At first Gewa and Ona could not think of a way to save Mea. Then Ona suddenly had a bright idea. He chose a large tree at the edge of the river and told Gewa to help him chop it down. Next, they cut off all the side branches. When they finished this, the two boys carefully pushed the trunk out into the river holding the end of it. The river carried the tree trunk until it hit the log that Mea was clutching. Ona cautiously climbed onto the log and started to walk along it towards Mea. He soon reached her and held out his hand to her. He helped her carefully onto the log and they both made their way back to Gewa waiting on the river bank.

Note
If there is time, you could suggest that the children illustrate their story.

LESSON TWO (Lesson Suggestion 14)

Objective
The children will learn how to administer mouth-to-mouth resuscitation and have practise at taking notes.

Preparation
Give out *Pupil's Book 3* to each child (page 7, Lesson 2).

Method
1 Study the illustrations.
2 Divide the class into pairs. Children follow directions as the teacher slowly reads out the passage again. (One child to be the patient, the other the rescuer. Then change over.)
3 Send children back to their seats. They must write down the main points of mouth-to-mouth resuscitation without looking at their books again.

Note
It would be wise to put a small piece of clean material or paper over the patient's mouth so the rescuer does not touch his mouth. This will stop germs being passed on.

Model Answer
Lie person on his back. Kneel beside him.
Tip his head back and support it.
Check that mouth and throat are clear.
Take in a breath, put your mouth over his and breathe out.
Shut his nose. Watch his chest to rise.
Remove mouth. Let him breathe out.
Blow into his mouth again.
Repeat until he starts breathing for himself.

SPELLING

LESSON ONE (Lesson Suggestion 22)

Objective
The children will be able to learn to spell this week's words.

Preparation
Give out *Pupil's Book 3* to each child (pages 8–9).

LESSON TWO

Select from Exercises A–E.

Preparation
Give out *Pupil's Book 3* to each child (page 8–9).

Answers

1 prefers	3 nearby crow	5 bruised
2 struggled	4 fireplace	

Exercise B (Lesson Suggestion 30)

Answers
slowly likable foolish regardless prettiest childish smiling beautiful inside invisible

Exercise C

Answers
deceive relieve grieve field tie

Exercise D — Down the River

Answers
Number 5: a pair of scissors, a pair of trousers, a pair of socks, a pair of pants
Number 15: fresh friend frost frown
Number 20: attention addition caution nation
Number 31: coming comes
Number 40: He threw the ball. He walked through the doorway.
Number 43: boxes churches hills branches
Number 47: travel collect go teach
Number 53: die thief pie relieve field
Number 59: going coming taking bringing
Number 63: hurry — rush, speak — talk, jump — leap

Exercise E

Answers
Baiyer Fly Kikori Markham May Musa Purari Ramu Sepik Waria

HANDWRITING (Lesson Suggestion 33)

Preparation
Give out *Pupil's Book 3* to each child (page 11).

READING

INTRODUCTION (Lesson Suggestion 34)

Objective
The children will be able to understand the background to the story, and the meaning of new words. They will read the story silently.

Preparation
Give out *Reader 3* to each child (pages 4–6), *'The Frog's Husband'*.

Method
1 Introduce the story. Talk about legends. Discuss other legends that the children know.
2 Follow Lesson Suggestion 34B.

LESSON ONE (Lesson Suggestion 34C)

Objective
The children will be able to answer questions about the story.

Preparation
Give out *Reader 3* (pages 4–6) and *Pupil's Book 3* to each child (page 12, Lesson 1).

Answers

1 The frog asks the first question.
2 He is lying on the river bank.
3 He feels cold and bruised because he was washed downstream by the river.
4 He was pushed into the river by his cruel father who hated him. He floated downstream and was washed ashore on the river bank.
5 The frog is the beautiful girl at the dance.
6 These are opinions.
7 My young brother is much stronger and much more handsome than I am.
8 amazed astonished surprised
9 He discovered that the frog was the beautiful girl.
  She heard a bird sitting on a branch nearby.
  He slipped and fell on the wet rocks.
  The water was sparkling in the sunlight.
10 ashore more poor wore law
  away today hooray okay relay
  fly sky high die cry

LESSON TWO

Objective

The children will be able to point to towns on a map by following directions.

Preparation

Give out *Pupil's Book 3* to each child (page 13). Tell the children to work in groups. One child reads out a direction, and the other children must point to the correct place on the map. Walk round the class checking the groups' work.

Answers

LESSON THREE

Objective
The children will be able to arrange sequence pictures in the correct order, and finish writing the story.

Preparation
Give out *Pupil's Book 3* to each child (page 14, Exercise B).

Answers
A 1 The children of Asemki village . . .
2 When they swung over the . . .
3 It was Morea's turn to . . .
4 It looked like a log at first . . .
5 By now the other children . . .

B The children all grabbed sticks and began beating at the water and yelling to scare the crocodile away, while Morea clung tightly to the vine. At last the crocodile swam away. Morea dropped into the river and swam quickly ashore.

Note
Answer B is only one possible suggestion. Children may come up with many other ideas.

LESSON FOUR

Objective
The children will be able to read for enjoyment.

Preparation
Give out *Supplementary Reader 3* to each child.

OR POETRY (Lesson Suggestion 40)

Preparation
Give out *Pupil's Book 3* to each child (page 15), '*The River*'.

Answers
1 Because it helps him in many different ways.
2 It washes away sweat and dirt. It can be used as a mirror. It is a drink. It provides fish for you to eat.
3 Fish and shrimps that live in the river.
4 drinking, washing, cooking, washing clothes, watering gardens

LESSON FIVE

Objective
The children will be able to play Reading Games.

Preparation
Give out *Reading Games for Grade 6* to each child (pages 68–70, Unit 27).

Method

1 Choose games for the children to play.
2 Mark their work using *Teacher's Notes* (pages 74–7).

LISTENING 28

LESSON ONE

Objective

The children will be able to listen carefully and follow the directions given them.

Preparation

Give each pupil a piece of paper and crayons or coloured pencils.

Method

1 Say: Listen carefully and do exactly as I say.
2 Then give directions for the children to follow, e.g:
Write your first name at the top right-hand corner of the page.
Now underline this with a coloured pencil.
Next I want you to quickly draw a bird at the bottom of the page on the left-hand side. Colour it blue.
On top of the bird draw an arrow pointing upwards about 10 centimetres long.
At the top of the arrow draw 6 steps going up, etc.
3 When you have finished giving directions, read out the directions again, this time drawing the answer on the blackboard. Children must compare their answers with yours on the board.

LESSON TWO

Objective

The children will be able to hear which word does not rhyme.

Preparation

Write the following lists of words on the blackboard (do *not* underline any words):

1 tell bell ball
2 tore sour poor
3 blind black unkind
4 borrow sorrow correct
5 tame team stream
6 around find around

Method

1 Read out the first three words.
2 Say: Which word does not rhyme?
Explain that 'tell' and 'bell' sound alike but 'ball' is different, therefore 'ball' does not rhyme.
3 After doing several more examples orally, ask the children to write down the words that do not rhyme in their books.

Answers

The underlined words do not rhyme.

TALKING

LESSON ONE (Lesson Suggestion 1C)

Objective
The children will practise last week's sentence pattern:
Which box is empty? The box on the table is empty.

Method
Point to the substitution table on the blackboard and revise it with the class.

LESSON TWO

Objective
The children will practise a sentence pattern they already know:
Have you ever been to Rabaul? No, I've never been to Rabaul.

Method
1 T: I've never been to Rabaul. Have you ever been to Rabaul?
  C: No, I've never been to Rabaul.
  T: Have you ever been to Wewak?
  C: No, I've never been to Wewak.
  T: Have you ever been to Salamaua?
  C: No, I've never been to Salamaua.
  T: Have you ever been to Sogeri?
  C: No, I've never been to Sogeri.
2 In groups, the children to practise this sentence pattern using the negative form of answer.

LESSON THREE

Objective
The children will be able to use a new sentence pattern:
Take this to the old man in the tradestore. Which old man? The old man with the beard.

Preparation
Give out *Pupil's Book 3* to each child (page 16).

Method
1 Hold up a small green leaf and a big green leaf.
  T: Which one do you want?
  C: The small green leaf in your right hand.
2 Ask questions about the picture on page 16. Children must give answers using this sentence pattern, e.g:
  T: Which woman is carrying her child on her back in a bilum?
  C: The woman who is digging in the front of the picture.
  T: Which woman is making a bilum?
  C: The woman sitting down on the left.

LESSON FOUR

Objective
The children will practise this sentence pattern:
Take this to the woman inside the house. Which woman? The woman wearing the blue laplap.

Method

1 T: Put this book on the shelf.
  C: Which shelf?
  T: The shelf over by the door.
2 Divide the class into pairs. Write the following on the blackboard:
  Bring me that cup please. Which cup?
  Bring me that book please. Which book?
  Pass me that pencil please. Which pencil?
  Give this to that child please. Which child?
  Put this in the desk please. Which desk?
3 In pairs, children practise this pattern, taking it in turns to give a description.

LESSON FIVE (Lesson Suggestion 1C)

Objective

The children will practise the new sentence pattern using a substitution table.

Preparation

Write the following table on the board:

Give me that	BOOK	please. Which book?
	PENCIL	
	CRAYON	
	BOX	
	RULER	

The	BLUE	book	ON	the teacher's table.
	RED		IN	
	GREEN		UNDER	
	LARGE			
	SMALL			

Give that	FRUIT	to	SALI	please. Which	FRUIT?
	VEGETABLE		KEPA		VEGETABLE?

Note

Remember to leave this on the board for next week.

ORAL EXPRESSION

LESSON ONE

Objective

The children will play a word association game.

Method

1 In this activity, the class has to think of words connected with a topic someone else has named. Each child must follow the last person, as quickly as possible, with a new sentence, e.g:
  1st child: Last Saturday we went to market and bought some *vegetables*.
  2nd child: Talking of *vegetables*, I have my own garden where I grow vegetables and *fruit*.
  3rd child: Talking of *fruit,* my *favourite* fruit is mangoes.
  4th child: Talking of *favourite* things, my favourite game is Tag.
2 Teacher should listen to ensure that children make sensible connections. If a child cannot think anything, you should start off a sentence for him.

LESSON TWO

Objective
The children will be able to make polite requests.

Method
Divide the class into groups. The leader becomes someone (e.g: a councillor, a diddiman, a teacher, a doctor, etc). Other children in the group make polite requests to him. If the request is polite, the leader replies, 'Yes, of course'. Otherwise, 'No, I'm sorry, I can't help you'. e.g:
Pupil: Will you teach me to drive your truck please?
Driver: Yes, of course, I will.
Pupil: I can come with you to town, can't I?
Driver: No, I'm afraid there's no room; I can't help you.

LESSON THREE

Objective
The children will be able to greet each other politely and know how to end a conversation.

Method
1 Revise greetings: Hello, Good morning, Good evening, How are you? Revise ways of ending a conversation: Goodbye, Goodnight, See you again, It was nice seeing you.
2 Pupils to work in pairs. They must greet each other, exchange a few sentences and then end the conversation.
3 Construct situations in which different forms of greeting are appropriate, e.g: two friends meeting; meeting a tourist from overseas; buying something at the tradestore; meeting an uncle of yours.

WRITTEN SENTENCES

LESSON ONE (Lesson Suggestion 2)

Objective
The children will be able to write good sentences about a picture.

Preparation
Give out *Pupil's Book 3* to each child (page 16, Lesson 1).

Possible Answers
1 The men are building a new fence around the garden.
2 The women are preparing the soil for planting.
3 The babies hang in bilums while their mothers work.

LESSON TWO (Lesson Suggestion 11)

Objective
The children will be able to change the sentences from singular to plural.

Preparation
Give out *Pupil's Book 3* to each child (page 17, Lesson 2).

Answers

1 women do gardens
2 men help fences
3 children go gardens their mothers help them
4 babies go their mothers carry them their bilums they work
5 mothers hang bilums they do
6 men trees gardens
7 they burned trees
8 they they seeds

LESSON THREE (Lesson Suggestion 21)

Objective

The children will be able to take the main points from a message to make a telegram.

Preparation

Give out *Pupil's Book 3* to each child (page 17, Lesson 3).

Possible Answers

2 REA. NEED HELP ON FARM IN HOLIDAYS STOP CAN YOU HELP? (NAME)
3 D.A.S.F. OFFICER. PLEASE SEND INSTRUCTIONS FOR MAKING COMPOST STOP ALSO FERTILIZER TO START IT OFF (NAME)
4 R.D.O. PLEASE SEND MORE SEEDS CARROTS PARSNIPS TURNIPS PEAS SOYBEANS (NAME)
5 JOHN. VEGETABLES ARRIVING ON WASI'S TRUCK 10 A.M. TOMORROW (NAME)

LESSON FOUR

Objective

The children will be able to answer questions using the correct sentence pattern.

Preparation

Give out *Pupil's Book 3* to each child (page 18, Lesson 4).

Answers

1 No, they don't.	5 No, they don't.
2 Yes, they do.	6 No, they don't.
3 Yes, they do.	7 Yes, they do.
4 Yes, they do.	8 No, they don't.

LESSON FIVE

Objective

The children will be able to use the words 'more' and 'the most' correctly.

Preparation

Give out *Pupil's Book 3* to each child (page 19, Lesson 5).

Answers

1 more	2 the most	3 more
1 more	2 more	3 the most
1 more	2 the most	3 more

WRITTEN COMPOSITION

LESSON ONE

Objective
The children will be able to read something, remember the main points and then write about it.

Preparation
Give out *Pupil's Book 3* to each child (page 20, Lesson 1).

Model Answer
'Bush Fallow Rotation' means that a piece of land is used for gardens for one year and then it is left to go back to bush. This is done because gardens use up lots of goodness in the soil. After five years, the same piece of land is used for gardens again. By then the goodness has returned to the soil.

LESSON TWO (Lesson Suggestion 14B)

Objective
The children will be able to write a paragraph from notes.

Model Answers
There are several disadvantages to the Bush Fallow Rotation method of gardening. First of all, it means that gardens are often scattered far away from the village, so that villagers have a long way to go to their gardens. Also there is a lot of hard work to be done, clearing the bush on new land each year to make new gardens. In many cases there is not be enough land belonging to the clan to make new gardens every year. Five years is a long time to wait until land can be used again as a garden.

SPELLING

LESSON ONE (Lesson Suggestion 22)

Objective
The children will learn how to spell this week's words.

Preparation
Give out *Pupil's Book 3* to each child (page 20, Spelling List).

LESSON TWO

Select from Exercises A–E.

Preparation
Give out *Pupil's Book 3* to each child (pages 20–1).

Exercise A (Lesson Suggestion 29)

Answers

1 sway	3 cautiously	5 upright
2 steel	4 shriek overflow	

Exercise B

Possible Answers

cardboard — The box was made from cardboard.
grandmother — My grandmother is very old.
basketball — We like to play basketball.
together — We went to the feast together last night.
underneath — I found Rewa asleep underneath the house.

Exercise C (Lesson Suggestion 32)

Objective

The children will practise a spelling rule.

Answers

half — halves, life — lives, loaf — loaves, knife — knives, shelf — shelves, wolf — wolves, thief — thieves

Note

Make sure the children learn that these words *do not* change: roofs, chiefs, reefs.

Exercise D

Answers

carpenter — hammer and nails
teacher — blackboard
farmer — cattle and crops
butcher — knife
driver — cars and trucks
plumber — water pipes
mechanic — engines
clerk — pen and paper

Exercise E (Lesson Suggestion 27)

Answers

Cameron S.O.
Canan K.M.
Crawford L.J.
Cremin M.
Croft E.P.
Crogan C.
Croke M.
Cronau N.A.
Crosbies Service Station

HANDWRITING (Lesson Suggestion 33)

Preparation

Give out *Pupil's Book 3* to each child (pages 22–3).

READING

INTRODUCTION (Lesson Suggestion 34)

Objective

The children will be able to understand the background to the story, and the meaning of new words. The will read the story silently.

Preparation

Give out *Reader 3* to each child (pages 7–9), *'Cyclone Hannah'*.

Method

1 Introduce the story. Discuss bad storms, hurricanes, and cyclones. Has anyone experienced one of these? Ask those children to describe what it was like, how they felt, etc.
2 Follow Lesson Suggestion 34B.

LESSON ONE (Lesson Suggestion 34C)

Objective

Children will be able to answer questions to show they understand the story.

Preparation

Give out *Reader 3* to each child (pages 7–9) and *Pupil's Book 3* (page 23, Lesson 1).

Answers

1 It was hotter than usual and dark storm clouds were gathering. The air was very quiet and still.
2 They might have heard a cyclone warning on the radio, or recognized the weather signs.
3 They had to leave their house because it was being ripped apart by the wind and was no longer sheltering them from the storm.
4 It grew dark because big black storm clouds were covering the sky.
5 The canoes were smashed to pieces by the cyclone.
6 centre
7 wreckage
8 weak
9 . . . their houses, gardens, belongings and canoes.
10 . . . very shaken and bewildered.

LESSON TWO

Objective

The children will be able to choose the correct answer to each question.

Preparation

Give out *Pupil's Book 3* to each child (page 24, Lesson 2).

Answers

1 c 2 b 3 c

LESSON THREE

Objective

The children will be able to write down the main points of a passage.

Preparation

Give out *Pupil's Book 3* to each child (page 24, Lesson 3).

Answers

a The scientists suggested that they plant special trees that were not affected by frosts, in their gardens.
b They could cover their gardens with banana and pandanus leaves.
c They could plant new types of plants which survive frosts.

LESSON FOUR

Objective
The children will be able to read for enjoyment.

Preparation
Give out varied reading material for children to choose from.

OR POETRY (Lesson Suggestion 40)

Preparation
Give out *Pupil's Book 3* to each child (page 25).

Answers
2 They sing to help themselves work steadily, in rhythm.
3 They are happy because they know they will have plenty to eat or sell at the market.
4 Everybody helps to harvest the yams.

LESSON FIVE

Objective
The children will be able to play Reading Games.

Preparation
Give out *Reading Games for Grade 6* (pages 70–3, Unit 28).

Method
1 Choose work for the children to do from these pages.
2 Mark their work from *Teacher's Notes* (pages 77–9).

LISTENING 29

LESSON ONE

Objective
The children will be able to identify the speaker without looking at him. (This is a game the children will enjoy.)

Method
1 First choose one person to come to the front of the room and stand with his *back* to the class.
2 Teacher points to a child in the class who must say only 'hello'.
3 The person standing in front must say who spoke. If he says the right person then he stays out the front and someone else has a turn at saying 'hello'. If he says the wrong person, then the person who spoke comes to the front of the room and he must then identify the person speaking.

Note
If the person out front finds this easy, suggest that the 'speakers' try to disguise their voices.

LESSON TWO

Objective
The children will be able to remember people by their number.

Method

1 Choose ten people to come to the front of the room.
2 Number these people from 1–10.
3 Tell those people to say their numbers out loud several times (in order).
4 Now, mix the children up by changing their order of places.
5 Choose a child to put them in the right order again so that they number 1–10.
6 When the child thinks he has them in the correct order, the ten children must call out their numbers.
7 Mix them up again and choose someone else to come and put them in the right order.

Note

After each child arranges the children, it might be an idea for the ten children to go back to their correct order.

TALKING

LESSON ONE (Lesson Suggestion 1C)

Objection

The children will practise last week's sentence pattern:
Give me the book please. Which book? The red one on the table.

Method

Point to the substitution table on the board and revise it with the class.

LESSON TWO

Objective

The children will be able to use a new sentence pattern:
Have you tidied your desks yet? We haven't tidied our desks yet.

Which girl made this	CAKE?	The one who's	HIDING	her face.
	DRESS?		GIGGLING	
	BASKET?		SCRATCHING	her head
	MAT?		YAWNING	

Which boy made this	BOW?	The one who's	SMILING.
	CANOE?		SCRIBBLING ON PAPER
	SPEAR?		FOLDING HIS ARMS
	FLUTE?		PULLING HIS EAR

Which	BOY	is	HURT?	The one who's	CRYING.
	GIRL		TIRED?		YAWNING.
	BOY		COLD?		SHIVERING.
	GIRL		SICK?		SWEATING.

Note

Leave this work on the board for next week's revision.

ORAL EXPRESSION

LESSON ONE

Objective
The children will be able to introduce people to one another.

Method
1 Divide the class into threes, one to introduce the other two, e.g:
Girl A: Mother, this is my friend Elizabeth. Elizabeth, I'd like you to meet my mother.
Girl B: I'm pleased to meet you, Mrs Kivia.
Mother: Hello Elizabeth, I'm pleased to meet you too.
2 Suggest other situations, e.g: introducing your cousin to your friend; introducing your father to your teacher, introducing yourself to a stranger.

Note
Teach children to shake hands firmly when they meet someone.

LESSON TWO

Objective
The children will be able to apologize in different situations.

Method
In groups, children act out situations where an apology is required, e.g: knocking someone over, tripping up someone, burning food, spilling water on someone, dropping paint on someone, dropping something heavy on someone's foot.

Apologies
I'm sorry, I'm very sorry, Excuse me, I beg your pardon.

LESSON THREE

Objective
The children will be able to state their own opinions.

Method
1 Choose six children to form a panel. Choose a chairman.
2 The chairman (or teacher) asks the class for questions which require personal opinions. Each member of the panel is asked to give his or her opinion on the subject and give reasons for thinking that way. The class could ask the panel questions like:
1 Do you think we should build a school library?
2 Do you think girls should wear jeans or trousers?
3 Do you think it's right to let women do all the work in the village?
4 Should we have exams at the end of every school year?

Note
Give the class time to think up their *own* questions. These examples are only suggestions.

WRITTEN SENTENCES

LESSON ONE (Lesson Suggestion 2)

Objective
The children will be able to write good sentences about a picture.

Preparation
Give out *Pupil's Book 3* to each child (pages 26–7, Lesson 1).

Answers
1 . . . the river banks where it is soft and moist.
2 . . . it will be soft enough to work.
3 . . . pots.
4 . . . many generations.
5 . . . on the fire until all the water has boiled away.
6 . . . to use.
7 . . . makes pottery.
8 . . . saucepans . . .

LESSON TWO (Lesson Suggestion 13)

Objective
The children will be able to use the correct punctuation.

Preparation
Give out *Pupil's Book 3* to each child (page 27, Lesson 2).

Answers
1 Pots are made at Yabob village in Madang. This is a popular tourist attraction.
2 Near Sigatoka in Fiji, people still make pottery in the traditional way. They make two types of pots.
3 One type is used for special drinking bowls, but cannot be used for cooking. The other is used as a cooking pot.
4 Large bowls and water pots are still made in the Chambri Lakes area. The people use traditional methods to make their pots.
5 The Motuans used to trade their pots for sago from the people of Kerema. The long journey made by canoe for this purpose was called the 'Hiri'.

LESSON THREE (Lesson Suggestion 13)

Objective
The children will be able to put quotation marks in the right places.

Preparation
Give out *Pupil's Book 3* to each child (page 28, Lesson 3).

Answers
2 'One method is to mould the shape of the pot by hand', he continued.
3 He picked up another piece of clay and rubbed it on his leg until it grew long and thin. 'Another method is to make the pots by using coils', he said.

4 'Sometimes people use a round stone', he said, showing us a large stone. 'You put clay around the stone and then beat it with a wooden paddle.'
5 'Of course the modern method of making pots', he said, pointing to a picture on the wall, 'is by using a potter's wheel'.

LESSON FOUR

Objective
The children will be able to answer questions about pottery.

Preparation
Give out *Pupil's Book 3* to each child (page 28, Lesson 4).

Answers
1 Village people today can buy ready-made saucepans which do not break easily.
2 Some are still used for cooking but many are sold to tourists.
3 It means it is put on a fire to 'cook', so that the clay becomes hard.
4 In the coil method, you roll the clay into long strips and coil it around and around until it forms a pot. (Other answers: shape by hand, stone and paddle, potter's wheel.)
5 When clay dries out it goes hard and crumbly, and you cannot shape it into pots.

LESSON FIVE

Objective
The children will be able to choose the best adverb to go in a space.

Preparation
Give out *Pupil's Book 3* to each child (page 28, Lesson 5).

Answers
1 cheerfully
2 angrily
3 carefully
4 sleepily
5 softly

WRITTEN COMPOSITION

LESSON ONE (Lesson Suggestion 16)

Preparation
Give out *Pupil's Book 3* to each child (page 29, Lesson 1).

Objective
The children will be able to write an imaginative story about a picture.

LESSON TWO

Objective
The children will be able to write a report.

Preparation
Give out *Pupil's Book 3* to each child (page 30, Lesson 2).

Method

1 Read the lesson introductions.
2 Study the picture carefully and discuss all the damage that was done to the classroom. How do you think the thieves got inside?
3 Decide on a date when the robbery took place.
4 Ask children to write a report on the robbery.

Model Answer

On Monday 21st October at 8.15 a.m. the Headmaster of Kelema Community School called me to investigate a break-in which took place at the school the previous evening.

The rascals had broken a window close to the door and reached through the window to open the door lock. A large amount of damage was done to the classroom. This include broken chairs, ink poured over books, paint thrown on the blackboard, books thrown on the floor and windows broken.

K200 in cash was taken from a money box on the teacher's desk and K30 worth of sports equipment was stolen.

The work was probably done by a group of rascals who know or even attend the school. However, as yet there are no clues as to who these people are.

SPELLING

LESSON ONE (Lesson Suggestion 22)

Objective

The children will learn how to spell this week's words.

Preparation

Give out *Pupil's Book 3* to each child (page 31, Spelling List).

LESSON TWO

Select from Exercises A–E.

Preparation

Give out *Pupil's Book 3* to each child (pages 31–2).

Exercise A

Answers

1 firewood
2 wicked
3 moist
4 generation/skills

Exercise B

Answers

shaking struggling imagining baking paddling weaving carving dancing preparing racing admiring diving

Exercise C

Answers

1 clay
2 bowl
3 baked
4 fired
5 respect

Exercise D (Lesson Suggestion 27)

Answers
Timber Preservation, Timber Yard, Tools, Tourist Agencies, Tourist Information, Tours, Towel Supplies, Towing Station, Toy Shops, Tractors, Trade Stores, Travel Agents.

HANDWRITING (Lesson Suggestion 33)

Preparation
Give out *Pupil's Book 3* to each child (pages 33–4).

READING

INTRODUCTION (Lesson Suggestion 34)

Objective
The children will be able to understand the background to the story, and the meaning of new words. They will read the story silently.

Preparation
Give out *Reader 3* to each child (pages 14–7), '*Maratsaip*'.

Method
1 Introduce the story. Tell the children that this story is a legend. Say how important it is that we remember the stories of our ancestors and hand them on to our children. If this is not done, all the old stories will be forgotten.
2 Follow Lesson Suggestion 34B.

LESSON ONE (Lesson Suggestion 34C)

Objective
Children will be able to answer questions to show that they understand the story.

Preparation
Give out *Reader 3* (pages 14–7) and *Pupil's Book 3* to each child (page 34, Lesson 1).

Answers
1 He thought they were stupid.
2 He respected the village traditions.
3 To teach him a lesson.
4 He covered himself in clay from the river and then hid in a hollow tree trunk close to where Thomas was chopping firewood. Then he made noises pretending to be Maratsaip. Thomas saw him and was very frightened.
5 Yes, he did believe that he saw a Maratsaip.
6 He exaggerates about the Maratsaip, and tells them that he was not afraid. he also says he did not run away, which is not the truth.
7 Because it was really only Rigo, covered in mud, and he is not that big.
8 The wink (closing one eye very quickly) was a message which meant that both Rigo and Kepa knew what had really happened.

9 Kepa was probably thinking that Rigo had played a very good trick because now Thomas was interested in village traditions and did not make fun of them any more.
10 He had to crouch down behind the bush to hide.
The clay was very moist.
A fierce animal leaped out from behind the bushes.

LESSON TWO

Objective
The children will be able to understand some abbreviations.

Preparation
Give out *Pupil's Book 3* to each child (page 35, Lesson 2).

Method
1 Read through the list of abbreviations with the class. Talk about their meanings. Read through the advertisement example.

Answers
A black Toyota automatic in excellent condition for sale. It is registered and is a 1977 model car. It is selling for K2,000 or the closest amount offered. Phone 72 1116 extension 17 during working hours and phone 26 1511 after hours.
For the second part of this answer, the children must make up their own advertisement. Make sure they use the correct abbreviations to do this.

LESSON THREE

Objective
The children will be able to find the sentence which does not belong in the story.

Preparation
Give out *Pupil's Book 3* to each child (page 35, Lesson 3).

Method
1 Read through the letter example. Ask the children which sentence did not fit in with the rest of the letter.
Answer: Last week I had a sore stomach.
2 Now tell children to read through the other paragraphs and write down the sentences which do not fit in.

Answers
1 He was almost thirteen years old.
2 I cleaned my teeth this morning.
3 Kote liked swimming.
4 He ate ten bananas.
5 Yesterday the sea was very blue and the sun shone on the water.

LESSON FOUR

Objective
The children will be able to choose the correct word.

Preparation
Give out *Pupil's Book 3* to each child (page 36, Lesson 4).

Answers

1 sore	3 rich	5 frightened
2 hungry	4 angry	6 clever

OR POETRY (Lesson Suggestion 40)

Preparation
Give out *Pupil's Book 3* to each child (page 37), *'Clay Pot'*.

Answers
pots admire pans important clay ground valuable

LESSON FIVE

Objective
The children will be able to play Reading Games.

Preparation
Give out *Reading Games for Grade 6* to each child (pages 74–6).

Method
1 Choose games for the children to do.
2 Mark their work using *Teacher's Notes* (pages 79–81, Unit 29).

LISTENING 30

LESSON ONE

Objective
The children will be able to recognize vowel sounds.

Method
1 Say two words which sound almost the same, e.g: ear air.
2 Next ask someone to use the first word in a sentence to show its meaning, e.g: My ear is sore.
3 Now ask someone to use the second word in a sentence, e.g: We breathe air.
4 Do the same with these words:

match — much	rid — red
bed — bad	cold — killed
come — calm	bill — ball

LESSON TWO

Objective
The children will be able to 'hear' the correct word.

Method
Write the following lists of words on the blackboard:

back	bag	pick	pig	crew	grew
peck	peg	anchor	anger	crane	grain
lock	log	crab	grab	clue	glue
wick	wig	crate	great	crease	grease
duck	dug	classes	glasses		

Method

1 First read down the lists. The children repeat them after you.
2 Next, read across. The children say them after you.
3 Finally, read only *one* word from each pair. The children must say the word that you said, or write down the word you said.
4 If you have extra time, you could point to a word and ask the children to use it in a sentence.

TALKING

LESSON ONE (Lesson Suggestion 1C)

Objective

The children will practise last week's sentence pattern:
Which boy is tired? The one who's yawning.

Method

1 Point to the substitution table on the board and revise it with the class.

LESSON TWO

Objective

The children will practise a sentence pattern they already know:
Have you finished writing? No, I'm still writing.

Method

1 T: Have you finished writing, Bill?
C: I'm still writing.
T: Have you finished working in your garden yet, Kele?
C: No, I'm still working in it.
T: Have you finished sewing that shirt, Mele?
C: No, I'm still sewing it.
T: Have you finished cutting the grass outside, Pel?
C: No, I'm still cutting it.
2 In groups, the first child must ask a question using this sentence pattern. The next child must answer it.

LESSON THREE

Objective

The children will be able to use a new sentence pattern:
He's the man I saw yesterday.

Method

1 This pattern is used to show that something happened to someone.
Set up a make-believe tradestore. Sell items to the children.
T: Yes, what would you like?
C: I'd like a packet of biscuits please.
T: That's forty-five toea please.
T: I sold her some biscuits. She's the girl I sold some biscuits to. Who is she?
C: She's the girl you sold some biscuits to.
Continue selling things to the children using this sequence.

2 T: I gave that little boy some money. He's the boy I gave some money to. Who is he?
C: He's the boy you gave some money to.
T: I gave that girl the key. Who is she?
C: She's the girl you gave the key to.
T: I quarrelled with the women. Who is she?
C: She's the woman you quarrelled with.

LESSON FOUR

Objective
The children will practise the sentence pattern:
He's the man I saw yesterday.

Method
1 Say two sentences. The children must put them together.
T: I saw the man. You told me about him. I saw the man you told me about. Who did I see?
C: You saw the man I told you about.
T: My sister knows that girl. You told me about her. Who does my sister know?
C: My sister knows the girl I told you about.
T: I met those boys. You asked me about them. Who did I meet?
C: You met those boys I asked you about.
T: You spoke to the girl. She plays basketball. Who plays basketball?
C: The girl I spoke to plays basketball.

LESSON FIVE (Lesson Suggestion 1C)

Objective
The children will practise the new sentence pattern using a substitution table.

Preparation
Write the following on the blackboard before this lesson:

Who is	HE?	He's the man I saw yesterday.
	SHE?	She's the woman I told you about.

I met those	GIRLS.	You asked me about them.	Who are they?
	BOYS.		Who did I meet?
	PEOPLE.		Who did I meet?

They're the girls you asked me about.
I met the boys you asked me about.
I met those people you asked me about.

I gave the	GIRL	a ripe	MANGO.	Who is	SHE?
	BOY		BANANA		HE?
	WOMAN		TOMATO		SHE?
	MAN		PAWPAW		HE?

SHE'S	the	GIRL	you gave a ripe	MANGO	to.
HE'S		BOY		BANANA	
SHE'S		WOMAN		TOMATO	
HE'S		MAN		PAWPAW	

ORAL EXPRESSION

LESSON ONE

Objective
The children will be able to remember a list of things, in the correct order.

Method
1 Divide the class into groups.
2 Leader begins: I went fishing last night and caught two lobsters . . .
Next child: I went fishing last night and caught two lobsters, five mackerel . . .
Next child: I went fishing last night and caught two lobsters, five mackerel, a large red emperor . . .
3 And so on, until everyone has a turn in the group. If someone goes wrong the rest of the group must say, 'Boo Boo!' The next person then continues the sentence.

LESSON TWO

Objective
The children will be able to discuss a set of pictures.

Preparation
Give out *Pupil's Book 3* to each child (page 38, Lesson 1).

Method
1 Look at the sequence pictures on this page.
2 Discuss these by asking the children questions about what is happening,
e.g: Why are the men chopping down a paper-mulberry tree?
What are they doing to the tree once it is chopped down?
What are the women doing? Why?
Why is a woman painting designs on the tapa? What type of paint do you think she's using? What will the tapa be used for?

LESSON THREE

Objective
The children will be able to use their imagination and express their thoughts in English.

Method
1 Use a rolled piece of paper or cardboard as a telescope.
Start by saying: I've got a telescope.
Class: What can you see through it?
T: I can see a ship. (Give the telescope to a child.)
C: What can you see?
C: I can see a ship sailing on the water.
2 That child then passes the telescope to another child who must build onto the story, using his imagination. When the story is finished (e.g: the boat sinks) the teacher then starts another story (e.g: I can see a house).

WRITTEN SENTENCES

Note
Teach only FIVE of the six lessons.

LESSON ONE (Lesson Suggestion 2)

Objective
The children will be able to write good sentences about pictures.

Preparation
Give out *Pupil's Book 3* to each child (page 38, Lesson 1).

Possible Answers
1 First, the men cut down the paper-mulberry trees.
2 Next, men remove the bark from the tree trunks.
3 Then women scrape the bark with a shell to remove the outside bark.
4 They then beat the bark with clubs to soften it.
5 Finally, someone paints a design onto the tapa cloth with twigs.

LESSON TWO (Lesson Suggestion 4)

Objective
The children will be able to change direct speech into reported speech.

Preparation
Give out *Pupil's Book 3* to each child (page 39, Lesson 2).

Answers
1 Ruth asked Elizabeth if she could beat the tapa by herself.
2 Phillip asked Tanu if he made that mask by himself.
3 Father asked if she carried that firewood by herself.
4 Rose asked if they went to market by themselves.
5 Ria asked if the dog got inside the house by itself.
6 Mondo said that he could make that kundu by himself.
7 Tina asked if Peter made the canoe by himself.
8 The teacher asked Solomon if he could work out that problem by himself.

LESSON THREE

Exercise A

Objective
The children will be able to choose the correct word to fit in a sentence.

Preparation
Give out *Pupil's Book 3* to each child (page 39, Lesson 3, Exercise A).

Answers

1 made	3 from	5 less	7 woven
2 wear	4 have	6 used	8 feeds

Exercise B (Lesson Suggestion 2)

Objective
The children will be able to write sentences about pictures.

Preparation
Give out *Pupil's Book 3* to each child (page 40, Lesson 3, Exercise B).

Answers
1 Two women are choosing colourful material from a tradestore.
2 This woman is cutting out a dress pattern.
3 She is sewing the material on a sewing machine.
4 The woman has made herself a new dress.

LESSON FOUR

Objective
The children will be able to match sentence beginnings with sentence endings.

Preparation
Give out *Pupil's Book 3* to each child (pages 40–1, Lesson 4).

Answers

1 d	3 e	5 a	7 h
2 c	4 b	6 g	

LESSON FIVE

Objective
The children will be able to answer questions with sensible answers.

Preparation
Give out *Pupil's Book 3* to each child (page 41, Lesson 5).

Possible Answers
1 It used to be the only form of cloth used by village people.
2 The paper-mulberry tree is usually used for tapa making.
3 The Kukukukus were famous for their bark cloth.
4 Fiji, Samoa, Tonga and the Wallis and Futuna Islands also make tapa cloth.
5 People make things like bags, skirts, and wall hangings to sell to tourists.
6 They are easier to obtain, last longer, are softer, more comfortable to wear and can be washed when dirty.
7 Wool, silk, cotton are used to make modern cloth.
8 You can make shoes, belts and coats from leather.

LESSON SIX

Objective
The children will be able to join two sentences using 'unless'.

Preparation
Give out *Pupil's Book 3* to each child (page 41, Lesson 6).

Answers
1 Unless it stops raining soon, we will have to stay inside.
2 Unless the doctor comes soon, this child might die.
3 Unless you study hard, you will not go to High School.
4 Unless you eat good food, you will get sick.
5 Unless you do the job properly, you will not get paid.
6 Unless you know your tables, you will not be good at Mathematics.
7 Unless you help me carry these tools, I will not come with you.
8 Unless you listen hard, you will not hear the questions.

WRITTEN COMPOSITION

LESSON ONE

Objective
The children will be able to list the main points of a story.

Preparation
Give out *Pupil's Book 3* to each child (page 42, Lesson 1).

Answers
Tapa is made from the inner bark of the paper-mulberry tree.
The tree grows straight with no side branches.
It is cut down when eight metres high.
They peel the bark off in one big piece.
They scrape off the outer green bark with a shell.
They wet and beat the inner strips.
Finally, they decorate the tapa cloth with dye.

LESSON TWO

Objective
The children will be able to write a story from notes and take notes from a story.

Preparation
Give out *Pupil's Book 3* to each child (page 42, Lesson 2).

Model Answers

A Simeon woke up at 6 a.m. as the sun was rising. He ate a quick breakfast of pawpaw and banana and had a wash in the river. Then he set off to market in the next village. It took him an hour to get there. When he arrived he met some of his friends and they chatted together for a short time. Simeon bought a bunch of bananas. Then he went to a tradestore nearby and bought himself a new knife. On his way home, a truck stopped and he got a lift home with his wantoks.

B (If there is time.)
Indonesia has about 1000 active volcanoes
Is most volcanic country in world
Java and Bali have over 130 volcanoes
Many 2–3,000 metres high

HANDWRITING (Lesson Suggestion 33)

Preparation
Give out *Pupil's Book 3* to each child (page 43).

SPELLING

LESSON ONE (Lesson Suggestion 22)

Objective
The children will learn to spell this week's words.

Preparation
Give out *Pupil's Book 3* to each child (page 44, Spelling List).

LESSON TWO

Select from Exercises A–E, or give a spelling and dictation test on the last four week's work.

Preparation
Give out *Pupil's Book 3* to each child (pages 44–5).

Exercise A (Lesson Suggestion 29)

Answers

1 luggage
2 packages
3 sensible
4 thorn
5 material

Exercise B (Lesson Suggestion 8)

Answers

1 made
2 reigns
3 wait
4 seen
5 weak

Exercise C (Lesson Suggestion 32)

Possible Answers
carried worried busily uglier tidily hungrier

Exercise D

Possible Answers
strong, wrong, long, wing, pond, jam, ton, not, got, slip, etc.
E K Q U W X Y

Exercise E

Answers

1 crops
2 clay
3 stored
4 trunk
5 beaten
6 thorns
7 dangerous

READING

INTRODUCTION (Lesson Suggestion 34)

Objective
The children will be able to understand the background to the story, and the meaning of new words. They will read the story silently.

Preparation
Give out *Reader 2* to each child (pages 23–6), '*The Red Suitcase*'.

Method

1 Introduce the story. Talk about travelling by plane. How many children have travelled on a plane? Sometimes luggage gets lost or sent to the wrong place, especially if it isn't marked correctly.

2 Follow Lesson Suggestion 34B.

LESSON ONE (Lesson Suggestion 34C)

Objective
The children will be able to answer questions to show that they understand the story.

Preparation
Give out *Reader 3* (pages 23–6) and *Pupil's Book 3* to each child (page 46, Lesson 1).

Answers
1 Bilums full of green coconuts and betel-nut, brown paper packages and boxes, a cage with a dog inside, and a big red suitcase were unloaded from the plane.
2 He saw his name on it.
3 He chopped a hole in the top of the suitcase with his axe.
4 He found a hairbrush, a pair of stockings, a bottle of perfume, a bra, a pair of high-heeled shoes and a pink night dress.
5 He asked his brother to send him some clothes, tinned meat and kaukau.
6 She said it could be used as a broom for sweeping the floor.
7 She filled them with oranges.
8 Kikoi must have felt very annoyed.
9 . . . pressing the silver buttons on the side.
10 . . . the airlines had labelled the luggage wrongly.
11 She would probably be very surprised to see the bilum. She might feel very angry that she had received the wrong luggage. She would probably ask the airline to find her suitcase, or pay compensation.

LESSON TWO

Objective
The children will be able to skim (read) quickly through a passage to find out the main points.

Preparation
Give out *Pupil's Book 3* to each child (page 46, Lesson 2, Exercise A).

Answers
1 Beqa
2 an eel
3 pleaded
4 their ancestors

LESSON THREE

Objective
The children will be able to tell fact from opinion.

Preparation
Give out *Pupil's Book 3* to each child (page 47, Exercise B).

Answers

1	a	fact	b	opinion
2	a	fact	b	opinion
3	a	opinion	b	fact
4	a	opinion	b	fact

LESSON FOUR

Objective
The children will be able to read for enjoyment.

Method
1 Give out varied reading material for the children to read, or *Supplementary Reader 3*.

LESSON FIVE

Objective
The children will be able to play Reading Games.

Preparation
Give out *Reading Games for Grade 6* to each child (pages 76–9, Unit 30).

Method
1 Choose some of these games for the children to do.
2 Mark their work using *Teacher's Notes* (pages 81–3, Unit 30).

TERM 4

WEEKLY UNITS OF WORK: LISTENING

Unit 31 1 Hearing different vowel sounds in words
2 Hearing different vowel sounds in words

Unit 32 1 Hearing sound differences in words
2 Hearing sound differences in words

Unit 33 1 Hearing different vowel sounds in words
2 Hearing different vowel sounds in words

Unit 34 1 Hearing different vowel sounds in words
2 Hearing different vowel sounds in words

Unit 35 1 Dividing words into syllables
2 Dividing words into syllables

Unit 36 1 Putting the correct stress on a word
2 Putting the correct stress on a word

Unit 37 1 Putting the correct stress on a word
2 Putting the correct stress on a word

Unit 38 1 Hearing stressed words in a sentence
2 Hearing stressed words in a sentence

Unit 39 1 Putting stress marks above the correct syllable in a word
2 Putting stress marks above the correct syllable in a word

WEEKLY UNITS OF WORK: TALKING

Unit 31 Revision of Unit 30's work
Revision: This shirt needs washing. This one doesn't need washing.
New sentence pattern: That's the book that was on the table.
Revision

Unit 32 Revision of last week's work
Revision: While Dani was cleaning the board, Gari put a book on the table.
New sentence pattern: He gave me a mango that he bought at the market.
Revision

Unit 33 Revision of last week's work
Revision: What will you take to the market? I might take the cabbages.
New sentence pattern: Pene has finished his maths but he hasn't finished his English.
Revision.

Unit 34 Revision of last week's work
Revision: We've been working since recess.
New sentence pattern: Unless he comes soon, we'll go without him.
Revision

Unit 35 Revision of last week's work
Revision: Why didn't Tanu come to school? Because he's very sick.
New sentence pattern: He said that he would go to Lae in August.
Revision

Unit 36 Revision of last week's work
Revision of Units 1–9

Unit 37 Revision of Units 10–18.

Unit 38 Revision of Units 19–26

Unit 39 Revision of Units 27–35

WEEKLY UNITS OF WORK: ORAL EXPRESSION

Unit 31
1 Making up stories
2 Making up stories
3 Making up stories

Unit 32
1 Making accurate oral descriptions
2 Using sequence signals
3 Describing objects

Unit 33
1 Making comparisons
2 Making comparisons
3 Describing pictures

Unit 34
1 Asking questions to find out information
2 Describing different objects
3 Asking each other questions

Unit 35
1 Discussing pictures
2 Giving directions
3 Asking questions in an interview

Unit 36
1 Solving a problem
2 Solving a problem
3 Speaking effectively on the telephone

Unit 37
1 Using a telephone
2 Passing on a message by telephone
3 Practising with a telephone

Unit 38
1 Preparing short talks
2 Giving a short talk
3 Holding a discussion

Unit 39
1 Making a play or mime
2 Performing a play
3 Miming actions

WEEKLY UNITS OF WORK: WRITTEN SENTENCES

Unit 31
1 Writing sentences about a picture
2 Punctuation
3 Writing descriptions to match pictures
4 Using 'for', 'since' and 'ago'
5 Putting in the correct pronoun
6 Practising known sentence patterns (optional)

Unit 32
1 Punctuation
2 Using 'much' or 'many'
3 Making notes
4 Writing sentences about pictures
5 Using pronouns instead of nouns
6 Practising known sentence patterns (optional)

Unti 33
1 Writing descriptions
2 Punctuation
3 Choosing the correct word
4 Putting words in the correct order
5 Changing from singular to plural
6 Using 'who' and 'which' (optional)

Unit 34
1 Writing sentences about pictures
2 Choosing the correct word
3 Answering questions
4 Writing imaginative sentences
5 Using quotation marks

Unit 35 1 Writing sentences about pictures
2 Punctuation
3 Reported speech
4 Using 'many are' and 'much is'
5 Choosing the correct word
6 Using phrases telling WHERE (optional)

Unit 36 1 Choosing the correct word
2 Writing the correct verb
3 Choosing the correct word
4 Using 'who' and 'which'
5 Using 'only'
6 Using phrases telling WHEN (optional)

Unit 37 1 Writing sentences about a picture
2 Punctuation
3 Using 'yet' and 'almost'
4 Writing about pictures
5 Writing the correct verb (optional)
6 Using ordinal numbers (optional)

Unit 38 1 Writing sentences about pictures
2 Writing a descriptive paragraph
3 Using commas
4 Choosing the correct word
5 Punctuation
6 Writing the correct form of the verb (optional)

Unit 39 1 Writing sentences about pictures
2 Using reflexive pronouns
3 Writing the correct form of the verb
4 Joining sentences with conjunctions
5 Using quotation marks
6 Reported speech (optional)

WEEKLY UNITS OF WORK: WRITTEN COMPOSITION

Unit 31 1 Writing sentences to match pictures
2 Giving directions

Unit 32 1 Filling in forms
2 Writing a personal letter

Unit 33 1 Writing a description
2 Writing an opinion

Unit 34 1 Following directions
2 Making notes

Unit 35 1 Writing an imaginative story
2 Writing about a chosen topic

Unit 36 1 Writing about funeral customs
2 Writing a personal letter

Unit 37 1 Writing a conclusion to a story
2 Writing about a rescue

Unit 38 1 Making notes
2 Expanding from notes

Unit 39 1 Expanding from notes
2 Writing a personal letter

WEEKLY UNITS OF WORK: SPELLING

Unit 31 seashore seaweed conch scales
necklace palm coconut splash (From Reader)
Family Group: Carvings
Spelling Exercises A–E

Unit 32 cheap crabs direction silent
bargain slippery childish float (From Reader)
Family Group: Weaving
Spelling Exercises A–E

Unit 33 warrior sign mass show
showground handcrafts chanting tourists (From Reader)
Family Group: Decorations
Spelling Exercises A–E

Unit 34 orphan jealous ugly secret
wander fright female male (From Reader)
Family Group: Copra
Spelling Exercises A–E

Unit 35 saddle handlebars crazy steer
yelled parcel brake steady (From Reader)
Family Group: Coffee
Spelling Exercises A–E

Unit 36 custom stretch jump unusual
length legend ankles path (From Reader)
Family Group: Burial Customs
Spelling Exercises A–E

Unit 37 science tears glasses control
shoulder spill obey pet (From Reader)
Family Group: Hunting
Spelling Exercises A–E

Unit 38 choose message trained sure
prove colourful useful delicious (From Reader)
Family Group: Mammals
Spelling Exercises A–E

Unit 39 sticky garfish current bait
kite steal web breeze (From Reader)
Family Group: Reptiles
Spelling Exercises A–D

WEEKLY UNITS OF WORK: HANDWRITING

Units 31–9 Model passage for the children to copy each week.

WEEKLY UNITS OF WORK: READING

Unit 31 Intro Reader: '*Gena's New Bride*' (Part 1)

1 Comprehension
2 Drawing conclusions
3 Recognizing exaggerations
4 Reading for enjoyment (Poetry)
5 Reading Games

Unit 32 Intro. Reader: '*Gena's New Bride*' (Part 2)
1 Comprehension
2 Drawing conclusions
3 Thinking up alternative titles
Drawing conclusions
4 Reading for enjoyment (Poetry)
5 Reading Games

Unit 33 Intro. Reader: '*Thief at the Show*'
1 Comprehension
2 Comprehension
3 Comprehension (a notice)
4 Reading for enjoyment (Poetry)
5 Reading Games

Unit 34 Intro. Reader: '*How the Coconut Palm was Made*'
1 Comprehension
2 Recognizing advertisement 'gimmicks'
3 Comprehension (a letter)
4 Reading for enjoyment (Poetry)
5 Reading Games

Unit 35 Intro. Reader: '*Wari's Bicycle*'
1 Comprehension
2 Matching pictures with captions
3 Following directions on a map
4 Reading for enjoyment (Poetry)
5 Reading Games

Unit 36 Intro. Reader: '*The Big Jump*'
1 Comprehension
2 Choosing the best headlines to match reports
3 Studying a poem
4 Reading for enjoyment
5 Reading Games

Unit 37 Intro. Reader: '*Simon's Pet*'
1 Comprehension
2 Comprehension
3 Correct order of events
4 Reading for enjoyment (Poetry)
5 Reading Games

Unit 38 Intro. Reader: '*Choosing a King*'
1 Comprehension
2 Comprehension (a letter)
3 Drawing conclusions
4 Reading for enjoyment (Poetry)
5 Reading Games

Unit 39 Intro. Reader: '*Spider Web Fishermen*'
1 Comprehension
2 Reading for understanding
3 Miming
4 Reading for enjoyment
5 Reading Games

LISTENING 31

LESSON ONE

Objective
The children will be able to hear different vowel sounds in words.

Preparation
Write the following lists of words on the blackboard before the lesson.

A shoe	B lose	C too	D look
A know	B foe	C sew	D bought
A ball	B fowl	C born	D bore
A mail	B weight	C wives	D way
A fire	B fair	C care	D bear
A score	B scar	C raw	D pour
A gate	B wait	C straight	D sat

Method
1 Tell the class to look at the words on the board.
2 Instruct children to get a pencil and piece of paper ready to write down their answers.
3 Say: I shall say each line of words once. Write down the *letter* in front of the word that sounds different from the others. (One of the underlined parts sounds different from the others.)
A shoe B lose C too D look
D look (sounds different from the others).
4 Now read through all these words slowly.
5 Mark their work by reading through all the words again and asking a child to say which words is different.

Answers
D D B C A B D

LESSON TWO

Objective
The children will be able to hear sound differences in words.

Preparation
Write the following lists of words on the blackboard before the lesson.

A rise	B race	C case	D face
A piece	B keep	C dive	D leave
A fizz	B licks	C six	D sticks
A tree	B shriek	C piece	D pick

Method
1 & 2 as for Lesson 1.
2 Read through the lists of words slowly.

3 Children must write down the *word* which sounds different.
   A rise B race C case D face
   A rise (sounds different)
4 Read through all the words again, this time asking children to say the word that is different. Children mark their own work.

Answers
rise dive fizz pick

TALKING

LESSON ONE

Objective
The children will practise the sentence pattern they learned in Talking, Unit 30, Lesson Four: Who is he? He's the man I saw yesterday.

Method
1 Write the substitution table from Talking, Unit 30, on the board. Revise it with the class.
2 Choose children to read out a sentence from the table.
3 Rub out the table and ask for further examples.

LESSON TWO

Objective
The children will practise a sentence pattern they already know:
This shirt needs washing. This one doesn't need washing.

Method
1 Hold up two socks. Say: This sock needs washing. It's very dirty.
   Point to the clean one: This one doesn't need washing. It's clean.
2 Point to a broken desk: This desk needs fixing. It's broken.
   Point to a good desk: This one doesn't need fixing.
3 Divide the children into groups to practise this sentence pattern.
   Give them some ideas, e.g: wall needs painting
   shirt needs mending
   hair needs brushing
   hands need washing

LESSON THREE

Objective
The children will be able to use a new sentence pattern:
That's the book that was on the table.

Method
1 Have a book on the table, a book in your bag and a book in the cupboard.
   Pick up the book on the table:
   T: This is the book that was on the table. Which book is this?
   C: That's the book that was on the table.
   T: Which book is this?
   C: That's the book that was in your bag.
   T: Which book is this?
   C: That's the book that was in the cupboard.
2 Show pictures, e.g: a dog.

T: That's the dog that bites people. Which dog is it?
C: It's the dog that bites people.
T: That's the bird that sings every morning. Which bird is it?
C: That's the bird that sings every morning.

3 Divide the class into groups. Leader must start by saying a sentence, e.g: That's the pencil I use every day. Which pencil is it? The rest of the group must answer. Then the leader chooses someone else to start.

LESSON FOUR

Objective

The children will practise this sentence pattern:
The book that's on the table is mine.

Method

1 Take a number of pupils' books and put them in different places.
T: The book that's on the table is mine. Which book is yours, Bari?
C: The book that's on the shelf is mine.
T: Which book is yours, Matina?
C: The book that's under the chair is mine.
T: Which book is hers?
C: The book that's under the chair is hers.

2 Tell a story: Here's a sad story of three dogs. The first dog bit a man. It was shot. The second dog got into a fight. It lost half its fur. The third dog crossed a road to chase a cat. It got run over.
T: Which dog was shot?
C: The dog that bit a man was shot.
T: Which dog lost half its fur?
C: The dog that got into a fight lost half its fur.
T: Which dog got run over?
C: The dog that chased the cat across the road got run over.

LESSON FIVE (Lesson Suggestion 1C)

Objective

The children will practise this sentence pattern using a substitution table.

Preparation

Write the following table on the blackboard:

The book that's	ON THE TABLE	is	MINE.
	UNDER THE CHAIR		HIS
	ON THE SHELF		HERS

The pen that was found	ON THE FLOOR	is	HENRI'S.
	IN THE BIN		MARIA'S
	OUTSIDE		KEMI'S

The house that was	BURNT DOWN	belonged to	MEA.
	BUILT LAST WEEK		PEL'S FATHER
	BURGLED		MY AUNTY
	BLOWN DOWN		MR AWANI

That's the child who	THREW THE STONE AT ME.
	HELPED ME CARRY THE FIREWOOD
	PUSHED OVER THE BUCKET OF WATER

Note

Remember to leave this work on the blackboard for revision next week.

ORAL EXPRESSION

LESSON ONE

Objective
The children will be able to make up stories.

Method
1 Give the children an outline of a story, e.g: a time (midnight), a place (in the bush), a sound (loud screams), the weather (thunder and lightning).
2 Divide the children into groups. Each group must expand the outline given by the teacher to make a story.
3 After five minutes, ask one person from each group to tell the rest of the class about the story they made up.

LESSON TWO

Objective
The children will be able to make up imaginative stories.

Method
1 Suggest two characters and an event, e.g: a policeman, a robber, a stolen car.
2 Divide the class into groups.
3 The leader of the group starts the story with one of the characters, e.g: A policeman was on duty one night, when he saw a car stopped by the side of the road.
The next child continues the story, e.g: He went up to it and looked in the window. He saw a man fast asleep in the front seat.
Each child following must try to make the story interesting and exciting, e.g: The policeman called to the man who immediately woke up. When he saw the policeman he looked frightened. He opened the car door and started to run away.

LESSON THREE

Objective
The children will be able to make up imaginative stories.

Method
1 As for Lesson Two.
2 You could write the following topics on the blackboard. Each group can choose which one they want to make a story about:
   1 a truck driver, a village man, a dead pig.
   2 a teacher, a pupil, a broken desk.
   3 a mother, a child, a radio.

WRITTEN SENTENCES

Note
Remember, you should teach only FIVE of the six lessons. Choose one lesson for homework, or for fast workers to do.

LESSON ONE (Lesson Suggestion 2)

Objective
The children will be able to write good sentences about a picture.

Preparation
Give out *Pupil's Book 3* to each child (page 48, Lesson 1).

Possible Answers
1 The men are carving tables and bowls.
2 The young boys are watching their fathers.
3 Two women are sitting in front of their houses.

LESSON TWO (Lesson Suggestion 13)

Objective
The children will be able to use the correct punctuation.

Preparation
Give out *Pupil's Book 3* to each child (page 48, Lesson 2).

Answers
1 The Trobriand Islanders are famous for their skilful carvings. These people have great pride in their work.
2 They use traditional tools such as stone adzes to make the carvings.
3 Carvings made from black ebony wood are worth a great deal of money.
4 The Trobriand carvers make special tables from one piece of wood. They show two figures holding up the top of the tables.
5 These carvers also make beautiful bowls, walking sticks, crocodiles, pigs, human figures and trays.
6 In the Manus Province, they make knives with driftwood handles and tortoise-bone blades.
7 Carvers use boars' tusks and sometimes the sharp teeth of large rats as scrapers, or for cutting patterns into the wood.
8 They also make traditional tools from bone, shell and stone flints.

LESSON THREE (Lesson Suggestion 2)

Objective
The children will be able to write descriptions to match pictures.

Preparation
Give out *Pupil's Book 3* to each child (page 49, Lesson 3).

Possible Answers
1 In the village of Baruni, near Port Moresby, carvers make round tables like these.
2 On Siassi Island, carvers make beautiful black bowls which often have lime or mother of pearl shell in a pattern around the edges.
3 The Sepik area is famous for its carved masks which usually look like faces and are highly decorated.
4 In the Sepik area, people make Kundu drums from a hollow piece of wood with lizard skin stretched over the top.
5 In Kanganamon, in the Sepik, decorated hooks are used for hanging baskets inside the house.
6 In Palembi, also in the Sepik, people carve flute stoppers in the shape of birds and other animals.

LESSON FOUR

Objective
The children will be able to use 'for', 'since' and 'ago' correctly.

Preparation
Give out *Pupil's Book 3* to each child (page 50, Lesson 4).

Answers

1 since	3 ago	5 for	7 ago
2 for	4 for	6 since	8 ago

LESSON FIVE

Objective
The children will be able to put the correct pronoun in the spaces.

Preparation
Give out *Pupil's Book 3* to each child (page 51, Lesson 5).

Answers

1 her	4 their	7 his it	10 their them
2 his	5 her	8 her they	
3 his	6 their	9 his he it	

LESSON SIX (Optional)

Objective
The children will be able to practise a language pattern.

Preparation
Give out *Pupil's Book 3* to each child (page 51, Lesson 6).

Answers

1 Yes she can.	3 No she can't.	5 Yes he can.
2 Yes he can.	4 No I can't.	

Possible Answers
6 Can they do that work by themselves?
7 Can you carry that firewood by yourself?
8 Can he lift that log?

WRITTEN COMPOSITION

LESSON ONE

Objective
The children will be able to think up captions to match the pictures.

Preparation
Give out *Pupil's Book 3* to each child (page 52, Lesson 1).

Possible Answers
2 'Oh boy! I've got a good one this time. It must be nearly as big as a shark.'
3 'Fire! Kela's still inside! I'm coming Kela! I'll save you. Climb out the window. Hurry, I'll catch you!
4 'Ow! I've fallen out of the tree and hurt my leg. I can't even walk. How am I going to get home?'

LESSON TWO

Objective
The children will be able to give directions.

Preparation
Give out *Pupil's Book 3* to each child (page 53, Lesson 2).

Answers
A Walk down to the end of this street and turn right. Take the first turn on your left and keep walking past the tradestores. Take the second turning on your left. The house you are looking for is the third house on the right hand side.
B b Continue down the main road, past the school and the football field. Take the first turning on your right, and you will find the hospital at the end of this street.
c Follow the main road and take the third turning on your left. Pita's house is the first house you come to at the end of the road, on the left hand side.

SPELLING

LESSON ONE (Lesson Suggestion 22)

Objective
The children will learn to spell this week's words. (They are from this week's story.)

Preparation
Give out *Pupil's Book 3* to each child (page 54, Spelling List).

LESSON TWO

Select from Exercises A–E (pages 54–6).

Exercise A (Lesson Suggestion 29)

Answers
1 scales
2 palm coconut
3 seaweed
4 splash

Exercise B

Possible Answers
grow grain green grass, brown breeze breathe brick, cloak climb cloud, crocodile cruel crash, drum dream drive, free frog fruit.

Exercise C (Lesson Suggestion 31)

Answers

Clues Across
1 seaweed
4 palm
5 smooth

Clues Down
1 scales
2 bowl
3 drum
6 tools

Exercise D

Answer
Meet me by the river at ten tonight.

Exercise E (Lesson Suggestion 27)

Answer
Chambri Lakes Curum River Kanganamon Kaningra Kusvenmas
Palambei Shamperi Torembi

HANDWRITING (Lesson Suggestion 33)

Preparation
Give out *Pupil's Book 3* to each child (page 56).

READING

INTRODUCTION (Lesson Suggestion 34)

Objective
The children will understand the background to the story, and the meaning of new words. They will read the story silently.

Preparation
Give out *Reader 3* to each child (pages 18–20), *'Gena's new Bride'* (Part 1).

Method
1 Discuss the sea and the creatures that live in it, such as turtles, sharks, whales, dugongs, etc.

LESSON ONE (Lesson Suggestion 34C)

Objective
The children will be able to answer questions to show they understand the story.

Preparation
Give out *Pupil's Book 3* to each child (page 57, Lesson 1).

Answers
1 Gena saw a beautiful mermaid sitting on a rock.
2 She was probably frightened of him.
3 He asked him to bring one hundred coconuts for his army before the moon rose in the sky.
4 He removed the musks by hitting the coconuts on a spike and tearing the husks off.
5 He told the children that the coconuts were for a bride price.
6 . . . the moon rose that night.
7 . . . water that comes out of your skin when you work had.
8 . . . a woman with a tail like a fish.
9 task dusk briefly

10 **Looking**	**Speaking**
peering	called
staring	asked
glanced	said
watch	cried
gazed	replied
	answered

LESSON TWO

Objective
The children will be able to draw conclusions from what they read.

Preparation
Give out *Pupil's Book 3* to each child (page 58, Lesson 2, Exercise A).

Answers
1 Hetti felt very nervous and afraid.
2 She sat stiffly in her seat; her fingers tightened their grip on the arm rests; she held her breath.
3 The hostess probably noticed that Hetti was nervous, because she came over to help Hetti.
4 The air hostess offered her a cold drink or a book to read. She probably did this to help her to relax and take her mind off the plane.

LESSON THREE

Objective
The children will be able to recognize exaggerations.

Preparation
Give out *Pupil's Book 3* to each child (page 58, Lesson 2, Exercise B).

Answers
1 I am very thirsty.
2 I am very hungry.
3 The wild boar was extremely big.
4 That book will take me a long time to read.
5 He can run very fast.
6 That bread is very hard.

LESSON FOUR (Lesson Suggestion 39)

Objective
The children will be able to read for enjoyment.

Preparation
Give out *Supplementary Reader 3* to each child.

OR POETRY (Lesson Suggestion 40)

Preparation
Give out *Pupil's Book 3* to each child (page 59).

Answers
1 They are the thoughts of an old man.
2 He is sad because village life has changed so much over recent years.

3 They have left the village to go to the towns.
4 The villages will soon be empty unless the children return to work and farm the land.

LESSON FIVE

Objective
The children will be able to do Reading Games.

Preparation
Give out *Reading Games for Grade 6* (pages 79–81, Unit 31).

Method
1 Choose games for the children to do.
2 Mark their work using *Teacher's Notes* (pages 83–6, Unit 31).

LISTENING 32

LESSON ONE

Objective
The children will be able to hear sound differences in words.

Preparation
Write the following lists of words on the blackboard:

A sign	B time	C lane	D fry
A fast	B star	C rather	D share
A hand	B end	C feather	D friend
A stitch	B wish	C match	D fetch
A century	B receive	C send	D shed
A instead	B heavy	C band	D lend
A tall	B recall	C torch	D cannot

Method
1 & 2 as for last week.
3 Read through each line of words slowly.
4 Children must write down the *word* which sounds different (one of the underlined parts sounds different from the others).
5 When finished, read through the lists again and ask children to say which word is different. Children mark their own work.

Answers
lane share hand wish shed band cannot

LESSON TWO

Objective
The children will be able to hear sound differences in words.

Preparation
Write the following lists of words on the blackboard:

A haul	B fell	C fall	D trawler
A shake	B break	C leave	D pain
A reign	B knew	C never	D lake
A dumb	B some	C murmur	D honey
A stored	B stalled	C passed	D crawler
A posted	B lifted	C roasted	D called

Method
1 & 2 as above.
3 Read through the lists of words slowly.
4 Children must write down the *word* with the different sound in it.
5 Read through the word again, asking the children for the answers.

Answers
fell leave lake money crawler called

TALKING

LESSON ONE

Objective
The children will practise last week's sentence pattern:
The book that's on the table is mine.

Method
1 Point to the substitution table on the board. Say examples from it.
2 Choose pupils to give examples from it.
3 Rub it out and ask for further examples.

LESSON TWO

Objective
The children will practise a sentence pattern they already know:
While Dani was cleaning the board, Gari put a book on the table.

Method
1 When two people do things at the same time, this is how we say it:
While Denipa was sweeping, Mary read her book.
While Pat was playing football, Kepa tidied the room.
2 Divide the class into pairs. Choose one pair to come to the front of the room. Each person must do something. The rest of the class says: While Gera was sweeping the floor, Lina cleaned the blackboard.
3 In pairs, children must do something and then say this sentence pattern.

LESSON THREE

Objective
The children will be able to use a new sentence pattern:
He gave me a mango that he bought at the market.

Method

1 Give a pupil a biro.
   T: I gave Meli a biro that I bought in the store. What did I do?
   C: You gave her a biro that you bought in the store.
2 Give a pupil a banana.
   T: I gave Gimoro a banana that I picked on the way to school. What did I do?
   C: You gave her a banana that you picked on the way to school.
3 Divide the class into pairs. One person says a sentence, e.g: The homework that I did last night is on my table. Where is it?
   The other person replies: The homework that you did last night is on your table.

LESSON FOUR

Objective

The children will practise this sentence pattern:
He gave me a mango that he bought at the market.

Method

1 Give several more examples as for Lesson Three.
   T: I gave him the rubber that I found under his desk. What did I do?
   C: You gave him the rubber that you found under his desk.
2 Explain that you can often shorten this pattern and leave out 'that'.
   T: Which book did you read? A: I read the book you gave me.
3 In groups, children must practise this patterns. Leader starts by saying: Which pencil did you use? Next child says: I used the one you gave me.

LESSON FIVE (Lesson Suggestion 1C)

Objective

The children will practise this sentence pattern using a substitution table.

Preparation

Write the following substitution table on the blackboard:

He gave me a	MANGO	that he bought at the	MARKET.
	PAWPAW	she	TRADESTORE
	GUAVA		
	SOURSOP		
	LOAF OF BREAD		
	SHIRT		

I	READ	the	BOOK	that I got from the	LIBRARY.
	ATE		ORANGE		ORCHARD.
	BROKE		CHALK		CLASSROOM.

Which	BOOK	did you	READ?	I	READ	the	BOOK	you gave me.
	FRUIT		EAT?		ATE		FRUIT	
	CRAYON		USE?		USED		CRAYON	
	SPEAR						SPEAR	

Note

Leave this work on the board till next week.

ORAL EXPRESSION

LESSON ONE

Objective
The children will be able to make accurate oral descriptions.

Method
1 Divide the class into pairs.
2 In pairs, the children must describe different places to each other, such as their homes, the village, the school, etc.
3 Give an example first by describing the school. Say where it is; its size; shape and colour; what its made from; what its like inside, etc.

LESSON TWO

Objective
The children will be able to use sequence signals when talking about something.

Method
1 Write the following sequence signals on the board: firstly secondly thirdly then next also finally
2 Give an example of how to use these words, e.g:
Cooking Rice — Firstly you must wash the rice. Secondly you must half fill a big pot with water. Then you must heat the water until it boils. Next, add the rice to the boiling water. Also remember to add some salt. Wait 20 minutes until the rice is cooked. Finally strain the water off the rice.
3 Divide the class into groups and give each group a topic, e.g: making coconut cream. The leader starts the story using 'firstly', then the next person continues, until everyone has a turn.

LESSON THREE

Objective
The children will be able to describe objects.

Method
1 Choose an object in the room and describes it to the class. They must guess what it is, e.g:
It is something very small and white. I use it every day when I teach you. Children must not use it unless I tell them to.
If the children cannot guess what it is, give them an easier clue — I write with it.
ANSWER: Chalk.
2 Divide the class into groups. The leader starts by describing an object in the room. Whoever guesses it first then has a turn.

WRITTEN SENTENCES

Note
Remember, teach only FIVE of the six lessons. Choose one for homework, or for fast workers to do.

LESSON ONE (Lesson Suggestion 13)

Objective
The children will be able to use correct punctuation.

Preparation
Give out *Pupil's Book 3* to each child (page 60, Lesson 1).

Answers
1 The people in the western islands of the Manus Province make finely-woven hats and bags. They use fibres from the leaf-buds of coconut trees.
2 In the Sepik, people use a river-grass fibre dyed in reds, browns and greens to make mats and bags.
3 In the Maprik area, people make a type of cane from sago palms. This fibre is very light and strong and it is used to make fish traps and food baskets.
4 Weavers from Siassi Island also use coconut leaf-bud fibre to make small bags for carrying betel-nut.
5 The Trobriand Islanders make woven mat squares from seagrass. People in Hong Kong, the Philippine Islands and in China also make this type of matting.
6 A Hagen axe is made of an adze which is firmly secured to a decorated, woven-cane handle. This weaving is very fine and decorated in designs of black and white.
7 Throughout Papua New Guinea, people make string bags called bilums. Sometimes they use creepers to make these bilums.
8 Some people make baskets from strips of pandanus leaf wrapped around a strong fibre from the coconut palm leaf.

LESSON TWO

Objective
The children will be able to use 'much' or 'many', and 'more' or 'the most' correctly.

Preparation
Give out *Pupil's Book 3* to each child (page 60, Lesson 2).

Answers

1 many	2 much	3 many
1 more	2 the most	3 the most
4 much	5 many	6 much
4 more	5 more	6 the most

LESSON THREE (Lesson Suggestion 14)

Objective
The children will be able to take notes.

Preparation
Give out *Pupil's Book 3* to each child (page 61, Lesson 3).

Answers
pass each leaf quickly through fire
boil leaf in fresh water for short time
cut off sharp edges in middle of leaf

dry strips of leaf in sun several days
roll strips into long coils and store

LESSON FOUR (Lesson Suggestion 16B)

Objective
The children will be able to write good sentences about pictures.

Preparation
Give out *Pupil's Book 3* to each child (page 62, Lesson 4).

Answers
1 Wamea wanted to run his own business, but he could not decide what to do. Suddenly he had an idea.
2 He picked up his bush knife and went off into the bush. He cut down long lengths of cane and put them over his shoulder. When he had enough, he returned home.
3 Wamea asked his friend Nipa to help him prepare the cane. They cut it into strips and soaked it in the river to make it soft.
4 Wamea then started to make a chair. He remembered making some cane furniture at High School, so he knew what to do.
5 After many weeks of hard work, Wamea used an empty village house to display his furniture. He put up a big sign on the house and a notice by the road. Soon many people came to buy furniture for their houses.

LESSON FIVE

Objective
The children will be able to use pronouns instead of nouns.

Preparation
Give out *Pupil's Book 3* to each child (page 63, Lesson 5).

Answers

1 They	3 she	5 her
2 them	4 We	6 them

LESSON SIX (Optional)

Objective
The children will practise using a sentence pattern they already know.

Preparation
Give out *Pupil's Book 3* to each child (page 63, Lesson 6).

Answers
1 Yes, I think he can./No, I do not think he can.
2 Yes, I think I will./No, I do not think I will.
3 Yes, I think she will.
4 Yes, I think they will.
5 Yes, I think I can.

Possible Answers
6 Do you think you will win the race?
7 Do you think it will rain today?
8 Do you think they will come tonight?

WRITTEN COMPOSITION

LESSON ONE (Lesson Suggestion 20)

Objective
The children will be able to fill in a form correctly.

Preparation
Give out *Pupil's Book 3* to each child (page 64, Lesson 1).

Answers
a 62745 (the number on the old postal order)
b K20.00 (the value of money of the postal order)
c John Pita (your first names)
d Gelang (your last name)
e P.O. Box 123, Boroko. (your address)
f (you sign your name)
g 24/8/82 (today's date)

LESSON TWO (Lesson Suggestion 17)

Objective
The children will be able to write a personal letter.

Preparation
Give out *Pupil's Book 3* to each child (page 65, Lesson 2).

Model Answer

P.O. Box 6142,
Boroko,
National Capital Province.

8th November 1982.

Dear Lucy,

Thank you very much for sending me a postal order for K20 to pay back the money I lent you. I should have written to you a long time ago, but I have been very busy. In fact I was so busy that I didn't take the postal order to the post office in time. It is now out of date, so I have to fill out a form to get a new one.

I hope you are well, and I look forward to seeing you in the holidays.

Love from your brother,

SPELLING

LESSON ONE (Lesson Suggestion 22)

Objective
The children will learn how to spell this week's words. (They are from this week's story.)

Preparation
Give out *Pupil's Book 3* to each child (page 65, Spelling List).

LESSON TWO

Select from Exercises A–E (pages 65–6).

Exercise A (Lesson Suggestion 29)

Answers
A 1 cheap 2 silent 3 slippery 4 float
B baskets fibres pandanus vines dyes

Exercise B

Answers
sign knee rustle whistle knuckle knot crumb doubt knock honesty

Exercise C (Lesson Suggestion 32)

Answers
hardly selfishly finally loudly stupidly completely cleverly dangerously silently carelessly

Exercise D

Answers

horse — foal	goat — kid	sheep — lamb
pig — piglet	lion — cub	hen — chicken
cat — kitten	dog — puppy	goat — kid

Exercise E

Answers
1 May I have a match to light this fire?
This match won't light because it's wet.
2 The football match was a great success.
We held a cricket match with that school last year.
3 These shoes do not match.
That shirt does not match your trousers.

HANDWRITING (Lesson Suggestion 33)

Preparation
Give out *Pupi's Book 3* to each child (page 67).

READING

INTRODUCTION (Lesson Suggestion 34)

Objective
The children will understand the background to the story, and the meaning of the new words. They will read the story silently.

Preparation
Give out *Reader 3* to each child (pages 21–2), '*Gena's New Bride*' (Part 2).

Method
Remind children about what happened in the story last week. Ask what they think will happen next.

LESSON ONE (Lesson Suggestion 34C)

Objective
The children will be able to answer questions to show they understand the story.

Preparation
Give out *Reader 3* (pages 21–2) and *Pupil's Book 3* (page 68, Lesson 1) to each child.

Answers
1 He told them to come back when the moon was high in the sky.
2 The Seashore Chief blowing his conch shell.
3 It was an army of huge red crabs.
4 The children laughed because it was a dugong.
5 He was very disappointed and astonished that such a thing had happened.
6 two legs
7 horn
8 sea-cow
9 ... he touched the mermaid before morning.
10 ... she slipped on a rock and he reached out to help her.

LESSON TWO

Objective
The children will be able to draw conclusions from what they read.

Preparation
Give out *Pupil's Book 3* to each child (page 68, Lesson 2, Exercise A).

Answers
1 b Tana was pleased to see Seveni.
2 c Hiari was worried.
3 The match was probably played at Keltiga School.
4 b Sileli was a Papuan.

LESSON THREE

Objective
The children will be able to think up alternative titles.

Preparation
Give out *Pupil's Book 3* to each child (page 69, Exercise B).

Possible Answers
1 The Frog's husband — The Magic Frog
2 Cyclone Hannah — Disaster at Tufi
3 Maratsaip — The Tree Trunk Spirit
4 The Red Suitcase — Mixed Luggage
5 Gena's New Bride — The Mermaid that Changed

Exercise C

Objective
The children will be able to draw conclusions from what they read.

Preparation
Give out *Pupil's Book 3* to each child (page 70, Exercise C).

Answers
1 He was going to mend the truck.
2 They were all too lazy and didn't feel like helping their father.
3 Peta did not really feel ill. It was just an excuse.
4 Father was thinking of a way to make the boys want to help him.
5 They knew they must help their father fix the truck or they would not be able to go to the party that night.

LESSON FOUR (Lesson Suggestion 39)

Objective
The children will be able to read for their own enjoyment.

Preparation
Give out *Supplementary Reader 3* and other reading material to each child.

OR POETRY (Lesson Suggestion 40)

Preparation
Give out *Pupil's Book 3* to each child (page 70).

Answers
1 She is making a string bag or bilum.
2 Twirling the fibre on her knee
With the palm on her hand
She weaves the string
Into figure of eight loops
All joined together
3 Vegetables and other crops; firewood, babies, clothes, sleeping mats.

LESSON FIVE

Objective
The children will be able to do Reading Games.

Preparation
Give out *Reading Games for Grade 6* to each child (pages 82–4).

Method
1 Allow children to choose a game to play.
2 Mark their work using *Teacher's Notes* (pages 86–8, Unit 32).

LISTENING 33

LESSON ONE

Objective
The children will be able to hear different vowel sounds in words.

Preparation

Remind children that vowels are A E I O U. Write the following list of words on the blackboard:

weave	wave	seem	same	pea	pay
reel	rail	leak	lake	eat	eight
weak	wake	read	raid	meal	mail
bee	bay	see	say	peel	pale
feed	fade	feel	fail		
		heat	hate		

Method

1 Read each pair of words. Tell the children to watch them on the board as you read them, and to listen to the difference.
2 Now read through the pairs again, this time telling the children that sometimes you will read *both* words, but other times you will read the same words twice, e.g: weave weave. If the children think you said two different words they must write down D (different). If they think you said the same word twice, they must write down S (same).
(Remember to make a note of this yourself as you call out the words.)
3 Now mark their work by calling out the answers.

LESSON TWO

Objective

The children will be able to hear different vowel sounds in words.

Preparation

Write the following list of words on the blackboard.

head	had	met	mat	when	one
men	man	guess	gas	many	money
bet	bat	end	and	pen	pan
beg	bag	bet	but	bled	blood
bed	bud	net	nut	ten	tin

Method

As for Lesson One.

TALKING

LESSON ONE

Objective

The children will practise last week's sentence pattern:
He gave me a mango that he bought at the market.

LESSON TWO

Objective

The children will practise a sentence pattern they already know:
What will you take to the market? I might take the cabbages.

Method

1 What will you do when you leave school?
Answers will start with: I might . . .
2 Explain that 'might' means that it may happen but it is not certain.
3 Divide the class in groups to practise this sentence pattern. Give other examples.
What will you do on Sports Day? I might enter the long jump.
What will you do in town? I might visit my wantoks.
What will you buy at the shops? I might buy a new knife.

LESSON THREE

Objective

The children will be able to use a new sentence pattern:
Pene has finished his maths but he hasn't finished his English.

Method

1 T: Pene, have you finished your maths?
C: Yes, I have.
T: Have you finished your English?
C: No, I haven't.
T: Pere has finished his Maths, but he hasn't finished his English.
Get the class to repeat this pattern.
2 Kila, have you cleaned the blackboard?
K: Yes, I have.
T: Have you cleaned the desks?
K: No, I haven't.
T: Kila has cleaned the blackboard but he hasn't cleaned the desks.
3 Divide the class into groups. Leader starts off: Sere, have you eaten all your food? Yes, I have. Muli, have you eaten all your food? No, I haven't. Sere has eaten all her food but Muli hasn't eaten all his food. Each child has a turn.

LESSON FOUR

Objective

The children will practise this sentence pattern:
Taman has finished but Belo hasn't.

Method

1 T: Taman, have you finished?
C: Yes, I have.
T: Belo, have you finished?
C: No, I haven't.
T: Taman has finished but Belo hasn't.
Get the class to repeat this.
2 Practise with other persons, e.g:
Teri has finished but you haven't.
We've all done our work, but they haven't.
3 Practise this pattern in groups.

LESSON FIVE (Lesson Suggestion 1C)

Objective

The children will practise this sentence pattern, using a substitution table.

Preparation
Write the following table on the board:

TAMAN	has finished but	BELO	hasn't.
JON		PIM	
KELA		GUAN	

TERI	has finished	his	work but	BEN	hasn't.
MARIA		her		MELI	

PIA	has washed the	DISHES	but	SHE	hasn't washed the	GLASSES.
KEP		CLOTHES		HE		DISHES
PEL		KAUKAU				YAMS

SARA	has eaten all	HER	food but	VELE	hasn't.
DANE		HIS		PEK	

Note
Remember to leave this table on the blackboard for next week.

ORAL EXPRESSION

LESSON ONE

Objective
The children will be able to compare two things.

Preparation
Make cards with the following written on them:
1st card: a bus and a truck.
2nd card: a football and a basketball
3rd card: a yam and a kaukau
4th card: a lizard and a crocodile

Method
1 Explain that when you compare things you point out what is *the same* about the two things, and then point out the *differences*, e.g: A bus and a truck are both large motor vehicles, but a bus is for carrying people, and a truck is usually for carrying things.
2 Divide the class into groups. Give each group a card. Each child must compare the two things written on the card.

Note
Encourage the child to use words like 'but' and 'however'.

LESSON TWO

Objective
The children will be able to compare things.

Method
1 Fellow steps 1 and 2 as above.
2 Use these examples:
a a village church and a village house
b modern clothes and traditional costume
c a canoe and a boat
d a cat and a cuscus
e a shirt and a dress
f shoes and boots
g a pen and a pencil
h a bed and a table

LESSON THREE

Objective
The children will be able to describe pictures.

Preparation
Give out *Pupil's Book 3* to each child (page 71, Lesson 1).

Method
1 Study the six pictures on this page.
2 T: Who can describe the woman in the first picture?
Which part of PNG is she from?
3 Do the same with the other pictures.

Answers
1 The first woman is from the Highlands.
2 The man underneath her is a Biami (Kukukuku) from the Morobe Province.
3 The man underneath him is a Mekeo from the Central Province.
4 The man at the top of the page is from the Sepik.
5 The man under him is a Huli wigman from the Southern Highlands.
6 The last woman is from the Trobriand Islands.

Note
If the children do not know any of these costumes, ask them to describe how people decorate themselves for special occasions in their area.

WRITTEN SENTENCES

Note
Remember, teach only FIVE of the six lessons. Choose one for homework, or for fast workers to do.

LESSON ONE (Lesson Suggestion 2)

Objective
The children will be able to write sentences describing one of the pictures.

Preparation
Give out *Pupil's Book 3* to each child (page 71, Lesson 1).

Model Answer
(Children choose only *one* person to describe.)
This Highland woman is wearing piece of laplap tied in a knot on her head, with a bilum on top of that. She is wearing many strings of beads and a kina shell around her neck. She also has shell bracelets on her arms, and has painted designs on her face.

LESSON TWO (Lesson Suggestion 13)

Objective
The children will be able to use punctuation correctly.

Preparation
Give out *Pupil's Book 3* to each child (page 72, Lesson 2).

Answers

1 The most important traditional things people use for decoration in the Highlands are wigs, aprons, furs, bird feathers and shells.
2 At singsings, people use drums, bones, oil and pig-grease, leaves, vines and earth paints. Today, people often buy paints, beads and cloth from the tradestore.
3 Pearl shells, bailer shells, conus shells and cowrie shells make good decorations.
4 People saw tiny nassa shells on to bark cloth and wear them around their forehead. People used to wear green-snail pieces in their ears or hair, but this is not so common today.
5 Sometimes people put pig tusks, wooden or bamboo pins, feathers and cassowary quills through their nose as decoration.
6 People keep bamboo tubes of oil squeezed from the red and yellow pandanus plant fruit. They use it for oiling the bodies and faces of men and women.
7 Highland men store shells and good feathers in their men's houses. They pack them in bark cloth, pandanus leaves, or in cardboard.
8 Sometimes women are tattooed for decoration. The tattoo marks are made by pricking the skin with something sharp, and then rubbing in charcoal mixed with blue dye.

LESSON THREE (Lesson Suggestion 8)

Objective
The children will be able to choose the correct word to fit each sentence.

Preparation
Give out *Pupil's Book 3* to each child (page 72, Lesson 3).

Answers

1 nose	3 hole	5 wear wood	7 worn
2 knot	4 new their	6 for sale	

LESSON FOUR

Objective
The children will be able to put names and pronouns in the correct order.

Preparation
Give out *Pupil's Book 3* to each child (page 73, Lesson 4).

Answers

1 Sapel, Masisa and I . . .
2 father and I . . .
3 Kana, Arua and I . . . .
4 Homoka and me . . .
5 My brother and I . . .
6 Molaki and me . . .
7 Ila and Molaki . . . I . . .
8 Hane and I . . .

LESSON FIVE (Lesson Suggestion 11)

Objective
The children will be able to change sentences from singular to plural.

Preparation
Give out *Pupil's Book 3* to each child (page 73, Lesson 5).

Answers
1 The wives of dancers often carry water in bamboo tubes to refresh them while they are dancing.
2 People in the Western Highlands take hair from women and children to make wigs for men.
3 For everyday wear, Highland men traditionally wear wigs covered with a woven net which may decorated with leaves, grass and fur.
4 Highland girls like to wear bright tradestore cloths tied at the head and hanging over their backs as a cloak which helps to keep them warm.
5 At the Hagen Show you often see dancers holding umbrellas as they dance, to protect the feathers in their head-dresses from rain.
6 Sometimes children like to stick hibiscus flowers into their hair so that their whole head becomes a mass of colour.
7 In some areas people make special head-bands from the hard backs of bright green scarab beetles.
8 In the Markham valley area, women still make earrings from the tiny wing-bones of fruit bats.

Note
The children do not have to do *all* these sentences.

LESSON SIX (Optional)

Objective
The children will be able to use 'who' and 'which' correctly.

Preparation
Give out *Pupil's Book 3* to each child (page 74, Lesson 6).

Answers

1 who	3 who	5 who	7 who
2 which	4 which	6 which	8 which

WRITTEN COMPOSITION

LESSON ONE

Objective
The children will be able to write a description.

Preparation
Give out *Pupil's Book 3* to each child (page 75, Lesson 1B).

Model Answer
This Mekeo woman is wearing a beautiful head-dress of flowers and feathers. She is wearing woven arm-bands. Around her neck she has many necklaces made from teeth and shells. She has some leaves tucked into her arm-bands.

LESSON TWO

Objective
The children will be able to express a personal opinion in writing.

Preparation
Give out *Pupil's Book 3* to each child (page 75, Lesson 2).

Model Answer
People sometimes use European things as part of their traditional dress. In this picture the people have used fish tin labels, safety-pins and keys, pipes, bottle tops, buttons and beaded belts and arm-bands. I think this is a good thing because it is interesting to use new things. OR I think this is a bad thing because these European things are not beautiful and they do not belong with traditional dress.

Note
Teacher to mark this work, making sure children give good reasons for their opinion.

SPELLING

LESSON ONE (Lesson Suggestion 22)

Objective
The children will learn how to spell this week's spelling words. (They are from this week's story.)

Preparation
Give out *Pupil's Book 3* to each child (page 76, Spelling List).

LESSON TWO

Select from Exercises A–E (pages 76–7).

Exercise A (Lesson Suggestion 29)

Answers

1 sign	3 mass	5 warrior
2 tourists handcrafts	4 chanting	

Exercise B (Lesson Suggestion 30)

Answers

possible	terrible	painful	hopeful
question	decoration	biggest	smallest
government	ornament	useless	fearless

Exercise C

Answers
carefully hopefully doubtfully cheerfully thoughtfully peacefully
1 She slept peacefully all night.
2 He limped painfully to the Aid Post.

Exercise D

Group Aa = B3
Ab = B1
Ac = B2

Exercise E (Lesson Suggestion 27)

Answers
Sare, B. Semeni, J. Semeni, Lakani. Sibe, B. Sibe, Benjamin L. Sor, Pem K. Sorda, M.

HANDWRITING (Lesson Suggestion 33)

Preparation
Give out *Pupil's Book 3* to each child (page 77).

READING

INTRODUCTION

Objective
The children will understand the background to the story, and the meaning of new words. They will read the story silently.

Preparation
Give out *Reader 3* to each child (pages 10–13), '*The Thief at the Snow*'.

Method
Talk about different 'shows' that the children have been to. Discuss what took place there. If no children have been to a show, then the teacher should describe what one is like.

LESSON ONE (Lesson Suggestion 34C)

Objective
The children will be able to answer questions to show they understand the story.

Preparation
Give out *Reader 3* (pages 10–13) and *Pupil's Book 3* (page 78, Lesson 1) to each child.

Answers
1 The long houses were built to provide shelter for visitors from other parts of the country who had come to the show.
2 The planes were bringing lots of visitors to the show from all over the country.
3 The lock was broken and was hanging loose. The door of the bank was slightly open.
4 He poured red paint outside the door so that the thief would stand in it when he came out, and leave red footprints behind him.
5 He probably thought that nobody would look there for stolen money, and he could come back later to pick it up.
6 very close to each other
7 centre
8 sausage sandwich
9 . . . his red feet.
10 . . . fierce looking masks made of mud.

LESSON TWO

Objective
The children will be able to answer comprehension questions.

Preparation
Give out *Pupil's Book 3* to each child (page 79, Lesson 2, Exercise A).

Answers
1 b 2 d 3 b

LESSON THREE

Objective
The children will be able to answer questions about a notice.

Preparation
Give out *Pupil's Book 3* to each child (page 79, Exercise B).

Answers
1 No it isn't.
2 One and a half hours.
3 In the morning between 8.30 am and 12.30 pm.
4 At 6 pm.
5 No.
6 At 8.30 am.

LESSON FOUR (Lesson Suggestion 39)

Objective
The children will be able to read for enjoyment.

Preparation
Give out *Supplementary Reader 3* to each child, or other reading matter.

OR POETRY (Lesson Suggestion 40)

Preparation
Give out *Pupil's Book 3* to each child (page 80).

LESSON FIVE

Objective
The children will be able to do Reading Games.

Preparation
Give out *Reading Games for Grade 6* to each child (pages 85–6).

Method
1 Allow children to choose work to do.
2 Mark their work using *Teacher's Notes* (pages 88–90, Unit 33).

LISTENING 34

LESSON ONE

Objective
The children will be able to hear different vowel sounds in words.

Preparation
Write the following words on the board:

cat	cut	sack	suck
cap	cup	ran	run
bag	bug	lamp	lump

Method
1 Say a sentence, putting in the first of the pair of words, e.g: I *cat* my finger.
Then say the same sentence, this time putting in the second word, e.g: I *cut* my finger.
2 Pupils write down the word that fits correctly, e.g: cut.

LESSON TWO

Objective
The children will be able to hear different vowel sounds in words.

Preparation
Write the following words on the board:

built	belt	pin	pen
did	dead	miss	mess
win	when	spilt	spelt

Method
As for Lesson One.

TALKING

LESSON ONE

Objective
The children will practise last week's sentence pattern:
Taman has finished but Belo hasn't.

LESSON TWO

Objective
The children will practise a sentence pattern they already know:
We've been working since recess.

Method
1 T: We will take a break now. We've been working since the bell went.
Class repeat: We've been working since the bell went.

T: How long have you been at school?
C: We've been at school since we were six.
T: How long have you been in your village?
P: I've been in my village since I was born.
T: How long have you been playing football?
C: I've been playing football since I was in Grade One.

2 Divide the class into groups. Children to practise this sentence pattern.

LESSON THREE

Objective

The children will be able to use a new sentence pattern:
Unless he comes soon, we'll go without him.

Method

1 Explain that 'unless' has the same meaning as 'if . . . not', e.g:
If he does *not* come, we'll go without him. This means the same as: Unless he comes soon, we'll go without him.

2 Practise with other examples:
Unless it rains, our crops will die soon.
Unless it stops raining, we'll have to stay inside.
Unless you pay that money, you'll get no more food.
Unless you finish your work, you'll get no dinner.

3 Divide the class into pairs to practise this sentence pattern.

LESSON FOUR

Objective

The children will practise this sentence pattern:
Unless he comes soon, we'll go without him.

Method

1 Write the following on the board:
Unless you finish that job, . . .
Unless you work hard, . . .
Unless you read the paper, . . .
Unless you go to High School, . . .
Unless you learn your tables, . . .
Unless you write neatly, . . .

2 In pairs, children must finish off these sentences.

LESSON FIVE (Lesson Suggestion 1C)

Objective

The children will practise this sentence pattern, using a substitution table.

Preparation

Write the following table on the blackboard:

Unless you	learn your tables, you'll be no good at Maths.
	wash you face, you'll get scabies.
	work hard at school, you won't go to High School.
	listen carefully, you won't know what to do.
	learn to spell, you won't be able to write stories.
	sharpen your pencil, you won't be able to write properly.

Note

Remember to leave this work on the board for next week's revision.

ORAL EXPRESSION

LESSON ONE

Objective
The children will be able to ask questions to find out information.

Method
1 Choose a child to leave the room.
2 The class thinks of an object (e.g: a broom).
3 The child returns and asks the class questions to work out what the object is, e.g:
Q: What do you do with it?
A: I'd clean the room.
Q: Is it a duster?
A: No, it isn't.
Q: Which part of the room would you clean with it?
A: I'd clean the floor.
Q: Is it a mop?
A: No, it isn't.
Q: Is it a broom?
A: Yes, it is.
4 Choose another child to go outside while the class chooses another object.

LESSON TWO

Objective
The children will be able to describe different objects.

Preparation
Have a box, some pieces of paper and a pen on your table.

Method
1 Choose one child to come out the front to your desk. She must write down the name of an object in large letters and then put the paper into the box.
2 The child says to the class: There's something in my box. Who can guess what it is?
3 One child asks: What does it look like?
4 The child out the front must describe the object written on paper.
5 Children can ask other questions that will describe the object, like:
How does it work?
How do you use it?
What is it made of?
6 When someone in the class guesses correctly, the person in front takes the paper out of the box and holds it up for everyone to read.
7 The person who guessed correctly then comes out the front.

LESSON THREE

Objective
The children will be able to ask each other questions.

Method
1 Divide the class into four groups.
2 The leader from each group must ask another group a question. If they answer correctly, put a point on the board for that group.

3 Each group has a turn at asking the question. At the end of the lesson, the group with the most points is the winning group.

Note
Encourage children to think up good questions about things they have studied at school this term.

WRITTEN SENTENCES

LESSON ONE (Lesson Suggestion 2)

Objective
The children will be able to write good sentences about pictures.

Preparation
1 Give out *Pupil's Book 3* to each child (page 81, Lesson 1).
2 Read this description of how copra is made, and discuss it with the class:

Possible Answers
1 The men are collecting fallen coconuts from under the trees.
2 They are cutting open the coconuts with sharp knives.
3 Now they are scooping out the meat with special knives.
4 Then they put the coconut meat on the copra dryer.
5 They put the dried coconut, called copra, into bags.
6 Then they load these bags onto trucks.

LESSON TWO

Objective
The children will be able to choose the correct word to go in the space.

Preparation
Give out *Pupil's Book 3* to each child (page 82, Lesson 2).

Answers
1 drying
2 dry
3 using
4 put
5 takes
6 does quicker
7 made
8 are
9 using
10 provide

LESSON THREE (Optional)

Objective
The children will answer questions about a passage.

Answers
1 Three days (4 bags in 1 day = 3 × 4 = 12)
2 Six bags (6 × 450 = 2,700)
3 The copra drier will hold more than three bags. (It will hold 1,500 nuts. 3 × 450 = 1,350 which is less than 1,500.)

4 It would take eighteen days to dry eighteen bags of copra.
5 It takes seven days.

LESSON FOUR

Objective
The children will be able to use their imaginations to think up different uses for half a coconut shell.

Preparation
Give out *Pupil's Book 3* to each child (page 83, Lesson 4).

Possible Answers
1 A bowl for mixing paints at a singsing.
2 A plant container.
3 Fill it with water and use it for mirror.
4 Use it as a cup.

LESSON FIVE (Lesson Suggestion 13D)

Objective
The children will be able to put in the quotation marks.

Preparation
Give out *Pupil's Book 3* to each child (page 83, Lesson 5).

Answers
2 'I'm taking it onto the wharf', the driver replied. 'Then it will be loaded aboard a cargo vessel.'
3 'How's the new copra drier going, Gena?' asked Semi.
4 'It certainly makes a lot more copra', answered Gena, 'and in only half the time'.
5 'Remind me to order some more copra sacks', said Mr. Awasai. 'We're nearly out of them.'
6 'Is it very expensive to build a drier like yours?' Semi enquired. 'I'd like to build one myself but I don't think I can afford it.'
7 'No', replied Gena, 'it's not expensive at all. The drier cost me only K100. However if you make the roof out of bush material, like sago or nipa, it costs even less'.
8 'Is that so?' said Semi stroking his chin thoughtfully. 'I just might build one myself'.

WRITTEN COMPOSITION

LESSON ONE

Objective
The children will be able to follow directions.

Preparation
Give out *Pupil's Book 3* to each child (page 84, Lesson 1).

Answers

A

B From Guan's house, you follow the river down until you come to the log crossing. Cross the log and go past Ana's and Tara's houses until you come to Ben's house. Follow the path beside Ben's house up the hill. Angon's house is half way up the hill.

LESSON TWO (Lesson Suggestion 14)

Objective

The children will be able to make notes.

Preparation

Give out *Pupil's Book 3* to each child (page 85, Lesson 2).

Model Answer

Simon, Karl: fetch saw dust from work shop
bring high jump stands and bar

Pita, Sia: will get the relay battons, hurdles, finishing tape, starting gun
fix one hurdle

Kini, Ketabu: get the equipment for the throwing events (e.g: shot put, javelin)

SPELLING

LESSON ONE (Lesson Suggestion 22)

Objective

The children will learn how to spell this week's words. (They are from this week's story.)

Preparation
Give out *Pupil's Book 3* to each child (page 86, Spelling List).

LESSON TWO

Select from Exercises A–E (pages 86–8).

Exercise A (Lesson Suggestion 29)

Answers

1 male female	3 ugly	5 fright
2 orphan	4 secret	

Exercise B (Lesson Suggestion 23)

Possible Answers
mate mile made mice match male mad met

Exercise C (Lesson Suggestion 32)

Answers

sitting	cutting	putting	getting	letting
fitted	stopped	hopped	fanned	knotted

Exercise D (Lesson Suggestion 23)

Possible Answers
sin see sea sun seat seed
win wee wheat weak
fin fee fun fear feel finish
bin bee beat bun bead
ginger green gun gear
hear hundred heel hint
pin peach peel punch

Exercise E

Answers
Group A1 — B1
A2 — B3
A3 — B2

HANDWRITING (Lesson Suggestion 33)

Preparation
Give out *Pupil's Book 3* to each child (page 88).

Note
Ensure that the children set the letter out exactly as shown in the model.

READING

INTRODUCTION (Lesson Suggestion 34)

Objective
The children will understand the background to the story, and the meaning of new words. They will read the story silently.

Preparation
Give out *Reader 3* to each child (pages 27–9), '*How the Coconut Palm was Made*'.

Method
Remind the children that regards are traditional stories, often used to explain why things are the way they are. Ask the children if they know any local legends.

LESSON ONE (Lesson Suggestion 34C)

Objective
The children will be able to answer questions to show they understand the story.

Preparation
Give out *Reader 3* (pages 27–9) and *Pupil's Book 3* (page 89, Lesson 1) to each child.

Answers
1 Tumis caught the dwarf because the dwarf was always frightening the young children in his village.
2 He promised to show Tumis how to make a net that would catch many fish every time he used it.
3 They were jealous because Tumis always caught plenty of fish while they only caught a few.
4 They took him far off into the jungle and left him there.
5 They planned to kill him and eat him.
6 parents
7 short
8 beating
9 . . . they fell for all Tumis' tricks.
10 . . . he tricked the witches many times.
11 amazed and surprised
12 They were jealous of Tumis and wanted to get rid of him.

LESSON TWO

Objective
The children will be able to recognize advertisement 'gimmicks'.

Preparation
Give out *Pupil's Book 3* to each child (page 90, Lesson 2).

Answers
a 2, b 2, c 3

LESSON THREE

Objective
The children will be able to answer questions about a letter.

Preparation
Give out *Pupil's Book 3* to each child (page 91, Lesson 3).

Answers
1 c, 2 a, 3 a, 4 b, 5 a

LESSON FOUR (Lesson Suggestion 39)

Objective
The children will be able to read for enjoyment.

Preparation
Give out *Supplementary Reader 3* and other reading material to each child.

OR POETRY (Lesson Suggestion 40)

Preparation
Give out *Pupil's Book 3* to each child (page 92).

LESSON FIVE

Objective
The children will be able to do Reading Games.

Preparation
Give out *Reading Games for Grade 6* (pages 87–90).

Method
1 Allow children to choose work from these pages.
2 Mark their work using *Teacher's Notes* (pages 91–2, Unit 34).

LISTENING 35

LESSON ONE

Objective
The children will be able to divide words into syllables.

Preparation
Write some words on the blackboard, e.g:
attack worker enlarge locate grumble lighten

Method
1 Tell the children that you are going to divide these words into syllables i.e: the parts of the word which you hear when you say the word. To do this, you must listen carefully.
2 Look at the first word on the blackboard — attack.

T: Who can say this word? (Pupil says it.)
T: Who can tell me how many syllables he used when he said 'attack'? (Answer: two) Write the word again on the blackboard, this time broken into syllables, i.e: attack – at-tack

2 Choose someone to say the next word. Ask the class how many syllables. Choose someone to write this on the board, broken into syllables.

Answers
at-tack wor-ker en-large lo-cate grum-ble light-en

LESSON TWO

Objective
The children will be able to divide words into syllables.

Preparation
Write the following words on the blackboard:
completely quickly suddenly anxiously exhibition display garden tractor condition plantation ceremonial address

Method
As for Lesson One.

Answers
com-plete-ly quick-ly sud-den-ly an-xious-ly
ex-hi-bi-tion dis-play gar-den trac-tor con-dit-ion
plan-ta-tion cer-e-mon-i-al ad-dress

STRESS MARKS OVER SYLLABLES

These words are to be used for Units 36 and 37. (The word with the correct syllable stressed is underlined for the teacher's benefit only. When you copy these words on the blackboard, do *not* underline the correct one.) Make sure you copy each word correctly.

A. át-tack B. at-táck
A. á-void B. a-vóid
A. sél-dom B. sel-dóm
A. ré-ceive B. re-ceiv́e
A. un-ús-u-al B. un-us-ú-al
A. cúl-tiv-ate B. cul-tiv́-ate
A. súc-ceed B. suc-ceéd
A. vál-u-a-ble B. val-ú-a-ble
A. pró-ducts B. pro-dúcts
A. ób-serve B. ob-sérve
A. ál-to-ge-ther B. al-to-gé-ther
A. pŕe-vent B. pre-vént
A. iḿ-poss-i-ble B. im-póss-i-ble
A. Á-mer-i-ca B. A-mér-i-ca
A. cón-tin-ent B. con-tin-ént
A. kán-ga-roo B. kan-ga-róo
A. góv-ern-ment B. gov-ern-mént
A. whén-ev-er B. when-év-er

A	B
A. mýs-ter-i-ous	B. mys-tér-i-ous
A. cór-rect	B. cor-réct
A. cól-our	B. col-oúr
A. méth-od	B. meth-ód
A. cá-noe	B. ca-nóe
A. cón-tain	B. con-taiń
A. má-lar-i-a	B. ma-lár-i-a
A. iń-sect	B. in-séct
A. iń-form	B. in-foŕm
A. cóm-pare	B. com-paŕe
A. tél-e-phone	B. tel-e-phoné
A. fór-get	B. for-gét
A. fúnn-i-er	B. funn-i-er
A. nót-ice	B. not-iće
A. dé-part-ment	B. de-párt-ment

TALKING

LESSON ONE

Objective
The children will practise last week's sentence pattern:
Unless he comes soon, we'll go without him.

LESSON TWO

Objective
The children will practise a sentence pattern they already know:
Why didn't Tanu come to school? Because he's very sick.

Method
1 Explain that we use 'very' to emphasise how sick he is. Give other examples:
That woman is very old. (Not just old but *very* old.)
That man is very tall.
That boy can run very fast.
2 T: Tane, can you reach that branch?
C: No, I can't reach it. It's very high.
T: Markus can you do that sum?
C: No, I can't. It's very hard.
T: How heavy is that log?
C: It's very heavy.
3 In pairs, one child asks the other child a question. The other must answer, using 'very' in his reply.

LESSON THREE

Objective
The children will be able to use a new sentence pattern:
He said that he would go to Lae in August.

Method

1 Write on the board: I will go to Lae in August. Ask a pupil to read it aloud.
C: I will go to Lae in August.
T: He said that he would go to Lae in August. What did he say?
C: He said that he would go to Lae in August.
Give more examples.

2 In pairs, one pupil explains to the rest of the class what the other pupil said, e.g:
A: I will become a farmer.
B: He said that he would become a farmer.
A: I will go hunting on Saturday.
B: He said that he would go hunting on Saturday.
A: I will never come back.
B: He said that he would never come back.

LESSON FOUR

Objective

The children will practise this sentence pattern:
He said that he would go to Lae in August.

Method

1 In groups, one person (the leader) makes a statement: I will go to market tomorrow after school.
The next person in the group reports what he said: He said that he would go to market after school tomorrow.
The next person then makes a statement, and so on, until everyone in the group has a turn.

LESSON FIVE

Objective

The children will practise this sentence pattern, using a substitution table.

Preparation

Write the following on the blackboard:
I will go to visit Rea tomorrow. He said that . . .
I will become a nurse when I leave school. She said that . . .
I will see that film tomorrow. He said that . . .
I will post this letter this afternoon. She said that . . .
I will give this parcel to my father. He said that . . .
I will sell my truck next week. He said that . . .
I will shoot that wild pig when I see him again. He said that . . .

Method

1 Teacher point to the blackboard and say the first sentence, then complete the unfinished sentence, e.g: He said that he would go to visit Rea tomorrow.
2 Choose pupils to complete the other sentences.
3 In groups, the children must complete one of the sentences on the blackboard.

Note

Leave this work on the board for next week.

ORAL EXPRESSION

LESSON ONE

Objective
The children will be able to discuss pictures and learn about coffee processing.

Preparation
1 Give out *Pupil's Book 3* (page 93, Lesson 1) to each child.

Method
1 Read out this description of how coffee is grown and processed. Discuss it with the children.
2 Study the pictures carefully.
3 Discuss what is happening in each picture.
4 For the correct answers to what is happening in these pictures, turn over to page 94 and look at the top of the page.

LESSON TWO

Objective
The children will be able to give direction.

Preparation
Give out *Pupil's Book 3* (page 103).

Method
1 Study the map of Popondetta on this page.
2 Show children how the Key works, e.g: Number 1 on the map is where the Hotel is, Number 2 is the Picture Theatre, and so on.
3 Give children an example, e.g: How would you get from the Anglican Mission to the Community School? Answer: Go north along Gona Rd, past the Oval, the Hotel, the Post Office, the small playing field and the High School. Take the fifth turning on your right. The Community School is at the end of this road.
4 Divide the class into groups. The leader in each group must ask for directions. One person in the group must say the directions while everyone follows them with their finger on their map.

LESSON THREE

Objective
The children will be able to ask questions in an interview.

Preparation
Write names of several famous people on the board.

Method
1 Pretend to be one of the famous people you have written on the board, e.g: a famous boxer. Children must ask you questions to find out about him, e.g:
Why did you become a boxer?
When did you first take up this sport?
How often do you have to train?
Do you have to get a lot of sleep?

What was your hardest fight?
How many titles do you have?

2 Now pretend to be another famous person. Choose different pupils to ask you questions.

WRITTEN SENTENCES

Note
Remember, teach only FIVE of the six lessons. Choose one for homework, or for fast workers to do.

LESSON ONE

Objective
The children will be able to choose the correct form of the verb.

Preparation
Give out *Pupil's Book 3* to each child (page 94, Lesson 1).

Answers

1 picking	5 taken
2 removed	6 packed
3 washed	7 send
4 dried	8 sold

LESSON TWO (Lesson Suggestion 13)

Objective

The children will be able to use the correct punctuation.

Preparation
Give out *Pupil's Book 3* to each child (page 94, Lesson 2).

Answers
1 Coffee grows best in the Highlands where the climate is mild, the soil is rich and the rainfall ideal.
2 Papua New Guinea exports most of the coffee to Australia, the United States of America, the United Kingdom and to Western European countries.
3 The main research centre for coffee is the Highlands Agricultural Experiments Station near Kainantu in the Eastern Highlands.

LESSON THREE (Lesson Suggestion 4)

Objective
The children will be able to change sentences from direct speech to reported speech.

Preparation
Give out *Pupil's Book 3* to each child (page 94, Lesson 3).

Answers
1 Mr Ravoa explained that the first coffee grown in this country came from Jamaica.

2 Mr Awo stated that the first coffee plantation was at Wau in the Morobe Province.
3 The plantation manager said that nearly all the coffee we export is mild Arabica.
4 He added that a different kind of coffee, called Robusta, is grown in some lowland and coastal areas.
5 Mr Charles said that in the early 1950's, coffee was planted in the Eastern and Western Highlands.
6 The Agricultural Officer explained that the coffee cherries are picked by hand and each tree is harvested many times during the season.
7 The Diddiman asked if we knew that coffee was now one of Papua New Guinea's biggest exports.
8 One of the students whispered that she still liked tea better.

LESSON FOUR

Objective
The children will be able to use 'much' and 'many'.

Preparation
Give out *Pupil's Book 3* to each child (page 95, Lesson 4).

Answers

1	many	are	6	much	is
2	much	is	7	many	are
3	many	are	8	much	
4	many	are	9	many	
5	much		10	much	is

LESSON FIVE (Lesson Suggestion 7)

Objective
The children will be able to choose the correct words to complete the passage.

Preparation
Give out *Pupil's Book 3* to each child (page 95, Lesson 5).

Answers
are growing is grows better

LESSON SIX (Optional)

Objective
The children will be able to use phrases telling WHERE something happened.

Preparation
Give out *Pupil's Book 3* to each child (page 96, Lesson 6).

Possible Answers
1 The children hid the pack of cards under the mat.
2 Kipa went down to the river for a swim.
3 They saw a ship on the horizon.
4 The fish swam around the bowl.
5 They took the vegetables to the market to sell.
6 Kila was hit in the face with the cricket ball.

WRITTEN COMPOSITION

LESSON ONE (Lesson Suggestion 16)

Objective
The children will be able to write an imaginative story.

Preparation
Give out *Pupil's Book 3* to each child (page 96, Lesson 1).

Model Story
(Do not read this out to the children until after they have completed their story, or they will copy it.)
One morning an old man found a pool by a waterfall which he had never seen before. He stopped to drink from the pool, but when he bent down he saw the reflection of a young, good-looking man in the pool.
'Who are you?' gasped the old man in surprise.
'I am you as you were many years ago, when you were young', said a voice.
'I wish I were young again', said the old man.
'You can become young again if you gave yourself to the spirit woman of the waterfall. She will give you back your youth.'
'How do I do that?' asked the man.
'All you have to do is join me!' said the reflection.
As the old man jumped into the pool, he heard a crackling laugh coming from the waterfall.
'Ha! Ha! you silly old fool, you have been bewitched!' laughed the voice.
Too late, the old man sank down, down, down to the bottom of the deep pool, never to come up again.

LESSON TWO

Note
There is no Lesson 2 for this week in *Pupil's Book 3*. Think up a topic for the children to write about. You might like to ask the children to write a poem or a play.

SPELLING

LESSON ONE (Lesson Suggestion 22)

Objective
The children will learn how to spell this week's words. (They are from this week's story.)

Preparation
Give out *Pupil's Book 3* to each child (page 97, Spelling List).

LESSON TWO

Select from Exercises A–E (pages 97–9) or give a spelling and dictation test on the last four weeks' work.

Exercise A (Lesson Suggestion 29)

Answers

1 handlebars saddle 3 steer 5 parcel
2 brake 4 steady

Exercise B (Lesson Suggestion 23)

Answers

chalk talk stalk town fish wish sound wound found hound
tough sold hold bold fold sigh high seam steam beam gleam

Exercise C (Lesson Suggestion 30)

Answers

1 cheerful	1 hurried
2 peaceful	2 taking
3 carefully	3 cried
4 thoughtful	4 coming

Exercise D

Turn back to pag 10 in *Pupil's Book 3* to play this game. If you have forgotten how to play it, the instructions are on page 9.

Exercise E (Lesson Suggestion 27)

Answers

Forestry	E–H	Fish	E–H
Boats	A–D	Cockroaches	A–D
Gardening	E–H	Yams	X–Z
Health	E–H		

HANDWRITING (Lesson Suggestion 33)

Preparation
Give out *Pupil's Book 3* to each child (page 100).

READING

INTRODUCTION (Lesson Suggestion 34)

Objective
The children will understand the background to the story, and the meaning of new words in this week's story. They will read the story silently.

Preparation
Give out *Reader 3* to each child (pages 30–3), '*Wari's Bicycle*'.

Method
Talk about bicycles. What do they look like? How do you ride one? Can anyone in the class ride one? If there is one at school, perhaps you could give a demonstration of how to ride it.

LESSON ONE (Lesson Suggestion 34C)

Objective
The children will be able to answer questions to show that they understand the story they read.

Preparation
Give out *Reader 3* to each child (pages 30–3), '*Wari's Bicycle*'.

Answers
1 He was expecting his bicycle to arrive.
2 He showed his excitement by singing.
3 He was chewing betel-nut.
4 He crashed into the river on it.
5 Wari said that because he felt embarrassed by what happened. He didn't want everyone to think that he was silly, so he blamed the bicycle.
6 He used the bicycle as a fishing reel.
7 John helped Wari by showing him how to ride a bicycle and then by holding the saddle while Wari tried to ride it.
8 A bicycle is something you ride on. It has two big wheels, a saddle which you sit on, and handle bars for steering. You start riding it by pushing it and then jumping up on to it. You sit in the saddle and hold the handlebars. Then your feet mush push the pedals around to make the bicycle move forward.

LESSON TWO

Objective
The children will be able to match pictures with their correct captions.

Preparation
Give out *Pupil's Book 3* to each child (page 101, Lesson 2).

Answers
Picture 1 Workers at a meeting.
Picture 2 Villagers instructed by a St. John's ambulance member build a rough stretcher from bush materials.
Picture 3 Carpentry and joinery students at Port Moresby Technical College working on a Lakatoi.
Picture 4 Work being done on the bridge at Kupa River.
Picture 5 Students taking part in a boat-building course, working on a light cargo and passenger boat.

LESSON THREE

Objective
The children will be able to follow directions on a map.

Preparation
Give out *Pupil's Book 3* to each child (page 103, Lesson 3).

Method
Ask the pupils to work in pairs. One child can have her book open at page 103, the other at page 104.

Answers

1 Hotel
2 market
3 small playing field
4 south of the town
5 Radio Station
6 Mission
7 Radio Station
8 Hotel
9 Picture Theatre
10 Administration Building

LESSON FOUR (Lesson Suggestion 39)

Objective
The children will be able to read for enjoyment.

Preparation
Give out *Supplementary Reader 3* and other reading material to the children.

Method
1 Allow children to read what they like.

OR POETRY (Lesson Suggestion 40)

Preparation
Give out *Pupil's Book 3* to each child (page 104).

LESSON FIVE

Objective
The children will be able to do Reading Games.

Preparation
Give out *Reading Games for Grade 6* (pages 90–3, Unit 35).

Method
1 Allow children to choose work to do.
2 Mark children's work using *Teacher's Notes* (pages 93–5, Unit 35).

LISTENING 36

LESSON ONE

Objective
The children will be able to put the correct stress on a word.

Preparation
Copy down the first six pairs of words from the list on page 00 onto their blackboard.

Method
1 Tell the children to look at the first pair of words on the board. There are two syllables in the first word 'attack'. A has the first syllable stressed át-tack while B has the last syllable stressed at-táck.

2 Say A, stressing the *first* syllable, and then say B, stressing the *last* syllable. Then ask the class which word was said correctly (Answer is B).
3 Now look at the next word in the list. Read it with the correct stress and ask the children whether you said the A word or the B word.
4 Go through all ten words doing as for 3.
5 Finish the lesson by reading through each word, pointing to the correct stress (A or B), with the children repeating each word after you.

LESSON TWO

Objective
The children will be able to put the correct stress on a word.

Preparation
Copy down the next seven pairs of words from page 00.

Method
1 Read through this list, stressing all the words correctly. Point to A if it is correct, or B if it is correct.
2 Now slowly read through each word again. Ask the children to write down A or B, whichever they think is the correctly stressed word.
3 Now read through the list again, pointing to the correctly stressed word (A or B) while the children mark their work.
4 Read through the list again, this time with the children repeating the correct stress after you.

TALKING

LESSON ONE

Objective
The children will practise last week's sentence pattern:
He said he would go to Lae in August.

LESSON TWO

Objective
The children will practise sentence patterns they already know:
What can you see in the mirror? I can see myself in the mirror.
Can you see yourself in the water? Yes, I can see myself. No, I can't.

Method
Turn back to Units 1 and 2, Lessons Three, Four and Five, to revise these sentence patterns.

LESSON THREE

Objective
The children will practise sentence patterns they already know:
What's he doing? He's washing himself.
When Waru looked in the mirror, he saw himself.

Method
Turn back to Units 3 and 4, Lessons Three, Four and Five, to revise these sentence patterns.

LESSON FOUR

Objective
The children will practise sentence patterns they already know:
Who did they buy the peanuts for? They bought them for themselves.
Did he build that house for himself? No, he built it for his brother.

Method
Turn back to Units 5 and 6, Lessons Three, Four and Five, to revise these sentence patterns.

LESSON FIVE

Objective
The children will practise sentence patterns they already know:
What did he do? He poured water on himself.
What did he buy himself? He bought himself a shirt.
Did anyone help Mailau to carry the box? No, he carried it himself.

Method
Turn back to Units 7, 8 and 9, Lessons Three, Four and Five, to revise these sentence patterns.

ORAL EXPRESSION

LESSON ONE

Objective
The children will be able to solve a problem.

Method
1 Present the class with a problem, e.g: Your sister has been bitten by a snake. What should you do?
Solution: You must get medical attention for her quickly.
Steps to take: A If possible, find the snake that bit her. Kill it and take it with you. (If you know exactly what type of snake it was, this is not necessary.)
B Carry your sister to a road and stop a PMV. Ask the driver to go straight to a hospital or Aid Post.
C Show the dead snake to the Medical Orderly or Doctor, or tell him what kind of snake it was. This will help him treat the wound correctly.
2 Divide the class into groups. Give each group the same problem. They must work out a solution.
3 After about ten minutes, ask each group leader to report their solution to the class. Compare solutions.

LESSON TWO

Objective
The children will be able to solve a problem.

Method
1 Present the class with a different kind of problem, e.g: The Local Government Council has offered to build you a school Library, if you can raise the funds for the building materials. However, the school has no money and so

you will have to raise the money yourselves to buy the materials. How can you do this?

2 Ask children to suggest various money-making projects and discuss them fully.

LESSON THREE

Objective
The children will be able to speak effectively on the telephone.

Preparation
If you have made telephones already during Expressive Arts, bring them out for this lesson.

Method

1 Teach the children how to start a conversation with a greeting, then to say why they are ringing.

2 When receiving a call, remember to greet the person politely, say who you are or who you work for, e.g:
Man: Hello! Rika's Tradestore.
Lisa: Hello. This is Lisa. May I speak to Rika please!
Man: Certainly. Just a minute please.

3 Tell how to end a telephone conversation, e.g:
Rika: I'll get those goods over to you by this afternoon.
Lisa: Thanks a lot Rika!
Rika: I'm glad to help. Goodbye.
Lisa: Goodbye.

4 Children make up telephone conversations in pairs.

WRITTEN SENTENCES

Note
Remember, teach only FIVE of the six lessons. Choose one for homework, or for fast workers to do.

LESSON ONE

Objective
The children will be able to choose the correct word.

Preparation
Give out *Pupil's Book 3* to each child (page 105, Lesson 1).

Answers

1 at	4 out	7 on	10 for
2 up	5 up	8 out	
3 up	6 up	9 up	

LESSON TWO

Objective
The children will be able to write the correct form of a verb.

Preparation
Give out *Pupil's Book 3* to each child (page 105, Lesson 2).

Answers

1 dies	called	
2 find	digging	
3 dies	kills	dead
4 smoked	tied	
5 wrap	woven	
6 dies	holds	
7 finished	called	

LESSON THREE

Objective
The children will be able to choose the correct word.

Preparation
Give out *Pupil's Book 3* to each child (page 106, Lesson 3).

Answers

1 tallest	3 many	5 further	7 louder loudest
2 more	4 much	6 longest	

LESSON FOUR

Objective
The children will be able to join two sentences by using 'who' or 'which'.

Preparation
Give out *Pupil's Book 3* to each child (page 106, Lesson 4).

Answers
1 This is my uncle who has just been to Australia.
2 This is the new fishing rod which he brought back with him.
3 This is his radio which I borrowed while he was away.
4 Over there is his house which he lives in with his family.
5 Here are his two daughters who go to the same school as I do.

LESSON FIVE

Objective
The children will be able to use the word 'only' to change the meaning of a sentence.

Preparation
Give out *Pupil's Book 3* to each child (page 107, Lesson 5).

Answers

1 Only I planted kaukau.	1 Peter was there and no one else.
2 I only planted kaukau.	2 The child was crying and not doing anything else.
3 I planted only kaukau.	3 There are three bananas left and no more.

LESSON SIX (Optional)

Objective
The children will be able to complete sentences using phrases that tell WHEN something happened.

Preparation
Give out *Pupil's Book 3* to each child (page 108, Lesson 6).

Possible Answers

1 The children woke up early to go fishing.
2 Uncle Raka will be visiting us next week.
3 The school holidays begin next Monday.
4 Pita bought his new bike last Friday.
5 Petrus arrived home last night.

WRITTEN COMPOSITION

LESSON ONE

Objective
The children will be able to write a story about funeral customs.

Preparation
Give out *Pupil's Book 3* to each child (page 108, Lesson 1).

Method
Discuss local funeral and mourning customs with the children.

Answers
You will have to decide which answers are right.

LESSON TWO

Objective
The children will be able to write a personal letter.

Preparation
Give out *Pupil's Book 3* to each child (page 109, Lesson 2).

Model Answer

Address.

Dear Arua,

I am very sorry to hear that you are unhappy in Boroko. I will send you some money to buy a ticket home. You can pay back the money later.

When you return to the village I would like you to think about coming into business with me. I have spoken to our local Diddiman and he wants me to grow soya beans. He told me what must be done to grow them, and says that our soil is just right for them.

This would be a good business for us both. We must start planting as soon as you arrive home. We are all looking forward to seeing you again soon.

From your brother,
Gumia.

SPELLING

LESSON ONE (Lesson Suggestion 22)

Objective
The children will learn how to spell this week's words. (They are from this week's story.)

Preparation
Give out *Pupil's Book 3* to each child (page 110, Spelling List).

LESSON TWO

Select from Exercises A–E (pages 110–11).

Exercise A (Lesson Suggestion 29)

Answers

1 jump	3 unusual	5 path
2 length	4 ankles	

Exercise B

Answers

old-fashioned	c
head-dress	a
life-time	b
tooth-brush	d

Exercise C

Possible Answers
1 They buried the body in a grave.
2 The wounded pig bled to death.
3 After the wedding there was a great feast.

Exercise D (Lesson Suggestion 28)

Possible Answers
Words beginning with 's': sing, slow, steal, snow, snake, spirit
Words ending with 'ing': ring, thing, bring, sting, tiring, mourning
Six-letter words: stones, letter, groans, scream, string, ankles
Section 2 sing, string, sewing, seeing, smiling
Section 4 drying, crying, trying, seeing, sewing

Exercise E

A1 Will you light that candle now?
Bb I will light the fire now.
A2 This wood is easy to carry because it is light.
Ba This one is very heavy but that one is light.
A3 It will soon be light and we will be able to see where we are going.
Bc We will go hunting as soon as it is light.
A4 He broke the light bulb with a stone.
Bd Turn off the light and go to sleep.

HANDWRITING (Lesson Suggestion 33)

Preparation
Give out *Pupil's Book 3* to each child (page 112).

READING

INTRODUCTION (Lesson Suggestion 34)

Objective
The children will understand the background to the story, and the meaning of new words. They will read the story silently.

Preparation
Give out *Reader 3* to each child (pages 34–7), '*The Big Jump*'.

Method
Explain that this week's story is about a custom from the island of Pentecost. Find the island on a map in your atlas.

LESSON ONE (Lesson Suggestion 34C)

Objective
The children will be able to answer questions to show that they understand the story.

Preparation
Give out *Reader 3* (pages 34–7) and *Pupil's Book 3* (page 113, Lesson 1) to each child.

Answers
1 The vines are cut only two days before the ceremony so that they did not have time to dry out and lose their stretchiness.
2 They perform this ceremony to prove their courage.
3 If they are not exactly the right length, the divers could hit the ground and be killed.
4 He probably felt very nervous and excited.
5 She held an old blanket which she would throw away after he made a successful jump. This meant that her little boy was now a man.
6 ... bend easily without breaking.
7 ... raised floor ...
8 ... tall ...
9 ... threw down some croton leaves. Then he clapped his hands three times over his head. He crossed his arms over his chest and closed his eyes.
10 ... a woman wanted to be rid of her husband. She climbed a tree and then challenged him to jump down. He jumped down and was killed, but she was not because she tied vines to her ankles.

LESSON TWO

Objective
The children will be able to choose the best headlines to match the news reports.

Preparation
Give out *Pupil's Book 3* to each child (pages 113–5, Lesson 2).

Method
1 Read the first news report to the children. Make sure they understand it. Then read out each headline and ask if it matches the report.
2 Do the same for the other two reports.

Answers
A Power Back On
B Pacific art goes on show
C 147 Hurt in Irian Quake

LESSON THREE (Lesson Suggestion 40)

Objective
The children will read a poem.

Preparation
Give out *Pupil's Book 3* to each child (page 116).

Method
1 Read through the burial chant.
2 Discuss what it means with the children.
3 What happens in your province when people die?
4 If you have time, you could suggest that the children write a short poem about:
 a how they felt when a close relative died
 b how they feel about dying

LESSON FOUR (Lesson Suggestion 39)

Objective
The children will be able to read for enjoyment.

Preparation
Give out magazines and library books.

LESSON FIVE

Objective
The children will be able to play Reading Games.

Preparation
Give out *Reading Games for Grade 6* (pages 93–6, Unit 36).

Method
1 Allow children to choose the games they want to play.
2 Mark their work using *Teacher's Notes* (pages 95–6, Unit 36).

LISTENING 37

LESSON ONE

Objective
The children will be able to put the correct stress on a word.

Preparation
Copy the next ten pairs of words on 350–1, on to the blackboard.

Method
1 Read out the first word, correctly stressed, in a sentence, e.g:
 That film was made in *A-mér-i-ca.*

2 Ask a pupil to say whether she thinks the stress was on A or B. (Answer B.)
3 Say the word again with the *correct* stress. Children repeat it after you.
4 Now do the same with the other words.

LESSON TWO

Objective
The children will be able to put the correct stress on a word.

Preparation
Copy the last ten pairs of words on page 00 on to the blackboard.

Method
1 Say each word slowly.
2 The children must copy down either A or B, depending on which word was stressed correctly.
3 When you have said all the words, read through them again, this time pointing to the correct stress.
4 Children mark their work.
5 Read through each word again. The class repeat each word after you.

TALKING

LESSON ONE

Objective
The children will practise sentence patterns they already know:
Can you make a kundu by yourself? Yes, I can.

Method
Turn back to Unit 10, Lessons Three, Four and Five, to revise this sentence pattern.

LESSON TWO

Objective
The children will practise sentence patterns they already know:
Can Mara get into the drawer? No, she's too big to get into the drawer.
Can this boy reach the top of the door? Yes, he's tall enough to reach the top of the door.

Method
Turn back to Units 11 and 12, Lessons Three, Four and Five, to revise these sentence patterns.

LESSON THREE

Objective
The children will practise sentence patterns they already know:
Can you lift the table? No, it's too heavy for me to lift.
Can Tunde wear this shirt? Yes, it's big enough for him to wear.

Method
Turn back to Units 13 and 14, Lessons Three, Four and Five, to revise these sentence patterns.

LESSON FOUR

Objective
The children will practise sentence patterns they already know:
Here's a good book for you to read.
It's bad for you to steal.
It's good for you to eat plenty of protein.

Method
Turn back to Units 15 and 16, Lessons Three, Four and Five, to revise these sentence patterns.

LESSON FIVE

Objective
The children will practise sentence patterns they already know:
He's going to draw it again. There's no need for him to draw it again.
Did they start the game before their friends arrived? No, they waited for them to arrive.

Method
Turn back to Units 17 and 18, Lessons Three, Four and Five, to revise these sentence patterns.

ORAL EXPRESSION

LESSON ONE

Objective
The children will learn how to use a telephone effectively.

Preparation
Take out telephones made during Expressive Arts.

Method
1 Divide the class into pairs.
2 Instruct the children to hold imaginary telephone conversations in pairs. Remind them of the lesson you had last week.
3 Suggest the following topics:
   a ringing an ambulance after an accident
   b ordering goods from a store
   c ringing the airport to find out when a plane is arriving
   d ringing the hospital to find out how your sister is

LESSON TWO

Objective
The children will be able to pass on messages by telephone.

Preparation
Take out telephones made already.

Method
1 Divide the class in threes.
2 One child rings another and gives a message. That child takes the message and passes it on to the third child.

Jon: Hello Mary, this is Jon. Can you tell mother that I won't be home tonight as I'm going to stay at Raka's place?

Mary: All right Jon, I'll pass on the message. We'll see you after work tomorrow.

Jon: Thank you Mary. Goodbye.

Mary rings Mother:

Mary: Hello. Mother, it's Mary here.

Mother: Hello Mary.

Mary: Jon just rang to say that he won't be home tonight because he's staying at Raka's place.

Mother: All right Mary, thank you.

LESSON THREE

Objective
The children will have further practise in using a telephone.

Method
1 Repeat Lesson One or Two. Tell the children to use different examples.

WRITTEN SENTENCES

Note
Remember, teach only FIVE of the six lessons. Choose one for homework, or for fast workers to do.

LESSON ONE (Lesson Suggestion 2)

Objective
The children will be able to write sentences about pictures.

Preparation
Give out *Pupil's Book 3* to each child (page 117, Lesson 1).

Answers
(Children should be able to write at least one sentence about the following weapons.)

a a bow and arrows
b a spear
c a pronged spear for fishing
d a rifle
e a stone club
f a bone dagger
g a ceremonial axe

LESSON TWO (Lesson Suggestion 13)

Objective
The children will be able to use the correct punctuation.

Preparation
Give out *Pupil's Book 3* to each child (page 117, Lesson 2).

Answers
1 The hunter crept up close to the cassowary's nest. He got ready to shoot with his bow and arrow.

2 Amos hunted the wild pig that had damaged his garden. At last he saw it digging up roots in the ground. He fired an arrow and hit the pig in its side.
3 Masori shot the eagle with a three-pronged arrow. He cooked it on the fire and shared the meat with Kerowa, who was with him.
4 Pima and Lurupu were lucky enough to find some large eggs in a nest. Pima thought they belonged to a bush turkey.
5 Temi noticed that something had been eating his bananas. That night, he sat near his banana tree to watch. Very soon, a large fruit bat flew onto his tree.
6 Sapel and Lakei laid fish traps in the river. Later on that afternoon, they returned to the place and found four small fish trapped in one of the nets.
7 Yoisi caught the small octopus in his hand and killed it quickly. Inky-black liquid filled the water around him.
8 Timon asked his father if he could have the tail of a cuscus to hang around his neck. His father shot one the next day and skinned it.

LESSON THREE

Objective
The children will practise writing a language pattern they already know:

Preparation
Give out *Pupil's Book 3* to each child (page 118, Lesson 3).

Answers
1 No, the food is not cooked yet, but it is almost cooked.
2 No, I have not finished the book yet, but I have almost finished it.
3 No, they have not crossed the river yet, but they have almost crossed it.
4 No, I have not done my work yet, but I have almost finished it.
1 Are you ready yet?
2 Has it stopped raining yet?
3 Have you eaten all the food yet?
4 Have they reached the sea yet?

LESSON FOUR (Lesson Suggestion 2)

Objective
The children will be able to write sentences about pictures.

Preparation
Give out *Pupil's Book 3* to each child (page 119, Lesson 4).

Answers
1 The cassowary is a large bird which cannot fly. Some people wear cassowary quills through their noses for decoration. Others use the leg bones to make daggers, and they eat the meat and eggs.
2 The Bird of Paradise has beautiful, long tail feathers. People use these feathers for decoration. The birds also provide food.
3 Possums are small furry animals with long, bushy tails. People use the fur for clothes and decorations. They eat the possum meat.

LESSON FIVE (Optional)

Objective
The children will be able to write the correct form of the verb.

Preparation
Give out *Pupil's Book 3* to each child (page 119, Lesson 5).

Answers

1 eating	3 scorching	5 captures	7 allowed
2 cooking eating	4 finds hatch	6 catch are	8 are

LESSON SIX

Objective
The children will be able to use ordinal numbers.

Preparation
Give out *Pupil's Book 3* to each child (page 120, Lesson 6).

Answers

Lari is first.	Tamu is second.	Keroa is third.	Warea is fourth.
Fono is fifth.	Mose is sixth.	Apu is seventh.	Nomba is eighth.
Paul is ninth.	Mark is tenth.	Temi is eleventh.	Haro is twelfth.

Vincent is thirteenth, or last.

WRITTEN COMPOSITION

Objective
The children will be able to complete a story.

Preparation
Give out *Pupil's Book 3* to each child (page 121, Lesson 1).
Suggestions for the type of answer children should write:

Feelings
You would feel very frightened. You might panic at first — not know what to do. When you see that he is still alive, you are relieved. If you can save his life, there will be no pay-back.

Actions
Rush to the nearest Medical Orderly; or get some men from your village to help carry the injured man back to your village. Get a truck to take him to hospital.

Result
If the man dies, then a Patrol Officer will want to hear your side of the story. The neighbouring tribe may demand compensation and you and your relatives may have to pay them in pigs, kina shells or money. You will probably have to go to court so that it can be decided if it really was an accident and not murder.

LESSON TWO

Objective
The children will be able to decide how best to solve a problem and write about it.

Preparation
Give out *Pupil's Book 3* to each child (page 121, Lesson 2).

Model Answer
I would climb out along the fallen tree trunk and try to grab the girl as she floats past. If the crocodile came near us I would strike it with my spear.

SPELLING

LESSON ONE (Lesson Suggestion 22)

Objective
The children will learn how to spell the new words for this week. (They are from this week's story.)

Preparation
Give out *Pupil's Book 3* to each child (page 122, Spelling List).

LESSON TWO

Select from Exercises A–E (pages 122–3).

Exercise A (Lesson Suggestion 29)

Answers

1 glasses	3 control	5 tears
2 obey	4 pet	

Exercise B

Answers
Zoo — wild animals are kept here
Prison — criminals are kept here
Airport — you catch a plane here
Cinema or Picture Theatre — you see films here
Hospital — doctors and nurses look after sick people here
Library — you borrow books here
Court — people who break the law go here
Post Office — you post letters here
Petrol Station — you fill up your car or truck with petrol and oil here
Bank — you put your money here so it is safe

Exercise C (Lesson Suggestion 30)

Answers
sitting digging cutting hopping hoping taking waking liking making shutting

Exercise D (Lesson Suggestion 33)

Method
1 Read the directions to this game carefully so the children understand how to play.
2 Give them several more examples and add up the points for each word, e.g: knee (15) sting (4) beak (15).
3 Set a time limit when they begin the game. Call out 'STOP' when the time is over. Children must then add up their points. The person with the highest score is the winner.

Note
The children do not have to use letters from each section in every word.

Exercise E

Answers

1 The scene out that window is beautiful.
I have seen that man before.
2 The herd of cattle belongs to my uncle.
I heard someone calling for help.
3 I have not been well.
That is a green bean.
4 That reed grows in the river.
I am going to read that book.
5 I will meet you at the market tomorrow.
We are having meat for dinner.
6 Did you steal that hat?
This knife is made of steel.

Note

Do not expect pupils to write sentences for all the words.

HANDWRITING (Lesson Suggestion 33)

Preparation

Give out *Pupil's Book 3* to each child (page 124).

READING

INTRODUCTION (Lesson Suggestion 34)

Objective

The children will understand the background to the story, and the meaning of new words. They will read the story silently.

Preparation

Give out *Reader 3* to each child (pages 38–41), *'Simon's Pet'*.

Method

Ask the children to tell you about any pets they keep.

LESSON ONE (Lesson Suggestion 34C)

Objective

The children will be able to answer questions to show that they understand the story read.

Preparation

Give out *Reader 3* (pages 38–41) and *Pupil's Book 3* (page 125, Lesson 1) to each child.

Answers

1 Simon found Billy at the foot of a coconut palm.
2 He was going to teach the bird to talk.

3 He flew onto his desk, knocking over all the bottles of water.
4 The teacher was called 'Old Thunderguts' because he had a very loud voice and often lost his temper.
5 The whole class was punished because no one would own up and tell the teacher who had said 'Old Thunderguts is an idiot'.
6 bad-tempered
7 test
8 . . . pretending that the bird spoke, when really he spoke.
9 . . . he was out of the room when the voice spoke, so the teacher knew it was not him.
10 bellow roar boom shout

LESSON TWO

Objective
The children will be able to answer questions about a story.

Preparation
Give out *Pupil's Book 3* to each child (page 125, Lesson 2, Exercise A).

Answers
1 b animals which are hunted
2 b at the bottm of the tree
3 He would probably hold up his hand in a 'stop' signal and then put his finger against his mouth, which means 'be very quiet'.
4 Kari was angry with Noke because the sneeze frightened the possum away.
5 b chewing at something with your teeth

LESSON THREE

Objective
The children will be able to list the correct order of events.

Preparation
Give out *Pupil's Book 3* to each child (page 126, Exercise B).

Answers
First fill large saucepan with water.
Put on fire to boil. Add salt. Cover with lid.
Next, add rice slowly when water boils.
Stir rice once, so it doesn't stick. Remove lid. Cook for 20 mins.
Later test rice by opening a grain.
If soft inside, rice is cooked.
Finally, tip away water.

LESSON FOUR (Lesson Suggestion 39)

Objective
The children will be able to read for enjoyment.

Preparation
Give out *Supplementary Reader 3* and other books to the class.

Method
Allow children to choose a story to read quietly.

OR POETRY (Lesson Suggestion 40)

Preparation
Give out *Pupil's Book 3* to each child (page 127).

Answers
1 father and son
2 The son wants to go hunting.
3 The father thinks his son is too young to go hunting. He is afraid that he will get killed.
4 Many answers possible. Teacher to look for logical reasoning.

LESSON SIX

Objective
The children will be able to play Reading Games.

Preparation
Give out *Reading Games for Grade 6* to each child (pages 96–8).

Method
1 Allow children to choose a game to play.
2 Mark their work using *Teacher's Notes* (pages 97–9, Unit 37).

LISTENING 38

LESSON ONE

Objective
The children will be able to hear stressed words in a sentence.

Preparation
Tell the children to have a pencil and paper ready.

Method
1 Read out the following sentences, stressing the underlined words (say that word stronger, but not louder).
2 Children must listen for the stressed word and write it down on their paper.
I saw him yesterday.
I saw him yesterday.
Peter took the knife home.
The tools are in the storeroom.
Are you going to dig your garden?
Today is a very sunny day.
I wonder when they will come?
Will you cook the dinner tonight?
My friend will drive the truck to Rabaul.
We are going to see the helicopter.
3 Read through the sentences again. Ask the children which word is stressed. Children will mark their own work.
4 Read the sentences again, stressing the underlined words. Children repeat each sentence after you.

LESSON TWO

Objective
The children will be able to hear stressed words in a sentence.

Method
As for Lesson One.

1 That tree was blown over by the wind.
2 Small puppies are very playful.
3 The little boy ran to his mother.
4 Your book is very neat.
5 Your book is very neat.
6 I won't allow you to have it.
7 Give me that money!
8 I'm not going to the party.
9 Are you going to build that house?
10 He has already gone.

TALKING

LESSON ONE

Objective
The children will practise sentence patterns they already know:
How long have you been sitting here? We've been sitting here since eight o'clock.
How long has he been standing? He's been standing for five minutes.

Method
Turn back to Unit 19, Lessons Three, Four and Five, to revise these sentence patterns.

LESSON TWO

Objective
The children will practise sentence patterns they already know:
Are you sure they'll come? Yes, I know they will.
Do you know who it is? Yes, I know who it is. No, I don't know who it is.

Method
Turn back to Units 20 and 21, Lessons Three, Four and Five, to revise these sentence patterns.

LESSON THREE

Objective
The children will practise sentence patterns they already know:
Who do you think it might be? I think it might be Samot.
Do you think it will rain tomorrow? Yes, I think it will. No, I don't think it will.

Method
Turn back to Unit 22, Lessons Three, Four and Five, to revise these sentence patterns.

LESSON FOUR

Objective
The children will practise sentence patterns they already know:
Do you think he'll win the race? I don't know, I hope so.
He's going to sweep the floor.

Method
Turn back to Units 23 and 24, Lessons Three, Four and Five, to revise these sentence patterns.

LESSON FIVE

Objective
The children will practise sentence patterns they already know:
Do you think it's going to rain? Yes, I do.
A large deadly spider is under the table.

Method
Turn back to Units 25 and 26, Lessons Three, Four and Five, to revise these sentence patterns.

ORAL EXPRESSION

LESSON ONE

Objective
The children will be able to prepare a short talk.

Preparation
Allow time for the children to work out what to talk about.

Method
1 Divide the class into groups.
2 Each group must work out a short talk on a chosen topic. They will give their talk to the class in the next Oral Expression lesson.

LESSON TWO

Objective
The children will be able to talk to the class about the topic they prepared in Lesson One.

Method
1 The leader of each group gives a talk to the rest of the class.

LESSON THREE

Objective
The children will be able to discuss matters that interest them.

Preparation
Take the class to look at something interesting near the school, e.g: a timber mill, a factory, an unusual plant, a waterfall, a walk along the seashore, etc.

Method
1 Return to the classroom and invite a discussion about what you saw.
2 Guide the discussion by asking questions beginning with: how, why, what, when.

WRITTEN SENTENCES

Note
Remember, teach only FIVE of the six lessons. Choose one for homework, or for fast workers to do.

LESSON ONE (Lesson Suggestion 2)

Objective
The children will be able to describe three animals in a picture.

Preparation
Give out *Pupil's Book 3* to each child (page 128, Lesson 1).

Possible Answers
1 Bats sleep during the day and hang upside down from trees. They hunt for food at night.
2 Possums have warm, furry coats and bushy tails. They live in trees. They eat fruit and leaves. They are active at night.
3 Bandicoots have long noses. They search for fruit and insects on the forest floor.

LESSON TWO

Objective
The children will be able to write a descriptive paragraph.

Preparation
Give out *Pupil's Book 3* to each child (page 129, Lesson 2).

Method
1 This lesson should be based on an animal studied recently in school.
2 Revise all the facts known about this animal and ask the children the questions set out in this exercise.
3 Children then write down their answers to make a good paragraph.

LESSON THREE (Lesson Suggestion 13)

Objective
The children will be able to use commas correctly.

Preparation
Give out *Pupil's Book 3* to each child (page 129, Lesson 3).

Answers
1 Bats, grey wallabies, rats and bandicoots are nocturnal animals, which means that they sleep during the day.
2 Bandicoots dig in the ground with their front legs to find grubs, insects and roots to eat.
3 Possums, tree kangaroos and sugar gliders all live in trees.
4 Horseshoe bats, tube-nosed bats, black-bellied fruit bats and many others all live in this country.
5 Fruit bats often raid gardens at night for pawpaws, bananas, mangoes and other soft fruits.
6 Possums can be different colours such as white, brown, grey, or even black, depending on where they live.

LESSON FOUR

Objective
The children will be able to choose the correct words.

Preparation
Give out *Pupil's Book 3* to each child (page 129, Lesson 4).

Answers

1 many	3 for	5 enough	7 since
2 too	4 ago	6 much	

LESSON FIVE (Lesson Suggestion 13)

Objective
The children will be able to use the correct punctuation.

Preparation
Give out *Pupil's Book 3* to each child (page 130, Lesson 5).

Answers
1 The Matschie's tree kangaroo is found only in the Huon Peninsula area, north of Lae.
2 One kind of deer, called Java Rusa, lives in swamp and grassland areas.
3 Another kind of deer, called Axis, is found near Madang.
4 Pure white possums have been found around Madang, but black ones live on Manus Island.
5 On Wednesday, Toki and I shot a strange animal in the forest.
6 Uncle Ravi told us that it was an echnida.
7 Last September, we were shown a film at school called 'Animals of the Rainforest'.

LESSON SIX (Optional)

Objective
The children will be able to write the correct form of the verb.

Preparation
Give out *Pupil's Book 3* to each child (page 130, Lesson 6).

Answers

1 finished	3 eaten	5 seen	7 started
2 finished	4 ate	6 will see	8 will start

WRITTEN COMPOSITION

LESSON ONE (Lesson Suggestion 14A)

Objective
The children will be able to take notes.

Preparation
Give out *Pupil's Book 3* to each child (page 131, Lesson 1).

Answers
Bats are the only flying mammals. Found everywhere except very cold countries. Two types: fruit-eaters and insect-eaters. Rest in day. Hunt at dawn or dusk. Fruit bats have big eyes – see well. Insect-eaters have large ears – hear well. Sleep hanging upside-down in sheltered places.

LESSON TWO (Lesson Suggestion 14B)

Objective
The children will be able to make a story from notes.

Preparation
Give out *Pupil's Book 3* to each child (page 131, Lesson 2).

Model Answer
Mammals are warm-blooded animals. Their young are born alive and not in eggs. They breathe air. The mothers provide milk for the young.
Many mammals are found in Papua New Guinea. Among these are flying foxes, possums, wallabies, sugar gliders, deer and pigs. People hunt most of these animals for their meat and fur.
Some mammals, such as dolphins, whales and dugongs, live in the sea. Even though they may look like fish and live in the water, they are mammals. They have large brains and are very intelligent. In many countries they are trained and taught to do clever tricks.

SPELLING

LESSON ONE (Lesson Suggestion 22)

Objective
The children will learn how to spell this week's words. (They are from this week's story.)

Preparation
Give out *Pupil's Book 3* to each child (page 132, Spelling List).

LESSON TWO

Select from Exercises A–E (pages 132–4).

Exercise A (Lesson Suggestion 29)

Answers

1 choose
2 colourful
3 delicious
4 trained
5 message

Exercise B

can/not day/light may/be birth/day rail/road air/port some/thing in/side fire/man her/self pea/nut cup/board black/board play/ground

Exercise C (Lesson Suggestion 30)

Answers

1 making	3 careful	5 patting	7 collecting
2 riding	4 peacefully	6 beautiful	8 closing

Exercise D (Lesson Suggestion 31)

Answers

```
  W
  H
W A L L A B Y
  L       A
  E       N
          D U G O N G
          I
          C
          O
        P O S S U M
          T
```

Exercise E

Note
Show the children how to make spelling clocks, and then how to make words with them. Keep the clocks and encourage the children to use them in pairs whenever they have time. If there is no time to make spelling clocks, draw one on the blackboard and keep changing the position of the hands.

HANDWRITING (Lesson Suggestion 33)

Preparation
Give out *Pupil's Book 3* to each child (page 135).

READING

INTRODUCTION (Lesson Suggestion 34)

Objective
The children will understand the background to the story, and the meaning of new words. They will read the story silently.

Preparation
Give out *Reader 3* to each child (pages 42–5), '*Choosing a King*' A Play.

Method

If your class has not read a play before, explain that it is a story which is acted by people who take the part of various characters. Read through the list of characters at the beginning of the play and choose people to take these parts. Whenever they see the name of the character they are playing, they must read the story.
(Children remain in their desks to read the play through the first time.)

Note

This play could be acted out fully, with the characters dressed up for their parts moving around the classroom. Costumes could be made during an Expressive Arts lesson. (The class may like to perform in front of the rest of the school.)

LESSON ONE (Lesson Suggestion 34C)

Objective

The children will be able to answer questions to show they understand the story.

Preparation

Give out *Reader 3* (pages 42–5) and *Pupil's Book 3* (pages 135–6, Lesson 1) to each child.

Answers

1 The bat.
2 The bat and the owl.
3 Catch fish.
4 The pigeon.
5 Bird of Paradise.
6 Parrot
7 Eagle.
8 . . . they discovered that they all had different talents and that it would be better to all work together instead of having a King.
9 The honey-eater found her some honey.
The kingfisher caught her a fish.
The eagle found her village.
The pigeon carried a message — her necklace.
The Bird of Paradise attracted the villagers' attention.
The parrot guided her father through the thick jungle by his bright feathers.
The bat guided her father by night.
The owl stayed to guard the girl.
10 The author probably wrote this play to show how everyone is different and everyone has their own special abilities. There is a message in the story that tells us that we are really all equal, and no one is better than anyone else.

LESSON TWO

Objective

The children will be able to read a letter, then answer questions about it to show they understand its meaning.

Preparation

Give out *Pupil's Book 3* to each child (page 136, Lesson 2).

Possible Answers

1 The main points are: a People in PNG are not interested in reading because books are written by foreigners in a foreign language.
b Books should be written by local people in local languages.
c Books are too expensive to buy. Village library centres should be set up so villagers can borrow books easily.
2 Most of these points are opinion.
3 No, the writer does not tell us.
4 Yes, the writer does exaggerate a little as some books have been written by local authors.
5 Yes, because it makes you suspicious of the arguments. (Pupils' answer could also be no, but they should give a reason for their answer.)
7 He suggests that they set up groups of local writers, editors and publishers to discuss how to produce good, cheap books for Papua New Guinea. He also suggests establishing village library centres.
8 If pupils agree with this letter then they should write out the letter again including phrases like 'I think', or 'I believe'.
9 If pupils disagree, then they should write a letter saying what they think about the issue. Teacher should look for logical arguments when marking this work.

LESSON THREE

Objective
The children will be able to draw conclusions from what they read.

Preparation
Give out *Pupil's Book 3* to each child (page 137, Lesson 3).

Answers

1 Three people.
2 Very old because she needed to use a walking stick and she had a croaky, husky voice.
3 She was very fond of Tom. I know this because she called him 'dear son' and patted him gently on the arm, which is a sign of affection.
4 Tom also felt very fond of his mother. He was quick to help her when she rose, and held the door open for her as she went out. He also told his wife that he was fond of his mother.
5 They are son and mother.
6 They are probably husband and wife. I guess this because Maria suggests it when she yells, 'It's a pity you never show that you're fond of your wife.'.
7 No, I don't think Maria likes the woman.

LESSON FOUR (Lesson Suggestion 39)

Objective
The children will be able to read for enjoyment.

Preparation
Give out *Supplementary Reader 3* and other books.

Method
Allow children to select stories to read.

OR POETRY (Lesson Suggestion 40)

Preparation
Give out *Pupil's Book 3* to each child (page 137).

Answers
1 At night.
2 The poet could see its shape and hear its faint squeal.
3 flying
4 When it is hanging from a tree.
5 Because it eats fruit from our trees.
6 It makes a faint squeal.

LESSON FIVE

Objective
The children will be able to play Reading Games.

Preparation
Give out *Reading Games for Grade 6* to each child (pages 98–102).

LISTENING 39

LESSON ONE

Objective
The children will be able to put the stress mark above the correct syllable in each word.

Preparation
Copy the following words on the blackboard. (Each word has the stressed syllable *underlined* for the Teacher's benefit only. Do *not* underline them on the blackboard.)

at-tack e-vil help-ful ed-u-ca-tion e-qual fin-all-y ad-ven-ture
stu-dent ad-van-tage bam-boo re-al-ize yell-ow in-ter-est-ed

Method
1 Do the first one for the class by saying at-tack with the stress laid on the second syllable. Show on the blackboard how to put the stress mark above the second syllable.
2 Now the children must copy down the next word. Say the word, i.e: é-vil, putting stress on the first syllable. The children say it and then put the stress mark where they think it should go.
3 Do the same with all the other words.
4 Now read out the words again, this time putting the stress mark in the correct place on each word, on the blackboard. Children mark their own work.

LESSON TWO

Objective
The children will be able to put the stress mark above the correct syllable in each word.

Preparation

Copy the following words on the blackboard. (Each word has the stressed syllable underlined for the Teacher's benefit only. Do *not* underline them on the blackboard.)

help-less them-selves sur-prise di-rec-tion moun-tain-ous wor-ker
trav-ell-er ord-in-ar-y in-tern-al man-a-ger mem-ber

Method

1 As for Lesson One.

OR

2 Instead of just saying the word as in Step 2, use each word in a sentence, putting the stress on the correct syllable of that word, e.g:
The children did not know which way to go. They felt hélp-less.

TALKING

LESSON ONE

Objective

The children will practise sentence patterns they already know:
Which box is empty? The box on the table is empty.
Take this to the old man in the tradestore. Which old man? The man with the beard.

Method

Turn back to Units 27 and 28, Lessons Three, Four and Five, to revise these sentence patterns.

LESSON TWO

Objective

The children will practise sentence patterns they already know:
Which boy is ill? The one who's holding his stomach.
He's the man I saw yesterday.

Method

Turn back to Units 29 and 30, Lessons Three, Four and Five, to revise these sentence patterns.

LESSON THREE

Objective

The children will practise sentence patterns they already know:
That's the book that was on the table.
He gave me a mango that he bought at the market.

Method

Turn back to Units 31 and 32, Lessons Three, Four and Five, to revise these sentence patterns.

LESSON FOUR

Objective

The children will practise sentence patterns they already know:

Pure has finished his maths but he hasn't finished his English.
Unless he comes soon, we'll go without him.

Method
Turn back to Units 33 and 34, Lessons Three, Four and Five, to revise these sentence patterns.

LESSON FIVE

Objective
The children will practise a sentence pattern they already know:
He said that he would go to Lae in August.

Method
Turn back to Unit 35, Lessons Three, Four and Five, to revise this sentence pattern.

ORAL EXPRESSION

LESSON ONE

Objective
The children will be able to use their imagination to mime and act.

Method
1 Divide the class into groups.
2 Each group must make up their own simple mime (acting without words) or play to perform to the rest of the class.
These could be based on:
sequence pictures — stories they know from books
village stories or legends — imaginative stories
3 Each person in the group must have a part to act. The leader will supervise her own group.
4 Teacher should help wherever needed.

LESSON TWO

Objective
The children will be able to act out a play in front of the class.

Method
1 Choose each group to act out the play they prepared in Lesson One.

LESSON THREE

Objective
The children will be able to mime actions.

Method
1 Explain that you are going to mime an everyday scene without saying a word. When you have finished the pupils must tell you what you did, e.g: You wake up (stretch your arms and yawn), get out of bed, wash your face and get dressed, then eat your breakfast.
2 Now choose individual pupils to come out the front and mime something.

The rest of the class must guess what they're doing, e.g: lighting a fire, making a spear, making a fence, preparing a meal.

3 This could also be done in groups.

WRITTEN SENTENCES

Note
Remember, teach only FIVE of the six lessons. Choose one for homework, or for fast workers to do.

LESSON ONE

Objective
The children will be able to write about three reptiles in the picture.

Preparation
Give out *Pupil's Book 3* to each child (page 138, Lesson 1).

Possible Answers

1 Freshwater crocodiles are found in rivers, swamps and lakes. They can grow up to four metres in length and are covered in very tough scaley skin. They have large jaws with many sharp teeth.

2 There are many different types of snake found in this country. Some are found in long grass and others in trees. Some are poisonous and some are not. They can be many different colours and lengths.

LESSON TWO (Lesson Suggestion 5)

Objective
The children will be able to chooes the correct reflexive pronoun.

Preparation
Give out *Pupil's Book 3* to each child (page 138, Lesson 2).

Answers

1 himself	3 myself	5 itself	7 themselves
2 yourself	4 himself	6 myself	8 yourself

LESSON THREE

Objective
The children will be able to write the correct form of the verb.

Preparation
Give out *Pupil's Book 3* to each child (page 139, Lesson 3).

Answers

1 has uses	3 found	5 grows	7 protects
2 seen	4 lives eats	6 has	8 are

LESSON FOUR

Objective
The children will be able to join sentences using suitable joining words.

Preparation
Give out *Pupil's Book 3* to each child (page 139, Lesson 4).

Answers
1 I cannot come now but I will come later.
2 Do you like tea or do you prefer coffee?
3 I fell asleep early because I was so tired.
4 He cannot read but she can.
5 I will go home now unless you want me to stay.
6 We stayed in the house until the rain stopped.
7 I will prepare the food while you light the fire.
8 He passed his exams because he studied hard.
9 I had a strange dream while I was asleep.
10 Will you come with me or will you stay here?
11 I will wait for you until you come back.
12 We will go without them unless they arrive soon.

LESSON FIVE (Lesson Suggestion 13)

Objective
The children will be able to add quotation marks to the correct places.

Preparation
Give out *Pupil's Book 3* to each child (page 140, Lesson 5).

Answers
1 'The boas are not more than a metre in length and are quite harmless', the teacher continued.
2 'Which is the most dangerous snake of all?' Anis asked.
3 'One of the most dangerous snakes is the Papuan taipan', Mr Siwai told the class. 'It is about two metres long and has a red stripe running along its back.'
4 'The death adder is also a dangerous snake', he continued.
5 'Young green tree pythons may be red or yellow in colour', said Mr Siwai. 'But when they reach one metre in length they change colour to a bright green.'
6 'That's just like one type of dragon lizard', said Rea. 'It can change colour from bright green to dark brown in just a few minutes.'
7 'That's true, Rea', said Mr Siwai. 'Does anyone know why it changes like that so quickly?'
8 'I think it does it as camouflage', Rea said. 'It can change its colour to suit the colour of the branch it is on so that its enemies won't see it.'

LESSON SIX (Optional)

Objective
The children will be able to change direct speech into reported speech.

Preparation
Give out *Pupil's Book 3* to each child (page 140, Lesson 6).

Answers
1 She said she would become a teacher when she finished High School.
2 He said he would go hunting next week.
3 They said they would come with us.
4 He said he would never come back to this village.

5 The girl said they would all pay for this.
6 He said he would be able to help you after dinner.
7 He said she would not be going to the dance.
8 He said he would help you (me) carry those vegetables.

WRITTEN COMPOSITION

LESSON ONE (Lesson Suggestion 14B)

Objective
The children will be able to expand a story from notes.

Preparation
Give out *Pupil's Book 3* to each child (page 141, Lesson 1).

Model Answer
Kone and I decided to build a raft. We finished it in a week and we were really pleased with it. We launched it in the river, both climbed aboard and floated downstream.

Suddenly, with no warning, our raft hit a tree trunk in the river and overturned. We fell into the water. I came up gasping for air and looked around for Kone. I saw his shape under the water so I took a deep breath and dived under. He was caught up in the branches of the tree trunk. I helped him to get free and we rose to the surface. He was exhausted, so I dragged him to the shore.

Kone was unconscious when I got him ashore so I gave him mouth-to-mouth resuscitation that we learned at school. At last he started to breathe by himself. He opened his eyes and coughed. I let out a sigh of relief.

LESSON TWO (Lesson Suggestion 17)

Objective
The children will be able to write a personal letter.

Preparation
Give out *Pupil's Book 3* to each child (page 141, Lesson 2).

Model Answer

Ward Three,
General Hospital,
Popondetta,
Northern Province.

19th November, 1982.

Dear Maria,

I am very sorry to hear that you were bitten by a snake. I hope you will be well again soon.

I'm glad that you reached the hospital in time for the doctors to give you special treatment. I am sorry that I cannot visit you in hospital but I will come and see you when you return home.

We are all thinking of you and looking forward to seeing you well again.

With love,

SPELLING

LESSON ONE (Lesson Suggestion 22)

Objective
The children will learn how to spell this week's words. (They are from this week's story.)

Preparation
Give out *Pupil's Book 3* to each child (page 141, Spelling List).

LESSON TWO

Select from Exercises A–D (page 142) or give a spelling list and dictation test on the last four weeks' work.

Exercise A (Lesson Suggestion 29)

Answers

1 current	3 bait	5 breeze
2 steal	4 web	

Exercise B (Lesson Suggestion 8)

Answers

1 seam	3 wait	5 waist	7 son
2 stare	4 would	6 tide	8 tale

Exercise C

Answers

1 rose	3 made	5 arrived at
2 received	4 caught	

Exercise D

Note
Teacher should do one or two examples before children do this exercise.

HANDWRITING (Lesson Suggestion 33)

Preparation
Give out *Pupil's Book 3* to each child (page 143).

READING

INTRODUCTION (Lesson Suggestion 34)

Objective
The children will understand the background to the story, and the meaning of new words. They will read the story silently.

Preparation
Give out *Reader 3* to each child (pages 46–8), *'Spider Web Fishermen'*.

Method
Talk about the many different ways of catching fish — using lines, nets, spears, traps. How many can the children describe? This story is about unusual method of fishing used on one of the islands of the Milne Bay Province.

LESSON ONE (Lesson Suggestion 34C)

Objective
The children will be able to answer questions to show they understand the story.

Preparation
Give out *Reader 3* (pages 46–8) and *Pupil's Book 3* (pages 143–4, Lesson 1) to each child.

Answers
1 They caught spiders to spin sticky webs which they used for catching fish.
2 Lokuia used to be powerful many years ago but one day he disappeared into the hills and no one saw him again.
3 They were spiders.
4 The current took the canoe to a strange beach.
5 They promised to set the spiders free and never catch them again.
6 They were caught in a strong current which carried them to the beach.
7 water
8 have seen before
9 . . . fastening the sticky ball of web to a long piece of bush rope and then tying the rope to the bottom of the kite. They flew the kite over the water and the ball of web skimmed over the surface. The garfish jumped out of the water and clamped his teeth into the ball and could not escape.
10 . . . send his spiders to cover the whole village with spider webs so they would be trapped inside their houses.

LESSON TWO

Objective
The children will read for understanding.

Preparation
Give out *Pupil's Book 3* to each child (page 144, Lesson 2).

Answers
1 Two boys got off the plane at Mt Hagen.
2 Two girls used buttons.
3 There was only one thing which they all grew.

LESSON THREE

Objective
The children will be able to mime how reptiles move.

Preparation
Give out *Pupil's Book 3* to each child. (Turn to Poetry, page 144, and the picture on page 138.)

Method

1 Read the poem about the Lizard.
2 Choose someone to mime the way a lizard moves.
3 Turn to the picture of reptiles on page 138. Ask children to mime one of these animals. The rest of the class must guess which animal is being mimed.

LESSON FOUR (Lesson Suggestion 39)

Objective

The children will be able to read for enjoyment.

Preparation

Give out *Supplementary Reader 3* and other books.

LESSON FIVE

Objective

The children will be able to play Reading Games.

Preparation

Give out *Reading Games for Grade 6* to each child (pages 102–9).

Method

1 Children choose some games to play.
2 Mark their work using *Teacher's Notes* (pages 102–6, Units 39–40).

LESSON SUGGESTIONS FOR LISTENING

INTRODUCTION

Good communication begins with listening. Children will not learn to communicate unless they learn to listen carefully. You must give the children a lot of practice in listening.
Listening must be stressed in *all lessons*. It is a good idea to *test* children sometimes to make sure they are listening properly and concentrating on what you are saying. You can do this by suddenly whispering or shouting, or by saying something completely ridiculous in the middle of a sentence to see if the children notice. But do this only when you notice that the children are not giving their full attention during a lesson.
Children who do not hear well should sit at the front of the classroom. Try to arrange for these children to do a hearing test.

LESSON SUGGESTIONS FOR ORAL EXPRESSION

INTRODUCTION

Children must learn to express themselves fluently in English. This will only happen if they are given many opportunities to practise their oral expression in meaningful situations.
Always encourage the children to use *complete sentences* for answers, not one-word answers.
During these lessons, give the children the opportunity to use as many as possible of the different sentence patterns which they have already learned. Remember, it is much easier for children to talk about something they have seen or done in a practical situation than in an unreal situation.
The suggested time allocation for Grade 6 is 60 minutes each week. This time could be broken into three 20 minute lessons. Arrange your timetable so that some Oral Expression time is allowed before a Written Composition lesson.

LESSONS SUGGESTIONS FOR TALKING

INTRODUCTION

The time allocation for this subject is for teaching sentence patterns. Some patterns are easy to learn, as they are merely extensions of patterns learned in earlier grades. Some patterns are difficult, and you may have to keep repeating these lessons for some time.
Do not go on to a new pattern until children *understand* the pattern they are learning. They must be able to use it properly in meaningful situations.
The sentence patterns set out in this course do not always have to be learned exactly as written. Teachers should think up more examples and give practice situations during other lessons where children can use these patterns. Use only the vocabulary known to the children for these drills. Children should learn to *say* the pattern correctly before they write it down.
Do not expect *all* pupils to learn *all* the sentence patterns listed in this course. It is better for them to learn *some* of them confidently at their own learning pace, so that they can use them correctly and confidently.

Group work is usually the best way to practice these patterns because everyone is able to *talk*. However, you must organize and supervise the groups carefully.

Each unit of Work for Talking consists of:

Lesson 1: Revision of last week's sentence pattern.
Lesson 2: Revision of Grade 5 sentence patterns.
Lesson 3: Learning of a new sentence pattern.
Lesson 4: Practice of new pattern.
Lesson 5: Practice, using a substitution table based on this pattern. (This will be left on the blackboard and used for Lesson 1 the following week.)

LESSON SUGGESTION 1

A Teaching a new statement

Method

1 Revise any known words and structures in the new sentence pattern, e.g: I'm going to walk to the store. She's going to sweep the floor.
2 Demonstrate the situation to the children by using aids or mime, e.g: Go to the window, put out your hand and say: I think it's going to rain.
3 Say the pattern several times.
4 The children repeat it.
5 Repeat the sentence pattern, substituting other words. Get the whole class to repeat each sentence, e.g: I think it's going to be a fine day. I think it's going to be a cloudy day.
6 Choose individual children to say the new pattern.

B Teaching a new question with a known statement

Method

1 Revise any known words or structures in the new sentence pattern, e.g: What did he buy?
2 Demonstrate the situation to the children, making use of any teaching aids available. Miming is also a valuable teaching aid, e.g: Mime a boy going to a shop and buying a new bush knife.
3 Say the sentence pattern clearly three times.
4 Say the pattern and get the whole class to repeat it, e.g: What did he buy himself? He bought himself a new bush knife.
5 Repeat the same sentence pattern, substituting other words. Get the class to repeat after you, e.g: What did she buy herself? She bought herself a new dress. What did they buy themselves? They bought themselves a new truck.
6 Then ask the question and select a pupil to answer, e.g: What did I buy myself? (Holding up the knife) A: You bought yourself a new knife.
7 Divide the class into small groups of about three. Two children in the group mime to a situation (with aids) while the third child must say the sentence pattern.
8 Walk around the room listening to each group.

C Practice from a substitution table

Method

1 Write the substitution table on the blackboard before the lesson begins (or use the one from last week).

I need some RICE	but I don't need any MEAT.
FRIENDS	ENEMIES
SHIRTS	SHORTS
SALT	OIL
WATER	FOOD
ADVICE	MONEY

2 Introduce the pattern, e.g: I need some rice but I don't need any meat.
3 Children repeat it.
4 Then substitute new words into the same pattern, e.g: I need some friends but I don't need any enemies.
5 Children repeat it.
6 Ask children to read out this pattern, substituting different words from the table on the blackboard.
7 Now ask children to make up their own examples.
8 Divide the class into groups to practise this pattern using the table on the blackboard as a guide.

LESSON SUGGESTIONS FOR WRITTEN SENTENCES

INTRODUCTION

Read out the instructions for each lesson and make sure the children understand what they should do. Read out the example given at the beginning of each lesson. If no example is given, discuss the first two or three sentences with the class, giving the correct answers. Make sure that *all* children understand fully what they must do before they do any written work. If time is short for written work, tell the children to write one-word answers.
Five minutes before the end of each lesson, correct each sentence orally with the children.

Note
Six lessons per week are set out in the *Using English* Books. As there is only time for *five* of these lessons, you should choose the five most suitable for your class. The sixth may be given for homework (or given to fast workers).

LESSON SUGGESTION 2

Writing sentences about pictures

Method
1 Talk about the pictures with the children before you ask them to write anything.
2 Ask the children to tell you what is happening in the pictures. Make sure they use complete sentences, not just words and phrases. Encourage the children to use sentence patterns they have learned.
3 Sometimes the children are asked to answer questions about the picture. Ask them to tell you possible answers before they write them down.
4 Help the children with the first two or three sentences by writing them on the blackboard.

LESSON SUGGESTION 3

Finding the sentence, phrase or word out of context

Method

1 Read the passage (or sentence, or list) out loud, or ask the class or a good reader to read it.
2 Ask which sentence, or phrase, or word, does not belong. Ask why?
3 Make sure that everyone understands *why* it does not belong.

LESSON SUGGESTION 4

Reported speech

This is reporting what someone has said, e.g: 'I am going to the gardens today', said Mary. (Direct speech.) Mary said that she was going to the gardens today. (Reported speech.)

Method

1 Remind the children that for reported speech they must:
   write the speaker's name at the beginning of the sentence
   not use quotation marks (')
   change pronouns from 'I' to 'she' or 'he'
   change the tense of the action word (verb) from 'am going' to 'was going'.
2 Write some examples on the blackboard and ask the class to help you change them into reported speech.

LESSON SUGGESTION 5

Reflexive pronouns

Method

1 These are either singular (only one) or plural (more than one), e.g:
   singular – himself.
   plural – themselves.
2 When teaching these pronouns you could write the following lists on the blackboard.

singular		*plural*	
my	myself	them	themselves
your	yourself	our	ourselves
her	herself	your	yourselves
him	himself		
it	itself		

3 Use these words in sentences, e.g:
   I can see myself in the mirror.
   He poured water on himself.
   Have you washed yourself?
   They made it by themselves.
   Did you enjoy yourselves at the party?
   We helped ourselves to the food.
4 Ask the children to use these words in sentences by themselves. If this is too difficult, ask them to choose the correct word to go in the spaces, e.g:
   She made the dress . . .
   The dog bit . . . on the tail.
   Did you make that basket by . . . ?
   I taught . . . to swim.

LESSON SUGGESTION 6

Completing written sentences/providing questions or answers

Method

1 Explain what the children will be doing.
2 Discuss the example given in the book if there is one.
3 Read out the sentence to the children and ask them for possible beginnings or endings, questions or answers. It is very important that they do this *orally* before they do any writing.
4 Write the first two or three sentences on the blackboard and get the class to decide on suitable answers. Write the answers on the blackboard and let the children copy them down.
5 Tell the children to complete the other sentences by themselves.
6 Walk around the room, helping children and correcting some of their work.

Follow Up

1 Choose pupils to read out their answers to the rest of the class.
2 Make sure that all sentences make sense and that children use sentence patterns they have learned.
3 Mark this work and ask children to write out the correct sentences if they have made mistakes.

LESSON SUGGESTION 7

Choosing the correct form of the verb

Method

1 Read through the example twice, using the first word in brackets and then the second word. (Sometimes only one word is given.)
2 Ask which word fits. Remind the children that the form of the verb will depend on whether the action took place now, in the future, or in the past.
3 Work out the first two or three sentences with the children on the blackboard.
4 Tell the children to complete all other sentences by themselves.

Follow Up

Read out the correct answers.

LESSON SUGGESTION 8

Choosing the correct word

Some words sound the same but have different meanings and are spelled differently.

Note

There is no easy way to teach the meaning of words. Whenever you come across two words that sound the same, explain that they have different meanings and are spelled differently, e.g:

blue and blew
My coat is blue. (colour)
The wind blew very hard.

The children must learn the correct spelling for the right meaning.

Method

1 Discuss the meaning of the words in brackets, e.g: (threw, through).
2 Give examples of how each word could be used in a sentence.

3 Do the first two or three examples on the blackboard for the children to copy.
4 Make sure the children understand the meaning of each word before they do any written work.

LESSON SUGGESTION 9

Apostrophes

Method

Explain that we use apostrophes to show 2 things:

1 That something belongs to someone or something, e.g:

The pig's tail (the tail belongs to the pig)
The girl's pencil (the pencil belongs to the girl)

Remind the children that if you are writing about *one* girl's pencil, you put the apostrophe *after* girl and *before* 's'.

If you are writing about *two or more* girls' pencils, the apostrophe goes *after* the 's'.

But if you are writing about a plural word that does not end in 's', you put an apostrophe then add an 's', e.g:

children	children's
men	men's
women	women's

2 Apostrophes are also used to shorten words, e.g: isn't (is not) (see Lesson Suggestion 10 — Contractions).

LESSON SUGGESTION 10

Contractions

Method

1 Explain to the children that the sentences as they are already written *are* correct, but that when we *talk* in English we usually shorten these words.
2 Discuss where you need to write apostrophes, i.e. where letters are missing from the words.
3 Write several examples on the blackboard.

Follow Up

Write the correct answers on the blackboard for children to mark themselves.

won't	will not	we'll	we will	that's	that is
haven't	have not	I'm	I am	he'd	he will
wouldn't	would not	can't	cannot	mustn't	must not
can't	cannot	your're	you are	aren't	are not

LESSON SUGGESTION 11

Rules for changing from singular to plural or plural to singular

Note

You will not cover all these points in one lessons. Simply explain the ones which are being taught in the lesson you are doing.

Method

1 Remind the children that you usually add 's' to a word to make it plural (to show that you mean more than one), e.g: girl girls, boy boys, teacher teachers,

2 Explain that you need to add 'es' to some words to make them plural, e.g: box boxes,
3 Explain that some words change completely in the plural, or change at least one letter, e.g: child children, man men, woman women, thief thieves,
4 Explain that when you change a singular noun to plural in a sentence, you often have to change the other words which relate to the noun, e.g:
The boy is washing his shirt (singular)
The *boys are* washing *their shirts* (plural)

LESSON SUGGESTION 12

Rules for changing tenses

Method

1 Remind the children that action words (verbs) change according to whether the action is:
happening now (present)
has already happened (past)
is going to happen (future)
2 Write examples on the blackboard:
Mary is giving her baby a bath. (present)
Mary gave her baby a bath. (past)
Mary will give her baby a bath. (future).
3 Ask the children to do some work orally before they do any written work.

LESSON SUGGESTION 13

Punctuation

Note

Most of the lessons on punctuation cover only one point at a time.

Method

1 Remind the children to use the correct punctuation mark.
2 Write several examples on the blackboard and discuss them with the children before you ask them to do any written work.

A Capital letters ABC

Capital letters are used in the following cases:

1 The first word of a sentence, e.g: This is a sentence.
2 People's names, e.g: Julius Chan.
3 Towns and cities, e.g: Boroko, Wewak.
4 Provinces and countries, e.g: Morobe Province, Papua New Guinea.
5 Rivers and mountains, e.g: Sepik River, Mount Hagen.
6 Days of the week, months, holidays, e.g: Monday, January, Easter.
7 Titles, e.g: The Chief Minister, Her Majesty the Queen.
8 Nationalities, e.g: Indonesians, Australians.
9 The word 'I'.
10 Organizations, e.g: The Red Cross Society.
11 Titles of books and magazines, e.g: *Using English*.
12 The first word of direct speech, e.g: He said, 'You are not listening carefully'.
13 Subjects at school, e.g: Mathematics, Agriculture.
14 Names for God and religious leaders, e.g: Jesus Christ, Buddha.

B Fullstops .

Fullstops are used:
1 At the end of a sentence.
2 To show that a word is abbreviated, e.g: P.O. Box (Post Office Box)

C Question marks ?

The question mark is used only with direct questions. e.g: What is your name? Who is that man?

D Quotation marks '

Quotation marks are used to show the exact words of the speaker, e.g: 'I told you not to open that parcel', said John.
These marks should also be used when quoting the exact title of a book for film, e.g: We went to see *'Close Encounters of the Third Kind'* last night.

E Hyphens -

Hyphens are used to join words which together make up another word, e.g: twenty-one, sailing-boat

F Commas ,

Commas are used to separate lists of items:

1 e.g: I bought some bananas, lemons, tomatoes, onions, potatoes and pumpkin tops at the market.
2 They are used before or after direct speech:
  e.g: 'I won't come', he said.
  He said, 'I won't come.'
3 They are also used to show differences in meaning.
  e.g: John, my friend, is coming to stay.
  John, my friend is coming to stay.
  (The first sentence explains that the friend coming to stay is called John. The second sentence tells us that the talker is telling John that a friend is coming to stay.)
4 Commas are also used at the end of each line (except the last) in addresses, e.g: Mr K. Tibbo, P.O. Box 663, Madang.

LESSON SUGGESTIONS FOR WRITTEN COMPOSITION

INTRODUCTION

By Grade 6, children should be able to write a composition of several sentences about a variety of topics. They should be able to use their imagination, to express their own ideas and to use the skills they have learned in all areas of English language learning.
It is very important that you introduce this subject in an interesting way so that pupils *want* to write their own stories. Most Written Composition lessons in the *Using English* books have introductions which you should read and discuss with the children before they write.

Where pictures are provided, you should disuss them with the children before they try to write. Encourage pupils to imagine that they are the people in the illustration. Ask how they would feel and what they would do in that situation. You must correct all written work with the pupils. Explain the mistakes. Discuss the main weaknesses privately with each pupil.
It is useful to provide a list of words on the topic before the children write. In many cases you will find useful words in the Family Lists in the *Using English* books.

LESSON SUGGESTION 14

A Note-taking

Method

1 Explain that note-taking is listing information in the order in which it is given, using key words, instead of full sentences.
2 Remind the children to use words like: first, second, third, firstly, secondly, next, after that, finally, last of all. These words tell you the order in which things happen.
3 Make sure that you read the passages several times, slowly and clearly, when you ask the children to take notice.
4 If they find it very difficult, ask them questions about the passage before you ask them to take notes.

B Making a story from notes

Method

1 Explain that this is the opposite of note-taking. Only the key words are supplied and the children must make complete sentences from the notes.
2 Explain that the key words give only the outline of the story, and provide clues as to what happened.
3 Discuss the key words or phrases given and ask what the children think they mean. Make some suggestions on the blackboard to start them off.

LESSON SUGGESTION 15

Choosing the best sentence to go with a picture

Children are given several sentences which are similar but not equally suitable.

Method

1 Discuss with the children what is happening in each picture.
2 Ask the children to choose which sentence is most suitable for the picture. Why do they think it is the most suitable?
3 Encourage the children to give logical reasons why the others are not suitable.

LESSON SUGGESTION 16

A Writing stories

Method

1 Read the introduction to each lesson which should stimulate the children's interest about the subject.

2 If there are illustrations, ask the children to describe what is shown in the pictures. Ask questions about the pictures.
3 Encourage the children to imagine how other people feel, what they think and why they do things.

B Sequence pictures

These help the children set out their stories in a sensible order.

Method

1 Ask the children to say what happens in each picture before they write anything down.
2 Write a list of useful words on the blackboard.

C Writing descriptions

Method

1 Encourage the children to write about what they can see, hear, touch or smell, when they describe things.
2 Encourage them to use describing words. Write lists of these on the blackboard at the beginning of a lesson and add the children's suggestions to these.
3 Ask some of the class to read out their descriptions.

LESSON SUGGESTION 17

Letter-writing

INTRODUCTION

It is important for children to know why letter-writing is a useful skill. Explain that letters will help them to:

1 keep in contact with friends and relatives
2 send and answer invitations
3 send thanks to someone for a gift
4 express sadness or regret
5 congratulate a friend
6 share ideas with a penfriend in another country

Business letters will help them to:

1 find out information
2 obtain mailed goods from a store
3 reply to an advertisement
4 apply for a job

Sometimes Grade Six pupils will be asked to write business letters for their parents or friends in the village.

Letters written in Written Composition lessons should be the kind of letters the children are likely to have to write in a real situation, now or in the future. Try to think up situations where the letters can really be posted.

Method

1 Teach the correct setting out of business and personal letters. (See Grade 6 Syllabus, pages 248–55.)
2 Teach the children to make a plan before writing the letter.
3 Teach the children to address the envelopes clearly and correctly. (See Grade 6 Syllabus, page 256.)

LESSON SUGGGESTION 18

Addressing envelopes

Method

1 Mr Kapita has a Post Office Box number. Miss Teta's address is c/o (or c/–).

2 Explain to the class that some people in towns pay money each year to use a Post Office Box. The person in the Post Office puts all their mail in their box, where it is collected by the person renting the box.

3 Explain that Miss Teta's address uses an abbreviation (c/–) which means 'care of'. Many people living in rural areas cannot collect mail from a Post Office, so the Post Office sends their mail in the care of the nearest mission, Patrol Post or school.

4 Explain to the children where to write the address,
the name of the person, with a comma after the name
the Post Office Box number (or place) followed by a comma
the name of the town or city — followed by a comma
the name of the province (or country) followed by a full stop
capital letters and full stops used for proper names
the correct placing and *cost* of the postage stamp

5 Give the children practice in addressing envelopes. Choose real addresses for the children to use.

6 When the children can do this correctly, show them how to put the sender's name (their own name) on the back of the envelope. Explain the reason for doing this. (If the letter does not arrive at the correct place, the Post Office will return it to the sender.)

LESSON SUGGESTION 19

Writing a report

INTRODUCTION

Children need to know that many people have to write reports about things they have seen or done, e.g: a newspaper reporter interviews people and then writes about what they said; teachers write 'reports' on their pupils' progress at school; councillors report on the running of markets and co-operatives.

Method

1 Teach the children how to change direct speech into reported speech, e.g:
direct speech: 'I think we should have more people on the committee', said Mr Giri.
reported speech: Mr Giri said that he thought they should have more people on the committee.

2 Children require the skill of note-taking (see Lesson suggestion 14) in order to take notes for their reports.

3 When writing a report from notes, those notes must be expanded into a good composition, e.g:
(notes) *School Sports Day*
Fine day — most children took part — many parents attended — events: running, high jump, long jump, hurdles, novelty races, relays — 'This is the best Sports Day we can remember', said Mr Awepa, the Head Teacher.
(Report) *Gaba School Sports Day*
On Wednesday, Gaba Community School held its annual Sports Day. The day was fine and most of the children from Gaba School took part in the sporting programme. It was good to see so many parents of the children

attending. Events for the day included running, high jump, long jump, hurdles, relays and novelty races. The Head Teacher, Mr Awepa, said that it was the best sports day they could remember.

LESSON SUGGESTION 20

Filling in forms

INTRODUCTION

Children have already learned to fill in simple forms. In Grade 6 they should be given further practice in filling in other forms, e.g: bank deposit and withdrawal slips, application for a driver's licence, enrolment forms for High School and any other forms teachers can obtain which are relevant.

Method

1 See Grade 6 Syllabus on Form Filling, pages 235–42.
2 Teacher should explain what the headings on forms mean, e.g: surname, address, occupation, etc.
3 Explain *why* these forms have to be filled in, *where* you can get them, and *where* they should be sent when filled in.

LESSON SUGGESTION 21

Telegrams

INTRODUCTION

In Grade 6 the children should learn what a telegram is and why it is sent. Explain that a telegram is a message sent by telegraph. The message is telegraphed to another place on a machine called a teleprinter. Explain that telegrams are usually used when you want to send an important message urgently or very quickly. Telegrams are expensive, so the message must be as brief as possible but still make sense to the reader.

Method

1 If possible, show the children a real telegram (which has been delivered) and a telegram form (from a Post Office).
2 Discuss particular messages with the children before you ask them to write telegram messages. Ask them which parts of the messages are the most important.
3 See Grade 6 Syllabus on Telegrams, pages 242–6.

LESSON SUGGESTIONS FOR SPELLING

INTRODUCTION

In Grade 6, children should learn to spell about 450 words in addition to the words they have already learned in earlier grades. However, children should be expected to spell only the words which they are likely to use in their written work.

The main purpose of this subject is to help the children memorize the correct order of letters in words.

Each weekly spelling section in the *Using English* books is divided into five short exercises. There will not be time to do all these, so you must decide which will be done. You should choose exercises which concentrate on pupils' weak areas. Some of the work could be given for homework.

Each weekly list is divided into two parts – a Weekly List and a Family Group. The Weekly List contains eight new words. These are either words with similar structures, or words taken from the Pacific Series Reader story for that particular week. The Family Group consists of eight words on a given topic. Pupils may know some of these already. Use the Family Group words throughout the week's work. Encourage pupils to use these words as reference lists to help them with written work.

The children are expected to learn how to spell all eight words from the weekly list. These words could be written down into the children's personal spelling lists for learning. They could also be written on the blackboard and left there all week. These could be tested at the end of each month either in a spelling test or dictation.

LESSON SUGGESTION 22

Learning to spell new words

Method

1 Explain the meaning of each word and give examples of how it can be used in a sentence.
2 Explain the following learning routine to the children:
   a Write down the new words in your book.
   b Look at the first word. Say it and then spell it.
   c Close your eyes. Say it and then spell it.
   d Open your eyes and look at the word again. Did you spell it correctly?
   e Spell it again.
   f Now do the same with the other words.
   g When you think you can spell all the words, give your book to a friend and ask her to test you.
   h If you spell a word wrong, put a small cross by it and learn it again.
3 While the children are learning these words, write the words from this week's Family Group on a wall chart. At the end of the lesson, read through these words with the class. Leave the chart on display all week.

Suggested method for using words from Weekly Spelling Lists

Method

1 Children have a separate spelling notebook. Children copy the words from the Weekly Spelling List into this notebook, numbering each week.
2 Children should be given a learning time where they carry out a–h (above).
3 Later in the week, children could test each other again in partners. Tester puts either a tick or cross in the space column. If the word is spelled wrongly, then the child must use it in a sentence under the list.

Week one

harm	above
harmful	abandon
hard	abillity
harbour	about

I did not have the ability the spell this word correctly.

Note

Always ask the children to *check* that they have copied the words correctly into their notebooks, otherwise they may learn to spell the words incorrectly.

LESSON SUGGESTION 23

Word-building

Method

1 Explain to the children that they can use groups of letters, or the letters from a given word, to make new words. They can use a few or many of the letters in each word. They can re-arrange the order of the letters.

2 Tell a child to jumble up the letters in the original word and write them on the blackboard in a new order. This makes it easier to see combinations of the letters.

e.g: Directions:

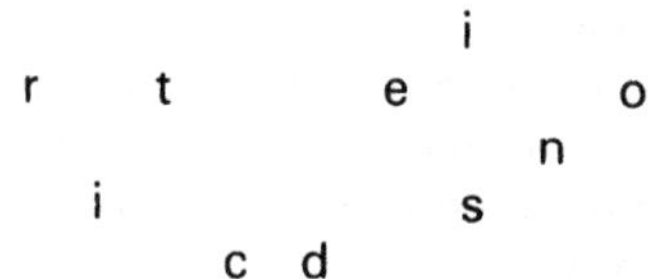

Possible words: tie, not, do, so, cent, nest, net, noise, toes, stone, credit, dirt, ride, etc.

3 Discuss possible new words before you ask the children to write anything down.

4 Ask some children to read out their lists of new word and you write their suggestions on the blackboard.

5 Tell the children to write any new words they learn into their spelling note-books.

Note

Some lessons ask the children to make words from a root word, e.g:
fly flies flier flying flown flight

Method

1 Give the children several examples. Write them on the blackboard.

2 Help the children by making them finish sentences which use these new words. (Do this out loud first.)

e.g: drive
I am . . . (driving)
He is a taxi (driver)
We . . . to town yesterday. (drove)
There was a wide . . . leading to the house. (driveway)

LESSON SUGGESTION 24

How to use words from the Family Group

Method

1 Read the words with the children and discuss the meaning of each one.

2 Teacher could make a Word Chart using these words. On large sheets of paper (made into a large book) write the topic, e.g: Clothes, at the top of the page, then underneath write the eight words.

3 Choose children (perhaps those who spell all their words correctly) to illustrate each word on the chart.

4 Use this chart frequently and have it open at this week's list. Refer to it whenever talking about that topic, and for Written Composition. Encourage children to come out and look at the chart.

LESSON SUGGESTION 25

Dictation

Method

1 There are only two lessons for spelling each week, so there will not be much time for dictation. However this is a good way of testing children's spelling of the words they have learned. You could give the class a dictation test at the end of each four weeks' word, in place of Exercises A–E.
2 Choose sentences containing the spelling words. Read them out slowly to the class, giving the children plenty of time to write them down.
3 When you have finished the test, read the sentences once more for the children to check their work.
4 Now collect papers and mark them. Put a cross beside each word that is spelled wrongly and give the papers back to the children. All words that were wrongly spelled, must be re-learned and used in sentences in Spelling notebooks, under that week's work.

LESSON SUGGESTION 26

Word chains

Method

1 This is a spelling game to make children think of words starting and ending with certain letters.
2 Point out that each word must start with the last letter of the last word, e.g: paint – time
rent – tear – real – lime – each – hear –
3 If the children find this lesson difficult, you could write a list of words on the blackboard, so the children can choose the correct words from it.

LESSON SUGGESTION 27

Alphabetical order

INTRODUCTION

Explain why alphabetical order is useful. Explain that is makes it easy to find names in the Telephone Directory or on the electoral roll, etc.

Method

1 Explain that when we write things in alphabetical order we sort them according to the *first* letter.
e.g: ball, candle, dog.
2 If several words start with the same letter, we sort them according to the *second* letter in each word.
e.g: best, bin, black, brush.
3 When the first two letters are the same, we sort them according to the *third* letter.
e.g: that, their, though, through, thumb.
4 Explain that when we put people's names into alphabetical order we sort according to the family name, and then according to the first name or initials.
e.g: Asi, H.T.
Asi, L.
Balik, Jacob
Calep, B.
Calep, Seth

LESSON SUGGESTION 28

Spelling intersection game

Note

Children should remember playing intersection games for spelling last year. They work the same way as intersection games for maths.

Method

1 Look at the circles; they overlap each other.
   In the area numbered 1, you must make up words containing 4 letters.
   In the area numbered 2, you must make up words beginning with 'p'.
   In the area numbered 3, you must make up words containing 'ai'.

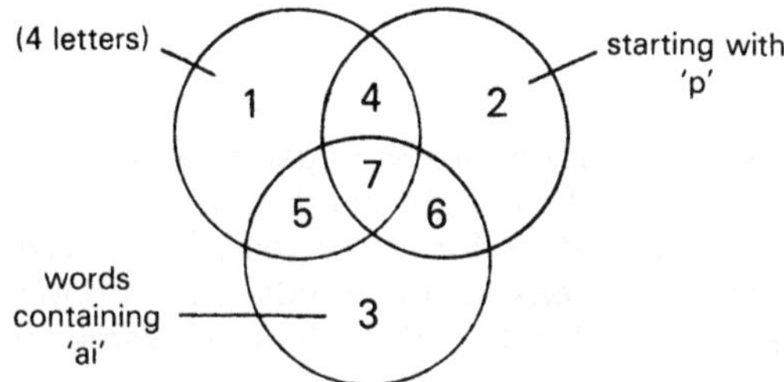

Words for number 4, must be as for numbers 1 and 2 (4 letters and begin with 'p', e.g: pond, pair).
Words for number 5, must be as for numbers 1 and 3 (4 letters with 'ai' in them, e.g: main, pain).
Words for number 6, must be as for numbers 2 and 3 (begin with 'p' and have 'ai' in them, e.g: pair, paint).
Words for number 7 must be as for numbers 1, 2 and 3 (4 letters, starting with 'p' with 'ai' in them, e.g: paid, pail).

LESSON SUGGESTION 29

Word meanings

Note

This is usually Exercise A for each week.

Method

1 Ask the children if they can tell you what any of the words mean. Discuss the meanings of all new words.
2 Give examples of how you can use the words.
3 Read out each sentence and ask the children which of the new words would fill the space.
4 Ask the children to write down the answers.
5 Walk round the classroom checking the children's work.
6 If a child spells a word wrongly in his notebook, he must use it correctly in a sentence. This ensures that the child knows the meaning of the word, and gives him practice in spelling the word.

LESSON SUGGESTION 30

Suffixes and prefixes

Method

1 Explain that you can change the meaning of a word by adding a prefix or suffix.
   A prefix goes at the *front* of a word, e.g: disobey
   A suffix goes at the *end* of a word, e.g: properly
2 A prefix often changes the word into its opposite meaning.
   e.g: obey/disobey   honest/dishonest
3 Children should learn to recognize suffixes and prefixes at a glance to help them when reading a new word.

LESSON SUGGESTION 31

Crossword puzzles

Method

1 Explain that crossword puzzles are word games where you have to work out the answers to clues to fit the right words into the white squares.
   Clues *across* give you ideas for the words written *across* the puzzle.
   Clues *down* give you ideas for the words written *down* the puzzle.
   When words cross each other, they share the same letter, e.g:

2 Discuss the clues with the children. Ask them questions about the clues to help them work out the answers.
   Sometimes the puzzle in the *Using English* book will have some letters written in. If the letters already written on the puzzle do not match your answer, then your answer is wrong.

LESSON SUGGESTION 32

Spelling rules

Note

These rules can be used as a guide when spelling words.

Method

The following spelling rules are taught in the *Pupil's Books*.

a When we add 'ing' to words ending with 'e', we leave off the 'e' before adding 'ing', e.g: take, taking.
b Put 'i' before 'e' except after 'c', e.g: thief, ceiling.
c When a noun ends in 'f', you must change the 'f' to 'v' and add 'es' to make it plural. (If it ends in 'fe', you must change the 'f' to 'v' and add 's'.) e.g: one calf, two calves, one knife, two knives.
d Change 'y' to 'i' before adding a suffix, e.g: hurry, hurried.
e When you add 'ly' to a word to make an adverb, you do not change any letters, e.g: slow, slowly.
f You can add 'ful' to a noun to make an adjective, e.g: pain, painful.
g When you have added 'ful' to a word, you can also add 'ly' to make an adverb, e.g: painful, painfully.

LESSON SUGGESTIONS FOR HANDWRITING

INTRODUCTION

At this stage, children should be encouraged to keep their writing neat and regular in size, slope and spacing.

You should always check that pupils hold their pens correctly and that they are sitting sensibly.

It is a good idea to walk round the class, pointing out children's errors and correcting them.

Children should copy the model passages from the *Using English* books as closely as possible. This is good practice in copying accurately. Pupils should read through their work to make sure they have copied the passage correctly. Ask them to read through each other's work sometimes.

LESSON SUGGESTION 33

Weekly work-plan

Method

1 Look at the fluency exercises with the pupils. Point out difficult areas and demonstrate these on the blackboard. Ask children to practise these in the air before writing in their books.
2 Now tell the children to look at the passage to copy. Look through it for difficult joins and demonstrate these on the blackboard.
3 Tell children to copy the model passage into their exercise books, making sure they copy accurately.
4 Walk round the classroom while the children are doing this. Point out any errors to the children.
5 Collect work for marking. Give some sort of praise to those who have tried to keep their work neat and legible, e.g: display their writing to the class, or give stamps or stars for good work.

LESSON SUGGESTIONS FOR READING

INTRODUCTION

The key to reading is understanding and enjoying what you read. If possible, give the children a wide variety of material to read.

Encourage pupils to work out new words for themselves by using word recognition skills they have learned. Many of these skills are taught in the *Using English* books.

The introductory lessons each week will take 30 minutes; the other reading lessons will last 20 minutes. Use the first 30 minutes of reading time each week to introduce the story, and any new words in it. Ask the children to read through the story silently.

Lesson One gives comprehension questions based on the story. Lessons Two and Three are reading exercises based on reading skills. Lessons Four and Five are spent on the following: reading for enjoyment, poetry, reading supplementary readers and reading games.

You can choose which of these activities to do for Lessons Four and Five, depending on what equipment you have. You should have *Reading Games for Grade 6* (and a copy of *Teacher's Notes* for this book) and *Supplementary Readers 1, 2* and *3*.

LESSON SUGGESTION 34

A Introductory lesson

Method

1 Try to introduce each story with some kind of interesting background material, e.g: *Reader 3, 'The Big Jump'*: Take out an atlas of the Pacific and find the island of Pentecost in the New Hebrides (now known as Vanuatu). Discuss rituals, e.g: initiation ceremonies in PNG; fire-walkers in Fiji.
2 If possible show pictures to do with the story, e.g: *Reader 1, 'Machele and the Heron's Leg'*: show a picture of a heron (bird).

B Learning new vocabulary

Method

1 Write the list of new words from the story on the blackboard. (These can be found in the Reader at the beginning of each story.)
2 Read through this list with the class, explaining the meaning of the words.
3 Let the pupils read the story silently.
4 When they have finished, read through the list of new words again. Choose pupils to say a word when you point to it, or to read aloud the sentence which contains the new word.
5 If there is time, ask the children questions about the story. Encourage them to find sentences in the story which tell the answers.

C Comprehension questions

Method

1 Ask the children to read out the list of new words which should still be written on the blackboard.
2 Read through the questions or sentences for Lesson One and ask the children to answer them orally. Discuss the answers with the children.
3 Then ask the children to write down answers to the questions, using good sentences, or to write the correct sentences from the book.

LESSON SUGGESTION 35

Context and picture clues

Note

This skill should be taught to the children, to help them work out the meanings of new words.

Method

Context Clue

1 Read the sentence containing the new word but say 'something' in place of that word, e.g: (Unknown word is Library)
T: We all to the '*something*' to get books to read.
T: Where do we go to get books to read?
C: To the library.
T: We all went to the *library* to get books to read.

Picture Clue

2 Where pictures are provided, use these to give clues to new words, e.g:
T: The man leaped out of his plane and opened his '*something*'.
T: Look at the picture. What did the man do after he leaped from the plane?
C: (looking at the picture) He opened his *parachute*.

LESSON SUGGESTION 36

Fact and opinion

Method

1 Explain that things that can be proved are called 'facts', e.g: There are twenty-three children in Grade 6.

'Opinions' are thoughts or feelings that people have about something which cannot be proved, e.g: I *think* this is the best school in Papua New Guinea.

2 Encourage the children to recognize the difference between what is fact and what is opinion, e.g: when reading a newspaper or magazine.

3 Ask the children how they feel about that opinion. They should be encouraged to think about something and give their *own* opinion rather than just accept what someone else thinks.

LESSON SUGGESTION 37

Following directions

Method

1 The best way to teach this skill is to use a map or draw a map on the blackboard which you can point to.

2 Choose one student to read out the directions while another student follows these directions on the map with a stick. If this student gets lost, then replace him with someone else.

3 Give the children practice at giving their own directions orally. If possible, follow these directions in a practical situation and see if the directions were correct, e.g: How to get to the river from the classroom. Choose someone to write down directions. She must read these out and the class must follow these to reach the river.

LESSON SUGGESTION 38

Correct order of events

Method

1 Read a short story to the children. Ask the children what happened first in the story; what happened next; what happened after that, etc, until the children can tell all the main events of the story in the correct order.

2 Next, write all the sentences of the story on the blackboard, in the wrong order.

3 Children have to sort them out into the correct order.

4 Discuss with the children why the next point will not make sense if it is in the wrong order.

LESSON SUGGESTION 39

Reading for enjoyment

Method

1 Children should be able to choose their own reading material during this lesson.

2 Try to provide as much variety as possible, e.g: New Nation magazine, Paradise, Post Courier, The Times, National Geographic magazines, library books.

LESSON SUGGESTION 40

Poetry

Note
This lesson is optional and should only be used if there is time.

Method
1 Read the poem aloud, slowly and clearly. Then read it a second time, or ask a child to read it.
2 Ask the children whether they like the poem. Do they understand what it is about? What is the poet trying to say?
3 Explain that poets often use words or phrases in unusual ways to try to make you understand something new.
4 Ask questions about the poem. The children should answer orally.